304. 2083 GEO

Geographies (
and Families

C000002394

304.
208
3
GEO

07378 963

University of Brighton

Aldrich Library
Cockcroft Building
Moulsecoomb
Brighton BN2 4GJ
Telephone 01273 642770

Online renewal http://library.brighton.ac.uk

om the vibrant
ilies.

es an overview
g geographies
f examples of
ross the globe.
g people and/
ng the context

course text for
l the social sci-
s of education,

gh University,
nunity, Society.
young people,
ion, inclusion,
een published
hy, Environment

This item must be returned on or before the last date stamped
A fine may be charged if items are returned late

LR.04.08.ISR.vL1

WITHDRAWN FROM
UNIVERSITY OF BRIGHTON
LIBRARIES

Geographies of Children, Youth and Families

An international perspective

Edited by Louise Holt

 Routledge
Taylor & Francis Group

LONDON AND NEW YORK

UNIVERSITY OF
BRIGHTON

2 4 DEC 2010

INFORMATION
SERVICES

First published 2011
by Routledge
2 Park Square, Milton Park, Abingdon, Oxon, OX14 4RN

Simultaneously published in the USA and Canada
by Routledge
270 Madison Avenue, New York, NY 10016

Routledge is an imprint of the Taylor & Francis Group, an informa business

© 2011 Louise Holt; individual chapters, the contributors

The right of Louise Holt to be identified as the author of the editorial
material, and of the authors for their individual chapters, has been
asserted in accordance with sections 77 and 78 of the Copyright,
Designs and Patents Act 1988.

Typeset in Baskerville
by Pindar NZ, Auckland, New Zealand
Printed and bound in Great Britain
by CPI Antony Rowe, Chippenham, Wiltshire

All rights reserved. No part of this book may be reprinted or
reproduced or utilised in any form or by any electronic, mechanical,
or other means, now known or hereafter invented, including
photocopying and recording, or in any information storage or retrieval
system, without permission in writing from the publishers.

British Library Cataloguing in Publication Data
A catalogue record for this book is available from the British Library

Library of Congress Cataloging in Publication Data
Geographies of children, youth and families: an international
perspective / edited by Louise Holt.
    p. cm.
    1. Children. 2. Youth. 3. Families. 4. Human geography. I. Holt,
Louise, 1975-
    HQ767.9.G46 2010
    306.85—dc22   2010028017

ISBN 13: 978-0-415-56383-3 hbk
ISBN 13: 978-0-415-56384-0 pbk
ISBN 13: 978-0-203-86330-5 ebk

This book is dedicated to my sister Sharon,
and also to Iola and Amelie.

Contents

THEME II
The home, family and intergenerational relationships 81

THEME III
Cities and/or public spaces 151

Illustrations

Tables

Contributors

Nafisah Abdul Hamed studied geography at the National University of Singapore (NUS), and for her honours year thesis researched and wrote 'Adult anxieties: regulation of spaces for young teenagers in Singapore'. Nafisah was awarded the 2007/2008 NUS Outstanding Undergraduate Researcher Prize for the individual category from the Faculty of Arts and Social Sciences. She received the Ministry of Education's Teaching Award in 2007 and went on to pursue the Postgraduate Diploma in Education in the National Institute of Education. She is currently teaching geography at Innova Junior College.

Michael Adjaloo is a research fellow at the Kwame Nkrumah University of Science and Technology, Kumasi, Ghana.

Stuart Aitken is Professor of Geography at San Diego State University. His books include *Geographies of Young People: The Morally Contested Spaces of Identity* (Routledge 2001), *Family Fantasies and Community Space* (Rutgers University Press, 1998), and *Putting Children in Their Place* (Association of American Geographers, 1994). He has also published widely in academic journals including the *Annals of the AAG, Geographical Review, Antipode, The Professional Geographer, Transactions of the IBG, Society and Space, The Journal of Geography* and *Environment and Planning A* as well as various edited book collections. His interests include film and media, critical social theory, qualitative methods, children, families and communities.

Kathrin Blaufuss completed a PhD in the Departments of Anthropology and Geography at Durham University. She currently works for the German NGO Forum on Environment and Development and coordinates the political activities of German NGOs regarding the UN Convention on Biological Diversity.

Mireia Baylina is Lecturer in Geography at the Autonomous University of Barcelona and member of the Geography and Gender Research Group of the same University. Her research interests include gender and rurality, gender and childhood and the teaching of Europe.

Phoebe Beedell is a freelance researcher and worked as a Research Associate at the University of the West of England on the ESRC-funded 'Identities, Educational Choice and the White Urban Middle-classes' research project. She has interests in psychosocial methodologies.

Victoria Ann Cook obtained her PhD from the University of Leeds. Before starting her PhD, Victoria worked as a secondary school geography teacher. Her research interests include researching with children, geographies of education and embodiment.

Olga den Besten is an independent researcher in social sciences, currently based in Paris. Since 2004 she has been working mainly in the field of child-hood studies, doing research in Russia, France, Germany and the UK. This work has focused on children's relationship with their urban environment, as well as on how children can contribute to changing their environment through participating in school-building projects. Among other qualitative methods, Olga has used visual methods in her research, in particular, mental maps drawn by children.

Julia Fionda is Professor of Law at Kingston University and holds an LLB (Hons) and a PhD (Southampton). Her teaching and research interests lie in criminal justice, youth justice and criminal law and her publications include *Public Prosecutors and Discretion: A Comparative Study* (Oxford University Press, 1995), *Legal Concepts of Childhood* (Hart Publishing, 2001) and *Devils and Angels: Youth, Policy and Crime* (Hart Publishing, 2005).

Margaret Greenfields is Senior Lecturer in Social Policy at Buckinghamshire New University. She is the co-author (with Colin Clark) of the 'standard' text-book for students and professionals working with nomadic families *Here to Stay: The Gypsies and Travellers of Britain* (UHP, 2006). In addition to her ongoing work with David Smith on housed Gypsy and Traveller communities she has undertaken a series of Gypsy and Traveller Accommodation Assessments for local and health/education authorities across England. Margaret has been a member of the Department of Community and Local Government advisory panel on Gypsy and Traveller matters and has worked closely with the Commission for Racial Equality during their exploration of inequalities facing Gypsy and Traveller communities. In addition to her Gypsy and Traveller research, Margaret has worked with lone-parent and same-sex families, grandparent-carers raising children, and has undertaken comparative international research into teenage pregnancy outcomes. Margaret has a particular interest in the provision of support services to families under stress or at risk of social exclusion as a result of their 'otherness' or poverty issues

Kate Hampshire is Senior Lecturer in Anthropology at Durham University. Most of her research is in sub-Saharan Africa, on health, well-being and mobility, with a particular focus on children and youth. She began working mainly in francophone West Africa; her PhD thesis (at UCL 1994–98) explored the social and demographic consequences of changing mobility patterns among Fulani agro-pastoralists in northern Burkina Faso, and in subsequent years she worked with pastoralist populations in Chad and Niger. More recently, Kate's research has diversified and expanded geographically. Her recent work in Africa includes a large project on child mobility in Ghana, Malawi and South Africa, with Dr Gina Porter; work among refugee youth in Ghana; and work in Niger on intra-household allocation of resources and impacts on child health. She is also currently working on a couple of UK-based research projects: one on the management and social consequences of infertility among British Pakistani Muslims, and another looking at the social capital impacts of children's participation in community arts projects.

Peter J. Hemming is a research fellow in the Centre for Child and Youth Research at Brunel University, working on an AHRC/ESRC-funded project on religion and youth. His PhD was completed at the University of Leeds in the School of Geography and School of Sociology and Social Policy and was entitled 'Religion and spirituality in the spaces of the primary school: social and political explorations'. Peter's research interests include children and young people, religion and spirituality, education spaces, community and citizenship, emotional geographies and qualitative and mixed-method approaches. He is also a former primary school teacher.

Sumi Hollingworth is Senior Research Fellow at the Institute for Policy Studies in Education (IPSE) at London Metropolitan University. She is a sociologist of education with research interests in urban sociology, social class inequalities and identity. She has worked on research exploring class, gender and ethnic inequalities, in the context of urban education. She is co-author of *Urban Youth and Schooling* (Open University Press).

Sarah L. Holloway is Professor in Human Geography at Loughborough University and Director of the Centre for Research in Identity, Governance and Society. Her research interests focus on the twin themes of children, youth and families and social geographies of in/exclusion. She is co-author of *Cyberkids: Children in the Information Age* (RoutledgeFalmer) and *Geographies of New Femininities* (Addison Wesley Longman) and co-editor of *Children's Geographies: Playing, Living, Learning* (Routledge) and *Key Concepts in Geography* (Sage).

Louise Holt is Lecturer in Human Geography at Loughborough University, and a member of the Centre for Research in Identity, Governance and Society. Her research interests focus on geographies of children, young people, families, and disability, and socio-spatial processes of exclusion, inclusion, embodiment and identity, and social capital.

John Horton is Lecturer in Social Sciences at the University of Northampton, UK. As part of the university's Centre for Children and Youth, he has worked on numerous research projects regarding children and young people's everyday geographies, experiences, and issues in diverse educational, institutional and recreational contexts. Broadly, John's research and publications consider how ostensibly banal childhood practices such as 'play', 'fun', 'mess' and 'popular culture' can seriously matter.

Kahryn Hughes is Senior Research Fellow in sociology of health at the University of Leeds. She is currently researching problem gambling funded by the ESRC/RIGT initiative and intergenerational exchanges in social exclusion as part of an ESRC Qualitative Longitudinal Research Initiative.

Robert Jago is Senior Lecturer in Law at the University of Surrey. He holds a BA (Hons) and MPhil (Cantab.) His teaching and research interests lie in criminal justice, family law and public law. He has extensive research experience in the field, having worked on projects evaluating young offender regimes (at Cambridge University) and parenting support projects (at Kent University).

Fiona Jamieson is Senior Lecturer in Education at the University of Sunderland. She has worked on the 'Identities, Educational Choice and the White Urban Middle-classes' project as a research associate. Her research interests centre around gender, social class and 'race' dimensions within education, equalities education and education policy.

Kate Kilpatrick has worked with humanitarian programmes in Southern and West Africa. She is currently Policy Manager for Conflict and Low-income Countries with the Fairtrade Labelling Organization in Bonn, Germany.

Peter Kraftl is Lecturer in Human Geography at the University of Leicester, UK. He has published numerous academic articles and policy reports, principally concerning children's experience of buildings, young people's everyday geographies, and theorisations of childhood. He is currently working on a UK Research Council-funded project exploring children's participation in the re-design of school buildings in the UK. Peter is Treasurer of the Geographies of Children, Youth and Families Working Group of the Royal Geographical Society (with IBG).

Peter Ohene Kyei is Rector of Pentecost University College in Accra, Ghana. He was a lecturer in the Department of Geography and Rural Development for many years at the Kwame Nkrumah University of Science and Technology (KNUST), Kumasi, Ghana. His research interest is in decentralization and poverty alleviation in rural Ghana and has worked with NGOs on their Strategies of Poverty Alleviation in Northern Ghana, on which he obtained his doctorate at the University of Durham, UK. He is a co-author of *NGOs and the State in the Twenty-first Century Ghana and India* (INTRAC, 2005) and a member of the research team on 'The Resilience of Liberia Youth in Budumburam Refugee Camp in Ghana', funded by the Nuffield Foundation.

Ruth Lewis is a research fellow at the London School of Hygiene and Tropical Medicine. After studying geography at the University of Leeds, she moved to the University of Edinburgh where she gained her PhD. Her research focuses on young people's sexual health, and particularly sexual behaviour and sexuality education. She is currently working on an ESRC-funded study of young people's sexual practices in the UK. Previous work has explored parent–child communication about sex, school-based sex education and childhood sexual abuse.

David Lulka is an independent scholar in San Diego. Most recently, he has published on issues related to nature/society debates in *Ethics, Place and Environment, Journal of Cultural Geography, Geoforum, Society and Space, Sociologia Ruralis* and *Great Plains Research*. His research puts a strong emphasis on conceptions of space and place, incorporating a focus on agricultural biotechnology, endangered species programmes in zoological institutions, and the teaching of evolution in schools.

Rachel Manning is Senior Lecturer in Social Psychology at University of the West of England, Bristol. Her research interests are informed by relationships between social and environmental psychology and are broadly focused on issues of pro- and anti-social behaviour. Her work has involved an examination of the implications of socio-spatial identities, the history and development of bystander intervention research in social psychology, and is supported by the use of multi-method research programmes.

Elizabeth S. Mathews is a doctoral student with the Geography Department and the National Institute for Regional and Spatial Analysis in the National University of Ireland, Maynooth. Her PhD examines issues of language, discourse and relations of power in the educational mainstreaming of d/Deaf children. She holds a master's degree in Deaf Education from Gallaudet University, where she studied under the Fulbright Deaf Studies Programme. Gallaudet is the world's only liberal arts university for d/Deaf people. Her research interests include critical pedagogy, the governance of disabled bodies through institutional spaces, and the research as a means of advocacy with minority community groups.

George Oppong Appiagyei Ampong holds a PhD (UK) and MSc (Ghana). George is Chief Executive Officer of Youth Development Foundation (YDF), Executive Secretary of Defence for Children International, Ghana

(DCI-Ghana), part-time Lecturer of University College of Management Studies (UCOMS) and Coordinator of the Kumasi Study Support Centre of the McGrath Institute of Business Australia (MIBA). He has also held a number of international positions including Temporary Advisor to UNAIDS, and ran numerous internationally funded projects of ILO and ADF and IDRC. Current interests include NGO sustainability and youth development.

Anna Ortiz Guitart is a Lecturer at the Universitat Autonoma de Barcelona and member of the Geography and Gender Research Group at the Department of Geography of the UAB. She has researched in a variety of issues such as gender geography, children's geographies, use and appropriation of public spaces, women's strategies and practices in reconciling work and family life and in obtaining promotion and power in academia, skilled migration in Mexico and qualitative methodology.

Frank Owusu Acheampong assisted on a series of Durham University-led, DFID-funded, research projects in Ghana. He is currently a doctoral student at Durham University Business School, investigating the effect of financial liberalization on SME financing in sub-Saharan Africa with Ghana as case study. This includes assessment of the demand and supply of SME financing, equity issues in SMEs, access to external finance with specific emphasis on geographic and gender equity and technological orientation. The final objective examines the effectiveness of government interventions that seeks to enhance SMEs access to finance. Email: f.o.acheampong@durham.ac.uk

Chris Philo is Professor of Geography at the University of Glasgow. Chris's research interests are diverse: ranging from geographies of mental ill-health, including asylum and post-asylum geographies, to various strains of social, cultural and animal geographies; and to the history and theory of human geography. Chris has published a large book out of his asylums research, *A Geographical History of Institutional Provision for the Insane from Medieval Times to the 1860s in England and Wales: The Space Reserved for Insanity* (Edwin Mellen, 2004), as well as a co-authored methodological text (with Paul J. Cloke *et al.*), *Practising Human Geography* (Sage, 2005). Chris has also researched and commentated upon the field of children's geographies.

Helena Pimlott-Wilson is a research associate and member of the Centre for Research in Identity, Governance and Society in the Department of Geography at Loughborough University. Her research is driven by an interest in the daily lives of children, particularly in relation to family life and education. In this regard, her research focuses on parental employment and work–life reconciliation from the perspective of children. Her research extends to explore the implementation of education policy in the local context and the role of the state in social reproduction.

Gina Porter is a senior research fellow in the Department of Anthropology, Durham University. Her research combines ethnographic approaches with a strong interest in spatial perspectives, reflecting her training as a geographer. Uneven power relationships and associated issues of exclusion are linking themes through her work, much of which has a strong gender component. She has undertaken field research in diverse contexts but considers herself primarily an Africanist. She is currently leading an interdisciplinary research project on children, transport and mobility in three African countries: Ghana, Malawi and South Africa. This builds on her long-standing research interest in daily mobilities in sub-Saharan Africa.

Maria Prats Ferret is a Lecturer and a member of the Geography and Gender Research Group at the Department of Geography of the Universitat Autonoma de Barcelona. Her main research interest is geography and gender. She is particularly interested in geographies of children and young people, time use, public spaces, development and African studies.

Julie Seymour is Senior Lecturer in Social Research in the Department of Social Sciences at the University of Hull, UK. A first degree in geography has enabled her more recent sociological research to maintain a focus on spatiality. Her research interests in family practices in home/work locations arise from a long-term interest in the distribution of resources (material, emotional, embodied, spatial) in the household and the negotiations and bargaining which surround these processes. Recent publications include research on children's emotional labour in *The Politics of Childhood* (Palgrave Macmillan, 2005) and 'Treating the hotel like a home: the contribution of studying the single location home/workplace', *Sociology*, 41(6) (2007). She is currently writing a book on family practices and spatiality, and editing (with Esther Dermott) a collection on displaying family.

Tracey Skelton is Professor of Human Geography at the National University of Singapore. Tracey has wide-ranging research expertise united by the themes of identity, sense of place, place/space and relations of power, notably gender, age, 'race' and 'disability'. Among her many notable publications is the landmark text edited with Gill Valentine, *Cool Places: Geographies of Youth Cultures* (Routledge, 1998), an inspirational publication within the field of geographies of children, youth and families.

David Smith is Senior Lecturer in Sociology and Social Policy at Canterbury Christ Church University. His first sole-authored book, *On the Margins of Inclusion: Changing Labour Markets and Social Exclusion in London* (Policy Press, 2005), won the Social Policy Association prize for Best New Publication in 2006. David's research interests include social exclusion, labour market restructuring, welfare reform, urban sociology and housing. Currently, he is working on a project with Margaret Greenfields on housed Gypsy and

Travellers and was involved in the East Kent Gypsy and Travellers Needs Assessment Survey. In addition, David has worked on, and has an interest in, ageing and social exclusion and on comparative analysis of pensions systems and pensions reform.

Gill Valentine is Professor of Human Geography at the University of Leeds. Gill's research expertise focuses upon social identities, citizenship and belonging; children and parenting; consumption cultures; and research methods. Within this framework, recent and ongoing research has investigated the role of the Internet in D/deaf people's inclusion in the information society; social geographies of alcohol consumption; understanding the marginalization and resistance of vulnerable youth; children's social networks, 'virtual communities' and online spaces; food consumption; parental fears and restrictions on children's use of space; and sexuality and space. Gill has published multiple influential works within geography and social sciences. Recent book publications within the field of geographies of children, youth and families include: *Public Space and the Culture of Childhood* (2004); *CyberKids: Children and the Information Age* (2003), with Sarah Holloway; *Towards Inclusive Youth Policies and Practices: Lessons from Young Lesbians, Gay Men and D/deaf People* (2003) with Tracey Skelton and Ruth Butler; *Children's Geographies: Living, Playing, Learning* (2000), with Sarah Holloway; and *Cool Places: Geographies of Youth Cultures* (1998) with Tracey Skelton.

Katya Williams is a Researcher in social policy. She worked on the Identities, Educational Choice and the White Urban Middle-Classes project. Her research interests relate to social class, young people's aspirations and post-16 choices in education. She is particularly interested in the factors that influence aspirations and how education can widen horizons.

Acknowledgements

This book emerged from the First International Conference on Geographies of Children, Youth and Families, held at the University of Reading, UK, in September 2007. I would like to thank all the participants at the conference for their contributions and discussions, and the contributors to the book for providing their chapters and presenting papers at the original conference. Particular thanks are due to Heather Browning for helping to organize the conference, and the University of Reading School of Human and Environmental Sciences for funding and support.

I would like to thank my mum and dad for their constant support. Special thanks to Darren.

1 Introduction

Geographies of children, youth and families: disentangling the socio-spatial contexts of young people across the globalizing world

Louise Holt

International perspectives

This edited collection brings together contributions from key established and emerging international scholars within the interdisciplinary field of geographies of children, youth and families. The inspiration for the book came from the First International Conference on Geographies of Children, Youth and Families, held at the University of Reading, UK, in September 2007. Many of the chapters were papers presented at this conference. The book represents a timely account of the field, coming ten years on from the highly influential text edited by Sarah Holloway and Gill Valentine, *Children's Geographies: Playing, Living, Learning.* Holloway and Valentine (2000) has proved to be a defining text, marking a shift towards the development of a definable sub-/interdisciplinary of geographies of children, youth and families.

In the intervening decade since the publication of *Children's Geographies,* the sub-/interdisciplinary field has burgeoned. A significant mass of emerging and established interdisciplinary scholars researching children and young people's spatialities present and publish their work in a variety of arenas, including specialist publications (e.g. *Children's Geographies; Children, Youth and Environment*) at bespoke conferences and conference sessions. For instance, there have been specialist sessions at every Annual Meeting of the Association of American Geographers and International Conference of the Royal Geographical Society with the Institute of British Geographers (RGS/IBG) during the last decade. The re-establishment of the Geographies of Children, Youth and Families Working Group of the RGS/IBG, and its recent promotion to the status of Research Group exemplifies the level of activity in the field in the UK. The activity within the UK is reflected in other international contexts.

Despite this vibrancy of scholarship about geographies of children, youth and families (and perhaps more specifically children as discussed below), there has not been in the last decade an attempt to bring together an edited collection providing a broad overview of the field of likely appeal to both undergraduate and postgraduate students and academics.[1] This edited collection addresses this gap. The book includes chapters from both established and internationally recognized scholars and emerging researchers in the field. All of the chapters attempt to integrate children and young people more fully within their diverse socio-spatial contexts; including the relatively neglected familial sphere.

Geographies of children, youth and families: some critiques and ways forward

In the following chapter, Holloway and Pimlott-Wilson outline some achievements and current issues facing geographies of children, youth and families. In this section it is therefore necessary for me only briefly outline the perceived gaps within the field which inspired the conference and subsequently this book.

The development of children's geographies has been underpinned by the adoption of the concept of the 'sociological child' (James et al., 1998), which has gone some way to destabilizing dominant, 'common sense' assumptions about children. Researchers investigating geographies of children now widely accept that young people have social agency, with children perceived as much more than adults-in-waiting, whose development proceeds along a series of pre-defined steps. A key emphasis of scholarship has been children's agency to reflect upon and affect change in their worlds.

Despite the many achievements of critical understandings of childhood, it is becoming apparent that such an approach also constrains and frames conceptual and theoretical debates. The book as a whole attempts to simultaneously overcome key limitations of the focus on children's relatively autonomous and reflexive agencies, and retain the advances of emphasizing the centrality of a reconfigured children's agency.

Existing publications in the field of geographies of children and youth have tended to conceptualize children as 'knowing' actors. This focus upon young people's agency has been pivotal to overcoming dominant societal perspectives of children and young people, which have been reproduced in many social science arenas. Such dominant accounts suggest that children are not competent actors who can engage meaningfully in political, cultural and academic forums. By contrast to earlier scholarship (and those which have not engaged with these critical studies), geographies and social studies of childhood have done much to incorporate the voices and experiences of young people; there has been an exceptional bourgeoning of research focusing upon the emplaced experiences of children and young people.

Despite the many contributions of emphasizing young people's agency, there are three strands of critique which can be levelled at the existing field: (1) the relative neglect of certain socio-spatial contexts (notably the family); (2) the exclusions associated with adopting modernist perspectives of agency; and (3) the frequent under-emphasis of 'structural' constraints.

First, the centrality of young people's agency has led to a tendency to neglect certain social and spatial contexts of childhood. Notably, critical social studies and geographies of children and youth have instigated a shift away from focusing upon children within their familial contexts (Punch, 2006). Attempts to address an early tendency to completely subsume children within the family underpin the current emphasis on children in non-familial contexts. Thus, until recently, there has been limited dialogue between researchers of the family and critical geographies of childhood, and the experiences of children and young people within family contexts has been relatively under-explored (although, see Holloway and Pimlott-Wilson, Chapter 2, for a different perspective; see also Bushin, 2009; Christensen, 2000; Holloway and Valentine, 2001; McIntosh and Punch, 2009; Punch, 2007, 2008; Young and Ansell, 2003; Valentine, 1997, for exceptions). This edited collection consciously seeks to enhance the dialogue between critical research into families and children and youth, by incorporating more fully the family as *one* key social context of childhood. Importantly, however, children and young people are not associated exclusively with, or subsumed within, families; in line with the broader field, other social contexts are explored in the book (the body, public space and/or the city, institutional spaces). To focus exclusively on the family could reproduce the limitations of earlier research wherein children were viewed as merely familial 'objects' rather than active subjects (James *et al.*, 1998).

Second, Ruddick (2007) suggests that the discourse of children's rights has often inadvertently reproduced narrow, dominant, modernist concepts of agency, as self-cohesive and independent. Ultimately, such a view 'others' those who are unable to express such autonomous individuality. This notion of agency, which has been pivotal to the development of geographies of children and youth and the incorporation of children's voices and experiences into academic discourses, is paradoxically integral to the marginalization within contemporary societies of children and young people (and others, such as disabled people) who cannot achieve this ideal of independence and autonomy. It is therefore inherently problematic that academic accounts of children have endeavoured to suggest that they can be autonomous 'sovereign' agents. In this context, it is unsurprising that the experiences of certain groups of children and young people, who are particularly marginalized by dominant accounts of agency, such as those with disabilities, have not been fully incorporated into geographies and social studies of children (Pyer *et al.*, 2010).

Finally, the focus placed upon agency has often implicitly underplayed the role of 'structures' which constrain and facilitate young people's experiences (Holt, 2006). In illuminating 'children's voices', critical researchers have arguably accorded 'epistemological privilege' to young people (Gallacher and Gallagher, 2008). However, in common with all agents, young people are not able to consciously trace all of the ways in which their lives are constrained and enabled by broader 'structural' conditions, including normative values about identity positionings (see also Holt and Holloway, 2006). Therefore, the epistemological privilege accorded to young people is problematic.

The three key critiques that I am levelling at the field of geographies of children, youth and families are a reflection of the general tendencies of the sub-/interdisciplinary field. Examples can be found of exceptions to all of these limitations, and I have indicated some (although clearly not all) of these in the discussion. Nonetheless, overall, I would contend that the field of geographies of children, youth and families is in danger of implicitly reproducing these three tendencies: to neglect certain socio-spatial contexts; to draw upon relatively uncritical, modernist notions of agency, and; to over-emphasize agency over structure. This edited collection begins to go some way to address these critiques.

Beginning to address these critiques: children and young people in diverse socio-spatial contexts – the contributions of the chapters

This edited collection endeavours to overcome these three critiques, without losing the central insight that *all* young people have the capacity to contribute to society and academic research. Emphasis in many of the chapters is placed upon the structural conditions that constrain and enable young people's expressions of agency within a variety of socio-spatial contexts, along with how children and young people negotiate, respond to, and can transform, these constraints. The family is one of the key socio-spatial contexts that is emphasized. As a whole, the book implicitly challenges the concept of the 'sovereign child agent', albeit placing a reconfigured children's agency at the core of analysis.

The edited collection brings together research from a variety of socio-spatial contexts, from Ghana to the USA; from Spain to Singapore; from the UK to Mexico. The range of national contexts facilitates an exploration of the commonalities and differences of the socio-spatial contexts and experiences of children and young people across the globalized world (Holt and Holloway, 2006), facilitating further exploration of structures that constrain and enable young people's practices.

The collection is divided into four interconnected themes which focus on different socio-spatial contexts of childhood at a variety of intersecting scales: (1) the body; (2) home, family and intergenerational relationships; (3) public space and/or the city; and (4) institutional spaces. In addition, there is a second overview chapter, in which Sarah Holloway and Helena Pimlott-Wilson explore more fully the achievements and challenges of children's geographies to date. They question some of the taken-for-granted assumptions of the problems currently facing the sub-/interdiscipline and suggest ways forward.

The first section, 'Bodies and identities', begins with Chris Philo's theoretical discussion of Foucault's figuration of children. Philo unravels children as an important, if understated sub-theme in Foucault's work; particularly within lecture series given at the Collège de France, only recently published in English; *Abnormal* and *Psychiatric Power*. Subsequently in this section, Peter Hemming discusses the role of both religious and secular embodied rituals and practices to the construction of 'communities' within and that extend without primary (elementary) schools in the UK. In Chapter 5, Ruth Lewis outlines the changing affective family boundaries of bodily modesty surrounding bathroom practices during the transition from child to teenager. Locking the bathroom door becomes a sign of a young person's desire for privacy, and an expression of agency over their bodily boundaries, largely respected within the family.

Lewis' chapter crosscuts with Theme II, 'The home, family and intergenerational relationships'. Chapter 6, by Kate Hampshire, Gina Porter, Kate Kilpatrick, Peter Ohene Kyei, Michael Adjaloo and George Oppong documents how forced migration and resettlement in a Ghanian refugee camp following the Liberian conflict has rendered precarious and uncertain, and in many cases transformed, traditional (inter-) generational relations and identities. In Chapter 7, David Smith and Margaret Greenfields assess the impact of, frequently coerced, settlement into housing, upon Gypsy-Traveller cultures and intergenerational roles and relationships. They point to experiences of racism and marginalization, but also to an increasing convergence between Gypsy-Travellers and settled communities, particularly among young people. The focus of Chapter 8 is how family life is (re)produced within single-location home/workplaces. Julie Seymour discusses how family practices are used to create a sense of family, often in relation to an idealized 'imaginary' family. In Chapter 9, Gill Valentine and Kahryn Hughes make a case for incorporating more fully a neglected range of familial ties (intergenerational, sibling and partnerships) into geographic research. Their empirical study of problem Internet gamblers highlights the importance of the emotional and practical support of a range of family relations to finding pathways out of problem gambling. Chapter 10 focuses specifically on parent–child familial relationships and the negotiation of the spatial freedom of children to use public spaces in Paris. Olga den Besten highlights the importance of internal family dynamics and the life-histories of parents in (re)producing particular cultures of parenting in relation to the spatial freedoms and restrictions of children.

The focus on how internal family dynamics facilitate or constrain young people's access to the public space of the city in Chapter 10 provides a link to the following section of the book 'Cities and/or Public Spaces'. In the first chapter in this theme, Mireia Baylina, Anna Ortiz and Maria Prats investigate the gendered experience of the city by children in Barcelona, Spain and Mexico City. Although children's practices in public space are gendered in both Barcelona and Mexico City, *access* to public space is constrained for both girls and boys and markedly gendered in Mexico City, with boys having more access to public spaces. Chapter 12, by David Lulka and Stuart Aitken, draws upon Nietzsche's challenge to history to unravel how the conflicts emerging from harbour seals beaching at Children's Pool, La Jolla, San Diego, pose questions about what is perceived to be the historically appropriate use of the pool. They propose an emphasis on flexibility rather than a potentially stultifying historical preservation to negotiate the competing interests of the children and seals.

Moving to rural public spaces in Southern Ghana, Gina Porter, Kathrin Blaufuss and Frank Owusu Acheampong explore the gendered experiences of young people's load carrying. They consider potential health and education impacts of load carrying and discuss an action research project in which low-technology Intermediate Means of Transport (IMTs) were introduced to contribute to addressing the transport gap. Chapter 14, by Tracey Skelton and Nafisah Abdul Hamed, offers a counterpoint to the Western-dominated literature about young people's (often restricted) use of public space, by exploring teenagers exclusion/marginalization from, and resistive use of, public space at night time in Singapore. Despite restrictive familial and state practices, Skelton and Hamid examine the strategies many teenagers employ to use public spaces at night. In the final chapter of this section, Chapter 15, Rachel Manning, Robert Jago and Julia Fionda unravel the socio-spatial impacts of current anti-social behaviour legislation, and in particular Anti-Social Behaviour Orders (ASBOs) on young people. Drawing upon interviews with young people subject to ASBOs and their families, along with professionals, they point to how problematic questions are raised about the ways in which ASBOs constrain young people from becoming active citizens and members of communities.

The focus on legal institutions in Chapter 15 provides a link to the final section, which focuses upon institutional spaces. The first chapter in this section, by John Horton and Peter Kraftl (Chapter 16) explores the neglected geographies of pre-school children's experiences of a Sure Start Centre. This chapter raises important questions about how to include the experiences of very young children in research and policy evaluation. Another relatively neglected group, middle-class young people, is the focus of Chapter 17. In this chapter Sumi Hollingworth, Katya Williams, Fiona Jamieson and Phoebe Beedell interrogate how young middle-class people who attend(ed) urban state secondary schools conceptualize educational and social inequalities: frequently reproducing dominant ideas about meritocracy despite their often radical political leanings. In Chapter 18, Elizabeth S. Mathews examines the socio-spatial positioning of an extremely marginalized group of young people, whose voices and experiences have been relatively neglected in the literature: d/Deaf children and youth. The chapter focuses upon the institutionalized practices that serve to configure deafness as a medical problem to be overcome and which structure children's educational options, resulting in a re-institutionalization of d/Deaf children via the mainstreaming process. In the final chapter of the book, Victoria Ann Cook explores how young people's ability to act as social agents in relation to fieldwork is constrained/enabled by their positioning as variably (in)competent as risk-takers in two state secondary (high) schools in the UK.

I hope that you, the reader, agree that each of the chapters individually makes an important contribution to geographies of children, youth and families. Although it would be too big a claim to state that this book is representative of current scholarship in the field, I would argue that the scope and contents of the chapter are broadly reflective of, and provide an insightful introduction to, research in the sub-interdiscipline. The contributors are situated within a variety of national and disciplinary contexts; although the book has 'geography' in the title, the authors' disciplinary affiliations are diverse, from anthropology to sociology. This diversity is expressive of geographies/sociologies/anthropologies of children, youth and families as a truly interdisciplinary field of the wider social sciences.

The book in its entirety, I argue, begins in a modest way to address some of the critiques levelled at the field in the first section of this chapter, particularly via the emphasis on how a diverse range of socio-spatial contexts constrain and enable children and young people's agency. Notable here is the international focus and the emphasis on the family. The voices and experiences of certain groups of young people who have been marginalized in the literature have been attended to: for instance, refugees in non-Western contexts, very young children, middle-class and d/Deaf young people. However, even ten years on from Holloway and Valentine's landmark text, geographies of children, youth and families feels like an emerging area of research. There is much to be done to explore new contexts, critique the scholarly field, address the critiques, and engage more fully with scholarship without the subdiscipline in the social sciences to challenge conventional notions of childhood, youth and the family.

Note

1 There have been excellent, more special appeal, edited collections, such as Horshelman and Colls (2009), Jeffrey and Dyson (2008), van Blerk and Kesby (2008) and Panelli *et al.* (2007).

References

Bushin, N. (2009) 'Researching family migration decision-making: a children-in-families approach', *Population, Space and Place*, 15: 429–43.

Christensen, P. (2000) 'Home and movement: children constructing family time', in S. L. Holloway and G. Valentine (eds) *Children's Geographies: Playing, Living, Learning*, London: Routledge, pp. 120–49.

Gallacher, L. A. and Gallagher, M. (2008) 'Methodological immaturity in childhood research: thinking through "participatory methods"', *Childhood*, 15: 499–516.

Holloway, S. L. and Valentine, G. (eds) (2000) *Children's Geographies: Playing, Living, Learning*, London and New York: Routledge.

Holloway, S. L. and Valentine, G. (2001) 'Children at home in the wired world:

reshaping and rethinking the home in urban geography', *Urban Geography*, 22: 562–83.

Holt, L. (2006) 'Exploring other childhoods through quantitative secondary analyses of large scale surveys: opportunities and challenges for children's geographers', *Children's Geographies*, 4: 143–55.

Holt, L. and Holloway, S. L. (2006) 'Theorising other childhoods in a globalised world', *Children's Geographies*, 4: 135–42.

Horshelman, K. and Colls, R. (eds) (2009) *Contested Bodies of Childhood and Youth*, London: Palgrave Macmillan.

James, A., Jenks, C. and Prout, A. (1998) *Theorising Childhood*, Cambridge: Polity Press.

Jeffrey, C. and Dyson, J. (2008) *Telling Young Lives: Portraits of Global Youth*, Philadelphia, PA: Temple University Press.

McIntosh, I. and Punch, S. (2009) '"Barter", "deals", "bribes" and "threats": exploring sibling interactions', *Childhood*, 16: 49–65.

Panelli, R., Punch, S. and Robson, E. (eds) (2007) *Global Perspectives on Rural Childhood and Youth: Young Rural Lives*, London and New York: Routledge.

Punch, S. (2006) 'Some methodological problems of research with children, and some practical solutions'. Keynote speech to Workshop 1 of Geographies of Children, Youth and Families Working Group of the RGS/IBG workshop series 'Methodological issues in researching with young people', RGS/IBG 16 February 2006.

Punch, S. (2007) '"I felt they were ganging up on me": interviewing siblings at home', *Children's Geographies*, 5: 219–34.

Punch, S. (2008) '"You can do nasty things to your brothers and sisters without a reason": siblings' backstage behaviour', *Children and Society*, 22: 333–44.

Pyer, M., Horton, J., Tucker, F., Ryan, S. and Kraftl, P. (2010) 'Children, young people and "disability": challenging children's geographies?' *Children's Geographies*, 8: 1–8.

Ruddick (2007) 'At the horizons of the subject: neo-liberalism, neo-consertvatism and the rightst of the child. Part One: from "knowing" fetus to "confused" child', *Gender, Place and Culture*, 14: 513–27.

Valentine, G. (1997) '"Oh yes I can." "Oh no you can't": children and parent's understandings of kids' competence to negotiate public space safely', *Antipode*, 29(1): 65–89.

van Blerk, L. and Kesby, M. (eds) (2008) *Doing Children's Geographies: Methodological Issues in Research with Young People*, London: Taylor and Francis.

Young, L. and Ansell, N. (2003) 'Fluid households, complex families: the impacts of children's migration as a response to HIV/AIDS in southern Africa', *The Professional Geographer*, 55(4): 464–79.

2 Geographies of children, youth and families

Defining achievements, debating the agenda

Sarah L. Holloway and
Helena Pimlott-Wilson

Introduction

Geographies of children, youth and families is a vibrant area of research. Over the past couple of decades the field has moved from being a minority concern, to one firmly established as a subdiscipline within geography with its own structures within geographical institutions, journals, conferences, culture and an increasing number of researchers. We take this rapid development of interest as the context for our chapter, in which we both seek to examine the defining achievements of the field to date, and debate our future agenda. In examining our progress, we trace the diverse roots of the subdiscipline exploring how these, alongside changing philosophical approaches in geography and developments in the wider world, have shaped our diverse approaches and achievements to date. We then reflect on three challenges facing us today: first whether our subdisciplinary structures and culture are a help or a hindrance to intellectual innovation; second, how we might best conceptualize the axis of social difference which lies at the centre of our field; and finally, in what ways we can best manage the tension between theoretical insight and the policy imperative in a changing political and economic climate.

Defining achievements

Children's spatial cognition and mapping abilities

The first of the roots of children's geographies we trace focuses on children's spatial cognition and mapping abilities. This form of research, which sits at the boundaries of children's geographies and developmental and environmental psychology, is one of the earliest types of research to emerge in the subdiscipline lead initially by Blaut and Stea (Aitken, 1994). They sought, through the Place Perception Project which they founded at Clark University, to examine whether young children could be taught to read maps by first teaching them to read aerial photographs (Blaut *et al.*, 1970; Blaut and Stea, 1971, 1974). Through the 1980s and 1990s a small group of researchers developed this approach, which refines Piagetian models of child development that suggest children cannot read maps until the age of seven or so (see Downs *et al.*, 1988; Liben and Downs, 1997), through cross-cultural studies which demonstrated that children as young as three have some map-reading abilities (Blades *et al.*, 1998; Blaut, 1991, 1997; Matthews, 1987, 1992, 1995; Sowden *et al.*, 1996; Stea *et al.*, 1997).

This approach to children's geographies, though initially very important, has not developed at the same rate as other areas of our field. Despite this, an examination of a twenty-first century example of this type of work demonstrates the importance of not othering or writing out more minor threads from our collective history. Blaut *et al.* (2003) use research with urban and rural children in the global North and South to demonstrate that children aged 3–5 years are able to interpret aerial photographs and simple maps to use these as way-finding devices in simulated and real circumstances. This might seem a long way from the type of research undertaken by many children's and young people's geographers. However, it is in thinking through the implications of their work that we start to see some commonalities. Blaut *et al.* argue that the implication of their research is that educational practice needs to be rethought: pre-literate children can, because of their proven ability to understand visual representations, be exposed to a much richer curriculum at a younger age. In this regard there are clear parallels with other branches of children's geographies as they envision children as more competent than conventional Piagetian models of childhood suggest. Furthermore, they also express an urgent desire to critique and improve policy, in this case educational policy, which shapes children's lives whilst also attending to the contexts in which different children live.

Families, feminism and children

A second impetus for research on geographies of children, youth and families comes from feminism and more broadly the changing nature of women's lives in the late twentieth and early twenty-first centuries. Following in a feminist tradition forged outside the discipline by writers such as Friedan (1963) and Gavron (1966) who named and challenged the isolation many women felt in the home, early feminist geographers sought to explore and make visible the lives of mothers raising families (Tivers, 1985). This focus on mothering developed during the 1980s and 1990s, with a two-fold pattern emerging in the research agenda. On the one hand, the increasing feminization of the labour force across the global North inspired a range of studies about the ways in which women manage the tension between paid employment and childrearing (England, 1996; Holloway, 1999), and about the employment relations between working parents and those who provide substitute care whilst they work (Gregson and Lowe, 1995; Pratt, 1999). Children themselves remained an absent presence in this literature, and especially in the case of pre-school children, the focus tended to be on how care was arranged for them, rather than on their subjective experiences of care. However, older children were more likely to make an appearance as subjects as well as the objects of care, with Fiona Smith and John Barker's (2000) research into children's views of after school clubs being an early example of this trend.

The twenty-first century has seen renewed interest in issues about work/life or work/family reconciliation. On the one hand, the continued growth of dual-earner couples has garnered interest in the ways they manage social reproduction in the contemporary city (Jarvis, 2005; Jarvis and Pratt, 2006; Schwanen, 2007; Schwanen and de Jong, 2008); on the other hand, the restructuring of the neo-liberal welfare state, and the associated shift from seeing women as dependents to potential workers, has also promoted debate about the importance of considering the ethic of care in debates about work-fare (McDowell, 2004, 2005). Here too there is a tendency to see children as the objects of care, but some contemporary research also moves beyond this to trace the notion of childhood embodied in current policy initiatives to promote dual-earner family models, and to explore children's views about parental employment and their experiences of living in working families (Holloway and Pimlott-Wilson, 2009; Pimlott-Wilson, 2008).

To characterize the literature on families, feminism and children as being entirely dominated by concerns about working families would, however, be to do it a gross disservice. Late twentieth-century research also focused on the moral geographies of mothering and parenting, examining how ideas about the ways children ought to be raised circulate through neighbour-hoods, influencing parents' (and thereby children's) experiences as they either choose to conform to, or reject, the local models of appropriate par-enting, for example in relation to spatial range (Valentine, 1997; Harden, 2000; see also Pain, 2006, for a more recent example). The twenty-first cen-tury has seen further developments in this area. Aitken's (2009) research has foregrounded the experiences of fathers, and builds on earlier research which reminds us that the role of men, as well as women, in families needs to be understood. We have also seen a move towards research which over-turns ideological constructions of unidirectional parental care *for* children to incorporate the voices of young carers, both in the global North (Stables and Smith, 1999) and global South (Robson, 2000, 2004; Robson *et al.*, 2006). Moreover, we have seen the emergence of studies which more fully incorporate the voices of children alongside those of adults in their explora-tion of family dynamics. Holloway and Valentine's (2001: 18) analysis of the micro-geographies of ICT usage in family homes illustrates the importance of 'adult-child power relations in shaping everyday sociospatial practices within the home'. Equally, Young and Ansell (2003), in their examination of HIV/AIDS migration in southern Africa, incorporate the views of children alongside other household members to give a more nuanced perspective of children's migration as part of extended family coping strategies (see also Bushin, 2009 on children's role in migration decisions).

In summary, this strand of research with feminist roots has done much to further interest in families, taking account of the views of both parents, and increasingly children, in studies which explore both the implications of the feminization of the labour force, and more broadly adult–child power relations in the context of family geographies.

Childhood, children and young people's geographies

The third strand of research on children's geographies, and the one that has seen the greatest explosion of interest in the past couple of decades, can again be traced back to the 1970s. Influential here is the work of Bunge (Bunge, 1973; Bunge and Bordessa, 1975), who focused on the spatial oppression of children in Detroit and Toronto through 'expeditions', which revealed children as the victims of social, economic and political forces in the adult-mediated built environment (Aitken, 1994). This pioneering attempt to place children on the geographical agenda did not initially gain momentum but myriad changes in the discipline, including those outlined above, brought a second wave of researchers who became interested in studying children in their own right to the fore. A few brief examples serve to illustrate this point. The success of research on children's mapping drew researchers, such as Matthews, into the field and he now considers children's environments in the broadest possible sense. Equally, the influence of feminism, and for some Marxism, on the discipline drew researchers such as Katz, Karsten and Valentine into studies of social reproduction and thence to children. Moreover, the developing influence of poststructural writings, with a common emphasis on including geography's others on the agenda, has informed the interest of researchers such as Aitken and Philo in children. Thus the move to study children's geographies, in the sense of their experiences as subjects in the world (rather than their mapping abilities, or as objects and to a lesser extent subjects of care), did not simply come from one source, rather it was influenced by a confluence of circumstances within the discipline.

Moreover, the development of research in this field was not solely shaped by events internal to the discipline, but also by external influences. Key has been geographers' engagement with others in the new social studies of childhood (James et al., 1998) who have emphasized the social construction of childhood, the temporal specificity of contemporary ideas about childhood, and the importance of conceiving of children as competent social actors in their own right, and avoiding characterizing them only as 'adults in the making rather than children in the state of being' (Brannen and O'Brien, 1995: 730). In addition, of course any social science discipline is also shaped by the outside world and the changing social, economic and political landscapes in the global North and South have also elevated children's position on the agenda, making considerations of their lives ever more essential in academia (Katz, 2004; Horton et al., 2008).

One of us has argued elsewhere that the key contribution that geographies of children and young people has made is to imbue new social studies of childhood with a sense of spatiality. This notion of spatiality is threefold: (1) emphasizing the importance of place (avoiding the danger of ethnocentrism at the same time as we draw lines of connection between different global/local places); (2) exploring the nature of the everyday spaces in and through which young people's lives are made (including spaces for playing, living and learning); and (3) tracing the importance of ideas about childhood in spatial discourses which inform socio-spatial practices in different sites (practices which then reinforce, or occasionally challenge, our ideas about childhood) (Holloway and Valentine, 2000a, 2000b). As authors of this chapter we both stand by the basics of this argument, but note that the volume of research now available dwarfs that which informed Holloway and Valentine's original review, and that some of this challenges us to nuance that argument in new ways. For one, the development of research considering the body over the past 15 years has increasingly made space for the embodied experiences of children and young people (Christensen, 2000; Evans, 2006; Holt, 2007; Colls and Hörschelmann, 2009).

Engagement with non-representational theory has induced debate about the partial and situated nature of representation, suggesting that the non-cognitive may be employed to inform our empirical engagements within research, including an interest in embodiment, affect, emotion, performance and practice (Horton and Kraftl, 2005, 2006; Lorimer, 2005; Jones, 2008; Woodyer, 2008). Additionally, research which has over the past decade highlighted children's and young people's experience of movement in, and across, various parts of the globe (Waters, 2003; van Blerk and Ansell, 2006; Punch, 2007; Hopkins and Hill, 2008; Adams, 2009; Bushin, 2009) challenges us to add an appreciation of mobility to this otherwise rather static sense of spatiality. To this more developed sense of spatiality, children's geographers have over the past decade also paid more attention to the temporal in the lives of young people, conceiving of them as both beings and becomings, and pointing to transitions during childhood and to adulthood (and the factors which create differentiated experiences of these) (Valentine, 2003; Punch, 2004; Hopkins, 2006; Langevang, 2007, 2008; van Blerk, 2008; Holdsworth, 2009).

Where we have seen continuity in the ensuing ten years since that review, is in the attention paid to the diverse nature of children's childhoods. At one level, researchers are concerned to explore different children and young peoples lives, for example focusing on issues to do with gender (Bettis and Adams, 2005; Costello and Duncan, 2006; Janssen, 2009), social class (Gough and Franch, 2005), race/ethnicity (Sporton *et al.*, 2006; Mand, 2009; de Leeuw, 2007), dis/ability (Skelton and Valentine, 2003; Holt, 2004), sexuality (Thomas, 2004; Gwanzura-Ottemoller and Kesby, 2005; van Blerk, 2008) and so on. At another level, there has been a concerted effort made to ensure that voices from the global South receive more attention, as although never excluded from the field, initially they attracted less attention than they ought to have done (Matthews, 1995; Kesby *et al.*, 2006; see *Children's Geographies* special issue 2007).

In addition to writing about a diversity of children, geographers have also sought to speak to a variety of other geographers. During the past ten years it has become increasingly easy to address an audience of other children's geographers as dedicated conferences and conference sessions have emerged, alongside the (re)emergence of journals such as *Children's Geographies* and *Children, Youth and Environments*, and there has been growing interest in the field by publishing houses. However, at the same time there have also been efforts by some to ensure that their research also reaches outside the confines of our subdisciplinary field. A few brief examples once again serve to illustrate this point.

Louise Holt's (2004) research on children and disability, speaks both to children's geographers but is also important in the way that it moves geographies of disability forward, broadening the field to incorporate those with emotional and behavioural difficulties. Sam Punch's (2001) research on children's household work in rural Bolivia, similarly adds both to our understanding of children's work, but also acts as a critique on debates about domestic labour which have been dominated by global North accounts of the conjugal division of labour, and ignore the importance of generational divisions of labour in the global South. More recently, Bethan Evans (2009: 2) explicitly attempts to mainstream children's geographies by 'illustrating the potential for geographies of childhood to gain from, and contribute to, recent geographical work on spatiotemporalities, biopolitics and pre-emption . . . and critical geographies of obesity, fatness, bigness and corpulence'.

Debating the agenda

What is lurking beneath the surface?

The first half of this chapter has established then both the diverse roots of the subdiscipline of children's geographies and traced its development from marginal interest from the 1970s onwards towards institutional respectability in the noughties. Aitken (2004: 171) comments on such developments that 'We have arrived. And I am worried'. He argues that while everything seems rosy on the surface, there may be hidden dangers facing us. In this second half of the chapter we want to explore three of the issues which have been lurking beneath, but over the past five years have bubbled to the surface, of geographies of children, youth and families.

Subdisciplinary structures and cultures

We begin with one of the concerns he raises in this editorial suggesting that the 'block politics' which sustained early researchers establishing the field might eventually turn it into a 'gated community' (see Aitken, 2004: 172–5). In effect his concern that the supportive networks of conferences and dedicated journals populated by like-minded academics eventually become spaces of security which we do not leave, meaning our research becomes ghettoized rather than spread through academe as feminism has been. Our reading of this is that while *Children's Geographies*, and *Children, Youth and Environments* both act as subdisciplinary homes, research on children, youth and families is also evident in most of the mainstream geographical journals (e.g. Robson, 2004; Kraftl, 2006; Crawley, 2009; Evans, 2009). The degree of integration in terms of conferences and conference sessions is perhaps a little less obvious but the process of mainstreaming children's geographies is well underway. There is, however, a need for constant vigilance, and to take the lessons learned in children's geographies out into wider geographical debates to ensure existing (and potential) subdisciplinary knowledges are neither overlooked nor sidelined in developing debates (see Holloway *et al.*, 2010, for an example of this).

Notwithstanding the need to take our arguments out in the wider discipline, there is no doubt that the institutional culture that dominates geographies of children, youth and families has been a comfortable one for many. The field, like feminist geography, which is one of its roots, sees a much greater representation of women than is evident in the discipline as a whole (Al-Hindi, 2000; Garcia-Ramon and Pujol, 2004; Blumen and Bar-Gal, 2006). The conference from which this book emerges attracted more female delegates than male (76 per cent and 24 per cent respectively), though the current volume of *Children's Geographies* is somewhat more evenly balanced. It is also a theme that has attracted significant numbers of lesbian and gay researchers, though the whiteness of geography as a discipline, and the level of educational qualifications required to work as an academic, means the field does remain exclusionary in other ways (Mahtani, 2004; Liu, 2006). Moreover, the culture in the field, by our estimation at least, is a supportive one, where researchers encourage other researchers, and the questions asked at conferences are more likely to be constructively complimentary than (constructively) critical. Our intension here is not to cast the gendering of the discipline as a causal factor in the development of its particular conflict-avoiding culture. This would not only involve gross levels of essentialism, it would also fly in the face of evidence elsewhere within geography where feminist debates are disproportionately populated by women without the emergence of a similar set of socio-cultural practices. Indeed, Vanderbeck (2008) has sought to question whether children's geographies is perhaps less critical than it ought to be. This in itself is an interesting question. Is it possible for the discipline to move forward together through collective intellectual endeavour, or does the development of knowledge depend upon a model where one geographer makes his or her reputation by critiquing the orthodoxy established by others? Whilst we find the former suggestion appealing, our own sense is that the lack of public critique stems as much from the still relatively small size of the field as from any of cooperative endeavour amongst its researchers. Perhaps we will only know 'we have arrived' as Aitken put it, when we feel more able to disagree.

Geographies of age and intergenerational relations

A second challenge which has been bubbling up to the surface during the noughties is about how we should conceptualize our field of interest as a subdiscipline. The question that has been raised is whether geographies of children, youth and families focuses on too narrow a section of the age spectrum. Paralleling developments elsewhere in geography – where the geographical interest in women morphed into a focus on gender, where work on dissident sexualities broadened to incorporate normative heterosexuality, and where interest in racialized minorities grew to incorporate an analysis of racism and whiteness – the call has in some quarters been for geographies of age or intergenerational relations. In Hopkins and Pain's (2007: 287) words:

> The study of age in geography is also undergoing striking change, with a recent explosion of interest in children and young people following a far more limited interest in the very old. Yet geographers have still to break out of the tradition of fetishising the margins and ignoring the centre. While work on age might still be accused of being, in many ways, adults' geographies (Maxey 2006; Weller 2006), there are no geographies of adults in sight.

Their argument is a compelling call to arms, and yet we still have our reservations. Quite apart from the fact that this argument infantilizes the very old in the way it excludes them from the category adult, there is a rich history of research on parenting within geographies of children, youth and families which deals with the issues facing adults raising families, and more broadly much of the literature in wider social, economic and political geography focuses on adults. To say though there are no geographies of adults in sight is simply not correct. It is true that geographers' growing interest in the young, and to a lesser extent the old, could have the unfortunate effect of normalizing those in the intervening years (Holloway, 2005) and that adulthood is often not examined as an explicit category (Vanderbeck, 2007). What is needed then is not necessarily a relative increase in the number of studies about adults, but more explicit recognition within these that this is one, amongst others, of the social categories they are dealing with (cf. Horton and Kraftl, 2008). We would, however, want to sound one note of caution here. In attempting to ensure that those in the intervening years between the bookend generations are explicitly studied as adults, we need to ensure that the older generations of adults are more fully attended to within the geographical literature. If geographers avoid this focus for fear of 'fetishising the margins', we run the risk of excluding this group, rejecting this focus for fear of exoticization before they have been fully included within the discipline. The battle to incorporate older adults into geography has not yet been won.

These critiques of geographical approaches to age have spurred calls for greater research into intergenerational relations:

> Given this compartmentalized character of much work on age, the geographies of intergenerationality – and particularly, extrafamilial intergenerational relationships – remain, in my view, substantially under-researched.
>
> (Vanderbeck, 2007: 202)

The qualification in Vanderbeck's argument (see also Hopkins and Pain, 2007) is important here. Intrafamilial intergenerational relationships have, as we discussed earlier in the section of feminism, families and children, been a source of interest to geographers who have explored adult–child power relations in the home. Extrafamilial intergenerational relationships too have formed a focus of study, for example in adults and young people's struggles over access to, and control of, public space. This is, however, an avenue of opportunity for geographers, and these authors argue persuasively that this could be more fully developed in different spheres in ways which make us think through the ever-changing meaning of generation and age which are always culture and context specific. While we would argue that the call to study intergenerational relations marks an evolutionary rather than revolutionary change, we too believe there is much to be gained from deepening this engagement.

'Alternative theory' and the policy imperative

The final issue facing the subdiscipline that we want to consider is that of the usefulness of academic research. On the one hand, Matthews (2005: 271) identifies the success of the field in foregrounding research on diverse children and young people but expresses his growing concern that there is a 'a trend towards empiricism for its own sake'. Comparing our field with feminist and disability research, he argues that academics have greater responsibilities when studying children's geographies because children are not in a position to challenge the sustaining hegemony (as say feminists might do) or become part of the academy (as someone with disabilities might do):

> Is it enough merely to disentangle, unfold and deconstruct the social milieu of every day life without further purpose or intent? For me, this is little more than cultural voyeurism, a somewhat sterile play space which to occupy. Do we not owe it to children to do much more? In essence,

> if children's geographies becomes an end in itself (Horton and Kraftl, 2005), is it not letting down those who so willingly give up their time, thought and emotions to be its 'subjects'.
>
> (Matthews, 2005: 271)

For Matthews, if we are to avoid becoming cultural raiders, we need to do something with the knowledge we produce other than circulate it amongst ourselves. Such calls for usefulness are now further being inscribed in our institutional structures in the UK at least, where political changes following the global economic crisis have seen an increased demand from funding bodies (ESRC, 2009) and assessments of research quality (HEFCE, 2009) for a demonstrable impact from academic research.

In geographies of children, youth and families this discourse about the need for usefulness has been articulated through debates about the potential merits of engaging with alternative contemporary theories. Horton and Kraftl (2005, 2006) too are concerned that children's geographies is becoming dominated by empiricism, but their response to this is very different:

> [W]e argue that although 'usefulness' is a very, very good thing, it is also not the *only* thing that 'Children's Geographies' could and should be about. In fact, our gut feeling is that it would be dispiriting, self-spiting turn for the worse if all *Children's Geographies* readers/contributors suddenly began to focus solely on being 'useful' . . . And we wonder: if 'Children's Geographies' was solely dedicated to being 'useful', would it be all that *interesting*, or engaging, critical, thought-provoking, progressive and sustainable? So, *vive la différence*: the more different things that 'Children's Geographies' can do, the better; and the more scope for open-ness and unpredictability that there can be in 'Children's Geographies', the better.
>
> (Horton and Kraftl, 2005: 131–2)

Rather than avoid the danger of endless empiricism through political engagement, Horton and Kraftl would do so through theoretical engagement with post-structural, post-feminist and non-representational theories and approaches, as they envision a subdiscipline which does not simply draw on, but also contributes to, these theoretical trends. In particular, their reading of these 'alternative contemporary theories' as they label them leads them to argue we might like to think more about: everydayness; material things; practices; bodies; affect; ongoingness and education; and spacings.

In emphasizing their differences we are to an extent setting these up as straw arguments and obscuring the complexity of their positions. Matthews does not, in fact, suggest an entire disengagement from theory; Horton and Kraftl themselves conduct policy-relevant work. Indeed, we could argue that in the sophistication of their arguments we see our answer to this dilemma. We can reject the dualistic understanding that research is either theoretically innovative or policy informing, and argue that the art of the academic is in writing up research in appropriate ways for different audiences. This is sometimes true, but we cannot convince ourselves that this is always the case. Some topics will simply be more interesting, some more useful to policy-orientated end-users, some more likely to generate exciting new theory and be 'more than useful' to use Horton and Kraftl's terminology. Perhaps this is an instance where as the subdiscipline develops we can move forward without agreement, being self-confident in our diversity, and recognizing that there is more than one way of doing geographies of children, youth and families.

Acknowledgements

Dr Sarah Holloway is a Philip Leverhulme Prize winner and gratefully acknowledges the Leverhulme Trust's support for her research.

References

Adams, M. (2009) 'Stories of fracture and claim for belonging: young migrants' narratives of arrival in Britain', *Children's Geographies*, 7(2): 159–71.

Aitken, S. C. (1994) *Putting Children in their Place*. Washington, DC: Association of American Geographers.

Aitken, S. C. (2004) 'Editorial: from dismissals and disciplinary inclusions; from block politics to panic rooms', *Children's Geographies*, 2(2): 171–5.

Aitken, S. C. (2009) *The Awkward Spaces of Fathering*. Farnham: Ashgate.

Al-Hindi, K. F. (2000) 'Women in geography in the 21st century – introductory remarks: structure, agency, and women geographers in academia at the end of the long twentieth century', *Professional Geographers*, 52(4): 697–702.

Bettis, P. J. and Adams, N. G. (eds) (2005) *Geographies of Girlhood: Identities In-between*, Mawhaw, NJ: Lawrence Erlbaum Associates.

Blades, M., Blaut, J. M., Darvizeh, Z., Elguea, S., Sowen, S., Soni, D., Spencer, C., Stea, D., Surajpaul, R. and Uttal, D. (1998) 'A cross-cultural study of young children's mapping abilities', *Transactions of the Institute of British Geographers*, 23(2): 269–77.

Blaut, J. M. (1991) 'Natural mapping', *Transactions of the Institute of British Geographers*, 16(1): 55–74.

Blaut, J. M. (1997) 'The mapping abilities of young children', *Annals of the Association of American Geographers*, 87(1): 152–8.

Blaut, J. M. and Stea, D. (1971) 'Studies of geographic learning', *Annals of the Association of American Geographers*, 61: 387–93.

Blaut, J. M. and Stea, D. (1974) 'Mapping at the age of three', *Journal of Geography*, 73: 5–9.

Blaut, J.M., McCleary, G. and Blaut, A. (1970) 'Environmental mapping in young children', *Environment and Behaviour*, 2(3): 335–49.

Blaut, J. M., Stea, D., Spencer, C. and Blades, M. (2003) 'Mapping as a cultural and cognitive universal', *Annals of the Association of American Geographers*, 93(1): 165–85.

Blumen, O. and Bar-Gal, Y. (2006) 'The academic conference and the status of women: the annual meetings of the Israeli Geographical Society', *Professional Geographer*, 58(3): 341–55.

Brannen, J. and O'Brien, M. (1995) 'Childhood and the sociological gaze: paradigms and paradoxes', *Sociology*, 29: 729–37.

Bunge, W. W. (1973) 'The geography', *The Professional Geographer*, 25(4): 331–7.

Bunge, W. W. and Bordessa, R. (1975) 'The Canadian alternative: survival, expeditions and urban change', *Geographical Monographs*, no. 2, York University, Toronto.

Bushin, N. (2009) 'Researching family migration decision-making: a children-in-families approach Population', *Space and Place*, 15(1): 429–43.

Christensen, P. H. (2000) 'Childhood and the cultural construction of vulnerable bodies', in Prout, A. (ed.) *The Body, Childhood and Society*. Basingstoke: Macmillan, pp. 38–59.

Colls, R. and Hörschelmann, K. (2009) 'The geographies of children's and young people's bodies', special issue, *Children's Geographies: the geographies of children's and young people's bodies*, 7(1): 1–6.

Costello, L. and Duncan, D. (2006) 'The "Evidence" of sex, the "Truth" of gender: shaping children's bodies', *Children's Geographies*, 4(2): 157–72.

Crawley, H. (2009) 'No one gives you a chance to say what you are thinking': finding space for children's agency in the UK asylum system', *Area*, early view.

de Leeuw, S. (2007) 'Intimate colonialisms: the material and experienced places of British Columbia's residential schools', *Canadian Geographer*, 51: 339–59.

Downs, R., Liben, L. and Daggs, D. (1988) 'On education and geographers: the role of cognitive development theory in geographical education', *Annals of the Association of American Geographer*, 78(4): 680–700.

England, K. (ed.) (1996) *Who Will Mind The Baby? Geographies of childcare and working mothers*. London: Routledge.

ESRC (Economic and Social Research Council) (2009) *ESRC Strategic Plan, 2009–2014: delivering impact through social science*. London: ESRC.

Evans, B. (2006) '"I'd feel ashamed": girls' bodies and sports participation', *Gender, Place and Culture*, 13(5): 547–61.

Evans, B. (2009) 'Anticipating fatness: childhood, affect and the pre-emptive "war on obesity"'. *Transactions of the Institute of British Geographers*, Early view *Note – due in print 2010*, 35(1).

Friedan, B. (1963) *The Feminine Mystique*. London: Gollancz.

Garcia-Ramon, M. D. and Pujol, H. (2004) 'Gender representation in academic geography in Catalonia (Spain): towards a masculinzation of the discipline?' *Journal of Geogrpahy in Higher Education*, 28(2): 111–19.

Gavron, H. (1966) *The Captive Wife: conflicts of housebound mothers*. London: Penguin.

Gough, K. V. and Franch, M. (2005) 'Spaces of the street: socio-spatial mobility and exclusion of youth in Recife', *Children's Geographies*, 3(2): 149–66.

Gregson, N. and Lowe, M. (1995) '"Homemaking": on the spatiality of daily social reproduction in middle class Britain', *Transactions Institute of British Geographers*, 20(2): 224–335.

Gwanzura-Ottemoller, F. and Kesby, M. (2005) '"Let's talk about sex, baby . . .": Conversing with Zimbabwean children about HIV/AIDS', *Children's Geographies*, 3(2): 201–18.

Harden, J. (2000) 'There's no place like home: the public/private distinction in children's theorizing of risk and safety', *Childhood: a global journal of child research*, 7(1): 43–59.

HEFCE (Higher Education Funding Council) (2009) *Research Excellence Framework: second consultation on the assessment and funding of research*. London: HEFCE. Available at: http://www.hefce.ac.uk/pubs/hefce/2009/09_38/09_38.pdf (accessed 30 October 2009).

Holdsworth, C. (2009) '"Going away to uni": mobility, modernity, and independence of English higher education students', *Environment and Planning A*, 41(8): 1849–64.

Holloway, S. L. (1999) 'Mother and worker?: the negotiation of motherhood and paid employment in two urban neighbourhoods', *Urban Geography*, 20: 438–60.

Holloway, S. L. (2005) 'Identity: age, sexuality and bodily ability', in Cloke, P., Crang, P. and M. Goodwin (eds) *Introducing Human Geographies*. London: Arnold, pp. 400–10.

Holloway, S. L. and Pimlott-Wilson, H. (2009) 'Geographies of education, parenting and childhood: the neo-liberal workfare state, social reproduction and the changing role of schools in 21st century Britain', Paper available from the authors, Department of Geography, Loughborough University, Loughborough, Leicestershire, LE11 3TU, UK.

Holloway, S. L. and Valentine, G. (2000a) 'Spatiality and the new social studies of childhood', *Sociology*, 34: 763–83.

Holloway, S. L. and Valentine, G. (eds) (2000b) *Children's Geographies: playing, living, learning*. London: Routledge, pp. 275.

Holloway, S. L. and Valentine, G. (2001) 'Children at home in the wired world: reshaping and rethinking the home in urban geography', *Urban Geography*, 22: 562–83.

Holloway, S. L., Hubbard, P. J., Jöns, H. and Pimlott-Wilson, H. (2010) 'Geographies of education and the importance of children, youth and families', *Progress in Human Geography*, 34: 583–600.

Holt, L. (2004) 'Children with mind-body differences and performing (dis)ability in classroom micro-spaces', *Children's Geographies*, 2(2): 219–36.

Holt, L. (2007) 'Children's socio-spatial (re)production of disability within primary school playgrounds', *Environment and Planning D: society and space*, 25(5): 783–802.

Hopkins, P. E. (2006) 'Youth transitions and going to university: the perceptions of students attending a geography summer school access programme', *Area*, 38(3): 240–7.

Hopkins, P. E. and Hill, M. (2008) 'Pre-flight experiences and migration stories: the accounts of unaccompanied asylum-seeking children', *Children's Geographies*, 6(3): 257–68.

Hopkins, P. and Pain, R. (2007) 'Geographies of age: thinking relationally', *Area*, 39(3): 287–97.

Horton, J. and Kraftl, P. (2005) 'For more-than-usefulness: six overlapping points about children's geographies', *Children's Geographies*, 3(2): 131–44.

Horton, J. and Kraftl, P. (2006) 'What else? Some more ways of thinking and doing 'Children's Geographies', *Children's Geographies*, 4(1): 69–98.

Horton, J., Kraftl, P. and Tucker, F. (2008) 'The challenges of 'Children's Geographies': an affirmation', *Children's Geographies*, 6(4): 335–48.

James, A., Jenks, C. and Prout, A. (1998) *Theorizing Childhood*. Cambridge: Polity Press.

Janssen, D. F. (2009) '"Where" "boys" "are": co-constructions of maturities-genders-bodies-spaces', *Children's Geographies*, 7(1): 83–98.

Jarvis, H. (2005) 'Moving to London time: household co-ordination and the infrastructure of everyday life', *Time and Society*, 14(1): 133–54.

Jarvis, H. and Pratt, A. C. (2006) 'Bringing it all back home: The extensification and "overflowing" of work', The case of San Francisco's new media households, *Geoforum*, 37(3): 331–9.

Jones, O. (2008) 'True geography [ ] quickly forgotten, giving away to an adult-imagined universe', Approaching the otherness of childhood, *Children's Geographies*, 6(2): 195–212.

Katz, C. (2004) *Growing up Global: economic restructuring and children's everyday lives.* Minneapolis, MN: University of Minnesota Press.

Kesby, M., Gwanzura-Ottemoller, F. and Chizororo, M. (2006) 'Theorising other, "other childhoods": issues emerging from work on HIV in urban and rural Zimbabwe', *Children's Geographies*, 4(2): 185–202.

Kraftl, P. (2006) 'Building an idea: the material construction of an ideal childhood', *Transactions of the Institute of British Geographers*, 31(4): 488–504.

Langevang, T. (2007) 'Movements in time and space: using multiple methods in research with young people in Accra, Ghana', *Children's geographies*, 5(3): 267–82.

Langevang, T. (2008) '"We are managing!": Uncertain paths to respectable adulthoods in Accra, Ghana', *Geoforum*, 39(6): 2039–47.

Liben, L. S. and Downs, R. M. (1997) 'Can-ism and can'tiansim: a straw child', *Annals of the Association of American Geographer*, 87(1): 159–67.

Liu, L. (2006) 'On being 'hen's teeth': interdisciplinary practices for women of color in geography', *Gender, Place and Culture*, 13(1): 39–48.

Lorimer, H. (2005) 'Cultural geography: the busyness of being "more than representational"', *Progress in Human Geography*, 29(1): 83–94.

Mahtani, M. (2004) 'Mapping race and gender in the academy: the experiences of women of colour faculty and graduate students in Britain, the US and Canada', *Journal of Geography in Higher Education*, 28(1): 91–9.

Mand, K. (2009) *Researching South Asian Children in Transnational Families: how, when, where?* Presented at Creative Research Methods Workshop, London South Bank University, 20 February 2009.

Matthews, H. (1987) 'Gender, home range and environmental cognition', *Transactions of the Institute of British Geographers*, 12: 43–56.

Matthews, H. (1992) *Making Sense of Place: children's understandings of large-scale environments.* Hemel Hempstead: Harvester Wheatsheaf.

Matthews, H. (1995) 'Culture, environmental experience and environmental awareness: making sense of young Kenyan children's views of place', *The Geographical Journal*, 161(3): 285–95.

Matthews, H. (2005) 'Editorial: rising four: reflections on the state of growing-up', *Children's Geographies*, 3(3): 271–3.

McDowell, L. (2004) 'Work, workfare, work/life balance and an ethic of care', *Progress in Human Geography*, 28(2): 145–63.

McDowell, L. (2005) 'Love, money, and gender divisions of labour: some critical reflections on welfare-to work policies in the UK', *Journal of Economic Geography*, 5(3): 365–79.

Pain, R. (2006) 'Paranoid parenting? Rematerializing risk and fear for children', *Social and Cultural Geography*, 7(2): 221–43.

Pimlott-Wilson, H. (2008) 'Children's experiences of parental employment: gender, class and work-life negotiations', unpublished PhD thesis, University of Liverpool.

Pratt, G. (1999) 'From registered nurse to registered nanny: discursive geographies of Filipina domestic workers in Vancouver, BC', *Economic Geography*, 75(3): 215–36.

Punch, S. (2001) 'Household division of labour: generation, gender, age, birth order and sibling composition', *Work, Employment and Society*, 15(4): 803–23.

Punch, S. (2004) 'The impact of primary education on school-to-work transitions for young people in rural Bolivia', *Youth and Society*, 36(2): 163–82.

Punch, S. (2007) 'Negotiating migrant identities: young people in Bolivia and Argentina', *Children's Geographies*, 5(1–2): 95–112.

Robson, E. (2000) 'Invisible carers: young people in Zimbabwe's home-based healthcare', *Area*, 32(1): 59–69.

Robson, E. (2004) 'Hidden child workers: young carers in Zimbabwe', *Antipode*, 36(2): 227–48.

Robson, E., Ansell, N., Huber, U. S., Gould, W. T. S. and van Blerk, L. (2006) 'Young caregivers in the context of the HIV/AIDS pandemic in sub-Saharan Africa', *Population, Space and Place*, 12(2): 93–111.

Schwanen, T. (2007) 'Gender differences in chauffeuring children among dual-earner families', *The Professional Geographer*, 59(4): 447–62.

Schwanen, T. and de Jong, T. (2008) 'Exploring the juggling of responsibilities with space-time accessibility analysis', *Urban Geography*, 29(6): 556–80.

Skelton, T. and Valentine, G. (2003) '"It feels like being Deaf is normal": an exploration into the complexities of defining D/deafness and young D/deaf people's identities', *The Canadian Geographer*, 47(4): 451–66.

Smith, F. and Barker, J. (2000) 'Contested spaces: children's experiences of out of school care in England and Wales', *Childhood: a global journal of child research*, 7(3): 315–33.

Sowden, S., Stea, D., Blades, M., Spencer, C. and Blaut, J. M. (1996) 'Mapping abilities of four-year-old children in York, England', *Journal of Geography*, 95(3): 107–11.

Sporton, D., Valentine, G. and Nielsen, K. B. (2006) 'Post conflict identities: Affiliations and practices of Somali asylum seeker children', *Children's Geographies*, 4(2): 203–17.

Stables, J. and Smith, F. (1999) '"Caught in the Cinderella trap": narratives of disabled parents and young carers', in Butler, R. and H. Parr (eds) *Mind and Body Spaces: geographies of illness, impairment and disability*, London: Routledge, pp. 256–68.

Stea, D., Elguea, S. and Blaut, J. M. (1997) 'Development of spatial knowledge on a macroenvironmental level: a transcultural study of toddlers', *Revista InterAmericana de Psicologia*, 31(1): 141–7.

Thomas, M. E. (2004) 'Pleasure and propriety: teen girls and the practice of straight space', *Environment and Planning D: Society and Space*, 22(5): 773–89.

Tivers, J. (1985) *Women Attached: the daily lives of women with young children*, London: Croom Helm.

Valentine, G. (1997) '"Oh yes I can." "Oh no you can't": children and parent's understandings of kids' competence to negotiate public space safely', *Antipode*, 29(1): 65–89.

Valentine, G. (2003) 'Boundary crossings: transitions from childhood to adulthood', *Children's Geographies*, 1(1): 37–52.

van Blerk, L. (2008) 'Poverty, migration and sex work: youth transitions in Ethiopia', *Area*, 40(2): 245–53.

van Blerk, L. and Ansell, N. (2006) 'Children's experiences of migration: moving in the wake of AIDS in southern Africa', *Environment and Planning D: society and space*, 24(3): 449–71.

Vanderbeck, R. M. (2007) 'Intergenerational geographies: age relations, segregation and reengagements', *Geography Compass*, 1(2): 200–21.

Vanderbeck, R. M. (2008) 'Reaching critical mass? Theory, politics, and the culture of debate in children's geographies', *Area*, 40(3): 393–400.

Waters, J. L. (2003) '"Satellite kids" in Vancouver: transnational migration, education and the experiences of lone children', in Charney, M. W., Yeoh, B. S. A. and T. C. Kiong (eds) *Asian Migrants and Education: the tensions of education in immigrant societies and among migrant groups*. London: Kluwer Academic Publishers, pp. 165–84.

Woodyer, T. (2008) 'The body as research tool: embodied practice and children's geographies', *Children's Geographies*, 6(4): 349–62.

Young, L. and Ansell, N. (2003) 'Fluid households, complex families: the impacts of children's migration as a response to HIV/AIDS in southern Africa', *The Professional Geographer*, 55(4): 464–79.

Theme I

Bodies and identities

3 Foucault's children

Chris Philo

Intoduction: Foucault, children, childhoods, children's geographies

Michel Foucault (1927–1984), the celebrated French intellectual, never had any children of his own. Nor has he usually been identified as a theorist or researcher *of* children and childhood, since these topics were apparently never much in his horizon of concern. Even so, this absence has not denied him a place in the emerging interdisciplinary field sometimes characterized as social studies of children and childhood. James *et al.*'s influential *Theorising Childhood* (1998, esp. ch. 3) contains numerous references to Foucault, while more recent texts such as Prout's *The Future of Childhood* (2004), Jenks's *Childhood* (2005; see also Jones, 2006) and Wyness's *Childhood and Society* (2006) all display a loosely Foucauldian concern for constructions of knowledge – the varying and contested 'regimes of truth' – framing how children become inserted into contextually shifting 'social spaces of childhood' striated by socio-structural and political-economic lines of power (and see also McNamee, 2000). In a more restricted register, insights from Foucault's best-known monograph, *Discipline and Punish* (Foucault, 1976), have featured in research on children, schools and education, with papers such as those by Cannella (1999) and Covaleskie (1993) setting an agenda some years ago that, in effect, dragged Foucault into the classroom. Mac Naughton's text *Doing Foucault in Early Childhood Studies* (2005) fuses the broader epistemological borrowings from Foucault evident in the likes of James *et al.* (1998) with claims about researching the micro-level dynamics of early-educational practice, at home as well as in school, while a study by Germeten (2000) is just one among many using Foucault to interrogate how time and space – both physical and 'pedagogical space' – are mobilized in the disciplining of school children. For all that, my sense is that these borrowings from Foucault remain relatively limited, relying heavily on relatively few passages from only a few of his writings, namely *Discipline and Punish* (Foucault, 1976) and, to a lesser extent, *The History of Sexuality, Vol. 1* (Foucault, 1979a).

The same is definitely true of the narrower subfield of children's geographies, and readers will only find the occasional nod towards Foucault in the subfield's founding texts such as Aitken's *Putting Children in their*

Place (1994), Valentine and Skelton's *Cool Places* (1998) and Holloway and Valentine's *Children's Geographies* (2000). There are exceptions, such as Wood and Beck's *Home Rule* (1994), which 'manages to domesticate Foucault[1] and breathe everyday life into him' (Katz, 2004: 10), and various mentions in Aitken's *Geographies of Young People* (2001) that draw upon him as a post-structural theorist of embodiment and sexuality. There are also exceptions in three unpublished PhD theses known to me (Benstead, 2001; Gallagher, 2005;[2] Kyle, 2006), all of which offer sustained engagements with *Discipline and Punish* and other of Foucault's writings on power in addressing the geographies of schools, the Boys Brigade and 'out-of-bounds' adventure courses for troubled youth. Another geography PhD project has mobilized Foucault's concept of 'governmentality' (Foucault, 1979b) in addressing citizenship education, positioning the latter as a 'governmental technology' (Pykett, 2004, 2006, 2007, 2009), and it is interesting the extent to which a constellation of concerns around education, schooling, citizenship and participation (see also Gaskell, 2008; Weller, 2003a, 2003b, 2007) – shading into questions about methodologies of the researcher in tackling such concerns – appears to be gradually emerging as a more-or-less explicit Foucauldian fringe around the edges of children's geographies.

A search of the journal in this subfield, *Children's Geographies*, for the period from first issue (2003) to the time of submitting this chapter (mid 2009) finds that Foucault has been cited in twenty-three papers and two book reviews (but with the suggestion of increasing citation rates over the past two years). In most cases, the engagement with Foucault is cursory, absolutely not a criticism of the papers nor a doubting of their worth, but it remains the case that comments tend to be gestural and only referencing the same two major texts as mentioned earlier (i.e. Foucault, 1976, 1979a). Echoing claims above, there are more substantial Foucauldian borrowings in nine papers on school, and in one case nursery school, spaces (Ansell, 2009; Catling, 2005; de Leeuw, 2009; Gallacher, 2005; Harker, 2005; Hemming, 2007; Holt, 2004; Newman *et al.*, 2006; Pike, 2008; also Barker *et al.*, 2010); herein the significance of power-knowledge, surveillance strategies and the materialities of disciplined – but sometimes unruly, differently abled or 'otherwise' different – children's bodies are variously explored. One of these papers, by Pike (2008; also Pike, 2010), is also the first piece in the journal to include 'Foucault' in the title – it is called 'Foucault, space and primary school dining rooms' – but there, as in its companions, it is the more 'generic' Foucault, rather than a Foucault with something specific to say *about* children, that is the prime inspiration. Several papers touch upon Foucault when considering methodological and ethical issues (e.g. Gallagher, 2008; Holt, 2006; Kesby, 2007; Jones, 2008), while Giddings and Yarwood (2005) quote from *Discipline and Punish* when discussing the 'panopticism' of rural childhoods as encouraging (some) rural children into self-regulation. In his review of a book on historical social policies directed at youth 'deviancy', meanwhile, Vanderbeck (2004) asks whether a 'Foucault or Donzelot' might be valuable for injecting a more *critical* stance into the account being given. This quick trawl through *Children's Geographies* certainly suggests a 'presence' for Foucault, if hardly a dominant one nor one going much beyond the most prominent coordinates within Foucault's *oeuvre*.

Returning to Foucault himself, therefore, it is perhaps now time to appraise whether, if we look again at his major texts and, more particularly still, if we acknowledge his other less familiar contributions, we might be surprised to find that, after all, he did spend time *specifically* discussing children and childhood. If this is true, then we need to ask about implications for the social studies of children and childhood, and more narrowly for scholars in the subfield of children's geographies. Such is the ambition of this chapter, which takes its immediate cue from the publication over the last few years of Foucault's public lectures from the Collège de France,[3] first in French and then in English. Indeed, it is evident that one set of lectures, those entitled *Abnormal*, given between 8 January and 11 March, 1975, takes the figure of the child – more specifically, the figure of the 'masturbating child' – as absolutely central to the whole architecture of what is being argued, while the previous year's set of lectures, *Psychiatric Power*, given between 7 November 1973 and 6 February 1974, also contain materials germane to this centrality of the child *as* child to the broader arc of what is being examined. The *Abnormal* lectures first appeared in English in 2003 (Foucault, 2003a) and the *Psychiatric Power* lectures in 2006 (Foucault, 2006), and my argument will be that these two lecture series *do* entertain provocative new ideas with the potential, if not completely to transform, then certainly to pose fresh challenges for toilers on children and childhood.[4]

In what follows, I will indicate something of these challenges, chiefly regarding the intimacies of surveillance and intervention in the 'claustrophobic' and often 'anxious' spaces of what evolves into the modern nuclear family. I acknowledge that my discussion will be primarily exegetical, reflecting more the Foucault scholar in me than the embedded children-childhood researcher, and I do assume a basic acquaintance with Foucault's major texts, principal concerns and ('archaeological' and 'genealogical') ways of working. I do not offer much evaluation of the historical 'truth' or otherwise of Foucault's evidence and interpretations, leaving crucial lines of empirical (re)inquiry to another day. In prefacing what I say about *Psychiatric Power* and *Abnormal*, I will briefly cover writing that is more widely known, albeit rarely if ever tackled head-on by children's geographers (at least not in the published literature: cf. Benstead, 2001; Kyle, 2006): namely, the brush with juvenile 'delinquents' in Foucault's best-known text, *Discipline and Punish* (Foucault, 1976). A confession is that I will say little about what Foucault implies, if in fragmentary fashion, about children and sexuality in *The History of Sexuality* series (Foucault, 1979a, 1985, 1986), notwithstanding certain points of connection with my arguments below. This neglect is partly because I intend to engage this series elsewhere, but in part it is because the substantive basis for the second two books in the series (Foucault, 1985, 1986) – taking the reader back to Ancient Greece and Rome – interrupts what can otherwise be a fairly coherent account of how Foucault illuminates the *recent* historical geographies of (Western) children and childhood.

Foucault's 'delinquents'

Discipline and Punish (Foucault, 1976) is perhaps Foucault's best-known and most 'sensational' text, not least for the horrific opening description of the execution in 1759 of Damiens the Regicide. It functions on at least three different levels: *empirically*, documenting the birth of the modern prison and an array of so-called 'panoptic' techniques for controlling populations that dispersed throughout eighteenth- and nineteenth-century Western Europe and North America; *synoptically*, envisioning the replacement of an older form of 'sovereign' power, predicated upon the spectacular violence of the scaffold and pillory, by a newer form of 'disciplinary' power, dependent on a much more subtle calculus of nagging demands, allied to constant surveillance, monitoring and censure, designed to convert rebellious hearts and minds into 'docile' and productive bodies; and *conceptually*, foreshadowing a new, thoroughly relational approach to power, not as something held in 'blocks' and imposed entirely repressively on others, but rather a phenomenon, a cluster of actions, spatially distributed, circulating through capillaries, relays and transmission points, as certain human groupings endeavour to impress their will upon the conduct of others (to make the 'will' of others precisely identical with that of themselves). It hardly needs saying that these components of *Discipline and Punish* have now become the routine stock-in-trade of much contemporary social science and cultural studies; and it is also true that the deeply spatial concerns of the text – its constant return to the 'arts' of 'distribution in space' – have attracted the attention of geographers,[5] while numerous works of historical, social, cultural, political and even economic geography have derived inspiration from the substantive and conceptual innovations dropping from almost its every page.

It can be argued that the figure of the 'delinquent', the troublesome adolescent, is a shadowy presence throughout *Discipline and Punish*. For instance, there is a sense that new disciplinary practices are likely to be most effective on younger prisoners, inmates and trainees arriving in prisons, religious and military institutions or other carceral facilities, being a more malleable 'material' than their older counterparts for whom prospects of reform have receded. There are also numerous references throughout the text to schools of one sort or another, notably drill-schools for young army recruits or conscripts, although we rarely catch sight, as it were, of actual children in classrooms or boy cadets marching on parade grounds. The most obvious brush with delinquents arises near the close of the text, though, when – in discussing the creation of a disciplinary 'carceral archipelago' – reference is made to the Mettray reformatory for boys, opened in the countryside near Tours, France, in the 1840s (Foucault, 1976: 293–6). In passing, it might be noted that, thanks to Foucault's highlighting of Mettray, this institution has since been subjected to rigorous historical-geographical scrutiny by Driver (1990), prompting follow-up studies of young people in reformatories (Ploszajska, 1994) and children in workhouses (Driver, 1993a).

The Mettray evidence is clearly pivotal to the overall logic of *Discipline and Punish*, and yet it is often ignored, sidelined when compared to the more familiar example of Bentham's ideal prison-house, the Panopticon, which is too readily taken as *the* spatial model of disciplinary power that Foucault envisages circulating in late-eighteenth- and nineteenth-century Western Europe and North America (for this critique, see Driver, 1985, 1993b; Elden, 2003; Hannah, 1997a, 1997b; Philo, 1989, 2001). The Panopticon's spatial logic depended on a central inspection tower from which all prisoners, fixed within their cells, would in principle be constantly visible, fostering in inmates a sense of being forever under surveillance, an external eye that is then gradually interiorized as the internal eye of conscience. Mettray's spatial logic was different, since here the boys, allocated to artificial 'families' or collectivities of boys to which they were supposed to feel loyalty, were relatively free to move around and to interact – they were in no way fixed in cells – but in so doing were set within a veritable 'forest of gazes', everyone looking at and checking up on everybody else to ensure that conduct always reflected well on the families (which were encouraged to compete against one another for points, credits and sometimes more tangible rewards). Foucault argues that the 'maturation' of panopticism, the coming-of-age of modern disciplinary power, can be dated to the opening and early running of Mettray, thereby clarifying that for him the Panopticon and Mettray, their surface differences notwithstanding, are *both* emblematic of this new form of power diffusing across the face of modern Europe (and beyond too[6]).

With the discussion of Mettray, then, Foucault does encounter children and young people, albeit not in the sense that their status really *matters* to the broader trajectories of argument being unfolded. In short, the relevant section of the text is not *about* children and young people as such, but rather takes an institution (Mettray), one that just so happens to have housed this particular population cohort, as indicative of another crucial form – a more dispersed, mobile, multiple form, compared to in the Panopticon – that modern disciplinary power could adopt. Actually, this is perhaps to underestimate the extent to which an institution run along the lines of Mettray, with its family focus and deep conviction about the reformability of its inmates, could *only* have worked on younger delinquents and not on their adult parallels. Even so, the former are still not squarely the focus of attention that they become in Foucault's later writings, and it is also true that a 'family' model was deployed in other carceral institutions reserved *solely* for adults: here I am thinking of the Tukes' York Retreat for the Insane, as briefly discussed by Foucault in his first major text, *Madness and Civilization* (Foucault, 1967; see also Philo, 2004a, esp. chs 2 and 6). This latter point might itself be reversed, however, prompting critical inquiry into why and how there might be an 'infantilisation' of adults in facilities like the York Retreat: in other words, the construct of childhood arguably remained central to such facilities, refracted through techniques designed to *reduce* the adult inmates involved to the level of 'children' subject to the paternalist power relations of the (bourgeois) family.

Foucault's 'mad children'

The *Psychiatric Power* lectures (Foucault, 2006 [henceforth *PP* for in-text referencing]; see also Elden, 2006; Philo, 2007a) were written about the same time that Foucault was reworking the text that was to become *Discipline and Punish* (Foucault, 1976). Indeed, it is clear that the basic materials of *Discipline and Punish* had already been tackled as part of two earlier, as yet untranslated, lecture courses that were given between 1971 and 1973 (see Foucault, 1997a, 1997b). *Psychiatric Power* is fascinating because it sees Foucault returning to the themes of his first major text, *Madness and Civilization* (Foucault, 1967) and quite explicitly subjecting them to a retrospective auto-critique which, in part, amounts to a recasting of said themes through the lenses of power fashioned in *Discipline and Punish*. Thus, he expressly follows the thread of 'psychiatric power', as the quite specific version of modern disciplinary power – albeit with quite deep historical roots, troubling the chronology of *Discipline and Punish* – arising in the situated encounters between 'the mad' and their physicians (the proto-psychiatrists of the nineteenth century, as Foucault sometimes calls them).

Less the 'archaeological' excavation of discourses surrounding and constituting the mad from the Medieval period onwards, as linked to both a political economy and a diversity of institutional responses, it is more the 'genealogical' inspection of specific 'psychiatric scenes' in which the play of power, the micro-strategies or tactics of physicians in seeking to control their mad patients, becomes the prime focus. Foucault here claims that the power *of* the emerging psychiatric profession was anchored in these micro-strategies, enacted and dispersed across the spaces of the asylum which – in a memorable description (*PP*: 181) – Foucault describes as an extension of the psychiatrist's own body, his[7] presence, authority and instructions being embodied through the countless interventions of his staff (the medical officers, the attendants, the matrons) in every corner of an establishment. Crucially, though, it was precisely in this power, in the knowledge of how to manage the routine disciplining of patients allied to a nagging insistence that they acknowledge the 'truth' of their own madness, not persisting in their own delusions, that psychiatry gained shape and status. It did *not* do so on the basis of any real expertise regarding 'madness' itself. Despite fierce claims to the contrary, the physicians had no great medical or 'psychological' insight into the underlying causes of madness; indeed, their understanding in this respect was entirely banal, a *pseudo*-knowledge unconvincing if subjected to serious critique, and hence unlike what physicians of physical pathology could legitimately demonstrate.

There are various other things going on in *Psychiatric Power* that should be mentioned, since they all relate to the theme of 'Foucault's children'. For instance, Foucault considers the tangled relationships arising in the later nineteenth century between mental science (aka psychiatry) and neuroscience, wherein (marginally) more convincing linkages did begin to be drawn between human bodies (or at least nervous systems) and certain species of more minor mental illness (the so-called 'nervous diseases') which appeared to share aetiological ground with the likes of epilepsy, paralysis and different species of 'convulsions'. He also inserts a stunning account of how hysteria and hysterics fitted into this picture, suggesting that hysterics in effect 'played' their physicians, inventing stable physical symptomologies but at the same time 'acting up', intruding a voice of 'madness' that constantly obsessed about sexuality, sexual abuse and sexual perversions, wholly unnerving their physicians. By this light, if somewhat hyperbolically, Foucault positions hysterics as 'the true militants of anti-psychiatry' (*PP*: 254), and in so doing also opens the gates to a new feminist critique and rereading of psychiatric history. What he also identifies, at the close of *Psychiatric Power*, is this very terrain of concern, intimately sexual, that is soon to be colonized by psychoanalysis; and in certain respects Foucault regards the latter as just another technology of disciplinary power, on a par with those tactics nurtured in the nineteenth-century asylum, but now brought to bare on the disruptions occasioned by the hysterics as they threatened to spill the worrying waters of sexuality over the damns built by the proto-psychiatrists.

More broadly, what is happening, in terms of Foucault's own conceptual development, is that he starts to take more seriously both 'the flesh' – the actual bodies of patients and others, even as refracted through countless interpretational grids – and 'the confession', meaning the diverse techniques deployed to encourage individuals to speak of their innermost thoughts, feelings, experiences and fears, often as bound up with the seemingly most basal dimensions of life, death and sex. In short, we witness here the first stirrings of the concerns for *biopower* and *biopolitics*, the power and politics of and over the very fundamentals comprising *life*: who and what is to live, taking what forms, with what functions and what potentialities, and how such matters are to be talked about, understood and mastered. Such will be the deepest well-spring of 'the later Foucault', whether analysing the governments of either whole populations or individual selves (the two constantly intersecting modalities of 'governmentality', wherein biopower and biopolitics fold into one another: for brief comments, see Philo, 2004b; Sharp *et al.*, 2000: esp. 12–19). More specifically, sexual conduct cannot but be flowing centrally through this well-spring, which is why all of Foucault's later work is configured as contributions to 'a history of sexuality' (see also Elden, 2005).

But what of children in *Psychiatric Power*? In two lectures, the sixth and ninth in the series, Foucault discusses the 'constitution of the child as a target of psychiatric intervention' and then the 'generalisation of psychiatric power and the psychiatrisation of childhood' (phrases from the abstracts to these chapters: respectively, *PP*: 123 and *PP*: 201). What he means here is that, over the course of the nineteenth century, the orbit of psychiatric power – the sites of its application – gradually filtered out of the asylum into other spaces, including those of the family. There were two faces of this development, the first being the initial signs of wishing to detect the origins of 'madness' in an individual's childhood, spurred by a kind of 'evolutionary' or at least 'developmental' model of the individual's life wherein what someone *becomes* as an adult is reckoned to be detectable – and thus in principle explainable – in various shifts within and affecting their personality, beliefs and behaviours *during* childhood. Such a notion may now seem obvious, intuitive even, but it needed to be invented; and of course it was to be psychoanalysis, notably in its popularized Freudian guises, that would end up making this notion so commonplace. It was precisely this sense of 'abnormality' in waiting, as it were, that then commended a host of interventions *in* childhood, designed to correct minor difficulties or 'deviances' in the child before he or she gets too old, and in effect to assert a control over delinquency and ultimately more serious criminalities *before* such problems even surface in an individual (or, for that matter, a population). This idea, incipient in *Discipline and Punish*, is duly brought to light for critical examination, although it is actually in the *Abnormal* lectures that Foucault is most fully to unearth its many angles and outcomes (as we will see shortly).

Intriguingly, though, Foucault also argues as follows:

> It seems to me that both the notions and apparatuses of psychiatric control were gradually imported into the family. With regard to the famous instruments of restraint found in asylums from around 1820 to 1830 – binding hands, holding the head up, keeping in an upright position, etc. – my impression is that, initially established as instruments of and within asylum discipline, they gradually advance and take root in the family. The control of posture, of gestures, of the way to behave, the control of sexuality, with instruments for preventing masturbation, etc., all penetrate the family through a disciplinarisation which develops during the nineteenth century and the effect of which is that, through this disciplinarisation, the child's sexuality finally becomes an object of knowledge within the family itself.
>
> (pp. 124–5)

This passage anticipates the general concern for sexuality, as well as the more specific issue of the masturbating child, that was indeed to be foregrounded in the *Abnormal* lectures. At the same time, it hints at certain geographies integral to regulating children's sexuality: a 'dressage' of the child's bodily comportment, in which micro-spatial controls loom large (binding hands, keeping the body 'straight', maintaining appropriate distances); and the constant surveillance of the child's body, its postures and gestures, in which other kinds of micro-spatial mechanisms also figure prominently.

The idiot child

Intriguingly, though, in the ninth lecture of *Psychiatric Power*, Foucault takes a detour into the psychiatrization, not of the ordinary child or, to put it another way, the potentially 'mad child' (*PP*: 202), but of the 'idiot' or 'imbecile' child (who comes to be called the mentally handicapped/retarded child or, nowadays, the intellectually or developmentally disabled child or even the child with learning difficulties). Such a child was definitively *not* 'mad', not mentally ill, but rather was the bearer of a congenital condition, perhaps with readily visible complications, that meant his or her intellectual faculties simply would not develop in the same way as was 'normal' for everybody else. What this implied was that idiocy was a key plank in thinking about development, about the supposedly 'normal' developmental biography for the 'normal' individual, which also meant that the adult idiot – even more so that the adult mad person – was often understood as perpetually locked into childhood: 'The idiot belongs to childhood' (*PP*: 209). On a broader canvas of historical development, moreover, the idiot was seen as closer to humanity's own 'childhood', its original and supposedly primitive states, as well as being roped into emerging debates about 'degeneration': the idea that physical and mental 'defects' can be inherited, but also exacerbated, across the generations, with idiocy in a child standing as the result of successive generations of degenerative transmission (and with it also being thought imperative that idiots not be allowed to procreate, the root of 'eugenicist' reasoning that was also on the rise during the nineteenth century[8]). These elements were all what might be called, in Foucauldian vocabulary, 'surfaces of emergence' for a nexus of thought-and-action in which children, idiocy, development abnormalities and psychiatric intervention – where the latter indexed more the tactics of practical power perfected in the asylum, not the wielding of a genuinely specialist knowledge – were all problematically spun together.

Idiocy had for long been considered as part of the same broad field in which madness was situated, even if only in the context of calling forth distinctions between the two; and the institutional history of idiocy – the carceral sites to where idiots were often consigned, including both general confinement and asylums that were properly for 'lunatics', together with the changing practices directed at them – has always paralleled, and at times converged closely with, that of madness. More narrowly, Foucault discusses a process whereby, in later-nineteenth-century France, there was 'the establishment of idiocy within the psychiatric space, a colonization of idiocy by psychiatry' (*PP*: 211); a process with various faces, but which also included the opening of wards or even specialist pedagogical centres where idiot children would be subjected to much the same play of disciplinary power as physicians had refined in their treatment of mad people. Arguably, though, there was an even more transparent sense that what occurred here was barely anything to do with underlying causes, which in the idiot's case were already taken to be almost entirely beyond alteration, and everything to do with *training*: with creating appropriate environments and enacting suitable performances that might enable the idiot child to be trained into a measure of docility and usefulness, thereby instituting tactics that could impose the will of the trainer, educator or physician over the many small 'refusals' endemic to idiot children.[9]

Thus, 'in this moral treatment of idiot children you find again the organization of a disciplinary space like that of the asylum,' depending upon, 'for example, learning the linear distribution of bodies, individual places, gymnastic exercises – the full use of time' (*PP*: 217). Foucault hence outlines how the 'psychiatric power' of the idiot ward, asylum or colony was so redolent of 'school power', the species of power effected *outside* the idiot's institutional setting: i.e. in supposedly 'normal' schools. Foucault briefly touches on the techniques used by Éduoard Seguin, a famous figure in the history of nineteenth-century 'education' for idiots, emphasizing how Seguin used his own body as a vehicle for controlling that of the idiot child: 'A.H. [an idiot child] was uncontrollably lively; climbing like a cat, slipping away like a mouse. . . . I put him on a chair and sat opposite him, holding his feet and knees between mine; one of my hands held his two on his knees, while the other constantly brought his mobile face back in front of me. Apart from eating and sleeping, we stayed like that for five weeks' (in *PP*: 217). There is indeed a whole historical geography to be written about the precise location, spatial layout and spatialization of embodied practices in idiot schools, and I made a minor start on such a project many years ago in an unpublished paper dealing with the English idiot asylums, colonies and schools opened in the second half of the nineteenth century (Philo, 1987). In this paper, I briefly reviewed aspects of Seguin's practice, given that it had become influential in England, including things like encouraging idiot children to work in gardens, and noting how 'pathological' it was reckoned when children were found not caring for, but lopping the heads off, flowers. At that point, I was unaware of Foucault's own claims about such matters, let alone his explicit discussion of Seguin, but here without doubt is one very geographical implication of Foucault's claims about children in *Psychiatric Power*.

Foucault's 'little monsters'

I would suggest that in the *Abnormal* lectures (Foucault, 2003a [henceforth *Ab* for in-text referencing]; see also Elden, 2001; Stone, 2004) we detect an aspect of Foucault – a set of arguments, richly illustrated with empirical evidence – that can only be dimly apprehended in the already-published corpus (the books, essays and interviews). There is something different going on here, material that, for whatever exact reason, never made it into print before now, probably because it was all part of a much grander design for the various volumes of the *The History of Sexuality* series upon which Foucault was still working when he died in 1984 (although it is likely the case that new interests, and an increasing fascination with digging into the depths of Ancient and early-Christian practices of 'writing the self', also pushed the emphases of *Abnormal* into the background: see Elden, 2005). Central to this 'something different', I would insist, is the figure of the child, the child with 'problems', the recalcitrant child, and most obviously the masturbating child.

It must be realized that the *Abnormal* lectures were written when the manuscript for *Discipline and Punish* (Foucault, 1976) was on the verge of its first publication in French (in 1975). Thus, at this stage, Foucault is already even further along that road noted above (when discussing *Psychiatric Power*) of shifting his interests from the ground of *Discipline and Punish*, and towards the grand shapes of his projected history of sexuality: one charting the many and diverse ways in which 'regimes of truth' regarding right and proper conduct have been historically constituted around the corporeality (and, indeed, the psychology) of human sexual contact. Set within this horizon, people have been encouraged to 'see' themselves, to 'confess' their sexual sins and longings, and thereby to fashion themselves as beings with contingently appropriate sexual appetites, desires and prohibitions (linked to wider constructions of health, well-being and their opposites). The first volume in *The History of Sexuality* series (Foucault, 1979a) very much codifies these concerns. At the same time, and as mentioned in relation to *Psychiatric Power*, the contours of a concern for 'biopower', and for the 'biopolitics' of life, death, class, race and 'nation', all of which would later feature in his claims about 'governmentality', are also beginning to take shape (and would be further elaborated in the next sessional lecture series, that was entitled '*Society Must be Defended*': Foucault, 2003b; see also Elden, 2002; Philo, 2007b). It is perhaps no exaggeration to propose that *Abnormal* really does mark a decisive hinge in Foucault's overall thinking, the irony being that its own contents are so little-echoed in the already-published works.

The thrust of the lectures is set in part by Foucault's debt to one of his teachers, Georges Canguilhem, and notably the latter's text *On the Normal and the Pathological* (Canguilhem, 1973;[10] see also Philo, 2007c). Canguilhem seeks here to track medical thinking (and practice) around the envisaged boundary between the normal and the pathological, or the healthy and the diseased, from the 1700s through to the present (meaning the mid twentieth century). Canguilhem expressly critiques the concepts of 'normal', 'abnormal' and 'norm', retrieving a whole span of manoeuvres within medicine whereby *describing* what *is* apparently 'normal' in terms of human bodily form and function – normal as in the most statistically frequent, the average or mean – becomes the basis for *setting* 'norms' of what *ought* to be the proper forms and functions of human embodiment. Such norms, parachuted into specifications for what would be required from medical intervention hence serve as the basis for countless techniques of 'normalisation' designed to convert anything perceived – or, in a more quantitative vein, measured – as 'abnormal' back into the sizes, shapes and conformations of what is taken as normal. Canguilhem commences to broaden the scope of his analysis to take seriously not just the sphere of medicine in its most limited sense, but also the spheres of public health, education and law, all of which in one way or another constitute interlocking (but always distinguishable) 'institutions' or 'systems' within which – and between which – the press of normalization upon all manner of 'problem' peoples, places and practices is effected.

This vision is what Foucault takes as the point of departure for his inquiries in *Abnormal* (see also Elden, 2001: 102–4), striving, at bottom, to excavate how the late eighteenth and nineteenth centuries – again very much in Western Europe and a little in North America – saw the emergence of quite specific figures of the abnormal: particular constellations of abnormality in relation to which the prime ambition became the early detection of signs of abnormality *within* individuals, the hope being that suitable 'operations' could then be performed on these individuals to prevent their abnormality becoming a truly pathological 'monstrosity' (complete with all of the challenges that such monstrosity might pose for good social order: see also pp. 39–41 below). By 'operations' here, I mean – following Foucault – not the physical interventions of medical authority, the flash of the surgeon's knife perhaps, but the countless methods increasingly deployed by the embryonic disciplines of the human psyche (psychiatry, applied psychology, psychoanalysis, and diverse programmes of education, training, socialization). These concerns readily follow from the focus on modern disciplinary technologies displayed in *Discipline and Punish*, where Foucault often hinted at the more 'psychological' dimensions necessarily accompanying, and in some measure being afforded or demanded by, the mechanical interventions enacted in the spatial forms of the Panopticon or Mettray. They also follow from the moves made in *Psychiatric Power*, when reflecting upon the diffusion of the 'psy-function' through diverse fields of human endeavour, and as linked to the material shapes of, say, Seguin's schools for idiots. Here, though, the specificity of children as the locus for much of this attention, as indeed the crucible for the birth of wide-ranging normalization objectives and procedures that Foucault now sees as decisive in the making of modernity, becomes even more transparent.

There are various things happening in *Abnormal*, including an argument about the problematic intersections of psychiatric and juridical discourses, arising in the early-nineteenth century and continuing to the present day, wherein the most banal comments about individual psychologies – 'He cuts the heads off cabbages', 'She never liked her mother'; i.e. ones that psychiatrists would likely disown in their own professional writing – nonetheless end up attaining a privileged status, precisely *because* spoken by so-called 'experts', in another realm, the courtroom, whose own specialist discoursing is happy to leave a 'space' for such nonsense (in effect to abrogate certain responsibilities for inferring guilt and innocence in cases of psychological complexity). There are other remarkable elements too, such as passages where Foucault explicitly draws upon Canguilhem when critiquing the model of *exclusion* as 'shunning' that had dominated his own earlier work, proposing instead the need to adopt a model of *inclusion* – or, to be more precise, a model of *inclusion-in-exclusion*, emphasizing the play of power relations within institutions like prisons, wherein it is exclusion as a pre-condition for 'redeeming' – when critiquing how modern societies tackle their varied 'problem' populations. In effect, Foucault provides more of the connective tissue in his own thinking between *Madness and Civilization* (Foucault, 1967) and *Discipline and Punish* (Foucault, 1976): between the banishment of lepers to the woods or lunatics to country asylums and the socio-spatial disciplines gestated within the 'plague town', the Panopticon and Mettray.

There is also a particular substantive sweep in *Abnormal*, though, and this entails tracing the tangled genealogies of three distinctive figures: the 'monster' (initially meaning the acutely deformed person, perhaps with two heads or fused legs, but also those whose 'physical sex' is uncertain, mixed or absent); the recalcitrant individual (who basically misbehaves in some way and is in need of 'correction'); and the masturbating child (in principle, this could be any onanist, adult or child, but attention is mainly directed to the young 'self-abuser'). It should be added immediately, as Foucault admits in concluding the lecture course, that the second figure remains under-developed in his analysis, although conversely it could be argued that it actually becomes sufficiently generalized – as the notion of the problematic person *liable* at any point to think and act wrongly, against the norms of the age – as in effect to enroll the other two. In practice, though, it is the monster and the masturbating child who dominate the lectures, and – to cut horribly into the grain of his argument – the claim is that the former, a very old figure but gradually rendered more familiar, more immediately recognizable as 'human', from the seventeenth century onwards, in part exactly when it becomes a matter of sexual ambiguities largely invisible under clothing, was eventually 'reduced' in scale to the 'tiny monster' of the little boy playing with himself. (I might add at this point that the vast majority of the discourses and practices of concern did concentrate on boys, although some mention was still made of girls.)

The chain of reasoning is complex and convoluted, but in essence it goes like this: the nineteenth-century monster increasingly became cast in terms *not* of appearance per se, but in terms of the 'monstrosity' of acts done or crimes committed, such as butchering a baby, raping one's mother or performing sexual acts with the dead. The core issue became trying to establish what might possibly be the cause of such appalling actions, partly insofar that the plausibility or otherwise of the (relatively novel) 'insanity defence' in a courtroom could be decided, but partly because it began to be asked if the inklings of such monstrosity might be located in an individual's pre-history, their childhood included. A whole apparatus of concern then latched on to the child, scanning it for signs of the possible latent monstrosities which might be released during the course of an individual's subsequent 'development'. A penetrating gaze thereby descended upon the child, so Foucault states, hunting for any signs of embryonic monstrosity, for little signals of the pathological in the seemingly normal (to return to the terminology of Canguilhem); and thereby nailing a massive discourse of 'abnormality' on to what surely most of us today – and quite likely many people even then – would be regarding as the most innocent of childish 'ways', 'habits' and 'foibles'. In this way childhood became pathologized, or at least many aspects of it became pathologized, taken as the scenes of gestation for all manner of evils, physical and mental, profoundly disturbing to the social order (and, of course, deeply shaming for the families implicated). In this way too, the child was 'psychiatrised', thus extending the reasoning in the *Psychiatric Power* lectures; which means that the generalization of psychiatry – of the 'psy-function' – that is heralded in these lectures was here even more securely anchored around the figure of the child. 'Foucault's children' hence become absolutely crucial to a much broader thread of argument, one that in effect stitches together a great many otherwise quite diverse facets of Foucault's *oeuvre*: madness, psychiatry and psychiatric power; delinquency, criminality and disciplinary power; sexuality, techniques of the self (and self-control) and biopower.[11]

The masturbating child

It is instructive to take a closer look at the evidence deployed by Foucault in the ninth lecture of the *Abnormal* course, which will also allow a few more connections to be drawn to the concerns of children's geographies; and here I will also provide more direct quotation of Foucault's own evocative words. Around the early 1700s and gathering pace into the 1800s, a 'noisy chattering' (*Ab*: 233) broke out, so Foucault claims, on the subject of masturbation, different from anything that had gone before, and formatted less as 'scientific analysis' and more as 'a veritable campaign' (*Ab*: 235):

> It takes the form of exhortation, advice and injunctions. It is a literature of manuals, some of which are intended for parents. Around 1860, for instance, we find handbooks for fathers on how to prevent children from masturbation. But there are also tracts intended for children, for the adolescents themselves. The most famous is the *Livre sans titre*, which does not have a title but includes illustrations; all the disastrous consequences of masturbation are analysed on one side and on the facing page there are depictions of the increasingly decomposed, ravaged, skeletal and diaphanous physiognomy of the exhausted young masturbator. This campaign also includes institutions for the cure or care of masturbators, tracts for remedies and appeals from doctors that promise families they will cure their children of this vice.
>
> (*Ab*: 235)

Apparently, there was even a 'wax museum' in turn-of-the-century France where children could be taken by the parents to see, in waxy embodiment, the health problems that they could suffer if their little hands should ever stray inappropriately to their private parts.

What we learn here, according to Foucault, is that the discourses forming this campaign were, surprisingly, not especially or overtly 'moralistic'; or at least the emphasis was not – one or two examples aside – on childhood masturbation leading to adult sexual perversity, but rather on such masturbations necessarily leading to all manner of illnesses (either a 'total illness', some kind of 'absolute' sick condition indexed by every symptom under the sun, or 'every possible kind of illness'). One description from an early-nineteenth-century French dictionary of medical science reads as follows:

> 'This young man suffered from the most complete apathy; to sight, he was entirely lifeless. He satisfied the call of nature wherever he happened to be. His body gave off a particularly nauseating odour. His skin was ashen, his tongue lolled, his eyes were sunken, all his teeth were loose, and his gums were covered with ulcers §that foretold a scorbutic degeneration. Death for him could only be a happy release from his lengthy suffering.' We recognize here the portrait of the young masturbator with its fundamental characteristics: exhaustion, loss of substance, an inert, diaphanous and dull body, a constant discharge, a disgusting oozing from within the body, the infection of those around him and the consequent impossibility of their approaching him . . .
>
> (*Ab*: 238)

If that was masturbation leading to total illness, with death lurking in the background, the scientific texts of the time more commonly identified myriad specific illnesses that might result from self-abuse as a child: everything from meningitis to encephalitis to bone disease, degeneration of bone tissues, heart diseases, diseases of the eyes, tuberculosis and, of course, 'madness' (or different types of mental disease). Foucault also identifies the genre of the so-called 'patient's letters', wherein individuals provided mini-biographies of their many bodily ailments as bound up with their indulging as children in the 'bad habit' of masturbation: dizzy spells, aching joints and limbs, coughing up blood, nervous attacks preventing arm movement, fainting fits, blood loss and heaven knows what else. (As an aside, it must be underlined that there was and is *no* respectable scientific evidence to substantiate such connections; and as another aside, it is clear that Foucault really enjoyed reading this part of his lectures.)

Foucault argues that what was occurring here was a 'scientific fabulation' discursively constituting 'the inexhaustible causal power of infantile sexuality' (*Ab*: 240), meaning masturbation, which managed to avoid being particularly 'moralistic' *about* sexuality as such – much remained unsaid, just inferred – while nonetheless wholeheartedly condemning the act of child-hood self-abuse (and note of course the negative connotations of self-*ab*use). More broadly, the pathologizing of sexuality was commencing – the association of physical and mental illness with improper sexuality – and thus opening up a whole terrain of reasoning, medical, moral and medico-moral, that very much remains with us today (albeit refracted through different concepts and vocabularies to those of the eighteenth and nineteenth centuries[12]). The question to the child became 'What have you done with your hand?', but only as the tip of an emerging iceberg of sexual pathology, and in this context moves were afoot to cast childhood (notably *pre*pubescent) masturbation as itself *ab*normal, not a normal part of childhood-to-adulthood development, but rather as something arising by chance, a curiously random outcome in those children who perhaps discover a certain pleasure in, say, scratching an itch in the vicinity of their genitals.

Alternatively, it was acknowledged that a child might be led astray by 'the involuntary . . . encouragement given by parents and educators while washing the child with those 'careless and tickling hands', as one text puts it' (*Ab*: 243–4), or then again there might be cases where the more willful encouragement of older siblings, servants, private tutors or even family members played a role. In the latter two scenarios, dangers were duly attached to the less-than-properly-or-assiduously-run household, and ultimately the blame shifted from the children to the parents, even or especially where they allowed others – other family members, nurses, underlings of all kinds – to take direct care of their progeny. As Foucault notes:

> [T]he parents are ultimately guilty since these problems occur because they do not want to take direct responsibility for their children. It is their lack of care, their laziness, and their desire for tranquility that is ultimately in question in children's masturbation. After all, they only needed to be present and to open their eyes. For that reason, and quite naturally, it is the parents and their relationship with their children within the family space that is called into question.
>
> (*Ab*: 244–5)

Thus:

> What is required . . . is essentially a new organisation, a new physics of the family space: the elimination of all intermediaries and the suppression, if possible, of domestics, or at least a very close supervision of domestics, the ideal solution being the infant alone in a sexually aseptic space. . . . The ideal situation, if you like, is the child alone with her doll or his drum. It is ideal but unrealisable. Actually, the family space must be a space of continual surveillance. Children must be watched over when they are washing, going to bed, getting up and while they sleep. Parents must keep a lookout all around their children, over their clothes

and bodies. The child's body must be the object of their permanent attention. This is the adult's primary concern. Parents must read their child's body . . . as the field of possible signs of masturbation.

(*Ab*: 245)

Foucault cites various 'experts' on such matters, including one tract of 1835 warning about the tell-tale signs of the boy who hands are 'never outside the bed' and who 'likes to hide his head under the blankets'. He generalizes to propose that we find here 'the little theatre of the family comedy and tragedy with its beds, its sheets, the night, the lamps, with its stealthy approaches [the parent checking on the child], its odours, and the carefully inspected stains on the sheets; the little drama that brings the adult's curiosity ever closer to the child's body' (*Ab*: 246–7). Children were made to sleep 'straight' in their beds, with hands visible, recalling that 'dressage' of the child's body mentioned earlier; and it was also proposed that difficult cases should have their hands bound or laced with ties connected to older siblings or parents who would thereby be alerted to any attempt by the masturbator to satisfy their urges. If the need arose, moreover, it was even proposed in the 1835 tract that parents 'should sleep beside the young masturbator, in the same room and possibly in the same bed, in order to prevent him from masturbating' (*Ab*: 247). Such a recommendation strikes us as very strange, of course, given how greatly the whole discourse of fears surrounding child sexuality, and adult predations thereon, has changed since the 1800s. Whatever, all of the above entails 'the instruction for the direct, immediate and constant application of the parents' bodies to the bodies of their children' (*Ab*: 247). Collectively, everything described here amounts to an intense micro-panopticism applied to the most intimate spaces of the child's body, bed, bedroom, sheets, clothes and inter-corporeal contact with siblings and parents. The most close-in micro-geographies of childhood are thereby disclosed, signalling a fresh terrain of concern for the study of children's geographies.

Furthermore, what Foucault also claims is that the very form of the European family was undergoing a dramatic transition. Whereas the aristocratic or bourgeois family form prevailing up to the mid 1700s was a somewhat loose affair, 'a bundle of relations of ancestry, descent, collateral relations, cousinhood, primogeniture and alliances corresponding to schemas of transmission of kinship and the division and distribution of goods and social status' (*Ab*: 248), something novel was now afoot. We therefore arrive at exceptionally provocative critical-historical statements about the reshaping of childhood and its geographies:

What is now being constituted is a sort of restricted, close-knit, substantial, compact, corporeal and affective family core: the cell family in place of the relational family; the cell family with its corporeal, affective and sexual space entirely saturated by direct parent–child relationships. . . .

By highlighting the child's sexuality, or more exactly the child's mas-
turbatory activities . . . parents were urgently enjoined to reduce the
large polymorphous and dangerous space of the household, and to do
no more than forge with their children, their progeny, a sort of single
body bound together through concern about infantile sexuality, about
infantile autoeroticism and masturbation. Parents! Keep watch over your
excited daughters and the erections of your sons because this is how you
will become fully and truly parents!

(*Ab*: 248–9)

Foucault hence traces the origins of the cell or nuclear family[13] to precisely
this growing discourse and fear around the figure of the tiny masturbator,
the self-abusing child, whose body must be placed in a field of constant vis-
ibility, inspectability and potential intervention as surely as must any prisoner
in their Panopticon cell. Here he finds the origins of that family form now
so common, so accepted as the norm and as what should be normal, within
the West at least (see below), yet so saturated with 'this epistemophilic
incest of touch, gaze and surveillance' (*Ab*: 249);[14] and in so claiming he
reverses what might be the usual direction of reasoning, seeing the modern
nuclear family as the product of proliferating concern about the masturbating child, rather than the latter as resulting from the rise of the nuclear
family.

The plausibility or historical accuracy of Foucault's account – as far as this
may be deduced from extant sources – cannot readily be judged here, my
chief objective being simply to summarize the trajectory of his provocations
for studies of children, childhood and children's geographies. But what I
must finally add is his observation that parents were supposed to be drawing
upon 'expert' literature, guidelines and – if, heaven forbid, the masturbating child *was* discovered in the family midst – practical, maybe institutional
treatments; so much so that the promise could be realized of family power
and medical power, including psychiatric power, fully articulating with one
other. As Foucault elaborates:

The parents-children relationship that is solidifying into a sort of
physical-sexual unit [a physical-sexual geography] must therefore be
consistent with the doctor-patient relationship; it must extend the
doctor-patient relationship. The father or mother who is so close to the
children's bodies . . . must at the same time be a father and a mother
who are diagnosticians, therapists and agents of health. But this also
means that their control is subordinate, that it must be open to medical
and hygienic intervention, and that they must call upon the external
and scientific authority of the doctor at the first warning signs. In other
words, at the very moment that the cellular family is enclosed in a dense,
affective space, it is endowed with a rationality that, in the name of illness, plugs it into a technology, into an external medical power and

knowledge. The new substantial, affective and sexual family is at the same time a medicalised family.

(*Ab*: 250)

Within this narrowed family space, sexuality was not to be spoken about as such; if it reared its head, then the 'experts' should be called in, and it is the latter who had the task of putting into words what the family had first made visible by watching over itself in its most intimate moments and locations. 'Essentially, the family must function merely as a relay or transmission belt between the child's body and the doctor's technique' (*Ab*: 251–2). Foucault then delights in recounting the sorts of 'technologies' that the doctors would utilize: inaccessible nightshirts, a sort of metal corset that parents could keep padlocked, a little cane that could be inserted in a boy's penis as a deterrent, a variety of acupuncture (or at least inserting needles near the groin), and so on. One or two experts even ventured that castration might be a remedy in extreme cases, while more of these male physicians were prepared to contemplate clitorectomies or cauterizations. More broadly, programmes of 'natural education' were in the air designed to ensure the correct, hence 'natural', course of child-to-adult development, something increasingly concerning the nation-state when reviewing the condition of its biopower (in another lexicon, the virility of its fighting 'manpower'). Within the institutional spaces of schools, moreover, and even more markedly in reformatories such as Mettray or training academies for the armed forces, embryonic 'professionals' of all hues joined forces in the crusade against masturbation by children, adolescents and young men.

Conclusion: Foucauldian children's geographies?

When initially conceiving of his work on the history of sexuality, Foucault envisaged a six-volume series of books covering a range of thematic topics: at least that is what is apparent from the back cover of the first volume published in French (*La volonté de savoir*, translated as Foucault, 1979a: see Elden, 2001: 93; 2005). The third book of this series was to be entitled *La croisade des enfants*, or 'The children's crusade', and it was doubtless intended to cover the issue of the masturbating child, the ground for which I have briefly mapped in this paper. Had such a book been published, of course, then Foucault would instantly have become a more central figure in social studies of children and childhood, as well as – in a more minor register – attracting more immediate attention in the subfield of children's geographies. That Foucault could still be a key reference-point for toilers on children and childhood, despite the non-publication of *Le croisade des enfants*, remains arguable; but a close reading of the *Psychiatric Power* (Foucault, 2006) and *Abnormal* (Foucault, 2003a) lectures, as begun here, surely does strengthen the case, opening up horizons for rethinking the place – both actual and possible – of children within the broader sweep of Foucault's mid- and later-career writings on disciplinary power, biopower, governmentality and the history of sexuality.

As indicated, a central plank of the *Psychiatric Power* and *Abnormal* lectures is the 'generalisation' of psychiatry, the dispersal of the 'psy-function', throughout many domains of mid- to later-nineteenth-century social life. As such, it is presented as a pivotal element within that 'swarming of the disciplines' discussed in *Discipline and Punish*, where Foucault deploys the term 'disciplines' in the double sense of both grounded tactics for 'disciplining' people and organized bodies of knowledge, practice and concern comprising modern academic subjects and their professional application. It is clear that these doubles of discipline were seen by him as inextricably entangled, which of course is wholly consistent with the still-grander optic of power/ knowledge (Gordon, 1980) through which Foucault increasingly spied the social world from the early-1970s onwards. But what also becomes apparent is that a crucial terrain across which this generalization of the psy-functions occurred, from at least the 1830s, was that of childhood, partly in a practical sense of it being in ordinary schools, idiot schools and other training institutions that certain tactics of psychiatric power could be readily enacted, but partly in the more conceptual sense of it being in childhood that 'experts' of all stripes increasingly looked for signs of developmental abnormalities that could, if unchecked in childhood, lead to all manner of disastrous social pathologies in adulthood. Hence we detect precisely that association between adult 'monstrosities' and the little badnesses of childhood, and still more specifically the tiny habits of children's self-abuse, that, according to Foucault, become elemental to the apparatuses of monitoring, intervening and legislating that grew up around childhood – as both an intensification of and further catalyst for an overall panopticism traversing society 'in the round' – during the nineteenth century. If there is any truth in such claims, then the relevance expands exponentially of careful research into the constitution and transformation of nineteenth-century childhoods: research that starts to matter not just for what it unearths in its own immediate field of study but for the implications running off into countless other domains of critical-historical inquiry. The historical geographies of childhood, and particularly inquiries into the nineteenth-century spaces of adult interactions with and 'operations' upon children, similarly grow in significance.

Foucault's reconstruction – even historical explanation – of increasingly cellular bourgeois families progressively 'homing' in on the spaces of the home, and even more minutely the spaces of their children's bedrooms and bodies, potentially provides fresh ammunition in thinking about certain core concerns of current children's geographies. The prominence of this increasingly hegemonic if idealized model of family life, and hence of the lifeworlds experienced by children caught within its parameters, can surely be mapped from the pages of both *Psychiatric Power* and *Abnormal* to the texts, or maybe better the subtexts, of many projects in children's geographies concerned with the spatialized dialectics of constraint and free-dom – the former too often, it seems, winning out over the latter – present in the boundaries placed around today's children, the landscapes of surveil-lance into which they are inserted, and so on. Indeed, countless studies in children's geographies now hedge around the form taken by the modern (Western) family, notably once attention is drawn to the bubble-wrapped geographies of today's chaperoned child – constantly located in or ferried around in spaces shared with parents or delegated adult guardians – whose every bump and burp, it seems, is monitored, docketed, interpreted and possibly acted upon.[15] Exactly in line with his oft-stated aim of writing a 'criti-cal history of the present', here, in *Psychiatric Power* and *Abnormal*, Foucault is effectively teasing out the conditions of emergence for a construct – the nuclear family, its operations and spaces, its dovetailing with other 'expert' systems and spaces – that has become a relatively unquestioned fundamental of the present age. In another vocabulary, he writes the 'pre-history' – dare I say the 'pre-historical geography' – of much that is staple fare, as either largely unremarked background or overtly inspected foreground, in existing work on children's geographies.

More specifically, and contrary to other commentators, Foucault sees the nuclear family as itself a product *of*, less a precondition *for*, changing dis-courses and practices surrounding child sexuality, themselves shaped within a much more expansive landscape of human 'monstrosity', developmental abnormalities and the necessarily incoherent intersections of psychiatry, medicine, judiciary and education. Work on children's geographies to date has tended to be fixated on the contemporary, even to the point of being presentist, and the rarity of historically attuned studies is only made the more remarkable by recognizing what *can* be accomplished when reading the exemplary papers of Elizabeth Gagen[16] (e.g. 2000a, 2000b, 2001, 2004, 2007; see also de Leeuw, 2009) – who sometimes will position herself as a children's geographer – on how the evolutionary theories of later-nineteenth-century US psychologists and educationists played through into the material spaces of organized playgrounds (to which families entrusted their little loved ones). And yet the potentials held within Foucault's *oeuvre* for forging a more Foucauldian and hence critical-historical branch of children's geographies, particularly once the new additions to this *oeuvre* are acknowledged, strike me as legion. While this is admittedly in the main a matter of academic interest, it is not entirely so, for an historical focus is always one revealing that 'things have not forever been thus' and hence could maybe be differ-ent again in the future. In other words, it is *not* Foucault's fault that 'we' (modern Westerners) seem obsessed by the nuclear family; he is precisely concerned to show how this eventuality has come about, thereby prizing open the door to a sustained *critique* of said eventuality. In short, things do *not* need to be like this, and we can perhaps imagine other possibilities for the family, for childhood, for children, for 'real' children's geographies as created and lived.

Acknowledgements

A version of this paper was given at the *Global Futures* 'Retreat', University of Washington, Seattle, WA, in August 2006, and another version at the *First International Children's Geographies* Conference, University of Reading, September 2007. Particular thanks are due to Jane Dyson, Craig Jeffrey and Ann Anagost (at the Washington event) and Louise Holt, Stuart Aitken, Sophie Bowlby, Sara Holloway, Cindi Katz and Mike Kesby (at the Reading event) for their organizational contributions and/or feedback on my presentations. Thanks as well to Louise Holt for putting this volume together, and for her supportive editorial presence. Thanks also to Jessica Pykett for both encouraging comments and the sight of her 2009 paper.

Notes

1   The reference is to perhaps Foucault's most forbidding book, *The Order of Things* (Foucault, 1970).
2   In a paper available online, Gallagher (2006?) has gone on to use an impressive range of Foucault's writings in reflecting critically about the themes of 'Foucault, power and participation', although the geographical dimensions here are minimal; while in another paper available online, Gallacher and Gallagher (2005) borrow Foucauldian notions of power-knowledge in critiquing standard participatory methods in research with children.
3   Based on audio tapes, supplemented by use of his lecture notes (although not strictly a publication of these notes, which is not permitted by a letter that Foucault wrote a year before his death stipulating 'no posthumous publications': Elden, 2001: 91). The standard of the editorial work on these materials, supplemented by richly noted reconstructions of the primary evidence and secondary literature upon which he was drawing, is exemplary.
4   A caveat, though, is that researchers of children and childhood *may* have some familiarity with the sorts of ideas carried in these lectures from the work of Jacques Donzelot, and more specifically the latter's text *The Policing of Families* (1979a). Donzelot was clearly influenced by Foucault, being one of a group of scholars around Foucault in the mid 1970s working on historical materials; and a case can be made that *The Policing of Families* represents a sustained out-working of themes from the *Psychiatric Power* and *Abnormal* lecture series. In the preface to the English edition of the former text, Donzelot (1979a: xxv) acknowledges that the 'we' who is responsible for what follows 'is not the royal one, of course; it refers to a team fashioned on the periphery of Michel Foucault and Gilles Deleuze.' Deleuze, meanwhile, provides a remarkably clear and thoughtful foreword, in which Foucault's influence upon Donzelot – including his emerging concern for 'biopolitics' – is underlined (Deleuze, 1979: xi, xiv [note 1]). See also Donzelot (1979b), and the extended review of his book (the original French text) in Hodges and Hussain (1979).
5   This is not the place to provide detailed lists of references to relevant studies: indeed, this chapter will be deliberately light in its referencing of secondary Foucauldian scholarship both inside and outwith human geography (once you start referencing this scholarship, it is hard to know where to stop!). However, see the Crampton and Elden (2007) edited volume for an indication of the remarkable range of borrowings from Foucault in contemporary human geography.

6 I am fully aware that there is a persuasive critique to be directed at Foucault for his Eurocentricism, and that postcolonial writings adopt a careful stance of critical engagement with Foucault, aware that his ideas (both broader concepts and substantive generalizations) may and should not 'travel' unscathed to places outwith Europe (and the West).

7 It was always a 'he': there were no female superintendents of Europe's nineteenth-century public asylums, although a handful of female proprietors of (fee-charging) private madhouses can be identified (Philo, 2004b, ch. 5).

8 The historical geographers Radford and Carter Park have written several excellent historical-geographical studies of idiot asylums, in both nineteenth- and early-twentieth-century England and Canada, and they have also considered the eugenics arguments surrounding – and to an extent justifying the remote, secluded locations of – such institutions (for references, see Metzel and Philo, 2005).

9 In parentheses, the simple observation must be made that, because comparatively few nineteenth-century idiots survived beyond early adulthood, institutional spaces for idiots were primarily occupied by idiot children; and hence idiot asylums and colonies were often chiefly, and expressly named as, idiot schools.

10 Published in English in 1973, embracing both Canguilhem's 1943 doctoral thesis and a substantial 1966 addendum. The English version also carries a very thoughtful introduction by Foucault.

11 It can be added here that various of the themes just noted, including a taste of the empirical materials used in the *Abnormal* lectures, did creep into Foucault (1979a).

12 It seems to be the case that childhood masturbation has largely ceased to be much of a concern today, albeit still not being seen as something to be encouraged. Clearly, the terrain of anxiety around children and sexuality has moved much more towards the threat of adult sexual predation *upon* children, coupled to concerns about what children might inadvertently – or perhaps even wilfully – access *about* sexuality through watching television programmes or, possibly now *the* great concern, using the Internet.

13 Foucault is clear that the core of his analysis only applies to bourgeois childhoods, to increasingly cellular bourgeois families progressively 'closing' themselves within the policed boundaries of a sparsely populated family home. The counterpoint for his inquiries on this score – pursued in the tenth lecture of the *Abnormal* course – is the working-class family which arguably retains, even down to the present, a more expanded social field involving many more adults who cross the boundaries and can be enrolled in the watching, care and direction of 'family' offspring.

14 Reflecting upon how middle-class parents internalize a 'privatized domain of practice as a locus for determining their social value as "good parents" [, one shot through with] . . . an intensified aura of sentiment surrounding family life' (Anagost, 2000: 391), Anagost (2000: 416 [note 11]) remarks on 'the ways in which all "modern" parents are positioned in a space of anxiety replete with paradox and contradiction'.

15 A key reference-point for me here is a plethora of studies – too many to begin referencing – in children's geographies and related subfields that have explored the diminishing lifeworlds of many children, chiefly the offspring of Western(ized) families: the point being that a whole raft of parental (and adult, policy-maker, 'expert') fears about the perils presently confronting children, including the likes of environmental pollution but mainly centring on the spectre of abduction and/or abuse by 'strangers', have spurred an upsurge in the 'cocooning' of children, with parents (and other adults) increasingly 'chaperoning' them from family homes to schools, leisure activities, sports events, friends' houses, etc. The

elemental unit here becomes the nuclear family, caught within the walls of its self-imposed 'cell', walls that arguably close down many possibilities for children's independent negotiation of the environments, physical and social, beyond said 'walls' (with another aspect being the increasing surveillance of children within these 'walls', including the likes of spying on their Internet access). Many papers in the journal *Children's Geographies*, as well as numerous PhD theses, have been documenting this development.

16 Gagen (2010) has actually anticipated something of my argument in this chapter with her own excellent outline suggestions for drawing upon Foucauldian claims (about surveillance, 'disciplining bodies' and 'governmentality') in childhood research, specifically work on children's geographies, and she also offers brief speculations about why a Foucauldian approach has not been adopted here previously. Her chapter unfortunately appeared too late to be incorporated more fully into my chapter; but I must extend my thanks to her for sharing it with me.

References

Aitken, S.C. (1994) *Putting Children in their Place*, Washington DC: Association of American Geographers.

Aitken, S.C. (2001), *Geographies of Young People: The Morally Contested Space of Identity*, London: Routledge.

Anagnost, A. (2000) 'Scenes of misrecognition: maternal citizenship in the age of transnational adoption', *Positions*, 8: 389–421.

Ansell, N. (2009) 'Embodied learning: responding to AIDS in Lesotho's education sector', *Children's Geographies*, 7: 21–36.

Barker, J., Alldred, P., Watts, M. and Dodman, H. (2010) 'Pupils or prisoners? institutional geographies and internal exclusion in UK secondary schools', *Area*, 42: 378–86.

Benstead, K. (2001) *Disciplining Leisure: A Foucauldian Analysis of Outdoor Adventure for Young People at Risk and Young Offenders*, unpublished PhD thesis, School of Geography, University of Edinburgh.

Canguilhem, G. (1973) *On the Normal and the Pathological*, Dordrecht, Holland/USA/Canada/London: D. Reidel Publishing Company [trans., orig. 1966].

Cannella, G.S. (1999) 'The scientific discourse of education: predetermining the lives of others – Foucault, education and children', *Contemporary Issues in Early Childhood*, 1: 36–44.

Catling, S. (2005) 'Children's personal geographies and the English primary school geography curriculum', *Children's Geographies*, 3: 325–44.

Covaleskie, J.F. (1993) 'Power goes to school: teachers, students and discipline', Proceedings of the 49th Annual Meeting of Philosophy of Education Society, Champaign IL, Philosophy of Education Society, pp. 79–85.

Crampton, J.W. and Elden, S. (eds) (2007) *Space, Knowledge and Power: Foucault and Geography*, Aldershot, UK: Ashgate.

de Leeuw, S. (2009) '"If anything is to be done with the Indian, we must catch him very young": colonial constructions of Aboriginal children and the geographies of Indian residential schooling in British Columbia, Canada', *Children's Geographies*, 7: 123–40.

Deleuze, G. (1979) 'The rise of the social', foreword to Donzelot, J. (1979) *The*

Policing of Families, Baltimore and London: Johns Hopkins University Press [trans., orig. 1977].

Donzelot, J. (1979a) *The Policing of Families*, Baltimore and London: Johns Hopkins University Press [trans., orig. 1977].

Donzelot, J. (1979b) 'The poverty of political culture', *Ideology & Consciousness*, 5 (Spring): 73–86.

Driver, F. (1985) 'Power, space and the body: a critical assessment of Foucault's *Discipline and Punish*', *Environment and Planning D: Society and Space*, 3: 425–46.

Driver, F. (1990) 'Discipline without frontiers? Representations of Mettray reformatory colony in Britain 1840–1880', *Journal of Historical Sociology*, 3: 272–93.

Driver, F. (1993a) *Power and Pauperism: The Workhouse System, 1834–1884*, Cambridge: Cambridge University Press.

Driver, F. (1993b) 'Bodies in space: Foucault's account of disciplinary power', in C. Jones and R. Porter (eds) *Reassessing Foucault: Power, Medicine and the Body*, London: Routledge, pp. 113–31.

Elden, S. (2001) 'The constitution of the normal: monsters and masturbation at the Collège de France', *Boundary 2*, 28(1): 91–105.

Elden, S. (2002) 'The war of the races and the constitution of the state: Foucault's *'Il faut defendre la société'*, *Boundary 2*, 29: 125–51.

Elden, S. (2003) 'Plague, panopticon, police', *Surveillance and Society*, 1: 240–53.

Elden, S. (2005) 'The problem of confession: the productive failure of Foucault's *History of Sexuality*', *Journal for Cultural Research*, 9: 23–41.

Elden, S. (2006) 'Discipline, health and madness: Foucault's *Le pouvoir psychiatrique*, *History of the Human Sciences*, 19: 39–66.

Foucault, M. (1967) *Madness and Civilization: A History of Insanity in the Age of Reason*, London: Tavistock [trans., orig. 1961: a full English translation has very recently been published].

Foucault, M. (1970) *The Order of Things: An Archaeology of the Human Sciences*, London: Tavistock [trans., orig. 1966].

Foucault, M. (1976) *Discipline and Punish: The Birth of the Prison*, London: Allen Lane [trans., orig. 1975].

Foucault, M. (1979a) *The Will to Knowledge: The History of Sexuality, Vol. 1* London: Allen Lane [trans., orig. 1976].

Foucault, M. (1979b) 'Governmentality', *Ideology and Consciousness*, 6: 5–21 [trans., orig. Collège de France lecture from 1976–1977].

Foucault, M. (1985) *The Uses of Pleasure: The History of Sexuality, Vol. 2*, London: Penguin [trans., orig. 1984].

Foucault, M. (1986) *The Care of the Self: The History of Sexuality, Vol. 3*, London: Penguin Books [trans., orig. 1984].

Foucault, M. (1997a) 'Penal theories and institutions [course outline for lectures at the Collège de France, 1971–1972]', in P. Rabinow (ed.), *Michel Foucault: Ethics, Subjectivity and Truth (Essential Works of Foucault, 1954–1984)*, New York: The New Press, pp. 17–21.

Foucault, M. (1997b) 'The punitive society [course outline for lectures at the Collège de France, 1971–1972]', in P. Rabinow. (ed.), *Michel Foucault: Ethics, Subjectivity and Truth (Essential Works of Foucault, 1954–1984)*, New York: The New Press, pp. 23–37.

Foucault, M. (2003a) *Abnormal: Lectures at the Collège de France, 1974–1975*, London: Verso.

Foucault, M. (2003b) *'Society Must be Defended': Lectures at the Collège de France, 1975–1976*, New York: Picador [trans., orig. 1997].

Foucault, M. (2006) *Psychiatric Power: Lectures at the Còllege de France, 1973–1974* [trans., orig. 2003], Basingstoke: Palgrave Macmillan.

Gagen, E.A. (2000a) 'An example to us all: child development and identity construction in early 20th-century playgrounds', *Environment and Planning A*, 32: 599–616.

Gagen, E.A. (2000b) 'Playing the part: performing gender in America's playgrounds', in S.L. Holloway and G. Valentine, G. (eds) *Children's Geographies: Playing, Living, Learning*, London: Routledge, pp. 213–29.

Gagen, E.A. (2001) 'Too good to be true: representing children's agency in the archives of the playground movement', *Historical Geography*, 29: 53–64.

Gagen, E.A. (2004) 'Making America flesh: physicality and nationhood in turn-of-the-century New York schools', *Cultural Geographies*, 11: 417–42.

Gagen, E.A. (2007) 'Reflections of primitivism: development, progress and civilization in imperial America, 1898–1914', *Children's Geographies*, 5: 15–28.

Gagen, E.A. (2010) 'Commentary: disciplining bodies', in Colls, R. and Horschelmann, K. (eds), *Contested Bodies of Childhood and Youth*, Basingstoke: Palgrave Macmillan, pp. 178–89.

Gallacher, L. (2005) '"The terrible twos": gaining control in the nursery?' *Children's Geographies*, 3: 243–64.

Gallacher, L. and Gallagher, M. (2005) 'Participatory methods in research with children: a critique', paper given at Emerging Issues in the Geography of Children and Youth conference, Brunel University, June 2005. Available at: http://www.geos.ed.ac.uk/homes/s0453363/brunelpaper.pdf (accessed 23 August 2007).

Gallagher, M. (2005) *Producing the Schooled Subject: Techniques of Power in a Primary School Classroom*, unpublished PhD thesis, School of Geography, University of Edinburgh.

Gallagher, M. (2006) 'Foucault, participation and power', unpublished paper. Available at: http://www.childhoodstudies.ed.ac.uk/uk/research/MGallagher.doc (accessed 23 August 2007).

Gallagher, M. (2008) '"Power is not an evil": rethinking power in participatory methods', *Children's Geographies*, 6: 137–50.

Gaskell, C. (2008) '"But they just don't respect us": young people's experience of (dis)respected citizenship and the New Labour Respect Agenda', *Children's Geographies*, 6, 223–38.

Germeten, S. (2000) 'Early childhood education in Norway: time as an indication for pedagogical space?', paper given at the 10th European Conference on Quality in Early Childhood Education, London, August–September 2000. Available at: http://extranet.edfac.unimelb.edu.au/LED/Eec/pdf/germeten1.pdf (accessed 23 August 2007).

Giddings, R. and Yarwood, R. (2005) 'Growing up, going out and growing out of the countryside: childhood experiences in rural England', *Children's Geographies*, 3: 101–14.

Gordon, C. (ed) (1980) *Michel Foucault: Power/Knowledge – Selected Interviews and Other Writings, 1972–1977, by Michel Foucault*, Brighton, UK: Harvester Press.

Hannah, M.G. (1997a) 'Space and the structuring of disciplinary power: an interpretive review', *Geofraska Annaler*, 79B: 171–80.

Hannah, M.G. (1997b) 'Imperfect panopticism: envisioning the construction of normal lives', in G. Benko and U. Strohmayer (eds) *Space and Social Theory: Interpreting Modernity and Postmodernity*, Oxford: Blackwell, pp. 344–59.

Harker, C. (2005) 'Playing and affective time-spaces', *Children's Geographies*, 3: 47–62.

Hemming, P.J. (2007) 'Renegotiating the primary school: children's emotional geographies of sports, exercise and active play', *Children's Geographies*, 5: 353–71.

Hodges, J. and Hussain, A. (1979) 'La police des familles', *Ideology & Consciousness*, No. 5 (Spring, 1979): 87–123.

Holloway, S.L. and Valentine, G. (eds) (2000) *Children's Geographies: Playing, Living, Learning*, London: Routledge.

Holt, L. (2004) 'Children with mind-body differences: performing disability in primary school classrooms', *Children's Geographies*, 2: 19–236.

Holt, L. (2006) 'Exploring "other" childhoods through quantitative secondary analyses of large scale surveys: opportunities and challenges for children's geographers', *Children's Geographies*, 4: 143–55.

James, A., Jenks, C. and Prout, A. (1998) *Theorising Childhood*, Cambridge: Polity Press.

Jenks, C. (2005) *Childhood*, London: Routledge.

Jones, O. (2006) 'Book review of Jenks's *Childhood*', *Children's Geographies*, 4: 401–2.

Jones, O. (2008) 'True geography [ ] quickly forgotten, giving way to an adult-imagined universe': approaching the otherness of childhood', *Children's Geographies*, 6: 195–212.

Katz, C. (2004) 'Commentary on Wood and Beck's *Home Rules*', in McKendrick, J. (ed.) *First Steps: A Primer on the Geographies of Children and Youth*, London: Royal Geographical Society with the Institute of British Geographers, pp. 10–11.

Kesby, M. (2007), 'Methodological insights on and from children's geographies', *Children's Geographies*, 5: 193–205.

Kyle, R. (2006) *Negotiating Youth Work: Moral Geographies of the Boys' Brigade in Scotland*, unpublished PhD thesis, Department of Geographical and Earth Sciences, University of Glasgow.

Mac Naughton, G. (2005) *Doing Foucault in Early Childhood Studies: Applying Poststructural Ideas*, London: Routledge.

McNamee, S. (2000) 'Foucault's heterotopia and children's everyday lives', *Childhood*, 7: 479–92.

Metzel, D. and Philo, C. (2005) 'Outside the participatory mainstream?', *Health and Place*, 11: 77–85 [introduction to theme section on 'Geographies of intellectual disability'].

Newman, M., Woodcock, A. and Dunham, P. (2006) '"Playing in the borderlands": children's representations of school, gender and bullying through photographs and interviews', *Children's Geographies*, 4: 289–302.

Philo, C. (1987) 'Convenient centres and convenient premises: the historical geography of England's nineteenth-century idiot asylums', *University of Hull, Department of Geography, Working Paper No. 3*.

Philo, C. (1989) '"Enough to drive one mad": the organisation of space in nineteenth-century lunatic asylums', in J. Wolch and M. Dear (eds) *The Power of Geography: How Territory Shapes Social Life*, London: Unwin Hyman, pp. 258–90.

Philo, C. (2001) 'Accumulating populations: bodies, institutions and space', *International Journal of Population Geography*, 7: 473–90.

Philo, C. (2004a) *A Geographical History of Institutional Provision for the Insane from Medieval Times to the 1860s in England and Wales: 'The Space Reserved for Insanity'*, Lewiston and Queenston, USA and Lampeter, Wales: Edwin Mellen Press.

Philo, C. (2004b) 'Michel Foucault', in P. Hubbard, R. Kitchin and G. Valentine (eds) *Key Thinkers on Space and Place*, London: Sage, pp. 121–8.

Philo, C. (2007a) 'Extended review of Michel Foucault's *Psychiatric Power*', *Foucault Studies*, 4: 149–63.

Philo, C. (2007b) '"Bellicose history" and "local discursivities": an archaeological reading of Michel Foucault's "*Society Must Be Defended*"', in J. Crampton and S. Elden (eds) *Space, Knowledge, Power: Foucault and Geography*, Aldershot: Ashgate, pp. 341–67.

Philo, C. (2007c) 'A vitally human medical geography? Introducing Georges Canguilhem to geographers', *New Zealand Journal of Geography*, 63: 82–96.

Pike, J. (2008) 'Foucault, space and primary school dining rooms', *Children's Geographies*, 6: 413–22.

Pike, J. (2010) '"I don't have to listen to you! You're just a dinner lady": power and resistance at lunchtimes in primary schools', *Children's Geographies*, 8: 275–288.

Prout, A. (2004) *The Future of Childhood: Towards the Interdisciplinary Study of Children*, London: Falmer Press.

Ploszajska, T. (1994) 'Moral landscapes and manipulated spaces: gender, class and space in Victorian reformatory schools', *Journal of Historical Geography*, 20: 413–29.

Pykett, J. (2004) 'Using debate to promote critical thinking in citizen education', report commissioned by the Teacher Training Agency. Available at: http://www.citized.info/pdf/commarticles/Jessica_Pykett.pdf (accessed 6 February 2009).

Pykett, J. (2006) *The Geographies of Citizenship Education in England: Spaces, Practices and Subjects*, unpublished PhD thesis, School of Geography, University of Bristol.

Pykett, J. (2007) 'Making citizens governable? The Crick Report as governmental technology', *Journal of Education Policy*, 22: 301–2.

Pykett, J. (2009) 'Pedagogical power: lessons from school spaces', *Education, Citizenship and Social Justice*, 4: 103–17.

Sharp, J.P., Routledge, P., Philo, C. and Paddison, R. (2000) 'Entanglements of power: geographies of domination/resistance', in J.P. Sharp, P. Routledge, C. Philo and R. Paddison (eds) *Entanglements of Power: Geographies of Dominance/Resistance*, London: Routledge, pp. 1–42.

Stone, B.E., (2004) 'Defending society from the abnormal: the archaeology of bio-power', *Foucault Studies*, 1: 77–91.

Valentine, G. and Skelton, T. (eds) (1998) *Cool Places: Geographies of Youth Cultures* London: Routledge.

Vanderbeck, R. (2004) 'Book review of Zieger's *For the Good of Children*', *Children's Geographies*, 2: 163–5.

Weller, S. (2003a) *Teenage Citizenship: Rural Spaces of Exclusion, Education and Creativity*, unpublished PhD thesis, Department of Geography, Brunel University.

Weller, S. (2003b) '"Teach us something useful": contested spaces of teenagers' citizenship', *Space and Polity*, 7: 153–71.

Weller, S. (2007) *Teenagers' Citizenship: Experiences and Education*, London: Routledge.

Wood, D. and Beck, R. (1994) *Home Rules*, Baltimore MD: John Hopkins University Press.

Wyness, M. (2006) *Childhood and Society: An Introduction to the Sociology of Childhood*, London: Palgrave Macmillan.

4 Building a sense of community

Children, bodies and social cohesion

Peter J. Hemming

Introduction

Over the last few years, communities have become the focus of a range of government policies and initiatives in the UK, particularly regarding the development of social cohesion between different ethnic and religious groups (Forrest and Kearns, 2001). These interventions have partly been a response to the 2001 riots in English Northern cities such as Bradford and Oldham, where anti-Muslim rallies organized by the far right led to violence between White and Asian youths. Debates about interfaith community relations have also impacted upon education institutions, for example through the recently introduced legal requirement for all English schools to demonstrate their commitment to promote social cohesion. This policy can be understood as an attempt to calm concerns that faith-based schools, in particular, may be guilty of contributing to ethnic and religious division through their selection procedures (Ouseley, 2001). Geographers have also started to recognize and investigate the spatial aspect of these debates, such as the extent of ethnic segregation in school neighbourhoods (e.g. Burgess *et al.*, 2005) but there has, as yet, been a marked lack of research on religion and social cohesion issues within educational spaces.

In this chapter, I draw on qualitative research to contribute to the above debates, specifically through a focus on the institutional spaces of primary (elementary) schools. I begin by offering a theoretical discussion on bodies, rituals and belonging to build a foundation for the arguments made in the chapter, followed by a brief outline of the research study from which this chapter draws. Next, I examine some of the ways in which the primary schools in my study encouraged social cohesion and a sense of community with particular reference to the role of embodied practices. The significance of embodied identities for inclusion or exclusion in these practices are then explored. Finally, I go on to illustrate how these processes interconnect with the wider localities and some of the implications of this for the social cohesion agenda.

Bodies, rituals and belonging

Over the last decade or so, geographers have begun to eschew the traditional Cartesian dualism of mind and body and the prioritization of thinking over doing, to accept the body as both a significant entity within space but also as a legitimate space in itself for geographical enquiry (Longhurst, 2001; Valentine, 2001). This has led to an engagement with the more embodied aspects of human life, such as emotions, affect and practice (Anderson, 2006; Davidson and Milligan, 2004; Tolia-Kelly, 2006). Simonsen (2007) has called for a 'geography of practice', which acknowledges the role of somatic experience in constructing meaning and relating to other people and our environment.

Recent work on citizenship and national identity has begun to explore the embodied nature of collective belonging, for example through the role of affective musical experiences for fostering nationalist sentiments (Wood, 2007). Geographical research on nationalism has also emphasized the importance of embodied ritual for creating a sense of togetherness. Sharp (1996: 98) draws on Bennington and Renan to argue that:

> The nation is created not through an originary moment or cultur-ally distinct essence but through the repetition of symbols that come to represent the nation's uniqueness. National culture and character are ritualistic so that every repetition of its symbols serves to reinforce national identity. [. . .] Each drawing of maps of nation-state territory, each playing of the national anthem or laying of wreaths at war memori-als, every spectatorship of national sports events and so on represents this daily affirmation of national identification.
>
> (1996: 98)

Similarly, Viroli (1995, cited in Turner, 2002: 49) has expressed the view that shared rituals, along with a common culture and landscape, are essential for enduring national identities and commitments.

The importance of embodied rituals for 'social cement' is not a new idea or concept, as ritual was central to Durkheim's analysis of the social function of religion for society. Durkheim (1915, cited in Turner, 1991: 45–52) used his study of Aboriginal Australian totemism to show how symbolic religious practices and rituals, and the emotional states that are influenced by them (collective effervescence), can work to re-establish and cement social rela-tionships within collectives. This analysis emphasized practice and action more than other accounts of religion (e.g. Weberian) that focused solely on thought and belief (Turner, 1991).

Neo-Durkheimians such as Mellor and Shilling (1997), have suggested that current sociological thinking has tended to neglect the importance of collective and individual embodied experiences of the sacred. They argue that religious practice, and the influence of religious practice, remains central to the cementing of social relationships within modern Western societies. At the scale of the community, Paolone (forthcoming) has examined how embodied rituals in a central region of Italy serve to teach young citizens membership of their local community through the enactment of symbolic processions. In this chapter, I will examine the role of both religious and secular rituals in building up a sense of embodied community in the primary school.

Study outline

The data in this chapter originates from a wider project on religion and spirituality in primary school spaces. The study was qualitative in nature and adopted a case-study approach to investigate a community primary school and a voluntary aided Roman Catholic primary school. Both of the schools were located in an urban area of the North of England, within multi-faith localities. The research involved a mixed-method approach including participant observation, semi-structured interviews with parents and teaching staff, paired interviews with children and a number of child-centred methods. This chapter will draw primarily from the observation and interview data. The majority of the research was focused on particular classes within Key Stage 2 (7–11 years old). In both of the focus classes, I worked as a general classroom assistant alongside my participant observer role but also carried out observations in the playground, hall and corridors throughout the school day.

The child and parent interview sampling strategy aimed to reflect the religious make-up of the focus classes. In the community school, this consisted of approximately 20 per cent non-White Muslim or Sikh, 40 per cent Black or mixed race Christian and 40 per cent White Christian or agnostic children. In the Roman Catholic school, the figures were 5 per cent non-White Muslim, 15 per cent Black or mixed race Christian (mostly Catholic), 20 per cent White Christian (non-Catholic) or agnostic, and 60 per cent White Catholic children. I conducted a total of ten parent interviews in each school, mostly with just one parent but occasionally with two, and three interviews with teaching staff in each school. In the case of the children, there were eleven pairs and one group of three at the community school and ten pairs and one group of three at the Catholic school, in order to avoid excluding children who wanted to take part.

Embodied communities

The concept of community can be understood in a number of ways, as highlighted by Bell and Newby (1976). They outline three definitions, including a neighbourhood community based on close geographical proximity, a collection of local social and political systems and institutions, and a body of individuals with close personal ties and obligations towards other members.

Wellman and Leighton (1979) prefer to separate the concepts of neighbourhood and community, arguing that traditional community collectives based in geographic localities have become increasingly dispersed across space. This position is extended by Castells (1996), who maintains that we are now living in a network society, shaped by new technologies, where people exist within webs of social connections and interactions.

More recent definitions of community therefore emphasize the existence of common values and bonds between people, in contrast to neighbourhood and territory (e.g. Smith, 1999). This way of thinking about community is relevant for educational institutions, in their attempts to create a distinct character or culture based on a community of shared values and mutual goals (Sergiovanni, 1994). Collective identities in schools are often built on factors such as language, culture, and religious and ethnic identity. Hall *et al.* (2002) give the example of supplementary religious schools as contexts where shared identity and belonging are of real importance for pupils and parents. Cohesive communities may also be formed through somatic as well as discursive processes, but little has been said about the role of embodied practices for building a sense of togetherness in educational space.

In the schools in my research, embodied practices and rituals played a major role in building a cohesive school community and a sense of belonging. Both of the study schools used rituals and practices of a non-religious nature on an everyday basis. These included whole-school assemblies, where lines of children would file into the hall, sit in rows and listen to stories and announcements from the teachers, and whole-school events such as sports days and talent contests. Singing was also a time when children would come together and take part in a collective musical act. The daily ritual of Wake Up! Shake Up! (www.wakeupshakeup.com) was an aspect of school life where children took part in physical exercises together on the playground or in the hall, to the sound of popular dance music. Classroom rituals including taking down chairs from tables, calling out names to the register, and sitting down together on the carpet, all worked to create a feeling of familiarity and community.

> It was also quite interesting watching the school take part in 'wake up shake up' to 'It's Raining Men' on Thursday morning. The whole school came together in the hall and all took part in moving and dancing together in a big corporate, corporeal event
>
> (Research diary extract, Catholic school)

These ritualistic events were a daily part of children's lives in school and they referred to them in the paired interviews, such as Aisha below, who mentioned singing and the daily Wake Up! Shake Up! whole-school activity.

INTERVIEWER: Do you ever do singing in assembly or do you ever have prayers, or do you ever think silently?

AISHA (Asian Muslim girl, community school): We don't have prayers, but we, like, sing when we get there.

INTERVIEWER: You do have singing? What kind of things do you sing? Oh you mean when you're walking in?

AISHA: Yeah when we're walking in and when we're sitting down. Mr W, at the end, the head teacher takes a song, like wake-up, shake-up, when everybody's tired and all that, we stand up and sing wake-up shake-up. Like in the morning you sing a song.

In addition to the non-religious rituals outlined above, the Catholic school was able to draw on a range of religious rituals for community building, (see also Paolone, forthcoming). These included class prayers, which were rhymes that the children knew off by heart and chanted four times a day; class worship, which entailed children sitting together on the carpet around a lighted candle; assemblies, which contained religious stories and prayers; and services or Mass, which were led by the local parish priest. The prayers in particular were very embodied as they involved chanting in unison as well as making the sign of the cross at the start and the end of each prayer. These religious practices were a major part of daily life in the Catholic school, in contrast to the community school, where religious rituals were very rare.

The morning started with the usual prayer, and I reflected how the whole event was completely embodied, from putting hands together, closing eyes, disappearing into that spiritual place, and making the sign of the cross at the start and the end of the prayer. The words were as follows:

Father in heaven you love me, you are with me night and day,
I want to love you always, in all I do and say,
I'll try to please you Father, bless me through the day,
Amen.

(Research diary extract, Catholic school)

Teachers at the Catholic school were quite clear about the cohesive potential of such practices and rituals, pointing to the way that they could help in managing class behaviour. Some of the parents also highlighted this community-building aspect of religious rituals.

INTERVIEWER: I mean with the religious side of assembly as well, do you think there are any other functions of assembly, any other things that you know, that it does apart from promoting the religious side?

SALLY (White Christian non-Catholic mother, Catholic school): It's a community. It's an encouragement of belonging together. Everybody's included and not felt like they're left out, you know, people can take part if they wish, you know . . .

One of the most striking examples of togetherness was the way in which teachers in the Catholic school told children that Jesus would always listen to their prayers when more than one of them was praying together. This idea was reflected in some of the interview quotes from children at the Catholic school, but also from a number of children at the community school, who referred to the few occasions when they had prayed at school.

INTERVIEWER: Right OK. What about when you do prayers in assembly, do you enjoy doing those?

NATHAN (White Catholic boy, Catholic school): Yeah.

QUINTON (White Catholic boy, Catholic school): Yeah.

INTERVIEWER: Yeah, what do you like about that?

NATHAN: You're talkin', you know you're talkin' to God and it says if there's more than one or two people, if there's two or three people, Jesus will be there prayin' as well.

The rituals and practices at the Catholic school went hand-in-hand with more discursive ideas that emphasized the existence of community in school. This was reflected in the way that teachers and parents talked about the community feel of the school and the fact that many of the Catholic children came from families with long histories of attending the school. The concept was also explicitly discussed with the children in assemblies, where their membership in the local community was considered alongside being part of God's community. The extent to which all children were full members of these embodied school communities will be the focus of the next section.

Inclusive communities?

Earlier in the chapter, I referred to Smith's (1999) concept of a community of common values and bonds. Often these common social bonds are produced through appeals to an 'imagined community' at the level of the nation, neighbourhood or institution, that promotes an idealized and romanticized notion of sameness and similarity (Anderson, 1983; Rose, 1990). Consequently, Young (1990) discusses how the ideal of community can result in the elevation of unity and homogeneity over diversity and difference, and hence the exclusion of individuals who do not 'fit in' for whatever reason. In the context of education, faith schools can sometimes create clear boundaries between their school community and wider society in order to effectively promote spiritual values (Valins, 2003). However, the changing religious make-up of English society has meant that some Christian schools, in particular, are increasingly experiencing more religiously and ethnically diverse intakes (Department for Children Schools and Families, 2007). This raises the question as to how far non-Christian pupils can be fully included in an 'imagined community' constructed on common Christian beliefs.

In my research, the concept of community in the two study schools implied both processes of inclusion and exclusion. Smith's (1999) community of common values and bonds was much more apparent in the Catholic school than the community school, partly because of the emphasis placed on it as part of the school's religious ethos, but also because of the high frequency of religious rituals enacted on a daily basis. Although the Catholic school did demonstrate a stronger sense of togetherness through those aspects discussed, children who were unable to take part in the religious rituals inevitably experienced a certain amount of exclusion, despite the school's efforts to include them. Pupils in this category (such as Ahmed below) did not necessarily view this as a problem, but it did serve to mark them as different in the context of these daily religious rituals. Similarly, Smith (2005) found in his study that assemblies and collective worship in primary schools were times where religious differences were reinforced through withdrawal or separate worship. In the Catholic school in my study, children from minority religions were only included in the non-religious rituals such as 'wake-up-shake-up' and singing practice, when the songs were more secular in nature.

INTERVIEWER: Ok, what about singing? Do you like singing the songs in assembly?

CRAIG (White Catholic boy, Catholic school): Most of them, 'cos we don't do a lot.

AHMED (Black Muslim boy, Catholic school): It depends what they are. Some of the songs I don't like singing, some of them I do, and some of them I can't sing 'cos I'm a different religion, and some of the things they say inside there, I can't really say.

INTERVIEWER: Oh, so how do you know, do you know which one's that you're meant to be singing?

AHMED: Yeah.

INTERVIEWER: Yeah. Is that just decided before you go in assembly?

AHMED: Yeah, and if I can't say something, I just won't sing.

INTERVIEWER: Right, so you know which one's you're meant to sing and which one's you're not?

AHMED: Mmm.

In contrast, the community school did not engender such a strong feeling of community and togetherness, as comparative use of religious rituals would not have been appropriate in that context. However, the school's emphasis on inclusion as part of its school ethos did mean that children could take part in the majority of events and rituals, unlike in the Catholic school. A good example of this was the school talent contest, and the Key Stage 2 Christmas nativity, which although Christian in nature, was generic enough to allow children from other religions to take part (see diary extract below). The only exception was the Key Stage 1 Christmas nativity, because it was held in the local church and some Muslim parents, in particular, felt uncomfortable about their children attending a church.

> The class went down to the hall for [the Key Stage 2 Christmas performance], which was again, an all singing and dancing, costume-laden event. The set was in front of an enormous cross on the wall, covered in flags from different nationalities. The cast was multicultural and the choir and narrators certainly had children from minority religions amongst them, including Muslims and Sikhs.
>
> (Research diary extract, community school)

Although embodied rituals helped to develop a cohesive community and a feeling of togetherness, they also had the power to exclude when grounded in a particular religious faith. The resultant community dynamics in my study schools were significant for making sense of the way that both schools engaged with their surrounding neighbourhood localities and the implications for building social cohesion on a wider scale. This issue is addressed in the next section.

Wider communities

Although writers such as Wellman and Leighton (1979), Castells (1996) and Smith (1999) have adopted definitions of community that emphasize common interests and networks over neighbourhood and territory, Larsen *et al.* (2006) argue that social relationships are still formed and constituted by embodied practices. Real-life encounters and pre-existing social connections and traditions are often much more important than digital communication technologies for developing communities (May 2002). Such arguments encourage a re-engagement with the actual physical meetings and practices that take place to develop social collectives, many of which occur within and around neighbourhood institutions. For example, Witten *et al.* (2003) point to the role that schools play in developing and maintaining social and community networks within their localities.

Both of the schools in my research did engage with their local neighbourhood communities to a certain extent, through events and community outreach projects. Even if merely acting as loci for local social networks, the embodied practices and meetings that occurred within and around the schools were important for contributing to the development of a wider community. Acts of engagement with the local neighbourhood community included taking children to distribute food to the needy at Harvest festival and organizing pupils to entertain elderly people at a nearby venue. The study schools also offered breakfast and after-school clubs to local families, invited parents in to school events, and contributed to local festivals and projects. In one parent interview at the community school, Mona explained some other ways in which the school engaged with the local neighbourhood community.

INTERVIEWER: In your knowledge, is the school active in the local community?

MONA (Asian Muslim mother, community school): Yeah, I mean I guess so, because, though I've not done anything it that area, I know that Sure Start, I've seen a few mothers carry the stair guards [. . .].

INTERVIEWER: Oh right.

MONA: They were being dispensed here at school for mothers, very inexpensive ones, so very affordable for mothers and I think it means a lot.

INTERVIEWER: Oh, so to stop the children, those guards to stop smaller children going down the stairs?

MONA: Yes. Those ones were being sold. And also I think every Monday they have fruit and vegetables that are sold on the campus at reasonable prices for people who can't afford to go to the supermarkets.

The type of community present within each school was also important for making sense of the relationship between the institutions and their wider religious communities. The community school had some informal links with the local Anglican Church and the vicar occasionally took assemblies in school but there were no formal ties with the Anglican community. In contrast, the Catholic priest from the local parish took a central role in services and events at the Catholic school, and parishioners would attend class services and Masses, as well as other religious events in the school building. The community school was therefore able to focus more on providing for the surrounding neighbourhood community, where as the Catholic school focused more on providing for the local Catholic community. The links with the Catholic school and parish tended to result in more parental involvement than in the community school, but often engaged Catholic parents more because of their religious character.

INTERVIEWER: What would you say the school's role is in the local community?

HEADTEACHER (female Catholic, Catholic school): [. . .] We definitely need to be more a part of the parishes that we serve. So we do through sacramental preparation, that sort of thing, get involved in the parishes, we do have services that the parishioners come in and spend time with us, so we need to be seen as part of the parish community and active members of the parish community. We have, we do collections at Christmas, sorry at Harvest that we give, go round to the local community, it's picked up by the church people and they pack it up and take it round to the needy in the community. [. . .] One of the things we are doing at the moment, I've put in a bid to the national lottery to develop a peace garden, which would be built on that side of the school, and we hope to invite lots of groups, other faith groups to use it, because it will be designed for small meetings and prayer groups and that sort of thing, reflection. So we're starting to sort of branch out into the community, but it's quite difficult because we're next to the community school . . .

In summary, although both of the schools were in the business of engaging with their local communities, the ways in which they did this were very different. The type of communities that existed within the institutions themselves also closely reflected the kind of relationship that they maintained with their wider localities. These differences had important implications for concerns about social cohesion between different ethnic and religious groups and these will be explored in the conclusion.

Conclusion

In this chapter, I have outlined some of the processes that took place within two particular primary schools to promote a sense of community and belonging. This feeling of togetherness was achieved through the repetition of embodied rituals, routines, practices and events and occurred in a non-religious sense in both of the schools. However, the Catholic school was also able to draw on a wide range of religious rituals for community building, leading to a more tightly knit but less inclusive collective, particularly for those children who were from minority religious backgrounds. In contrast, the community school took a much more inclusive approach that, because of the fewer rituals used, resulted in a slightly weaker sense of togetherness. This pattern was repeated through the ways in which both schools engaged with their wider communities. The Catholic school focused more exclusively on the local parish community, where as the community school had more of an inclusive responsibility towards the neighbourhood community. These processes again highlighted the importance of embodied meetings and practices for making sense of the concept of community.

These findings have important implications for the social cohesion debate introduced at the start of the chapter. The British government currently remains committed to the role of religion within the education system and is keen to stress the place of faith-based schools in promoting social cohesion between different ethnic and religious groups (Department for Children Schools and Families, 2007). While it is certainly the case that some faith schools may be able to work towards developing social cohesion, for example through the encouragement of positive encounters between children from different backgrounds (Hemming, forthcoming), this research has shown that religion also has the potential to exclude. In both institutional space and the wider locality, the Catholic school in my study was much better placed to facilitate a sense of belonging amongst members of the Catholic community than forge networks and connections between members of different communities. Put another way, the Catholic school was better at bonding social capital than bridging social capital (Flint, 2007; Putnam, 2000).

By this, I do not wish to suggest that faith-based schools necessarily work against the development of social cohesion, as I have shown evidence to the contrary elsewhere (Hemming, forthcoming). The nature of the qualitative case-study approach in this study means that it is not possible to make generalizations about faith schools or community schools and the enormous diversity in the state school sector also militates against drawing conclusions of this kind (Jackson, 2003). However, what this study does show is that a naïve assumption that faith schools are good for promoting social cohesion, as current government rhetoric appears to suggest, may well be misplaced. The situation is certainly much more nuanced than this and more research is urgently required to unravel some of this complexity.

References

Anderson, B. (1983) *Imagined Communities*. London: Verso.

Anderson, B. (2006) 'Becoming and being hopeful: towards a theory of affect'. *Environment and Planning D: Society and Space*, 24, 733–52.

Bell, C. and Newby, H. (1976) 'Communion, communalism, class and community action: the sources of new urban politics'. In D. Herbert and R. J. Johnston (eds), *Social Areas in Cities*, vol. 2. Chichester: Wiley.

Burgess, S., Wilson, D. and Lupton, R. (2005) 'Parallel lives? Ethnic segregation in schools and neighbourhoods'. *Urban Studies*, 42(7), 1027–56.

Castells, M. (1996) *The Rise of the Network Society*. Oxford: Blackwell.

Davidson, J. and Milligan, C. (2004) 'Embodying emotion, sensing space: introducing emotional geographies (editorial)'. *Social and Cultural Geography*, 5(4), 523–32.

Department for Children Schools and Families (2007) 'Faith in the System'. Nottingham: DCSF Publications.

Flint, J. (2007) 'Faith schools, multiculturalism and community cohesion: Muslim and Roman Catholic state schools in England and Scotland'. *Policy and Politics*, 35(2), 251–68.

Forrest, R. and Kearns, A. (2001) 'Social cohesion, social capital and the neighbourhood'. *Urban Studies*, 38(12), 2125–43.

Hall, K. A., Ozerk, K., Zulfiqar, M., and Tan, J. E. C. (2002) '"This is our school": provision, purpose and pedagogy of supplementary schooling in Leeds and Oslo'. *British Educational Research Journal*, 28(3), 399–418.

Hemming, P. J. (2011, in press) 'Meaningful encounters? Religion and social cohesion in the English primary school'. *Social and Cultural Geography*, 12.

Jackson, R. (2003) 'Should the state fund faith-based schools? A review of the arguments'. *British Journal of Religious Education*, 25(2), 89–102.

Larson, J., Urry, J. and Axhausen, K. (2006) *Mobilities, Networks, Geographies*. Aldershot: Ashgate.

Longhurst, R. (2001) *Bodies: Exploring Fluid Boundaries*. London and New York: Routledge.

May, C. (2002) *The Information Society*. Cambridge: Polity.

Mellor, P. A. and Shilling, C. (1997) *Re-forming the Body: Religion, Community and Modernity*. London: Sage.

Ouseley, H. (2001) *Community Pride not Prejudice*. Bradford: Bradford Vision.

Paolone, A. R. (2011, in press). Spaces of ritual: informal education in an Italian village. *Social and Cultural Geography*, 12.

Putnam, R. D. (2000) *Bowling Alone: the Collapse and Revival of American Community*. London: Simon and Schuster.

Rose, G. (1990) 'Contested concepts of community: imagining Poplar in the 1920s'. *Journal of Historical Geography*, 16, 425–37.

Sergiovanni, T. J. (1994) *Building Community in Schools*. San Francisco, CA: Jossey-Bass.

Sharp, J. P. (1996) 'Gendering nationhood: a feminist engagement with national identity'. In N. Duncan (ed.), *Bodyspace: Destablilizing Geographies of Gender and Sexuality*. London: Routledge, pp. 97–108.

Simonsen, K. (2007) 'Practice, spatiality and embodied emotions: an outline of a geography of practice'. *Human Affairs*, 17, 168–81.

Smith, D. M. (1999) 'Geography, community and morality'. *Environment and Planning A*, 31, 19–35.

Smith, G. (2005) *Children's Perspectives on Believing and Belonging*. London: National Children's Bureau for the Joseph Rowntree Foundation.

Tolia-Kelly, D. P. (2006) 'Affect – an ethnocentric encounter? Exploring the "universalist" imperative of emotional/affectual geographies'. *Area*, 38(2), 213–17.

Turner, B. S. (1991) *Religion and Social Theory*, 2nd edn, London: Sage.

Turner, B. S. (2002) 'Cosmopolitan virtue, globalisation and partriotism'. *Theory, Culture and Society*, 19(1–2), 45–63.

Valentine, G. (2001) *Social Geographies: Space and Society*. Harlow: Prentice Hall.

Valins, O. (2003) 'Defending identities or segregating communities? Faith-based schooling and the UK Jewish community'. *Geoforum*, 34, 235–47.

Wake Up! Shake Up! Available at: www.wakeupshakeup.com (accessed 12 October 2010).

Wellman, B. and Leighton, B. (1979) 'Networks, neighbourhoods, and communities'. *Urban Affairs Quarterly*, 14, 363–90.

Witten, K., Kearns, R., Lewis, N., Coster, H. and McCreanor, T. (2003) 'Educational restructuring from a community viewpoint: a case study of school closure from Invercargill, New Zealand'. *Environment and Planning C: Government and Policy*, 21, 203–23.

Wood, N. (2007) '"It's like an instant bond": Emotional experiences of nation, primordial ties and the challenges of/for diversity'. *The International Journal of Diversity in Organisations, Communities and Nations*, 7(3), 203–10.

Young, I. M. (1990) 'The ideal of community and the politics of difference'. In L. J. Nicholson (ed.), *Feminism/Postmodernism*. London: Routledge, pp. 300–23.

5 Shutting the bathroom door

Parents, young teenagers and the negotiation of bodily boundaries at home

Ruth Lewis

Introduction

This chapter explores the negotiation of bodily boundaries between young teenagers and their parents at home. As many young people report feeling awkward about their physical development during puberty, it is perhaps unsurprising that they tend to become increasingly private about their time in the bathroom. While privacy has been a central theme in a range of work exploring the micro-geographies of domestic space (Allan and Crow, 1989; Sibley and Lowe, 1992; Madigan and Munro, 1999; Gurney, 2000a, 2000b; Mallett, 2004; Robinson *et al.*, 2004), the socio-spatial dimensions of inter-generational interactions concerning the bathroom appear to have received minimal attention within the literature. Despite its relative marginalization in analyses of home, I contend that the largely tacit negotiations over young people's solitary time in the bathroom are key to the management of pubertal bodies within families. As such, this chapter contributes to a growing body of work which explores the construction of affective boundaries within families (Halley, 2007; Gabb, 2008). Furthermore, by highlighting the significance of parent–child bathroom negotiations within accounts of 'growing up', this chapter responds to calls for greater documentation of young people's self-definitions and their own views on the transition from childhood into teenage years (Valentine, 2003; Weller, 2006).

Domestic privacy and the bathroom

Although home may provide elements of privacy for families from 'outsiders', this does not necessarily secure privacy for its individual members from each other (Allan and Crow, 1989: 5). Notions of individual privacy within families may be difficult to acknowledge where they are in tension with 'dominant ideas about family togetherness' (Madigan and Munro, 1999: 65). Certainly, empirical evidence indicates that a climate of openness within families is both highly valued and much claimed by contemporary parents, although teenagers report strategies to secure privacy from their family members (Brannen *et al.*, 1994; Solomon *et al.*, 2002; Kirkman *et al.*, 2005).

Giddens' (1992) framing of intimacy as a process achieved through mutual self-disclosure and ongoing dialogue has been challenged by attention to non-verbal and embodied strategies of disclosing intimacy (Jamieson, 1998; Gabb, 2008). Therefore, understanding the often tacit negotiation and contestation of bodily privacy within families is essential for a more sophisticated analysis of both physical intimacy within parent–child relationships, and the ways in which domestic space is lived.

In her discussion of the spatial ordering of domestic privacy, Twigg (1999) highlights the internal structuring of the home in terms of privacy and intimacy, with certain areas, such as the bathroom, more intensely associated with personal life. However, Twigg (1999: 391) critiques the conception of domestic space in a fixed sense, asserting that this provides 'a static account of social relations in the home'. Similarly, Mallett (2004: 77) challenges early work on domestic space which argued that certain rooms in the family home were gendered (e.g. the kitchen as female space, the shed as male, etc.), citing 'increasing recognition that rooms or spaces in the family home are not effectively gendered [. . .] rather it is the activities that are performed in these spaces at given times and in given relational contexts that reflect and/or subvert particular ideas about gender, age and role'. Drawing on Gurney's (2000a) concept of 'corporeal vulnerability', Twigg contends that privacy should be reconstituted around the body. This dynamic conceptualization of privacy is relevant for this study, where perceptions of the appropriate use of the bathroom are not fixed, but shift over time as children's bodies physically develop.

While this chapter focuses on the changing use of the bathroom over families' life course, bathroom practices are also shifting over time. Therefore, it is important to situate these familial interactions socio-historically. Hand *et al.* (2005) discuss changing contexts of bodily cleansing over the centuries, highlighting the transition from communal, public bathing in the Graeco-Roman period, to the location of washing within the domestic sphere. However, although bathing/showering has long been a domestic practice, it continues to evolve; for example, Hand *et al.* (2005) note the increasing frequency of bathing and showering, which has been reframed as a daily, rather than weekly, activity in contemporary times. They also argue the late-modern valuing of immediacy and convenience has led to the increasing popularity of en-suite facilities and the 'hyper-privitization' of showering. Despite this trend towards multiple bathrooms, all the participants in this study appeared to be sharing a 'family bathroom'.

The study

This chapter draws on qualitative data from empirical research which explored parent–child communication about sex and sexuality. Parents and young people (aged 11–15) from 23 families were individually interviewed between November 2005 and June 2006. The research was based in a Scottish city and all participants were interviewed in either their own home or that of a family member. Of the 32 parents who were interviewed (including biological and 'social' parents), 21 were female and 11 male. All the parenting couples were male–female. Of the 29 young people interviewed, 17 were girls and 12 boys. In five families, two siblings participated and one girl asked to be interviewed with a friend.

The sample included a diverse range of family forms: eleven young people lived with both biological parents; eight were living in lone-mother households; seven lived in blended families; two lived between two families and one girl lived independently from her parents. Parental occupations included managerial, professional and manual classifications. Eight fathers and six mothers were employed full-time, while six mothers and two fathers worked part-time. The nine mothers and one father not currently employed described themselves variously: unemployed/'on benefits' (4); 'housewife'/ 'home-maker' (3); voluntary worker (2) and studying full-time (1). Reflecting the city's ethnically homogeneous population, all but two of the families were White, two were Black African and one boy's father (with whom he no longer had contact) was Black American, while his mother was White British. Pseudonyms have been used to maintain the anonymity of participants.

As the study conceptualized 'communication' in the broadest sense, it extends the existing research focus on parent–child *talk* about sex, to illustrate the subtle and nuanced ways in which information and ideas about sex and sexuality are indirectly and non-verbally conveyed between parents and children. Parental surveillance and management of their children's pubertal bodies emerged as a significant mechanism through which notions of 'appropriate' sexuality were implicitly communicated within the families. These included interactions over the clothing and presentation of young people's bodies in 'public' spaces, which echoes other research (Rawlins, 2006). However, many participants also talked about the management of bodily modesty at home. Often grounded within talk about bathroom interactions, these accounts elucidate one of the broader themes of the research relating to the ongoing negotiation of 'appropriate' boundaries between parents and children in the early teenage years. It is worth noting that participants were not asked directly about their families' bathroom interactions; the numerous accounts from individuals across the sample emerged spontaneously from participants themselves, often in response to questions about any changes within their family 'over the past couple of years'.

Learning to cover up: the evolution of bodily modesty within families

Morgan (1996: 134) highlights the affinities between the words 'family' and 'familiar', noting that, 'to be familiar with another person is to have some bodily knowledge of that other, through the hand or the eye'. Indeed, in early childhood, parents usually have intimate knowledge of their children's bodies through processes of body care, such as washing and (un)dressing. A further way in which parents look after their children's bodies is through teaching them about bodily modesty. This was often cited by mothers in this study as an important early role in their children's sexual learning. For example, although rarely mentioned by young people themselves, mothers described a variety of ways in which they had conveyed notions of appropriate bodily boundaries to their young children outside the home, as illustrated by this mother's response to a question about parental involvement in sex education:

> As a parent you should be explaining things about their bodies when they're little, y'know, 'yeah don't poke that in there' [*laughs*] y'know and giving them an idea of what's appropriate and not appropriate when they're little and like in a big communal changing room don't have them outside y'know? Say 'aye we're goin' in here and we'll shut the door and we'll get changed, that's fine', so you're startin' to put into them, oh we need to do that when we're here 'cos it's not appropriate for that man I've never seen before in my life to see my bum, y'know, just starting to filter it in.
>
> (Brenda, mother)

In this extract, Brenda described the need for parents to implicitly convey a sense of bodily modesty to young children, specifically identifying 'bums' as something which should be hidden from public view. Mothers reported communication about other bodily boundaries, including teaching children not to touch their own or each other's genitalia, and not to allow themselves to be touched by 'strangers'. Like Brenda, most of these mothers seemed to feel a subtle process of 'filtering in' was an appropriate way to convey these notions of privacy, although a minority also said they had more explicitly discussed the need to 'cover up' with their children. However, children were not only taught to conceal parts of their bodies *in public*, but as they grew older, parents and young people described a process of erecting boundaries of modesty *within* their families. As Gabb (2008: 83) argues:

> Genital and other erotic areas of the body, such as women's breasts, are accorded a particular status in Western culture. This normative (moral) modelling continues into the home and is inculcated through ideas of 'good parenting'. Social norms of modesty dictate what must be concealed from children's eyes, especially once they reach puberty and become aware of their own sexuality and sexual identity. Children likewise learn to manage the sexual potentialities of their bodies. From an early age they learn that their 'privates' must be kept hidden and that areas 'down there' are too secret even to name.

In particular, the significance of solitary time in the bathroom emerged from participants' accounts of the shifting boundaries of 'appropriate' physical contact between parents and children. Clearly bathrooms are inextricably linked with bodily practices involving elements of nakedness, such as washing, urinating and defecating, amongst others. It is perhaps, therefore, unsurprising that this room appeared to hold particular significance in parents' and young people's understandings of their negotiations over bodily privacy. Certainly, the ways in which these spaces were used within most families appeared to evolve as children grew older. Possibly due to their corporeal associations, bathrooms were frequently reported by parents to be the location of early discussions with their children about sex and bodies, particularly talk about genitalia, reproduction and the importance of bodily hygiene. Several parents described bathrooms as communal spaces when children were younger, where there was often more than one person in the room at the same time, and family members regularly bathed or showered together. As children grew older, however, such practices appeared to become identified as inappropriate, particularly across genders, as reflected in the following quotations from two fathers' interviews:

> Obviously when they're younger you share a bath with them and have a good laugh y'know and when they reach a certain age you stop doing that and with a girl it's – well I mean now we wouldn't do that obviously, *absolute* privacy now [. . .] but I mean it's never been an issue, I've never really thought about it to be honest, it's just something that naturally has come about.
>
> (Mike, father)

> We have privacy at like bath-times with all the children, Emily [6] and Michael [7] up till recently have shared baths even up to six months ago they used to share a bath but we just decided it's about time we maybe separate them now y'know?
>
> (Don, father)

Rather than being verbally acknowledged between family members, the evolution of these boundaries of physical intimacy appeared to be largely tacit; indeed, as Mike notes above, it just seemed to '*naturally come about*'. By separating siblings, or by a parent stopping bathing with a child, this implies such intimate knowledge of each other's bodies is no longer appropriate. As such, these changes in bathing practices seem to be a key way in which ideas about bodily modesty are communicated within families. Furthermore, emphasis on the segregation of male and female bodies in the bathroom appears to be part of the process through which sex starts to be defined within most families as heterosexual. Drawing on accounts from non-heterosexual women who have been mistaken for men in *public* toilets and bathrooms, Browne (2004: 338) writes:

> The physical sexed segregation of bathrooms reproduces the illusion of a natural, biological binary separation of sex and physically (re)places bodies within dichotomous sexes ordering these sites.

Unlike public toilets and changing rooms, domestic bathrooms are not usually (at least not in this study), 'designated' male or female, but are generally used by all family members, whatever sex. Over time, however, co-occupation between parent–child and sibling dyads of the opposite sex appears to be considered more inappropriate than those of the same sex, and thus family bathrooms become (hetero)sexed spaces in which bodies are policed.

In the context of widespread concerns about sexual abuse and discourse about male sexual predation, fathers may experience confusion about what constitutes appropriate conduct with their children, and anxieties about the *misinterpretation* of physical intimacy (Morgan, 1996; Kirkman *et al.*, 2002; Gabb, 2008). Indeed, as girls became physically mature and developed a growing awareness of their sexuality, anxieties were particularly commonly expressed in relation to the management of bodily boundaries between fathers and daughters. That is not to suggest these participants were sexually aroused by each other, but rather that their behaviour appeared to be shaped by cultural codes of appropriate conduct between fathers and teenage daughters. Both generations described withdrawing from the more intimate hugs and kisses of earlier childhood, and again the bathroom emerged as significant site for the negotiation of bodily boundaries. For example, one mother described her husband, John's, recent avoidance of the bathroom when occupied by their eldest daughter, Beth (12):

> John I've noticed recently he'll, he tries to avoid goin' in the bathroom when Beth's there.
>
> RL: Whereas he might not do that with the younger ones?
>
> No, he would go in or whatever whereas I think if he knows Beth's in the bath or whatever now he's, I mean it's no' that she's said 'oh dinnae come in now' or whatever, it's just obviously he feels that she's beginning to develop a bit and maybe she's wantin' some space to herself or just a bit of privacy – it's a kind of subconscious thing isn't it, you just read the signals like the shut door or whatever.
>
> (Sheila, mother)

In the few families where their mother's new male partner had recently moved into the house, girls expressed heightened sensitivity to these boundaries, as illustrated by Hannah, who reported a variety of additional measures she took to ensure her bodily modesty around her mum's boyfriend,

Dave:

> If I'm in my room my door's closed and if I'm in the bathroom it's locked, yeah and I wear a dressing gown if I'm around the house, 'specially with Dave around the house now.

RL: Has that kind of changed things, having Dave in the house?

> Yeah, it means I'm actually wearing more clothes, it used to happen that I'd wear shorts and a strappy top around the house but with Dave being in the house I've started wearing a bra and wearing more clothes.
>
> (Hannah, 15 years old)

Hannah went on to state it was Dave's awkwardness which she was responding to by 'wearing more clothes' at home. Mostly, however, young people said their increasing bodily privacy was because of their own embarrassment. For example, one girl described her awkwardness about the prospect of her stepfather coming into the bathroom when she was getting changed, noting that her mother did not seem to appreciate her discomfort:

> I'll go like that, 'Mum, he might come up!', and then she'll go, 'come on, he brought up two girls!', and I mean fair enough her saying that but it's, it's different because it's you, do you know what I mean, it's different.

RL: Cos you weren't one of the ones that he brought up?

> Exactly exactly, because I've only known him what four, five years, so I mean I wouldn't like go around parading [*laughs*].
>
> (Lorna, 15 years old)

Lorna indicated her discomfort may be related to not having known her stepfather since she was younger, although her mother, Shona, appeared to feel his involvement in raising two other girls (with his previous wife) should ameliorate her embarrassment. Shona also raised the issue of bodily modesty when she described Lorna's varying comfort being partially clothed in her stepfather's presence: '*when we go on holiday she walks about in her bikini and all the rest of it in front of him, but I mean she wouldn't walk about in her underwear here*'. This reflection implies meanings of 'appropriate' bodily modesty between parents and children may be contextual;[1] while a bikini may be considered acceptable attire on a family holiday, just wearing one's underwear around the house may be perceived differently, despite involving a similar level of nudity.

Although most young people said they increasingly sought bodily privacy from their parents, Lucia (14) was a rare exception who still appeared to be comfortable being naked around her father, Jeremy. Lucia's mother, Judith, seemed relaxed about this, remarking that once her daughter started feeling 'sexually attractive towards boys', she would inevitably instigate greater bodily privacy from her father. However, although Judith described trying to reassure her husband, he nevertheless expressed concern:

> I find this almost amazing but it's still there that y'know I can walk into the bathroom when she's in the shower and she doesn't mind at all, erm, and y'know she's developed [*gestures to indicate breasts*].

> RL: But she's comfortable?

> Yeah, yeah, I mean I do, do I knock? I do sort of half tap the door now, 'cos I'm beginning to feel almost slightly awkward, although I try not – I feel perfectly comfortable, it doesn't worry me at all really, but I sometimes think, oh, y'know is this ok? And I sometimes think of other fathers and daughters of Lucia's age and I think, I wonder if so-and-so marches into his daughter? Is that right?

> (Jeremy, father)

Despite claiming to feel 'perfectly comfortable', Jeremy's 'half tap' on the door indicated his uncertainty about whether it was appropriate for him to see his daughter naked now she had developed breasts. Indeed, although Jeremy seemed keen to maintain a climate of openness with his daughter, his questioning of whether their co-occupation of the bathroom was usual or even 'right', implies the powerful force of cultural norms in shaping intimate conduct, and illustrates 'the contested barriers between what constitutes public concern and what remains legitimate private practice' (Gabb, 2008: 88).

This chapter has so far explored how perceptions of appropriate conduct and intimate behaviour within families shift as children grow older. In the next section I consider the significance of young people's regulation of these boundaries of physical intimacy within understandings of the early teenage years.

Reading the signs: bodily privacy and the transition to teenage years

In her call for a more coherent focus on teenagers' geographies, Weller (2006: 97) highlights 'the complex transitional positioning of young teenagers – situated between childhood, youth and adulthood', arguing for greater documentation of young people's own views on the 'boundary crossing' into teenage years (see also Valentine, 2003). Rather than the arbitrary age-based definition of 'teenagers', the vast majority of parents and young people in this study seemed to sway towards behavioural understandings of the transition from childhood to teenage years. Certainly, young people's increasing desire for bodily privacy was a prominent theme across both generations' accounts of the shifting dynamics of their parent–child relationships in recent years. In particular, although it rarely seemed to be remarked upon between parents and children, shutting the bathroom door was reported by both generations to be an important sign that young people were 'growing up'.

When co-occupied, bathrooms are spaces in which young people's physical development may potentially be observed by parents, as suggested by these extracts from two mothers' interviews:

> In the bathroom, y'know when they are going into the shower, I'm always curious to see how far she is growing [pubic hair] because I'm just curious, I just say, 'just show me!', 'Mum! Don't, no!'
>
> (Betty, mother)

> I saw them [sisters, Natasha and Natalie] in the bathroom and they'd come out and put their pyjamas on and I said, 'you'll have to wear bras now'.
>
> (Joan, mother)

As the majority of young people expressed some awkwardness and embarrassment about their changing bodies, it is perhaps unsurprising that many described resisting these opportunities for corporeal surveillance. Indeed, when asked to reflect on any changes in their relationship with their parent/s in recent years, about half the young people – particularly girls – spontaneously talked about becoming more private about their time in the bathroom:

> I lock the bathroom door 'cos I really don't want somebody to walk in when I'm in the shower.
>
> (Sarah, 13 years old)

> I used to not mind her [mother] coming into the bathroom when I was having a shower and stuff but now I like, I don't feel that comfy doing that and stuff [. . .] I lock the door when I go to the toilet too, I spoke to my friends and they say that they do the same as me but I hope my mum doesn't think I'm being too closed up or anything . . .
>
> (Francesca, 14 years old)

As Francesca noted, her increasing desire for bodily privacy was reflected on with friends and appeared to be an important component of her understanding of 'growing up'. Francesca's mother also described the significance of her daughter's evident discomfort being in the bathroom together, noting that she took this as a cue for initiating discussion with her about sexuality. Generally, however, young people's increasing desire for bodily privacy was not something parents and children reported explicitly acknowledging with one another.

Based on their study of the rules that exist in family homes, Wood and Beck (1990: 12, emphasis added) discuss the symbolic significance of the front door into the house, noting, 'the door is a valve but it is also a *sign*.' If this symbolism is considered in relation to the bathroom, the shutting and locking of the door appears to be understood within families as a sign of the occupant's desire for privacy. This was clearly articulated by Sheila, when talking about her 14-year-old son:

> I think he just maybe started shuttin' the door or something, whereas y'know if I'm in the bath I rarely shut the door, it's maybe ajar or some-thing like that which is no' kinda like an invitation to come in but it's allowed, well if the door's shut y'know there's somebody that's no' wantin' you to go in.
>
> (Sheila, mother)

In this extract, Sheila clearly distinguishes between the meaning of a door that is closed and one that is ajar. While this was not something which they had ever discussed together, she had interpreted her son's closing of the door as a signal of his desire for privacy. Indeed, when parents were asked to talk about any changes in their relationships with their children in recent years, the significance of shutting the bathroom door was invoked in a third of the parents' accounts, as illustrated by the following extracts:

> Cos even the wee ones now eh, like they go in the bath and obviously the bathroom door stays open so we can see what they're up to . . . but erm I think she started getting, I'd say probably nine-ish, ten, that's when she [12-year-old daughter] started to sort of want to lock herself in, be a bit more private and get a bit more privacy.
>
> (Shelley, mother)

> He's quite private about gettin' changed now, he goes in and locks the door [. . .] aye, if you walk in the shower room it's [mimes covering genitals] up wi' the towel kinda thing.
>
> (Terry, father)

> I s'pose growing a beard and shaving, you see all that happening but y'know you don't go in the bathroom, they lock the doors and that kind of stuff, that's them growing up.
>
> (Sandra, mother)

By commenting on those bodily changes visible to parents, such as male facial hair, Sandra implicitly alluded to those which tend to be hidden from view. Indeed, another mother, Kim, described how her knowledge of her 13-year-old son's body had dramatically reduced as he had 'grown up':

> Y'know you're used to going in and bathing them or whatever so any changes like y'know getting hair on his body I don't see cos of course now I sort of see him, his arms and from the neck up sort of thing [. . .] there was a much more relaxed vibe about that when he was younger and now he's more sort of pulled back or, 'I'm in the bath, don't come in Mum!'
>
> (Kim, mother)

Therefore, despite parents' many regulatory practices concerning their children's bodies, through shutting and even locking the bathroom door, young people exercise agency in regulating the boundaries for knowledge of their own bodies. Although shutting a door might seem incidental, parents' and children's accounts indicate its significance in terms of understandings of growing up, and the shifting boundaries of appropriate physical intimacy over time. This demonstrates the importance of looking beyond accounts of verbal communication within families, as non-linguistic actions, such as shutting a door, play an important role in shaping affective boundaries.

Conclusion

Commenting on her research concerning older people's bodily care, Twigg (2003: 143) remarks:

> Nothing could be more mundane and everyday than the processes of body care [. . .] These processes are assumed to be both too private and too trivial for comment, certainly too trivial for traditional academic analysis. They belong with those other aspects of private life which we are socialised to pass over in silence.

Indeed, while families' bathroom interactions are, by definition, concerned with micro-processes, these apparently mundane and everyday actions are not outside wider discursive concerns. First, by examining young teenagers' strategies to secure bodily privacy from their family members, this chapter contributes to earlier literature which disrupts notions of the home as a private space within a public/private dichotomy (Allan and Crow, 1989; Edwards and Ribbens, 1998; Sibley and Lowe, 1992). Second, through consideration of the shifting micro-geographies of home as children grow up, this chapter responds to appeals for analyses of domestic space to not only consider gender, but also its intersection with sexuality, age and generation (Mallett, 2004).

Furthermore, this research resonates with a growing body of work concerned with practices of intimacy and sexuality within families (Gabb, 2008). While debates about breast-feeding, sleeping with babies and practices of body care have focused attention on physical intimacy and the 'politics of touch' between parents and younger children (Gabb, 2004; Halley, 2007), there has been relatively little sociological discussion of how families with teenage children negotiate bodily intimacy. This chapter contributes important empirical evidence concerning the negotiated management of boundaries of bodily modesty between parents and young teenagers. Contrary to Sibley's (1995) argument that parents tend to establish boundaries within the domestic environment, and children have only limited opportunities to carve out their own space, the young people in this study appeared to exercise considerable agency in regulating boundaries of knowledge of their bodies, which largely seemed to be respected by parents. Of course, negotiations of privacy within domestic settings evolve with developments in housing over time (Allan, 1989). Indeed, it will be interesting to see how the trend towards multiple bathrooms within homes may influence the negotiation of bodily boundaries between parents and children in years to come.

Note

1 See Cover (2003) for fuller discussion of the contextual significance of nakedness, and slippage between sexual and non-sexual frames of nakedness.

References

Allan, G. and Crow, G. (1989) *Home and Family: Creating the Domestic Sphere*, Basingstoke: Macmillan.

Brannen, J., Dodd, K., Oakley, A. and Storey, P. (1994) *Young People, Health and Family Life*, Buckingham: Open University Press.

Browne, K. (2004) 'Genderism and the bathroom problem: (re)materialising sexed sites, (re)creating sexed bodies', *Gender, Place and Culture*, 11(3): 331–46.

Cover, R. (2003) 'The naked subject: nudity, context and sexualisation in contemporary culture', *Body and Society*, 9(3): 53–72.

Edwards, R. and Ribbens, J. (1998) 'Living on the edges: public knowledge, private lives, personal experiences', in Ribbens, J. and Edwards, R. (eds) *Feminist Dilemmas in Qualitative Research: Public Knowledge and Private Lives*, London: Sage.

Gabb, J. (2004) '"I could eat my baby to bits": passion and desire in lesbian mother-children love', *Gender, Place and Culture*, 11: 399–416.

Gabb, J. (2008) *Researching Intimacy in Families*, Basingstoke: Palgrave Macmillan.

Giddens, A. (1992) *The Transformation of Intimacy*, Cambridge: Polity Press.

Gurney, C. (2000a) 'Accommodating bodies: the organisation of corporeal dirt in the embodied home', in McKie, L. and Watson, N. (eds) *Organising Bodies*, Basingstoke: Palgrave Macmillan.

Gurney, C. (2000b) 'Transgressing private-public boundaries in the home: a sociological analysis of the coital noise taboo', *Venereology*, 13: 39–46.

Halley, J. (2007) *Boundaries of Touch: Parenting and Adult–Child Intimacy*, Chicago: University of Illinois Press.

Hand, M., Shove, E. and Southerton, D. (2005) 'Explaining showering: a discussion of the material, conventional, and temporal dimensions of practice', *Sociological Research Online*, 10(2).

Jamieson, L. (1998) *Intimacy: Personal Relationships in Modern Society*, Cambridge: Polity Press.

Kirkman, M., Rosenthal, D. and Feldman, S. (2002) 'Talking to a tiger: fathers reveal their difficulties in communicating about sexuality with adolescents', in Feldman, S. and Rosenthal, D. (eds) *Talking Sexuality: Parent–Adolescent Communication*, San Francisco, CA: Jossey-Bass.

Kirkman, M., Rosenthal, D. and Feldman, S. (2005) 'Being open with your mouth shut: the meaning of "openness" in family communication about sexuality', *Sex Education*, 5(1), 49–66.

Madigan, R. and Monro, M. (1999) '"The more we are together": domestic space, gender and privacy', Chapman, T. and Hockey, J. (eds) *Ideal Homes? Social Change and Domestic Life*, London: Routledge.

Mallett, S. (2004) 'Understanding home: a critical review of the literature', *The Sociological Review*, 52(1): 62–89.

Morgan, D. (1996) *Family Connections: An Introduction to Family Studies*, Cambridge: Polity Press.

Rawlins, E. (2006) 'Mother knows best? Intergenerational notions of fashion and identity', *Children's Geographies*, 4(3): 359–77.

Robinson, V., Hockey, J. and Meah, A. (2004) 'What I Used to Do On My Mother's Settee': spatial and emotional aspects of heterosexuality in England, *Gender, Place and Culture*, 11(3): 417–35.

Sibley, D. and Lowe, G. (1992) 'Domestic space, modes of control and problem behaviour', *Geografiska Annaler Series B, Human Geography*, 74: 189–98.

Solomon, Y., Warin, J., Lewis, C. and Langford, W. (2002) 'Intimate talk between parents and their teenage children: democratic openness or covert control?', *Sociology*, 36(4): 965–83.

Twigg, J. (1999) 'The spatial ordering of care: public and private in bathing support at home', *Sociology of Health and Illness*, 21(4): 381–400.

Twigg, J. (2003) 'The body and bathing: help with personal care at home', in Faircloth, C. (ed.) *Aging Bodies: Images and Everyday Experience*, Oxford: Altamira Press.

Valentine, G. (2003) 'Boundary crossings: transitions from childhood to adulthood', *Children's Geographies*, 1(1): 37–52.

Weller, S. (2006) 'Situating (young) teenagers in geographies of children and youth', *Children's Geographies*, 4(1): 97–108.

Wood, D. and Beck, R. (1990) 'Do's and Don'ts: family rules, rooms and their relationships', *Children's Environments Quarterly*, 7: 2–14.

Theme II

The home, family and intergenerational relationships

6 The search for belonging

Youth identities and transitions to adulthood in an African refugee context

Kate Hampshire, Gina Porter, Kate Kilpatrick, Peter Ohene Kyei, Michael Adjaloo and George Oppong Appiagyei Ampong

Introduction

Young people are widely thought to be affected disproportionately by conflict and displacement (Machel, 2001; Berman, 2001). However, over recent years, there has been a shift within the literature, to focus on the resilience of young people affected and displaced by war and their ability to overcome adversity (Boyden, 2003). Young people may be more adaptable than their elders to rapid social change and better able to take up new livelihood opportunities, sometimes reversing intergenerational flows of wealth and support (Vincent and Sorenson, 2001; Chatty and Hundt, 2001; Swaine, 2004). Such transformations can have important consequences for intergenerational relations. Supporting elders economically can enable young people to establish a role for themselves within a community and become adults (Hinton, 2000; Mann, 2004). Conversely, older people may feel threatened by intergenerational role reversals which challenge social norms around relations of authority and respect (Boyden *et al.*, 2002; Swaine, 2004; Kaiser, 2006).

Experiences of conflict and exile can lead to changes in generational categories and boundaries. It can be almost impossible for some young people to achieve full adult status in the context of a refugee camp and dependence on UNHCR, although the liminal spaces between childhood and adulthood can also provide new opportunities (Utas, 2003, 2005; Turner, 2004, 2006; Kibreab, 2004; Harrell-Bond, 2000). Mapped onto this is the struggle that young people face in the search for meaningful identities, in the transnational context of refugee camps. The recent interest among social scientists in transnationalism and cosmopolitanism has focused largely on those who migrate for economic reasons. Ballard (1994: 31) has described young British South Asians as 'competent cultural navigators', shifting between multiple cultural worlds (see also Cohen, 1997; Gardner, 1995). As we shall see, the search for meaningful identities is crucial for young refugees, many of whom have never seen, or are too young to remember, 'home'.

In this chapter, we trace the processes through which intergenerational relations are re-negotiated and played out in Buduburam refugee settlement in Ghana. We highlight the ways in which young people have sought to make sense of who they are, and to become adults, in the context of protracted exile. We argue that, while young people demonstrate great resourcefulness in negotiating identities and transitions, there can be costs, both to young people and to the wider community, of very rapid social change.

Conflict in Liberia and the Buduburam refugee camp

The conflict that led to Liberians fleeing to Ghana and other West African countries began in December 1989, although it had its roots in the last 150 years of Liberian history, since the founding of the country in 1821 as a colony for freed US slaves. By the official end of Liberia's war, in1996, there had been some 200,000 casualties, and approximately 750,000 refugees as well as 1.4 million internally displaced persons, out of a pre-war population of 2.8 million (Dick, 2002a, 2002b).

The Buduburam refugee settlement was established in 1990 in Gomoa District, some 35 km west of Accra. Spatially, the camp is divided into twelve official zones, with four 'Gaps': areas within the camp, inhabited largely by young ex-combatants, but outside of the officially recognized organization of the camp. Material assistance was provided initially by the UNHCR but, following the 1997 elections, the UNHCR shifted focus to voluntary repatriation and gradually scaled down the humanitarian support (Dick, 2002a, 2002b). At the time of fieldwork, there were reported to be over 41,000 Liberian refugees and asylum seekers resident at Buduburam (UNHCR Ghana, 2005).

Researching youth: methodological approaches

Intensive fieldwork was conducted in Buduburam refugee settlement over a four-month period (Jan–May 2005), largely by three experienced Ghanaian researchers, with short visits from UK researchers. The aim was to generate emic perspectives on social change, as seen by the refugees (see Hampshire *et al.*, 2008). The definition of youth was left deliberately unspecified, in order to elicit local interpretations and meanings. As we shall see, 'youth' emerged as a contingent category, shaped in part by the experience of conflict and becoming refugees. 'Youth' was generally seen by camp inhabitants to encompass a broad range of ages, and in what follows, we define 'youth' as anyone self-identifying as such. In practice, this tended to extend to the mid thirties for most people (at age 35, church members transfer from 'youth' to 'elders' groups, an important transition for many).

A multiple-method qualitative approach was adopted in order to facilitate cross-checking and triangulation of data, to increase reliability. Nineteen focus group discussions were held, twelve with groups of young people and seven with elders. Groups were composed of six to ten people and were in most cases homogeneous with respect to generation and gender. Thirty individual interviews were conducted: ten semi-structured interviews with young camp inhabitants, eight life history interviews with older Liberians, and twelve key informant interviews with representatives of camp-based organizations and local government. We succeeded in interviewing a broadly representative cross-section of ages, genders and ethnic/tribal affiliations within the camp. In addition, two senior secondary school students kept 24 hour photo-diaries, using disposable cameras and one other kept a detailed daily diary for two months. The three Ghanaian researchers participated in daily life and took detailed field-notes in the form of an ethnographic diary based on detailed observations (Geertz, 1973; Sanjek, 1990).

All interviews and focus groups were conducted in English, and were fully transcribed and coded for topics (see Miles and Huberman, 1994). Subsequent analysis used grounded theory: theory generated from the data rather than imposed (Glaser and Strauss, 1967). Data generated from the narratives represent transformed reality: rather than an objective real-time account of changes, they represent participants' own analysis of social change. The coded data were searched for emergent patterns, using a series of validity checks (Miles and Huberman, 1994). Throughout the research process, regular meetings were held with a small consultative group of key stakeholders and camp residents. Additionally, two workshops were held for camp inhabitants, which enabled people to comment on, and make changes to, the findings and analysis.

This study was given ethical approval by the Durham University Ethics Advisory Committee. There are clearly serious ethical implications of conducting research with young people who have lived through conflict and displacement, in particular the possibility of re-evoking emotional and psychological trauma and falsely raising hopes and expectations. These concerns were discussed at the consultative group meetings before research commenced, and mitigating steps were taken.

Life in Buduburam refugee settlement

Without exception, our informants, both young and old, pointed to the day-to-day difficulties experienced by those living in Buduburam. Major problems identified by those self-identifying as 'youth' included: very limited educational and livelihood opportunities; high living costs (accommodation, education, healthcare, food, water and sanitation); insufficient external support and loss of family members; risks associated with the need to engage in dangerous or illegal livelihood activities (prostitution, drug trafficking, armed robbery); and perceived lack of control over their lives and future prospects. A substantial proportion of camp residents were receiving regular remittances from family abroad, particularly from the USA. Those lacking adequate remittances were more likely to be pushed into risky and illegal livelihoods strategies.

As noted above, in 1997, the UNHCR began withdrawing humanitarian support, as it was deemed safe to return to Liberia, and by 2000, all UNHCR assistance had been withdrawn, as part of a regional policy (Dick, 2002a, 2002b). As it became clearer that the situation in Liberia was far from stable, the UNHCR reintroduced limited support for 'vulnerable groups' but, by 2005, when this study was conducted, the focus had again shifted to repatriation. (Since our fieldwork, repatriation has accelerated dramatically and refugee status has been withdrawn.) The gap left by the gradual removal of refugee status and UNHCR support was not filled, since the residents of Buduburam were not Ghanaian citizens and, as such, had few rights and limited access to services. Many complained that they could not work formally outside the camp without a work permit, which was very difficult to obtain, and this pushes people into insecure, informal sector work.

This context of widespread economic insecurity and uncertainty underpins many of the tensions and ambiguities in youth identities and intergenerational relations that we describe below.

Youth and transnational identities

In Buduburam, 'youth' as a social category, defined not by chronological age but by inability to achieve full adult status (see below), has assumed a great importance in camp life. There is a strong generational 'youth' identity, based on camaraderie and mutual support. '*We live as a group*', said one young man.

The search for meaningful identities was central to young people's quest to overcome their feeling of not belonging anywhere, and of having little control over their destinies. Many young people in Buduburam had lived for most, or even all, of their lives in Ghana. Yet, most felt keenly their Liberian nationality, and Liberia was referred to in many interviews as 'home', even by those who were so young when they left Liberia that they had little or no recollection of the country. 'Liberia is like a mother,' said a 22-year-old man who had left Liberia as a young child, 'you can eat outside, but if I don't eat food cooked in my house, like my mother's own food, I won't be happy.'

However, for many, the question of national identity was more ambivalent, with elements of being partly Ghanaian too. The extent to which young people identify as Liberian or Ghanaian can depend on particular good or bad encounters with local Ghanaians, as the following focus group exchange between young women shows:

'I am Liberian – I don't have any Ghanaian friends.'

'I feel both, because I have some Ghanaian friends in Tema.'

'I feel both. My mother is Ghanaian and my father Liberian. I am attending a Ghanaian school in Kasoa.'

'I feel Liberian, because in Liberia I went through the struggle. [She went on to recount an incident of being cheated by two Ghanaian market traders].'

Language was another important factor, with those able to speak Twi (the local Ghanaian language) identifying more strongly with Ghanaian nationality than those who could not (see also Porter *et al.*, 2008). Some young people had spent shorter periods of time in exile in other West African countries, and claimed that they more quickly felt part of the country because they could speak the language. (In many other Anglophone West African countries, the national language – English – is more widely spoken than in this part of Ghana.)

'I felt more Nigerian when I was in Nigeria. I was able to speak the language. I was treated as one of them.'

'In Guinea they treated me as one of them because I could speak the language.'

Attachment to Liberian identity seemed to be stronger for many younger people than for the older generation. As one older woman explained, 'I think the young people feel more like Liberians. Most of our youth dress more like the Americans, and play their songs too. So they feel more Liberian than Ghanaian. The dress code and music makes them feel more Liberians than Ghanaians. . . . The older people dress more like Ghanaians'.

Liberian identity was also associated with the strong connection that many young people felt to America, in particular black American youth culture, which was very prominent. 'On the camp, you feel connected to the USA, you have a friend or relative there,' said a young man in a focus group, whose friends agreed: 'Most people plan to go to the USA', 'USA is the land of opportunity first.' One teacher, speaking in a consultative group meeting, said, 'Nowadays, if they had money for nursery to PhD education in Ghana or go to the US, they'd go to the US . . . a boy told me, "I prefer being in America on the dung pile than in Africa."'

The connections with America were not just affective ones: for many on the camp they offered vital material support. Remittances from family members abroad – particularly those in the USA – were an important source of financial support for many camp inhabitants, and were seen by many as the key differentiating factor between those living within the camp. Young people were often pivotal in maintaining links with family abroad, through mobile phones and the Internet. Many young people spent a lot of time in the many Internet cafés in the camp, soliciting new sponsors from abroad and keeping in contact with existing ones.

However, for many young people, the sense of not quite belonging anywhere was acute: 'I have not been to any country since I came here. I will be a stranger in Liberia. I don't have any country' (young man). Indeed, the experience of having lived through, and in many cases having been actively involved in, the war, and the subsequent displacement had become, for many, a key aspect of identity: 'My life has been different because in the war I saw so many things, and people who have not seen this would not understand. This has changed my life . . . you have been killing so many people and your eyes are red' (young woman). Here, identity had become disconnected from a single place or sense of nationality. Instead, young Liberian refugees embodied cosmopolitan, transnational forms of identity (for similar examples, see Cohen, 1997; Gardner, 1995; Ballard, 1994), encompassing aspects of many different national identities, but not rooted exclusively in any of them, and with disruption and forced displacement as a key aspect of that identity.

Transitions to (and from) adulthood

Transitions to adulthood in the camp were marked by strong ambivalence. On the one hand, because of the economic situation, young people were frequently obliged to assume economic responsibilities associated with adulthood at an earlier age than they might have done in Liberia. Many of the livelihood opportunities on the camp were seen to be more accessible for young people than for elders, including sex work (often in the form of women making a living from 'gifts' from boyfriends), heavy manual labour, and violent crime such as armed robbery. Moreover, as noted above, young people typically learned the skills needed to use Internet facilities, enabling them to maintain ties with friends and families abroad (and even create new Internet-based relationships) more effectively than elders, and thus to receive remittances.

There were many accounts of intergenerational role reversals within the household, with children providing for parents and elders becoming increasingly dependent on youth incomes for their own survival:

> Now the 16-year-old girls are supporting their parents, and the parents don't ask them where they get the money, because they need it. It was different before the war.
>
> (Young woman)

> Now a 50-year-old man may be depending on a 20-year-old boy, because he gets remittances from the USA.
>
> (Young man)

> Back home, we didn't have the system of young people working – the

parents were responsible for their upkeep, but here you can't provide for them.

(Elderly man)

In many cases, transitions to adulthood happened very suddenly, as in the case of a young woman, who told us, 'I was fifteen and my father had no resources to support three children, so I started being an adult.' This was a commonly expressed view: 'Even a 12-year-old girl is not a youth because of the things she has to do to survive in the camp here', explained one young man, while another told us, 'Children on the camp . . . are forced to be men at a tender age, going for food, paying for school fees.' Experience of the conflict was also seen to have contributed to the premature propulsion of youth into adulthood and consequent shifts in intergenerational relations of power and authority: 'During the war, children had guns, so they had power over older people,' explained one elderly man.

One the other hand, because it was almost impossible for most people ever to provide adequately for a family, there was a sense of full adulthood being delayed indefinitely. In other words, there developed an increasingly protracted 'in-between' period, of being neither a child nor a full adult, able to participate fully in social and domestic life. This feeling of indefinite liminality (Utas, 2003) appeared to underpin many of the difficulties expressed by camp inhabitants about the relationships between the generations.

The blurring of boundaries between youth and adulthood worked in both directions, leading sometimes to reversals in life-course chronologies and infantilization of elders (described also by Turner, 2004). Many elders were, in their own terms, losing their adult status through becoming obliged to depend on their children for support:

'My daughter from London sends me money and gives me instructions as to what to use the money for. She is making decisions for me.'

'This is exactly what is happening. They decide what the money should be used for. My daughter sends $50 and dictates for us how long the money should last, and what we should eat and buy.'

(Focus group of elderly women)

The rapid development of 'youth culture' within the camp and increasing idealization of youth led some older people to adopt aspects of youth culture. This was driven partly by economic necessity, with older women adopting youth dress to attract 'boyfriends', whose 'gifts' were critical for economic security. But it was not only economic necessity that drove some older people (in particular women) to adopt aspects of youth culture and dress. Many believed that old age was no longer valued, while youth had become prized. Addressing someone as an old woman or man used to be seen as a mark of respect; now some began to see it as an insult, as one older woman explained: 'Some old women now refuse to be called old women. You want to give them respect by calling them old woman but they are angry.'

Negotiating new forms of youth identity: life in the Gaps

The most extreme changes in generational identities and transitions arguably occurred in the four 'Gaps': youth ghettoes, consisting mostly of young men and some young women, embracing a culture based strongly on Rastafarian identity. Many of those living in the Gaps were ex-child combatants, who fled Liberia and arrived in Ghana alone.

'We are homeless people, orphans.'

'People without support.'

'We buried our parents a long time ago.'

'I came without any family. That's why I'm here. I need friends to share with.'

'We are not real brothers and sisters, but we are friends, and we call one another brother and sister.'

The Gaps provided an arena in which new forms of youth identity in the camp were worked out. They represented liminal spaces within the camp – places in which the usual rules of social behaviour did not apply, and where even the camp authorities turned a blind eye to illegal activities like drug use. To 'outsiders', those living within UNHCR-designated zones of the main camp, the Gaps were typically seen as dangerous, lawless places. However, those inside presented a very different view: one of an alternative youth culture based on a cosmopolitan mix of Black American/Rastafarian and Liberian national identities.

The new forms of youth identity being constructed within the Gaps were based on an explicit rejection of 'tribal' or ethnic divisions. Ethnic divisions were typically downplayed throughout the camp. In the rest of the camp, this was done partly for expediency – to make life possible for those from ethnic groups on opposite sides in the conflict who are obliged to live in close proximity to one another, but in the Gaps the rejection of ethnic affiliation formed a central part of the construction of new identities. While American English had become a lingua franca throughout the camp, in the Gaps it was the only language permitted, with use of Liberian 'tribal' languages proscribed:

'All different tribes and nationalities live here.'

'We don't regard tribe – we are one. No one asks which tribe you are from.'

In the absence of elders and extended family support, the Gaps were characterized by a strong sense of camaraderie, mutual support and sharing: 'If someone needs money, others help him out. Each person gives a bit, even if it is only small small.' This applied to a wide range of needs – from help with medical costs to digging the grave when a Gap member died. Gap inhabitants also emphasized the importance of non-violent conflict resolution, with many contrasting this to their previous experiences of being coerced into fighting in Liberia:

'There is common understanding.'

'If there is an argument, whenever someone gets angry, someone says, "Look, my man, what you are doing is not good."'

'We find some neutral ground. And we separate the two people physically. Then two groups form and talk to each person and reason with them. After everything is resolved, they all have a smoke [of marijuana] together.'

(Exchange between Gap members)

Change and ambivalence in intergenerational relations

Most camp inhabitants, both young and old, regretted the dramatic changes they observed in the ways in intergenerational relations and life-course trajectories. However, it would be wrong to portray all intergenerational relationships as fraught with difficulty and mutual hostility. Many young people expressed the importance of advice and emotional support provided by elders in their families and the wider community.

'My mother advises me, she directs me for a good future. She knows I am going through difficulties.'

'The old people have experience. They can counsel you and give you the encouragement to continue in life.'

'They encourage us that this is not the end of life.'

(Focus group of young women)

In turn, while many elders were deeply critical of young people's attitudes and lack of respect for their parents, they understood and were sympathetic to their plight:

'If I were a younger person in this camp where my parents don't support me financially . . . it would be difficult. It is more difficult to be a youth now in this camp [than it was for us when we were young].'

'Some too are frustrated. Their parents are dead, so they decide to live their lives anyhow.'

(Focus group exchange between women elders)

It was, perhaps, because both young people and elders shared the frustration of not being able to fulfil the social responsibilities of adulthood that intergenerational relations were marked by some ambivalence. While it was very common for people to talk about intergenerational differences and conflict, there was also a strong sense that everybody, young or old, was in the same boat and suffering from the same problems.

Even in the Gaps, which appeared to represent the extremes of breakdown of 'normal' social relations and traditional gerontocracy, these had been replaced by transformed forms of social support and obligation. One of the Gaps even had a father figure – an older man, to whom the youth deferred for important decisions (although by living in the Gap, the old man had effectively forfeited his place in mainstream camp society). More generally, there was a deep ambivalence, felt by youth and elders, about the change towards a youth-oriented culture, and a sense of longing for a more stable (although perhaps illusory) past, in which 'proper' relations of youth deferring to elders were maintained.

Conclusions

Young people in Buduburam found themselves caught 'betwixt and between' in multiple ways. Not quite Liberian, and determinedly not Ghanaian, many felt that they did not belong anywhere. Youth identity had become disconnected from a single place or sense of nationality, as young people adopted cosmopolitan, transnational forms of identity, with the USA being a prominent feature of both youth identities and aspirations. The need to feel connected with abroad (particularly the USA) also had a material basis, with remittances playing a crucial role for many. More adept at using the Internet and mobile phones than their elders, young people were pivotal in creating and maintaining these transnational relations.

Young people were trapped somewhere between childhood and adulthood, unable to fulfil either role properly. Changes in the economic roles associated with young people and elders were seen to have led to the re-shaping of intergenerational relations of authority and respect. Moreover, the boundaries between different generational categories (childhood, youth, adulthood) appeared to have shifted and become blurred. In the most extreme cases – the Gaps – young people appeared to have opted out of intergenerational relations altogether, creating instead new forms of intragenerational relationships. Nonetheless, the changes, and people's feeling about these, were marked by ambivalence, with considerable sympathy for the plight of others.

Clearly, these changes did not necessarily come about purely as a result of the conflict and forced migration. However, it is likely that the experience of conflict, exile and concomitant economic hardship accelerated processes of social change (see also Kaiser, 2006). We argue that, although young long-term refugees often demonstrate a strong degree of resilience and resourcefulness, there may be price to be paid, in terms of social consequences. On top of the daily struggle to meet basic physical needs, many refugees (young and old), have struggled to make sense of who they are and how they fit into a rapidly changing social world.

Acknowledgements

This study was funded by the Nuffield Foundation. We thank Penny Nagbe, Morris Kormazu and Kester Miller, our camp-based research assistants, for their invaluable contribution to the project. We also wish to acknowledge the enormous assistance given by the Liberia Welfare Council, the Camp Commandant, CBOs and NGOs which are based or work in the camp, and the very many other individuals within the camp who made this study possible.

References

Ballard, R. (ed.) (1994) *Desh Pardesh: The South Asian Presence in Britain*, London: Hurst.

Berman, H. (2001) 'Children and War: current understandings and future directions', *Public Health Nursing*, 18(4): 243–52.

Boyden, J. (2003) 'Children under fire: challenging assumptions about children's resilience', *Youth, Education and Environments*, 13(1).

Boyden, J., de Berry, J., Feeny, T. and Hart, J. (2002). 'Children affected by armed conflict in South Asia: a review of trends and issues identified through secondary research', RSC Working Paper No. 7, January 2002, Oxford: Refugee Studies Centre.

Chatty, D. and Hundt, G. (2001) 'Lessons learned report: children and adolescents in palestinian households: living with the effects of prolonged conflict and forced migration', Oxford: Refugees Studies Centre, Oxford University.

Cohen, R. (1997) *Global Diasporas: An Introduction*, London: UCL Press.

Dick, S. (2002a) 'Liberians in Ghana: living without humanitarian assistance', New Issues in Refugees Research, Working Paper No. 57.

Dick, S. (2002b) 'Responding to protracted refugee situations: a case study of liberian refugees in Ghana', Geneva: UNHCR Evaluation and Policy Analysis Unit.

Gardner, K. (1995) *Global Migrants, Local Lives: Travel and Transformation in Rural Bangladesh*, Oxford: Carendon Press.

Geertz, C. (1973) *The Interpretation of Cultures*, New York: Basic Books.

Glaser, B. G. and Strauss, A. L. (1967) *The Discovery of Grounded Theory: Strategies for Qualitative Research*, New York: Aldine.

Hampshire, K., Porter, G., Kilpatrick, K., Kyei, P., Adjaloo, P. and Oppong, G. (2008) 'Liminal spaces: changing inter-generational relations among long-term Liberian refugees in Ghana', *Human Organization*, 67(1): 25–36.

Harrell-Bond, B. (2000) *Are Refugee Camps Good for Children?* UNHCR New Issues in Refugee Research, Working Paper 29, August 2000.

Hinton, R. (2000) 'Seen but not heard: refugee children and models for intervention', in C. Panter-Brick and M. Smith (eds), *Abandoned Children*, Cambridge: Cambridge University Press.

Kaiser, T. (2006) 'Songs, discos and dancing in Kiryandongo, Uganda', *Journal of Ethnic and Migration Studies*, 32(2): 183–202.

Kibreab, G. (2004) 'Refugeehood, loss and social change: Eritrean refugees and returnees', in P. Essed, G. Frerks and J. Schrijvers (eds), *Refugees and the Transformation of Societies: Agency, Policies, Ethics and Politics*, Oxford: Berghahn Books.

Machel G. (2001) *The Impact of War on Children*, UNICEF/UNIFEM; London: Hurst.

Mann, G. (2004) 'Separated children: care and support in context', in J. Boyden and J. de Berry (eds), *Children and Youth on the Front Line*, Oxford: Berghahn.

Miles M. B. and A. M. Huberman (1994) *Qualitative Data Analysis*, Newbury Park, CA: Sage.

Porter, G., Hampshire, K., Kyei, P. Adjaloo, M., Oppong, G. and Kilpatrick, K. (2008) 'Linkages between livelihood opportunities and refugee-host relations: learning from the experiences of Liberian camp-based refugees in Ghana', *Journal of Refugee Studies* 21(2): 230–52.

Sanjek, R. (1990) *Fieldnotes*, Ithaca: Cornell University Press.

Swaine, A. (with Feeney, T.) (2004) 'A neglected perspective: adolescent girls' experiences of the Kosovo conflict of 1999', in J. Boyden and J. de Berry (eds), *Children and Youth on the Front Line*, Oxford: Berghahn.

Turner, S. (2004) 'New opportunities: angry young men in a Tanzanian refugee camp', in P. Essed, G. Frerks and J. Schrijvers (eds), *Refugees and the Transformation of Societies: Agency, Policies, Ethics and Politics*, Oxford: Berghahn Books.

Turner, S. (2006) 'Negotiating authority between UNHCR and "the people"', *Development and Change*, 37(4): 759–78.

UNHCR Ghana (2005) *Statistical Report of Asylum Seekers and Refugees in Ghana*, Accra: UNHCR Ghana.

Utas, M. (2003) 'Sweet Battlefields: Youth and the Liberian Civil War', Uppsala University Dissertations in Cultural Anthropology, Uppsala: Uppsala University.

Utas, M. (2005) 'Building a future? The reintegration and remarginalisation of youth in Liberia', in P. Richards (ed.), *No Peace, No War: An Anthropology of Contemporary Armed Conflicts.* Athens, OH: Ohio University Press; and Oxford: James Currey, pp. 137–54.

Vincent, M. and Sorensen, B. R. (eds) (2001) *Caught Between Borders: Response Strategies of the Internally Displaced*, London: Pluto Press.

7 Travellers, housing and the (re)construction of communities

Margaret Greenfields and David Smith

Introduction

Considerable evidence exists that ethnic minority communities are more likely to reside in areas where levels of unemployment and social deprivation are higher than average (Wetherell *et al.*, 2007). However, research has tended to focus on 'visible' minority communities and/or newly arrived A8 migrants who (initially at least) often settle in well-established ethnic enclaves (Spencer *et al.*, 2007; Markova and Black, 2007).[1] Over time, second generation migrants and immigrants with particular skills which enhance their labour-market position demonstrate a tendency to move (or at least aspire to move) from their place of first settlement (Platt, 2004). Mapping historical ethnic minority migration patterns (e.g. the post-war movement of East End Jews to the relatively affluent reaches of North West London) allow a socio-spatial picture to emerge which demonstrates for many, a shift away from impoverished localities as their economic and cultural capital increases (Dench *et al.*, 2006; Webster, 2003). While migrants commonly struggle to gain access to the social and economic rewards of assimilation and escape urban ethnic localities, urban anthropologists have noted the tendency for Gypsies and Travellers to remain in low-income urban neighbourhoods for longer than other minority groups (Kornblum, 1975). Gypsy and other travelling communities in London and other urban centres dating back several generations have been recorded (Mayall, 1988; Griffin, 2008).

This chapter focuses predominantly on the experiences of first settlement for Gypsy and Traveller families (thus equating to place of first residence for non-UK-born migrants) and on the construction and maintenance of ethnic identity among those 'long-term' housed who may have spent all, or most, of their lives in conventional housing. For many, adapting to an often hostile environment with semi-enforced residence in conventional housing involves the conscious recreation of 'site' (or 'traditional') social patterns. Indeed younger Gypsies and Travellers, many of whom have spent the majority of their lives in housing, invoke an approximation of their elders' internalized world view. This inevitably involves the importation of their own experiences and expectations of Gypsy culture and also adherence to an idealized conceptualization of that culture, as a synecdoche for nomadism and being 'outside' of mainstream (sedentary) society.

The authors have developed a particular interest in the experiences of Gypsies and Travellers living in housing, recognizing that as a group they have frequently experienced even greater social marginalization than 'nomadic' Gypsies and Travellers. The transition into housing, lack of familiarity with bureaucratic requirements associated with such accommodation, separation from family members and a familiar cultural milieu combined with pervasive prejudice and racism from the wider society can lead to extreme distress and social dislocation (Cemlyn *et al.*, 2009). For a high percentage of housed Gypsies and Travellers social separation from 'non-Travellers' leads to a concurrent withdrawal into mono-ethnic groups, which adhere to culturally reified 'Gypsy and Traveller values'. In turn, membership of such a relatively closed community increases the likelihood of these individuals developing 'parallel lives' with potentially diminished access to a full range of capitals which may enhance their social mobility and life chances (Loury *et al.*, 2005). There are also countertendencies to this process with increasing social interaction and integration with the wider community, particularly among the younger generation of Gypsies and Travellers. This process is not necessarily resulting in assimilation but instead new understandings of what it means to be a Gypsy or Traveller in contemporary society based on an acknowledgement, and awareness, of the fluid and evolving nature of ethnic identities. The adaptability and resilience of Gypsy and other nomadic cultures to resist assimilation has been noted in a variety of national and historical contexts (Bancroft, 2005). While broader structural factors have increasingly brought nomadic communities into urban locations on a more or less permanent basis over previous decades the essential nature of their world view remains unchanged and they represent a 'clear case of a culture that is within but outside the dominant system' (Sibley, 1981: 15).

In seeking to unpick the dimensions of social exclusion experienced by housed Gypsies and Travellers and how this is offset through the recreation of community, we concentrate on 'geographical place' as a locus of inclusion/exclusion. Since the 2004 Housing Act, local authorities have been obliged to conduct accommodation and needs assessments of Gypsies and Travellers residing in their area (GTAAs). This chapter draws on data from GTAAs on which the authors have worked as researchers and authors, as well as findings from a small-scale 'follow-up' research project into housed Gypsies and Travellers undertaken in the West of England by one of the authors (Home and Greenfields, 2006). In addition we report from two studies that the authors have recently completed with housed Gypsies and Travellers in East Kent (South East England) and emerging findings from further 'work in progress' conducted in that region. The chapter draws on 37 interviews with formerly nomadic Gypsies and Travellers and two focus groups: one with young Gypsies and Travellers aged between 13 and 21 as part of the West of England study and a focus group undertaken with housed adult Gypsies and Travellers in the East Kent region. The majority (78 per cent) were residing in local authority housing or housing association properties with the remainder in a variety of housing tenures.

Gypsies and Travellers in housing

It has been estimated that there are 300,000 Gypsies and Travellers in the UK (CRE, 2006). Of these, the percentage living in housing may be as high as two-thirds. The pace of transfer from sites into (largely) public sector housing in the past five decades has been driven by relentlessly assimilationist policies that have sought to outlaw the culture and lifestyle of travelling. These include the closing off of and subsequent decline in 'stopping places'; draconian policies for unauthorized camping; inequities in the planning system; a shortage of official site capacity and a desire by those with no legal stopping place to avoid constant harassment and eviction. Evidence exists that in certain locations up to half of every generation of Gypsies and Travellers have transferred into housing throughout the latter half of the twentieth century (Richardson *et al.*, 2007).

Although little research has been conducted into the psycho-social impacts of residence in housing for Gypsies and Travellers it has been recognized in law that requiring someone who expresses a strong 'cultural aversion' to 'bricks and mortar' accommodation to move into a house is akin to requiring a house dweller to reside in 'a rat infested barn'.[2] Parry *et al.*'s (2004) Department of Health-funded study found that Gypsies and Travellers have the lowest health status of any other BME group in the UK with particularly high rates of depression and anxiety. Psychological ill-health was associated in particular with residence in housing, findings further supported by Matthews (2008). Evidence suggests that racism and hostility from sedentary communities profoundly exacerbate the negative impacts of settlement for members of these communities (Cemlyn *et al.*, 2009). Accordingly, the research team sought to highlight Gypsies and Travellers routes into, and experiences of, housing. In addition data was collected in order to map the inter-ethnic relationships that exist, or develop, between housed Gypsies and Travellers as well as the intra-ethnic relations between Gypsies and Travellers and their 'sedentary' neighbours. Exploring networks of social relations allowed for a consideration of the roles of neighbourhood and ethnic identity in shaping the structure of local community relations.

Routes into housing

The average duration of residence in housing for interviewees from the South West was ten years and seven years in the South East. Romany Gypsies had typically lived in housing for longer periods than had Irish Travellers who were more likely to report an 'in and out' pattern of house-travelling-house residence. In both areas certain trends were identified in relation to respondents' movement into housing that can be classified as 'shortage of sites/evictions/homelessness'; 'family reasons/other' and 'health/education of household members'. Under the 1996 Housing Act a person is classed as homeless if he or she has a caravan but no place to legally reside in it and over 60 per cent entered housing through this route due to a lack of legal stopping places. Significant numbers of participants reported feeling coerced into housing, generally through the twin mechanisms of planning enforcement and a shortage of official sites. One young man from the West of England focus group noted that 'The Council wanted us off the site and offered new housing so my parents did it'; while a woman housed for three years in East Kent reported:

> There were no spaces on the [council] site and I could not stay with my parents as they would lose their planning permission. When my dad died the council wouldn't even allow us to stay on their land to comfort my mum.

Coerced settlement was universally regarded as an assault on their traditional way of life: 'We're all in houses now. We don't want to be here but there's nowhere the Gypsies can go no more'. Even for the minority who had entered housing willingly, generally through becoming too old to travel or to gain access to health services or the education system a strong aversion to 'bricks and mortar' was reflected in their comments. One commented that:

> You can't get the kids into school when you're on the road they won't take them. I don't like it here it's a house. We're here for the kids schooling and 'cos we couldn't get planning [permission] on our own land.

Thus the 'choice' to enter housing is shaped by pervasive institutional racism such as reluctance by many schools to accept nomadic children and the unwillingness of many GPs to register Gypsies and Travellers without a permanent address. It was particularly noteworthy that over two-thirds of interviewees reported they would willingly give up their house in exchange for a place on the local authority site.

Transitions into housing

For many respondents moving into housing involved a significant social upheaval including isolation from extended family members, while simultaneously having to adapt to living in bricks and mortar (Greenfields, 2009). Unsurprisingly, significant numbers of initial housing placements break down within a relatively short period of time. A quarter of local authorities responding to Pat Niner's survey said the majority of Gypsy and Traveller tenancies ended within a year and 16 per cent said about half ended within a year (2003: 56). The move into housing also appear to have specific gender dimensions as problems of isolation are felt (or acknowledged more) by women. As one Traveller woman recalled during a focus group in the South East:

> It's one of the loneliest things that can happen to a travelling woman. It's alright for the men . . . men aren't in the house 24 hours, the men probably won't come in until eight o'clock and they've been out all day and they just go to bed but we've been there all day. It's been really, really hard.

Participants in both study areas made frequent reference to the psychological impact of settlement and subsequent social isolation that can result in the absence of kin and other Gypsies and Travellers. One woman commented, 'I get trouble with my nerves now and the panic attacks started when I went into a house', while another reported that she was 'on diazepam and a bottle of vodka a day' adding 'I would give my life to be on site with my mum'. In a study conducted in the Kent region by one of the authors, separation from family and kin was the most frequently cited reason for wishing to move out of housing and return to a site (Smith, 2008). As noted above, mental health is often disproportionately affected by movement into housing to the extent that the physical illness which triggered their move may come to seem less important than hitherto: '[Our] health is better on one hand because we have access to a doctor but worse because my wife hates it here and is on pills – depressed.' Despite women being more likely to report depression and isolation, young Traveller men in housing – frequently socially and culturally isolated and often multiply excluded through low levels of education and skills, unemployment and a lack of positive role models – rarely sought help from professional agencies (Levinson and Sparkes, 2003). A mistrust of health and associated services and highly gendered attitudes towards acknowledging depression or seeking help preclude most young men from requesting support. Many respondents report an anecdotal rise in drug and alcohol abuse amongst young Gypsy and Traveller men when the break up of kinship structures that can follow the transition into housing means that social control systems break down. In the Kent study one woman pointed to the relationship between forced settlement and the alienation and cultural trauma experienced by many young men:

> You have a drive down the High Street and have a look at the boys I grew up with . . . they're out of their head on drugs or on Tennants Super because they're getting rid of the day, there's no point in them having a day. They're all stuck in houses now, all stuck in the council estates, they don't want to be there but where are they going to go?

Identity and cultural capital

In addition to the frequently damaging emotional consequences of settlement in housing, the symbolic impacts of such a transition were highlighted by a number of participants. A common concern was that if respondents lived in housing and did not have adequate contact with relatives and other Gypsies and Travellers that their culture would become 'diluted'. Several recently settled interviewees expressed a concern that 'the worst thing is when you move into housing, they count you as . . . part of the population. You're not a Gypsy any more'. The fear is that not only do the mainstream population consider that once resident in housing a person is no longer a Gypsy or Traveller, but friends and relatives who still live on sites or travel may also become more distant from the housed individual thus exacerbating their isolation.

The symbolic centrality of 'travelling' to housed Gypsy and Traveller identity was reinforced repeatedly throughout interviews and focus groups. Over 65 per cent of respondents noted that they 'travelled' at some point in the year, even if only to attend one or two culturally important horse fairs or other key social occasions. The possession of a caravan and thus owning the ability to 'get up and go if you want to' was a significant marker of cultural capital. However, the imposition of local authority/social landlord regulations against stationing a caravan outside a property or concerning the duration that a rented property can be left vacant were often bitterly resented. Comments such as 'I'd love a trailer outside for when my family come but we're not allowed' were common. These restrictions combined with a lack of transit (short-term) sites pose particular difficulties in maintaining family relations and attending occasions such as weddings and funerals. One housed woman noted that 'I don't get to see my family very often as I'm in a house now and if there was a transit site round here they could visit more often'.

The emphasis on 'caravan dwelling/travelling' dominated the discourse of older respondents and those relatively new to housing as cultural markers of identity. Younger participants by contrast, were clear that Gypsies and Travellers are not defined purely by nomadism and do not lose their identity or culture when housed. While travelling was recognized as an important component of cultural identity the younger participants were more likely to emphasize factors such as ethnic origins, identification with central norms and values and recognition of changing community dynamics. These merged to form a hybridized identity which was not uncritical of their elders discourse. For many young people their understanding of what it meant to be a 'Gypsy' or a Traveller' consisted of a recognition of the changing nature of their communities, which was closer to the conceptualization of an ethnic group recognized in legislation and based on the principles of descent and a common cultural heritage. A member of the youth focus group in the West of England commented:

> What bugs me is that just because we live in a house and don't go travelling that you're not Travellers. It doesn't mean that at all, you're still Gypsies even though you don't go travelling. My Nan always lived in

wagons and when I get older I want to live in them and go travelling – I don't want to live in a house.

A young mother, who was part of the focus group, noted the resilience of Gypsy and Traveller identity and was adamant that this would not be weakened despite the demise of nomadic lifestyles. She commented that:

> It will never disappear, because my kids, all these little kids, and their kids – there'll still be Gypsy generations even 20 years down the line. When mine grow up they'll say 'my mum was a Gypsy'.

Conflict and discrimination in housing

Conflict is common between Gypsy and Travellers and their sedentary neighbours. Analysis of a series of GTAAs found that between 60 and 70 per cent of housed Gypsies and Travellers reported experiencing racist or discriminatory comments from neighbours. In the South West study area 65 per cent of housed families had experienced racism from non-Gypsy neighbours while in the South East study this was the experience of 70 per cent of respondents. Typical comments, one by the informant below, included:

> When I was in my first house, I used to get on with the neighbours but if anything happened, the fault was always ours.

In both study areas many respondents are housed by social landlords on what are seen locally as 'sink' estates. Perceptions of their estates tended to be negative and housed Gypsies and Travellers levelled the same criticisms and stereotypes of their settled neighbours as the settled population level at them. The major areas of contention centred on perceptions that both groups considered their neighbours to be 'dirty'; that their children were rude and unruly and that 'they're all thieves who can't be trusted'. One woman who had been housed for nine years on an estate in East Kent commented that 'most gorgers [non-Gypsies] on my estate are filthy dirty and would argue over a penny piece as most are scag-heads'. The imputation of criminality and drug addiction to their 'settled' neighbours often curtails family travelling as several respondents felt it was unsafe to leave their houses empty as 'it's not safe to go away – we'd be burgled – so we leave some of the older boys at home if we are away'. Conversely, there is a widespread acknowledgement that 'gorgers' would blame members of the Gypsy and Traveller community for any crime in their locality, meaning that they were unable to escape the negative labelling that attached to their community. One young man, housed for the majority of his life, remarked that 'we stick together if there's trouble but because people know we're Gypsies they always point to us whenever there's trouble'.

Poor relationships with neighbours featured more prominently in the narratives of respondents who experienced the most unhappiness in housing. When asked to identify positive aspects of residence in housing, the ability to avoid eviction and access to running hot water were the most frequently cited benefits. Significantly, given the importance of kinship ties the presence of relatives in the local area (whether on sites or in housing) was regarded as critically important in sustaining a tenancy: one respondent could find nothing good about housing except that 'my sister's near though and I like that' Another noted that 'all my family lives near here and that is the only good thing'. In the absence of close family members living locally, other Gypsy and Traveller families in the neighbourhood were often accepted as a proxy kin-group. Interviewees in both locations and of all ages stressed that the presence of an extended community group lessened some of the problems associated with housing and diminished the fear that cultural values would be lost through settlement. For individuals who had experienced racist violence or threats, the presence of other Travellers enhanced their sense of protection and belonging to a neighbourhood:

> I got family all over this estate there's so many of us the gorgers wouldn't dare give us any trouble that's the best thing about being here me aunts and cousins are always in our place.

'Traveller estates' and (re)creating community through the mutual exchange system

Given the importance of creating and sustaining a community network in the face of policy-driven settlement and frequent local hostility, patterns of 'migration-networks' are emerging which essentially mirror 'chain-migration' in other BME groups (Haug, 2008). Initially, Gypsies and Travellers may have been offered accommodation in 'hard to let' estates and thus found themselves living in proximity to others from their community after the closure of local sites. In the South East study, for example, a number of respondents were moved onto the same streets on the same estates after mass evictions from local stopping places. Many who entered housing after these evictions still feel betrayed that 'they [council] told us if we got off the marshes and went into houses they'd build sites for us and we could move back onto the sites. It never happened.' More recently, evidence of conscious choice over residence has begun to emerge in both study areas.

Local authority and social landlord housing officers report that on certain estates in both localities the population comprised of up to 50 per cent Gypsy and Traveller households with initial housing allocation failing to account for the size of the population. Not only are second and subsequent generations likely to request accommodation on the same estates as their own parents and siblings, but the impact of elective transfer has a cumulative effect as other residents transfer out when a locality gains a reputation as a

'Gypsy area' (Clark and Greenfields, 2006). Gypsies and Travellers then utilize their own social networks to build communities by passing information on potential 'swaps' or vacancies and enquiring whether friends or relatives wish to live locally. This allows for a high level of mobility within housing. In the South East study area just under half of a sample of 103 housed Gypsy and Traveller households had moved at least once in the previous five years, including over 20 per cent who had moved three times or more (Smith, 2008: 19). One housing officer in the South East noted:

> They are very mobile within housing and don't stay put for long. They're moving around and using houses like wagons. The lifestyle doesn't stop just because they're in housing. It's all done through ties and someone knows someone who wants to move onto this or that street and we'll get them turning up having arranged a three- or four-way exchange.

A further consequence of the long-established presence of Gypsies and Travellers on certain estates is that over time a degree of social and cultural convergence with their non-Traveller neighbours is occurring. Despite the rhetoric favouring marriage between community members, there are signs of increasing rates of intermarriage (or parenting relationships) with non-Travellers amongst both the young adult generation and, in some cases, their parents. Indeed a number of the younger focus group participants were either a product of, or were themselves in, 'mixed' relationships:

> 'My Mum and Dad are Travellers – not my sister's [Dad] though. We have different Dads.'

> 'There are various mixed marriages on the estate between gorgers and Travellers and I think it is quite healthy.'

Despite the increasing rate of mixed relationships and the changing conceptualization of 'Gypsy and Traveller identities', which is emerging from this process, such relationships are not without their problems and cultural tensions. As one participant in the South East study commented:

> It can be hard and I for one feel sorry for them, they've got the mum's family having a go about 'those dirty Pikeys' and the dad's family slagging off 'those bloody gorgers' and the kid's stuck in the middle pulled both ways.

Many of the problems facing Gypsy and Traveller youth such as inadequate and incomplete education, low literacy and skill levels, unemployment and the erosion of traditional family structures are also experienced by marginalized working class youth regardless of ethnicity. When combined with shared spatial residence an awareness of shared sets of problems and common solutions may emerge (MacDonald and Marsh, 2005). Interestingly, young people in both localities reported that youth resident on their estates had a highly ambivalent attitude to Gypsy and Traveller culture and observed a process of convergence between young Gypsies and Travellers and dispossessed working class youths.

> 'People say "oh they're – Travellers that, Travellers this, Travellers the other" but really deep down inside they'd love to be a Traveller, 'cos they dress up like Travellers, they wear gold earrings and they talk like us.'

> 'Some people [at school] do say to us "I wish I was a Traveller".'

However, this convergence of lifestyles is not welcomed by all, particularly older members of the community, who spoke critically of the Gypsy 'imitators' whose alleged standards of behaviour provided a means of differentiating the pretender from the 'genuine' Gypsy.

> There are loads of Travellers round here and loads of wannabe Gypsies as well. They're the worst they make it bad for the rest of us. When you tell the gavvers [police] they ain't Gypsies they say it's hard to tell these days.

This distancing from groups who may be categorized alongside Gypsies and Travellers but who do not meet the symbolic values of Gypsy/Traveller culture has been observed in other studies. Powell (2008) observes that 'the dialectic of identification and disidentification is played out within the context of an external threat' – in this case both those deemed as inauthentic and the settled population (2008: 98). The dynamic nature of community and ethnic relations on the participants' housing estates reveals a complex and contradictory picture. A cohesive and close knit community that reformulates an approximation to 'traditional' Gypsy and Traveller culture is maintained through a combination of adaptive strategies and social segregation based on the threat from their 'settled' neighbours on one hand, and a distinct cultural identity on the other. At the same time the boundaries of these divisions are becoming steadily blurred as identities have adapted and evolved in response to external change. One young woman – who analysed her own situation in terms of a choice between a culturally 'authentic' but increasingly untenable life of travelling, or settlement into housing and marriage offered a perceptive insight into the changing cultures of house-dwelling Gypsies and Travellers:

> What I think is happening is that because we have third, second and first generations on the estate there is a culture – to use the term – that is evolving . . . So you've got the Travellers of 30, 40 years ago that originally came onto the estate all those years back, and now you've got the generations coming on. And the culture is evolving.

Conclusion

Evidence from both study locations indicates that social relationships between Gypsies/Travellers and other residents of the estates are distinguished by a considerable degree of mistrust and antipathy. Social distance is maintained both by racist stereotypes and prejudice against Gypsies and Travellers but also by many Gypsy and Travellers' beliefs over their own superiority in relation to 'gorger' society. However, as McVeigh cautions, this parallel should not be taken too far since what is significant is the different degree of social power available to sedentary and Gypsy-Traveller society (McVeigh, 1997). As a diverse range of socially and economically marginalized groups become increasingly spatially concentrated and segregated into social and public sector housing, social relations between Gypsies and Travellers and others residing in their neighbourhoods are also marked by increasing cultural and social interrelations and convergence. As Gypsies and Travellers are becoming an increasingly prominent social group within some localities as a nomadic life becomes progressively more difficult to maintain, their influence on local neighbourhood cultures and socio-economic dynamics is likely to become of greater importance. The merging of communities and daily contact within schools and social settings means that young people are beginning to create a hybridized Gypsy/Traveller identity which is reflective of the changing social dynamics which surround them and which, to some extent, takes account of the common experiences and location of residents of socially excluded and deprived locations. For older Gypsies and Travellers, however, or those in the transitional situation between site and house, a desire to (re)create a traditional community (albeit in bricks and mortar) with a strong and supportive network of kin relations and intra-group social contact within the local Gypsy and Traveller community remains paramount and a key to the retention of bonding capital, with impacts for the nature of local social relations.

Notes

1 A8 refers to migrants to the UK from the eight EU accession countries (the Czech Republic, Estonia, Hungary, Latvia, Lithuania, Poland, Slovakia and Slovenia).
2 *Clarke v SSETR [2002] JPL 552.* In this case the Court of Appeal held that when a Gypsy sought planning permission for a caravan site and had a 'cultural aversion' to bricks and mortar, it could breach his human rights to take account of an offer of conventional housing that had been made to him.

Bibliography

Bancroft, A. (2005) *Roma and Gypsy-Travellers in Europe: Modernity, Race, Space and Exclusion,* Aldershot: Ashgate.
Cemlyn, S., Greenfields, M., Burnett, S., Matthews, Z. and Whitwell, C. (2009) *Inequalities Experienced by Gypsy and Traveller Communities: A Review,* London: Equality and Human Rights Commission.

Clark, C. and Greenfields, M. (2006) *Here to Stay: The Gypsies and Travellers of Britain*, Hatfield: University of Hertfordshire Press.

Commission for Racial Equality (CRE) (2006) *Common Ground: Equality, Good Race Relations and Sites for Gypsies and Irish Travellers: Report of a CRE Inquiry in England and Wales*, London: Commision for Racial Equality.

Dench, G., Gavron, K. and Young, M. (2006) *The New East End: Kinship, Race and Conflict*, London: Profile Books.

Greenfields, M. (2009) *Gypsies, Travellers and Accommodation*. A Race Equality Foundation *Briefing Paper*, London: Race Equality Foundation.

Griffin, C. (2008) *Nomads under the Westway: Irish Travellers, Gypsies and Other Traders in West London*, Hatfield: University of Hertfordshire Press.

Hammar, T., Brochmann, G. and Tamas, K. (1997) *International Migration, Immobility and Development: Multidisciplinary Perspectives*, Oxford: Berg Publishers.

Haug, S. (2008) 'Migration networks and migration decision-making'. *Journal of Ethnic and Migration Studies*, 34: 585–605.

Home, R. and Greenfields, M. (2006) *The Dorset Gypsy Traveller Accommodation Assessment*, Chelmsford: Anglia Ruskin University.

Kornblum, W. (1975) 'Boyash Gypsies: Shantytown Ethnicity', in Rehfisch, F. (ed.) *Gypsies, Tinkers and other Travellers*, London: Academic Press.

Levinson, M. and Sparkes, A. (2003) 'Gypsy masculinities and the school-home interface: exploring contradictions and tensions'. *British Journal of Sociology of Education*, 24(5): 587–603.

Loury, G., Modood, T. and Teles, S. (2005) *Ethnicity, Social Mobility and Public Policy: Comparing the US and the UK.* Cambridge, MA: Harvard University Press.

MacDonald, R. and Marsh, J. (2005) *Disconnected Youth? Growing up in Britain's Poor Neighbourhoods*, Basingstoke: Palgrave Macmillan.

Markova, E. and Black, R. (2007) *East European Immigration and Community Cohesion*, York: Joseph Rowntree Foundation.

Matthews, Z. (2008) *The Health of Gypsies and Travellers in the UK*, London: Race Equality Foundation.

Mayall, D. (1988) *Gypsy-Travellers in Nineteenth-century Society*, Cambridge: Cambridge University Press.

McVeigh, R. (1997) 'Theorising sedentarism: the roots of anti-nomadism', in Acton, T. (ed.) *Gypsy Politics and Traveller Identity*, Hatfield: University of Hertfordshire Press.

Niner, P. (2003) *Local Authority Gypsy/Traveller Sites in England*, London: ODPM.

Parry, G., Van Cleemput, P., Peters, J., Walters, S., Thomas, K. and Cooper, C. (2004) *The Health Status of Gypsies and Travellers in England*, Sheffield: ScHARR.

Platt, L. (2004) *The Intergenerational Social Mobility of Minority Ethnic Groups*, ISER Working Paper, Colchester: University of Essex.

Powell, C. (2008) 'Understanding the stigmatization of Gypsies: power and the dialectics of (Dis)identification', *Housing, Theory and Society*, 25(2), 87–109.

Richardson, J., Bloxsom, J. and Greenfields, M. (2007) *East Kent Gypsy Traveller Accommodation Assessment*, Leicester: De Montfort University.

Sibley, D. (1981) *Outsiders in Urban Societies*, New York: St Martin's Press.

Smith, D. (2008) *Sittingbourne Gypsy and Traveller Survey*, Canterbury: Canterbury Christ Church University; Amacus Housing Association; Canterbury Gypsy Support Group.

Spencer, S., Rhus, M., Anderson, B. and Royaly, B. (2007) *Migrant's Lives Beyond the*

Workplace: The Experiences of Central and Eastern Europeans in the UK, York: Joseph Rowntree Foundation.

Webster, C. (2003) 'Race, space and fear: imagined geographies of racism, crime, violence and disorder in Northern England', *Capital and Class*, 80: 63–90.

Wetherell, M., Lafleche, M. and Berkeley, R. (eds) (2007) *Identity, Ethnic Diversity and Community Cohesion*, London: Sage.

8 On not going home at the end of the day

Spatialized discourses of family life in single-location home/workplaces

Julie Seymour

Introduction

This chapter draws on a study of family practices in family-run hotels, pubs and boarding houses in the UK. One focus of the research is the spatiality of such locations; that is, the dynamic of space and social life in the construction of everyday family life where this occurs alongside a business. While such single-location home/workplaces may constitute a comparatively 'atypical case' (Mitchell, 1983), their 'inverted' spatiality makes explicit those processes and practices which are often less visible in situations where the home and workplace are situated in discrete locations. More broadly, they show how family practices are also enacted in locations other than the domestic thus preventing family research from being confined to specific locations.

The fluid and dynamic nature of the concept of spatiality finds resonance in that of family practices. Both address the continual and socially constructed nature of their 'realization' (Keith and Pile, 1993: 6) and the role played by both structure and agency in producing particular configurations within specific locations. Importantly, a 'family practices' perspective incorporates, but keeps separate, consideration of the activities of everyday family life and the discourses of 'the family' (Morgan, 1996). A family-practice focus on actions *and* discourse therefore 'allows the researcher to map the interplay of the influence of socially and historically constructed discourses of family life with the biographies of the specific individuals involved' (Seymour, 2007: 1098). As a result, the *doing* of family life is revealed as a structurative process of combining the pragmatic demands of the specific situation people find themselves in (the family they live with) with the aspiration of producing in Gillis' phrase (1996: xv) the 'imagined family we live by'. Through family practices, families reproduce themselves literally and ideologically (Dallos, 1997). An earlier article (Seymour, 2007) has focused on the activities element of family practices in hospitality establishments, particularly the creation of spatial boundaries. This chapter will focus on the issue of the discursive construction of family life by interviewees and the role of spatiality in this.

Data collection took place in 2001 and occurred in two UK east coast seaside resorts; one in the North of England and one in the South East. The data consist of three types of qualitative interview: 15 in-depth interviews with parents running hotels (7), pubs (2) and boarding houses (2) who were currently bringing up, or had recently brought up their families in these workplaces; 6 interviews with individuals or couples who had raised families or grown up in such establishments in the 1960s and 1970s (four hotels, one pub, one boarding house), and secondary data analysis from 50 oral-history interviews relating to involvement in the tourist industry in one northern seaside town during the early and middle twentieth century.[1] The primary data interviews were carried out by the author with at least one proprietor and, where appropriate and possible, with both. In addition, children who were currently living in the establishments who were prepared to be interviewed were included, resulting in a further four interviews with children. Access was initially through written communication via local Hotelier Associations and later in the project through snowballing. All the interviews but two (at the interviewees' requests) were taped and transcribed. (For more discussion of this technique of 'comparative cross-sectional inquiry', see Seymour, 2005.)

It has long been recognized that interview data must be treated as an intersubjective performance or a situated interaction (Layder, 1994). That is, interviewees are conscious that their dialogue with the interviewer is a presentation of self and as such they will actively construct their narrative utilizing appropriate discourses rather than uncritically regurgitating them. The interview data for this study then reveals two issues. One is the way in which spatiality emerges from the data as a key element in the informants' descriptions of both what constitutes a 'proper' family life and whether they felt able to achieve it. The second is how informants presented these spatialized discourses in a performative way in the interview to explain the extent to which they could achieve the family ideal to which they aspired. Before presenting these results, a brief contextual review will consider how spatiality has been discussed in the research on the social study of childhood.

Researching children and spatiality

This research project has followed the endorsements of McNamee (2007) and others (Brannen and O'Brien, 1996; Jensen and McKee, 2003) not to isolate children from their families. As McNamee (2007) says, in classic socialization theory, children were previously 'subsumed into accounts of the family'. In response, the new paradigm of the social study of childhood 'metaphorically removed' them from the home and the school in order to make them visible but as she and other authors (Seymour and McNamee, forthcoming) suggest, it is time to reintegrate them into these key sites. This is not to once again render them invisible but to recentre them in crucial sites as competent social actors. This research then uses interviews from a range of family members including children, recognizing all participants as active agents.

The research drawn upon in this chapter will develop the social/spatial study of childhood since much previous work such as Sibley's (1995) study of the construction of boundaries by children or that on parental risk anxiety and the perceived problem of 'stranger danger' (Scott *et al.*, 1998) seem to assume that all domestic spheres were only private domains. Similarly Mayall (1998) in her study of the management of children's bodies demarcates the 'public world of the school' and the 'private world of the home'. For children living in hospitality establishments the boundaries between public and private are much less sharply delineated.

Additionally, in many studies of global North societies, the economic and commercial role of children in the home has been largely unexplored (although see Song, 1999; Seymour, 2005; van der Hoek, 2005) leading to a lack of recognition of the particularity of the spaces in which it occurs. Hence James *et al.* (1998) refer to children's worlds as consisting of the home, the school and the city. Similarly, Holloway and Valentine (2000) discuss how children's lives are enacted in the street, the playground, the school and the home. To this should be added the impact on global North children's spatialized lives of the home as workplace.

As a result, when Holloway and Valentine (2000) encourage us to recognize the interconnections that exist between households, their immediate locality and the wider world especially in relation to children, studies such as the one outlined in this chapter provide examples where these interconnections are not spatially distinct. In addition, the growing number of people who work at or from home (Felstead *et al.*, 2005) means that the single-location home/workplace may become the experience of more families and children.

An emerging topic: defining a 'proper' family life in spatial terms

Interviewee definitions of a 'proper' family life have often focused on the form or membership of the family group (O' Brien *et al.*, 1996; Ribbens and Edwards, 1999; Mason and Tipper, 2006) or on eating meals together (James, 2007). Here the focus will be on how people living in hotels, pubs and boarding houses define what they consider to be a 'proper' family life and to what extent sharing their home location with their workplace aids or hinders its acquisition. The topic emerged when several informants contrasted their experiences of family life in a hotel, pub or boarding house with those of what they described as an 'ordinary family life' (Interview 7), a 'normal life' (Interview 9) or a 'proper life' (Interview 16). This initially appeared to suggest that, for some of those living in such dual locations, working at home was not providing the setting required to achieve the family life to which they aspired.

Key themes emerged in interview discussions about a 'proper' (normal or ordinary) family life with the following elements being frequently mentioned:

- time together with *all* family members (especially meals)
- undisturbed family time
- the ability to give children attention
- the freedom of the family home (spatial, aural, psychological)
- celebrating public holidays with just the family (e.g. Christmas, Easter).

In sum, the ideological discourse of a 'proper' family life involved time and activities spent together with other family members – and ideally only other family members.

The reality of combining work and home life in one location often meant that the experiences of the interviewees did not match those of the aspirational 'model'. This was often seen as a function of living and working in a hotel, pub or boarding house and informants compared their lifestyles with those of other family members or staff whose separate work and home sites meant they were able to carry out family practices which more closely resembled the discourse of a 'proper' family life.

> [W]hereas the others [staff] they can all go home at the end of the day, they can do what they like and nobody's none the wiser. Here we don't, we are constantly, everybody knows what's going on at all times, you've no private life at all.
>
> (Interview 16, female, living and working in own family-run hotel)

They reported non-resident family members' responses to their dual location. For example, one informant's sisters could never understand

> [h]ow you could live in that home with other people in the same house as you . . . If you don't know nothing else . . . but my sisters could never understand it . . . couldn't possibly have anyone live in the house.
>
> (Interview 2, female, ex-boarding house owner)

An important dimension here of the definition of a 'proper' family life is clearly the control of space and those who inhabit that space. The idyllic family life is expressed here by family members through boundaries (the front door) and the symbolic meaning given to them and as Valentine has expressed (2001) it is the meanings people give space which turns it into place.

Yet not all family responses were negative. One interviewee's sister-in-law who was brought up in an old people's home voiced no dissent since '[s]he just thinks it's the norm' (Interview 11, female hotel owner) presumably having experienced a spatially different model of family life from that of the dominant discourse.

Achieving a 'proper' family life in a single-location home/workplace

For some interviewees, achieving a 'proper' family life was an unrealizable ideal in a single-location home/workplace. For a second group, the nature of a family hotel allowed a degree of flexibility in the workplace which enabled the performance of family practices. Finally, for a third group of interviewees, the business was deliberately entered into because it was perceived as being perfectly structured to allow the combination of work and family life. This then begins to raise the questions both of which factors permit or limit the performance of a 'proper' family life, but also how much people actively construct its achievement in spatialized terms in interviews.

An unrealizable ideal in the single-location home/workplace

For one interviewee, working and living in the same location precluded a 'proper' family life by (his) definition.

JS: What's a normal family life?
INTERVIEWEE: Well, *having a job you go out to and come back* with money in your
    pocket and spend it on your family.
                    (Interview 9, male, ex-publican, my emphasis)

This definition is rather surprising from someone who had been in the catering industry all their working life, echoing as it does an expectation of the separation of home and workplace. Effectively, it presents a discourse of a 'proper' family life which is primarily spatially defined, occurs discretely from the place of employment and which can never be achieved in a single-location home/workplace.

This differs from the viewpoint of another interviewee who lived in her parents' hotel with her husband and several young children. She did not define the workplace as necessarily needing to be distinct from the home but focused on the negative impacts that the spatial constraints of bringing a family up in a business location had for her children. This is shown by her response when asked:

JS: What's a proper life then?
INTERVIEWEE: Proper life, where they [the children] can get up, get what they
    want for breakfast, wake them. You don't have to worry about whether
    it's tidy. You can go out, come back when you like, take the kids, pick
    them up from school, not have to rush about, not . . . I mean they're
    literally, they can't do what an average child would do. They can't just
    come in and put TV on and go help themselves to some biscuits out the
    kitchen. They can't just go into the freezers and grab something out.
    They can't just get an ice lolly, 'cos most kids, if they go into a house and

they get something out the fridge and they don't close the door, it's not a problem . . . that [one – hotel fridge] it is.

> (Interview 16, female, living and working in
> own family-run hotel)

Their situation was made more complex by the fact they had to share their 'private' space with other hotel employees.

JS: Do you feel you can create a boundary between . . .?

INTERVIEWEE: No, in fact, to put anything in the hotel washrooms, you've got to go through our private living quarters to them. To take the rubbish bins out, you've got to go through our living quarters to get to the bins, so, there's isn't even an area that you could say staff don't go in and we'll go. Many a time they'll go get changed and they'll get changed in our back living quarters and then they'll throw their uniform down, so you're constantly tidying up after them, so there's, you have no home life whatsoever.

> (Interview 16, female, living and working in
> own family-run hotel)

These responses draw a stark picture of a family life curtailed by business requirements. It is worth noting though that the two interviewees quoted were among the ones in my sample where the spatial boundaries between home and workplace were most rigidly upheld in that the children did not enter the pub or hotel (although it has been seen that the small living quarters of the family in Interview 16 were frequently breached by staff). Both were families with several young children and the last respondent quoted was working in, but did not own, the family business. Hence it appears that a combination of factors including stage in the life cycle, position as employee rather than as proprietor (and with few other staff in the establishment) but also determination to maintain firm boundaries led to the strongest feelings of family life being imposed on by the business imperative. While the construction by these interviewees of a 'proper' family life was literally unachievable in a single-location home/workplace the role of boundary setting and a non-permeable model of family practices also appears relevant.

It appeared that for these interviewees a 'proper' family life could only be achieved through a spatial relocation of home and workplace to discrete (or at least protected) domains. Another female hotelier who found family activities curtailed by the business resolved this by disaggregating family practices from their traditional location. With her husband and two children, she created family space outside the business location through eating away from their home and commented: 'If we want time together we go out for a meal' (Interview 17). That is, one practice which contributed to doing a 'proper' family life had developed through a deliberate withdrawal from the home (and work) location.

A model of permeable practices in the single-location home/workplaces

Elsewhere I have talked about how the concept of permeability between home life and work is particularly useful to this research topic (Seymour, 2001) and how, when both activities are occurring in the same location, there is potential for permeability to be a two-way process. This develops Goffman's (1959) ideas of front-stage/back-stage to introduce more spatial fluidity. Goffman's dramaturgical boundaries could appear overly static with specific physical locations in hotels, pubs and boarding houses envisaged as places where activities from only one arena take place. Hence hotel receptions, dining rooms and guest lounges are front-stage and kitchens and bedrooms are back-stage. In contrast, by focusing on the dynamic processes of family practices (Morgan, 1996; Seymour, 2007), a more fluid use of work and home space/time is revealed. Hence, many interviewees spoke of ways in which the nature of the business accommodated or even encouraged greater permeability of home and work life. This operated in both directions.

Home permeating into work when in the same location

INTERVIEWEE: The thing is when you're living in a place like this and you're working on the job, you can do your washing and your ironing, and cleaning gets done. For the few years I was out of it, you go to work, that's it. You go out at eight o'clock in a morning, and you come home at tea time and then you've got it all to start.

JS: Same to do again, yeah.

INTERVIEWEE: And you think 'Oh my goodness, when I used to live in it, I had all this done' you know.

(Interview 12, female, hotel owner)

For another mother of school-age children the advantages of working in the home were:

We're here all the time. We don't have to. I mean, if they're ill, we're here. If there's any emergency, we're here. You're not relying on anybody else, you're there all the time. That's got to be the first and foremost. And at the end of the day, if anything does go wrong, blood's thicker than water and your family will come first.

(Interview 17, female, hotel owner)

Even the woman working in her family's hotel (Interview 16) acknowledged that this employment set-up allowed her and her sisters to combine serving breakfast with the school run since whoever had a day off took the numerous children in the family to school. Hence certain aspects of the hospitality industry allow some dimensions of the desired 'proper' family life to be achieved when they are in the same location.

Work permeating into home when in the same location

The disadvantage of this permeability, however, is that proprietors are rarely off-duty and cannot take sick leave if the establishment is open. The ideology of a 'proper' family life also included the ability of parents to give their children uninterrupted attention. Although the parents interviewed felt their children suffered from the lack of *their* attention due to the demands of guests, children who were interviewed mentioned favourably the interaction with guests which often included presents and trips out. This appeared to compensate in some degree to the lack of parental attention. Indeed, some parents referred obliquely to average *annual* attention citing long periods out of season (winter), money earned and holidays abroad as balancing out the times when they were unavailable due to work demands.

Indeed, children's resistance to parental control and boundaries can use the impact of the workplace on the imaginary of 'proper' family life (through the enforced absence of their parents due to the business) as a bargaining tool. One female hotelier described how she could counteract her publican mother's demands that she stay in as a teenager with the phrase 'What for? So I can stay upstairs on my own, watching television?' (Interview 17). The children brought up in hotels, pubs and boarding houses have often shown creative agency in using their atypical family situations to their advantage (Seymour, 2005).

Similarities with those not working in/from family home: the limitations of spatial influence

Finally, it was recognized by some respondents that the discursive ideal of the 'proper' family life did not reflect the reality of lived experience either for those in the hospitality industry or in families where the parents were employed in spatially discrete workplaces. This was particularly mentioned in relation to families spending time together as their children grew older as the following accounts illustrate:

> You don't get quality time together, you miss out on some quality time. Weekends, I would say weekends, we don't have the weekends to spend as a family like we used to do but then again like I said my kids are at that age where they wouldn't have spent time with us anyway. I mean we're honoured to see (son) aren't we really?
>
> (Interview 17, female, hotel owner)

So for many of the people interviewed in this study, bringing up a family in a hotel, pub or boarding house was aided by the degree of flexibility inherent in the business location and the pragmatic recognition that for many (most?) people the reality of the family they live with rarely matches entirely the discursive 'imagined family we live by' (Gillis, 1996: xv).

A 'perfect trade' (-off): choosing the single-location home/workplace

For a small number of the hoteliers I interviewed, combining the home and workplace in one location had been a deliberate choice which they thought would allow for ease of childcare and other domestic activities. In effect, it was providing a single place in which to carry out the synchronized time that Morehead (2001) describes mothers working away from the home have to perfect. This view of the benefits of family life in a hotel had often been transmitted through the generations as the following quotation from the mother of school-age children describes:

> I was brought up in a shop . . . My mother's idea, *perfect trades are like this*. If you have a shop you're always there when your children come home. If you have a hotel, you're always there when your children come home. The children might complain that you're always working but you're there.
> (Interview 10, female, hotel owner, my emphasis)

Indeed, the work–home balance had been built into reproducing the generations as she went on to explain:

> I don't know what other hoteliers do, but we planned our children, to have them in winter, because it would be inconvenient for your business to have them in the summer, and so the birthdays are in winter and it was quieter, February and April. Well, April can be a bit awkward 'cos that could be over Easter, but, you know, February was better.
> (Interview 10, female, hotel owner)

Another female ex-hotelier discussed how, in the late 1950s, she was happy to move from teaching to running a hotel so that she and her husband could start a family. So the role of spatiality is key in some families as to when, and perhaps even whether, children came into being. This is significant as many lay perceptions of what constitutes a 'proper' family life require the presence of children (Campbell, 1985).

Children's accounts of a 'proper' family life

One interviewee brought up in a hotel considered that the children of hoteliers and boarding house owners were 'pushed from pillar to post' and the business came first (Interview 12). As part of the interview, I asked the children currently living in hospitality establishments, and adults who had grown up in a hotel, pub or boarding house, whether they thought family life in a hotel was different from that of people in private houses and, if so, in what way. Their responses were mostly positive about their experiences including:

- This was the family life we knew so it didn't seem strange.
- Other children they knew also lived in such establishments.
- They understood the demands of the business on their parents.
- Children in private houses were jealous of them living in hotels.

For example:

> By the time I realized there were alternatives, I'd got to like the way we did things.
>
> (Interview 4, adult son of ex-hotel owner)

Changes in children's spatial experiences of family life in hospitality establishments

The expectation that running a hotel, pub or boarding house allows parents to be in the same location as their children during the day contrasts with the data from the oral history interviews which described providing tourist accommodation in the mid twentieth century. Here accounts refer to sick children being hidden in stores so as not to lose bookings, sleeping in attics and tents outside to free up their bedrooms for guests and being sent away from the home after breakfast not to return until after the visitors had eaten their tea. The oral history accounts act as a reminder that the discourse of a 'proper' family life and parental–child relations have changed considerably over the past 50 years. Historical accounts of children not feeling left alone by their parents because they were used to 'playing out' contrast with some current practices of children being required to remain in the home due to fear of 'stranger danger' (Furedi, 1997). In addition, the pressure for greater parental supervision, and particularly input in children's education, places stronger demands on parents to physically be with their children for significant periods of time when in the home. This highlights the changing spatialities of the discourses of family life, childhood and parenthood. These recent influences feed into a construction of an idyllic but largely unattainable discourse of a 'proper' family life whether parents work within the home or at a separate location.

Conclusion: utilizing spatialized discourses of family life

For interviewees, the expressed satisfaction with their ability to conduct a 'proper' family life in an atypical spatial setting varied with their own childhood experiences, the age and number of their children, their relationship to owning the business, the number of staff in the establishment and to some extent the degree to which the hospitality lifestyle was perceived as a positive choice. It appeared that increasing the degree of permeability between workplace and home led generally to more positive responses from all family members although as has been shown by the data from Interview 16, there can be too much permeability, in this case from the business into family life.

Yet the issue of interviews as performance should be acknowledged. The spatialized discourses articulated in these presentations of a 'proper' family life could be examples of talk-in-interaction (Frith and Kitzinger, 1998) as much as rigidly held beliefs.

For some informants the construction of a 'proper' family life appeared to consist precisely of those activities which living and working in a hotel, pub or boarding house effectively denied them. That is, it was constructed as an ideal which could never be attained due to the demands of the business or its spatial location. These appeared to be the parents who were most dissatisfied with bringing up their family in a hospitality establishment. In contrast, the discourses of other interviewees presented 'proper' family life as something which could be achieved through the adoption of permeable work/family practices or indeed, an ideal which *became* possible through employment in one's own hospitality establishment.

This confirms that in interviews people do not simply draw on existing discourses when questioned but actively select and present aspects of them which will allow them to present the best case for the account on which they are collaborating with the interviewee. Thus although individuals may never be able to achieve fully in practice the discursive ideal of a 'proper' family life, they can, to some extent, construct the accounts of their lives to present their current family settings in the best possible light or to provide strong arguments as to why the failure to achieve what they consider to be a 'proper' family life is outside their control. This intersubjective approach to interviews is a specific instance of the wider practice of the strategic use of discourses and activities which result in the varied performance of family, and other, practices which people carry out in their everyday lives.

Acknowledgements

The interviews were funded by the Millennium Commission as part of the Looking Back, Looking Forward project carried out by the North Yorkshire Museums Department. I am grateful to the project's organizer, Karen Snowden, the interviewers and particularly the interviewees who allowed secondary analysis.

References

Brannen, J. and O'Brien, M. (1996) 'Introduction', in J. Brannen and M. O'Brien (eds) *Children in Families: Research and Policy*, London: Falmer Press.

Campbell, E. (1985) *The Childless Marriage: An Exploratory Study of Couples Who do not Want Children*, London: Tavistock.

Dallos, R. (1997, 2nd ed.) 'Constructing family life: family belief systems' in J. Muncie, M. Wetherell, M. Langan, R. Dallos and A. Cochrane (eds) *Understanding the Family*, London: Sage.

Felstead, A., Jewson, N. and Walters, S. (2005) *Changing Places of Work*, Basingstoke: Palgrave Macmillan.

Frith, H. and Kitzinger, C. (1998) 'Emotion work as a participant resource: a feminist analysis of young women's talk-in-interaction', *Sociology*, 32: 299–320.

Furedi, F. (1997) *Culture of Fear: Risk-taking and the Morality of Low Expectation*, London: Cassell.

Gillis, J. R. (1996) *A World of their Own Making: Myth, Ritual and the Quest for Family Values*, Cambridge, MA: Harvard University Press.

Goffman, E. (1959) *The Presentation of Self in Everyday Life*, Harmondworth: Penguin.

Holloway, S. and Valentine, G. (2000) 'Spatiality and the new social studies of childhood', *Sociology*, 34: 763–83.

James, A. (2007) 'A proper dinner', *Times Higher Education Supplement*, 25 May 2007: 16.

James, A., Jenks, C. and Prout, A. (1998) *Theorizing Childhood*, Cambridge: Polity Press.

Jensen, A. and McKee, L. (eds) (2003) *Children and the Changing Family: Between Transformation and Negotiation*, London: RoutledgeFalmer.

Keith, M. and Pile, S. (eds) (1993) *Place and Politics of Identity*, London: Routledge.

Layder, D. (1994) *Understanding Social Theory*, London: Sage.

McNamee, S. (2007) 'Childhood' in *The Blackwell Encyclopedia of Sociology*, Oxford: Blackwell.

Mason, J. and Tipper, B. (2006) *Children, Kinship and Creativity*, Working Paper, University of Manchester, Morgan Centre.

Mayall, B. (1998) 'Children, emotions and daily life at home and school', in G. Bendelow and S. Williams (eds) *Emotions in Social Life. Critical Themes and Contemporary Issues*, London: Routledge.

Mitchell, J. C. (1983) 'Case and situation analysis', *The Sociological Review*, 31: 187–211.

Morehead, A. (2001) 'Synchronizing time for work and family: preliminary insights from qualitative research with mothers', *Journal of Sociology*, 37: 355–69.

Morgan, D. H. J. (1996) *Family Connections. An Introduction to Family Studies*, Cambridge: Polity Press.

O'Brien, M., Alldred, P. and Jones, D. (1996) 'Children's constructions of family and kinship', in J. Brannen and M. O'Brien (eds) *Children in Families: Research and Policy*, London: Falmer Press.

Ribbens, J. and Edwards, R. (1999) 'Breaking out from our circles of assumptions: contingent categories in researching "step-families"', in S. Ali, K. Coate and W. wa Goro (eds) *Belonging: Contemporary Feminist Writings on Global Change*, London: UCL Press.

Scott, S., Jackson, S. and Backett-Milburn, K. (1998) 'Swings and roundabouts: risk anxiety and the everyday worlds of children', *Sociology*, 32: 689–705.

Seymour, J. (2001) '"Dinner is at seven": prescribing and protecting family practices in hotels, pubs and boarding houses', *Working Paper No. 7*, Centre for the Social Study of Childhood, Hull: University of Hull.

Seymour, J. (2005) 'Entertaining guests or entertaining the guests: children's emotional labour in hotels, pubs and boarding houses', in J. Goddard, S. McNamee,

A. James and A. James (eds) *The Politics of Childhood: International Perspectives, Contemporary Developments*, Basingstoke: Palgrave Macmillan.

Seymour, J. (2007) 'Treating the hotel like a home: the contribution of studying the single location home/workplace', *Sociology*, 41: 1097–114.

Seymour, J. and McNamee (forthcoming) 'Being parented? Children and young people's engagement with parenting activities', in J. Waldren and I.M. Kaminski (eds) *Learning from the Children: Culture and Identity in a Changing World*, Oxford: Berghahn.

Sibley, D. (1995) 'Families and domestic routines: constructing the boundaries of childhood', in S. Pile and N. Thrift (eds) *Mapping the Subject: Geographies of Cultural Transformation*, London: Routledge.

Song, M. (1999) *Helping Out: Children's Labor In Ethnic Businesses*, Philadelphia, PA: Temple University Press.

Valentine, G. (2001) 'On-line dangers? Geographies of parents' fears for children's safety in cyberspace', *Professional Geographer*, 53: 71–83.

van der Hoek, T. (2005) 'Growing up in poverty, while living in an affluent society: personal experiences and coping strategies of Dutch poor children', in J. Goddard, S. McNamee, A. James and A. James (eds) *The Politics of Childhood: International Perspectives, Contemporary Developments*, Basingstoke: Palgrave Macmillan.

9 Geographies of 'family' life

Interdependent relationships across the life course in the context of problem Internet gambling

Gill Valentine and Kahryn Hughes

Introduction

In this chapter we address the relative lack of attention paid to family life by geographers. We begin by outlining the ways in which family has been included in the discipline, contrasting this with sociological approaches to the family, to outline the limits of geographers' engagement. In the second part of the chapter we use an empirical case study of adult problem Internet gamblers and their significant others to make a case for the importance of 'family' (in terms of both material and emotional support) throughout the life course and consequently to demonstrate why geographers need to pay more attention to personal and intimate relations.

Geographies of family life

The family primarily emerged as a topic within geography through early feminist research which argued that social reproduction is not separate from production but rather is a foundational process to capitalism (WGSG, 1984). This work, however, was in essence about the household as unit of production – about how people organized everyday living and related to capitalism (for example, through women's unpaid domestic labour and childcare), rather than the wider range of familial relationships.

In a context in which the growth of women's participation in the labour market has exceeded the social provision of care for both the young and the elderly this research subsequently evolved into a focus on women's role/obligations as mothers (e.g. Holloway, 1998, 1999; England, 1996; McKie *et al.*, 1999, 2001) and the complex practical and moral choices which they face about how to combine paid work and caring responsibilities. In doing so, much of this work was oriented around models of family life from the global North. This work, however, was extended from this specific domestic context, by Pratt (1999) and others, to think about how parenting and childcare relationships are performed or maintained through transnational care chains; as well as how they are done differently in different geographical contexts (e.g. England, 1996). While representing a significant body of work that has made an important contribution to understandings of social reproduction in the context of globalization, this research has largely remained focused on the practical organization of care rather than on the emotional ties, the meaning and quality of relationships, and the 'doing' of intimacy within 'families' defined more broadly (though see Valentine and Skelton, 2003).

Little or no consideration has been given by geographers in the global north to other forms of familial relationship, for example between: adult children and their adult parents; siblings; grand-children and grandparents; and wider familial networks of aunts/uncles, cousins, etc. This relative absence is even more noticeable when set against sociological research which has addressed how family obligations are negotiated and maintained within, and between, generations for several decades (e.g. Finch, 1989; Brannen *et al.*, 2004). Geographers are only just beginning to think about how 'family' is stretched across the life course and to talk about intergenerational relations through a geographical lens. In particular, Vanderbeck (2007: 16) draws attention to the need for geography to adopt, what he terms 'a less compartmentalized approach to issues of age within geography', and to consider 'the diverse geographies of intergenerational relationships existing both within and between societies'.

In other words, the whole affective register of familial connections and practices, including erotic and non-erotic relations has been largely neglected. Yet, thinking about our relationships with others occupies a significant amount of most people's time and structures a lot of our thinking. What Gillis (1996) has termed 'the families we live by' – in other words the image of the relationships we aspire too – also remain a powerful force in shaping how we live our lives. Indeed, as the work of Wood and Beck (1994) hints, everyday spaces like the home are often produced, at least in part, by adults as instantiations of their own childhoods. As such the 'family' in its widest sense is a peculiar absent presence in the discipline of geography.

The family might seem an odd concept to advance as a focus for research within children's geographies in the light of queer critiques of hetero-patriarchal life (Bell, 1991) and given that both Giddens (1991) and Beck and Beck-Gernsheim (1995) claim that profound changes are occurring in relationships in the context of contemporary processes of individualization, detraditionalization and increased self-reflexivity. They argue that in the transformation from industrial society to new modernity traditional ideas and expectations about social relations are being reworked. The pre-ordained path of school, paid work, courtship marriage and parenthood is now less clearly marked. Rather, there has been a weakening of class ties, a decline in reliance on authorities such as the church, and a decoupling of some of the social behaviours and attitudes that used to be attached to marriage and family life (Beck and Beck-Gernsheim, 1995). Such that Beck-Gernsheim (2002: 22) claims that: '[I]ndividual self-fulfilment and achievement is the most powerful current in modern society.'

In this context Giddens (1992) argues that traditional forms of close personal relationships encumbered by kin and community obligations are being replaced by the pursuit of 'pure relationships'. These are relationships that are entered into for their own sake in the pursuit of happiness, and are sustained only as long as they are fulfilling. For example, the greater importance placed on having a 'good' marriage and the pursuit of individual pleasure, has produced higher divorce rates as individuals feel less obliged (e.g. by the church, marriage vows, community tradition, etc.) to stay in unsatisfactory relationships. While mobility as a product of economic globalization has also been presumed to undermine or threaten families as more members no longer live their daily lives in the same place.

Yet, we would argue that notwithstanding this social change, nonetheless 'family' defined in the broadest sense, still remains a form of relationship that most people strive to create for themselves and are still attached to (through birth, adoption, marriage, and by processes such as the transmission of values, inheritances and so on). In particular, Giddens' (1991) thesis of pure relationships and plastic sexuality has marginalized the significance of intergenerational relations across the life course and obscured the relational basis of people's affective lives. For example, repetitive sociological studies of intergenerational relations suggest that despite rapid socio-economic change and the growth of individualistic values and different forms of living arrangements, people still remain committed to reciprocal care and support (financial, emotional and instrumental) of kin (Finch and Mason, 1993; Brannen *et al.*, 2004) and that intra-familial generations remain intimately interdependent (Phillipson, 1998; Valentine, 2006). Finch and Mason (1993) for example argue that responsibilities between parents and children for each other are not a fixed set of obligations that expire at a particular age; rather they evolve over the life course through negotiation. This process is both relational, in that responsibilities are a product of familial interactions between individuals over time, and context specific, in that these relations are often embedded in particular material situations.

As David Morgan (1996) has observed the changes in patterns of intimate relations in western societies since the 1960s (e.g. growth of lone parent families, reconstituted and blended families, public emergence of families of choice and so on) do not spell the death of the 'family', but paradoxically reinforce its importance as a fundamental social unit albeit 'done' in an increasingly complex and diverse range of ways. Rather, what is changing is the way that people are 'doing' family and what affective relations or structure constitute personal relationships (Morgan, 1996).

Jamieson (1998) has mapped, what she argues is a shift in the nature of personal relationships from being functional to affective and emotionally intense. This is most evident in relations between parents and children. In the face of serial adult relationships, Beck and Beck-Gernsheim (1995) claim, that it is children who have become a more reliable source of love. In particular, the traditional social distance between parents and their offspring is alleged to be breaking down in an individualized culture as adults sacrifice their 'natural' authority for closer, democratic relationships with their children (Jamieson and Toynbee, 1989; Valentine, 2004). With this change in parenting styles has come greater parental anxiety about the need to be a 'good parent' and to provide appropriate material and social opportunities for their children even into adulthood and beyond (Beck and Beck-Gernsheim, 1995). This is reflected in debates about the importance of both 'family' time, and 'family' togetherness (e.g. Charles and Kerr, 1988; Holloway and Valentine, 2003). These practices are increasingly not just regarded as part of family life but to actually constitute 'family'. Through such interactive processes families inherit, negotiate, shape and rework their own conceptions of 'family'. What is evident in all the studies that capture different ways of 'doing' families is the enduring power of relations of love and care that persists throughout the life course.

As feminist geographers (WGSG, 1984) have long argued in relation to processes of social reproduction, part of the reason studies of intimate relations may be relatively neglected by the wider discipline of geography is that these relations are assumed to be 'private' and informal and thus not worthy of attention. Yet as Cole and Durham (2007) argue, broad scale processes and intimate matters have been historically intertwined, such that intimate social relations have played a crucial role in shaping the emergence of modernity, the development of capitalism and the dynamics of postcolonial encounters. Concomitantly, they point out that widespread social and economic changes, particularly the rise of market-based liberalized economies and their entanglements with state policies, have provided new contexts that are reshaping the way that people forge intimate social relations to form new social hierarchies that constitute globalization in various sites around the world. Indeed, Cole and Durham (2007) go onto observe the paradox, that at a moment in time when many policies and economic practices assume a subject freed from the obligations of social ties and traditions to make choices in a global economy; the rolling back of the welfare state and financial insecurity that characterizes contemporary neo-liberal economies mean that many people are increasingly dependent on family or other intimate relations for material and moral support.

In the remainder of this chapter we want to demonstrate the importance of 'family' throughout the life course in providing both material and emotional support by focusing on a case study of adult problem Internet gamblers. The material presented here is based on two waves of life history interviews with 26 self-identified problem Internet gamblers (20 men, 6 women), and a one-off, in-depth semi-structured interview with a 'significant other' (such as a partner, adult parent, sibling or child), nominated by the problem gambler. Participants were recruited from across the UK in both rural and urban areas, all the interviewees were white British. They were aged from 19 to 55 years old, their occupations ranged from unemployed through to professional, and they engaged in a diverse array of Internet gambling activities including, for example, bingo, slots, poker, and sports betting (including on football, rugby, cricket, tennis, golf, horse racing, dogs, etc.). When the term 'gambler' is employed to describe the interviewees in the remainder of the chapter this is used as shorthand for problem Internet gambler.[1]

Problem gambling and the family: individual problems; shared lives

For every individual with a gambling problem it is estimated that somewhere between a further five to seventeen other individuals are adversely affected by it (Lesieur, 1984). Yet, Krishnan and Orford (2002) point out that research into the effects of problem gambling on gamblers' families has been limited and has not addressed family coping in detail. Indeed, much of the academic work on problem gambling adopts an individualistic model. This is both in terms of data collection – which normally employs surveys or interviews with individual gamblers alone, rather than seeking relational accounts from their significant others – and in terms of its analysis, which commonly focuses on the gamblers' behaviour/experiences largely abstracted from the complexities of their wider social relations.

Where gambling research has focused on 'the family' it has commonly done so through the lens of the spousal relationship, in particular the impact of male problem gamblers' behaviour on their wives (Lorenz and Yaffee, 1988). There is little evidence about how problem gambling is constituted through relationships with other family members such as adult parents, children, siblings and so on. Yet, Internet gambling is often embedded in day-to-day household life and thus a range of significant others and their practices, are deeply implicated in the development, recognition and management of Internet gambling as a problem.

When Internet gamblers first disclose a 'problem', it is partners (who in this sample were mainly women) or mothers who were usually the first to be told or to discover the gambling problem. This is not surprising given that other research has identified that much of the emotional work within families is done by women. Indeed, their power within households commonly derives from their domestic knowledge of, and control over, other members' activities and middle-class women often work hard to manage and suppress confrontations to produce an image of familial or domestic harmony. Siblings were also commonly one of the first to be enrolled in the gamblers' secrets. This was because they usually had the resources to provide financial assistance, for example by paying off the gambler's debts or providing long-term or short-term loans, which was not always available from a parental generation now in retirement. In some cases help was sought from a sibling by the gambler not for financial but rather emotional reasons, because the brother or sister themselves had experienced personal problems (e.g. debts, relationship problems) and so it was assumed they would have a level of understanding (both about having a problem, and the difficulties of negotiating this within the family) not shared by others. Here, siblings often took on important mediatory roles in negotiating the disclosure and management of the Internet gambler's problem for them with other family members, including the gambler's own spouse. In this sense, addressing a gambling problem does not just involve a one-off leap of disclosure but can also become a continuous dialogue between members within the family, in which the responsibility for transmitting information about the problem is transferred from the gambler to others. This informant (Valerie) describes her brother's role in both taking on the responsibility to disclose her problem to others in their family, and in supporting her to confide in her mother.

> My brother came down and I said . . . I've got into online gambling and I've made a mess. And he went, 'What do you mean you've made?' . . . but I only told him £12,000 I didn't tell him the full amount. So he contacted . . . I don't know what others [family members] said because he actually contacted them all. Only one that we did have to go and tell and that were my mum, which he took me up. And he went in and he said, 'You want a cup of tea Ma, want a bit of whiskey in it? . . . Our Val's got something to tell you'. So she's going, 'What? What do you mean?' Alright, stay there, he'll make you a cup of tea, whiskey.
>
> (Woman, forties, instants)

Yet in 'coming out' about their problem to significant others the Internet gamblers effectively transferred the problem onto them (cf. Valentine and Skelton, 2003). Unlike, Valerie quoted above, several of the gamblers forbade the person or people they had confided in from discussing the issue with others. While in other households the family member who had been confided in chose of their own accord not to disclose their significant other's gambling problem to wider social relations because of fears that this information might spill over to them, spoiling their own and their family's identities as well. Some kept the problem gambling a secret in order to protect older relatives, siblings or children from anxiety and worry. In this way, problem gambling sometimes became closeted as a shameful secret. This had the consequence of leaving those family members who were aware of the gambler's problem isolated from any support.

Problem gamblers and significant others commonly became more open about the issue within the wider family and social networks when it appeared to be under control. In this sense, the disclosure of a gambling problem was not just a one-off event but became, for some, an ongoing narrative that evolved in the telling. Those family members told about 'the problem' had, in turn, to decide if, and how, to be open about it within their wider networks. As such, the disclosure of a gambling problem was not just something that was done in, or to, the family but rather was a process that was negotiated both with other individual family members and as a collectivity.

Financial and emotional theft from the family

Problem Internet gambling resulted in debts for the informants of between £10,000 and £144,000. Yet, the harms which caused the interviewees most distress were not financial but rather the emotional and personal complications that arose from their problem gambling. In order to carve out the time-spaces to gamble within the home, the problem gamblers had commonly reshaped family practices in such a way that they were either physically or emotionally absent from everyday family life (e.g. on the Internet all times of day and night, so not spending time together with partners in the same space; or being in a room with children but without looking after them or listening to them). This problem gambler and a problem gambler's wife describe gambling as effectively emotional theft (of time and commitment) from other family members:

> It was stealing off me family, you know, me wife and me kids, plain and simply that's what it was . . . you know stealing . . . and I was always very moody and very narky . . . because I'd been up all night gambling on the Internet. And then afterwards and was then rackin' me brain thinking well how could I get that [money] back.
>
> (Man, twenties, sports betting)

> I found out that during the Monday and Friday [when she worked] . . . instead of looking after the boys which is what he was supposed to be doing with the two littlest ones who were at home, here he is he's obviously been sitting on the Internet and gambling . . . They were fed and changed and things like that, but emotionally they hadn't been looked after during the day and that was very hard, very hard to take . . . I'd be fine for a few days and then the anger and resentment would build up and I'd sort of snap at him.
>
> (Wife of a gambler)

Several of the informants described completely withdrawing socially and emotionally from family and friends; while others recalled how their lives spatially contracted as they became reluctant to leave the home or engage in 'normal' family activities, like gardening. This interviewee describes how it was only when she stopped gambling that she realized how it had constrained her life and impacted on her familial relationships with both her husband and adult sons:

> [Since stopping gambling] . . . we just seem to be more content. I mean we had a week off last week . . . we had a lovely week. We were pottering about in our garden and we were out for a few drives and out for a meal and we had a lovely time . . . to think I would have been either stopping

in and doing the gambling, I'd have been far too wound up to even, well I wouldn't have been doing the gardening for kick off . . . And I wouldn't have felt comfortable going out, I would have made every excuse under the sun not to go. So that's been one thing that's changed. And my relationship to my sons is on a different level I would say now, a better level.

(Woman, fifties, instants and bingo)

As these quotations hint many of the informants felt guilty at the impact their gambling had had on their families and not being the child, partner or parent that they feel they ought to be. In this sense, the interviewees experienced a loss of self. The gamblers' family members described emotional losses: including the loss of trust, the loss of the imagined honest relationship they thought they had, and spoiled identities as well (i.e. as failed partners or parents because they had been unaware of the gamblers problem or the problem gambler had chosen gambling in effect over them). Many of these emotional consequences were not necessarily immediate, when the gamblers' problems were disclosed, but rather surfaced over time as familial relationships were renegotiated. Indeed, there is some evidence that gambling can contribute to family breakdown (e.g. Griffiths, 2004), with one informant claiming that problem Internet gambling has the potential to be as destructive of family life as drugs such as heroin. This man describes the impact of his gambling on his mother and adult siblings:

The pain my demise has caused my Mum and brothers, they'll still be hurt long after I've recovered. You know they'll have wounds for a long time . . . you never lose people's love but you lose their trust [edit] I feel particularly bad, like my brother's having work done on his house but you know he lent me thousands to bail me out and that's slowed down the progress of his house as well as causing him worry. But my Mum's in her sixties and I've probably . . . stolen years off her life, you know, in terms of anxiety and worry . . . you know for every addict, you know, you then look at all the people closest to them and then you see how the problems becomes a much bigger problems. It's like ripples in pond isn't it?

(Man, forties, poker)

Pathways out of gambling: the role of the family

Family support was crucial in forging pathways out of problem gambling. This often took the form of loans or outright payments of debts. Partners returned to work. In one case an adult gambler's parents even returned to work in order to provide financial help. In particular, money was commonly passed intergenerationally, that is vertically from parent to adult child, rather than just horizontally between partners/siblings. In this sense pathways out of problem gambling entailed participation and support from extended as well as immediate family. Financial control – such as bankruptcy, signing over power of attorney, and handing over credit cards – was often taken over by other family members (including parents and adult children). Peter, who is in his thirties, describes the way his father assumed financial control of his affairs:

> [W]hen I went home [to his parents' home following a gambling related suicide attempt], within five days all my debts were consolidated into one payment to my Dad per month, no interest . . . and all my cards were cut up, all my accounts were closed. The only account I have is the current account with the same bank of which my Dad dines with the manager, you know [*laughs*] . . . I told him [his father about his gambling debts] the Monday and on the Tuesday morning we were straight down to the solicitors . . . who he [his father] uses all the time and sat in the front of the bloke who he works with all the time, you know, it must have been embarrassing for him. And then my bank manager and then to the doctors, you know.
>
> (Man, thirties, slots/instants)

These 'self-correcting' strategies reflected on the capacities and capabilities of families to come to the rescue, both financially and emotionally, of the Internet gambler. Beck and Beck-Gernsheim (2002: 105) have argued that in the context of contemporary individualized family life 'identity struggles' can break out as members pursue their own right to a personal lifestyle in ways that impacts on the wider family. Such intra-familial transfer of resources caused tensions within families about how financial support was weighted towards somebody who had got into financial difficulty through gambling, rather than to those who had demonstrated responsibility with money.

Several of the informants had stolen money from employers or other family members to sustain their gambling or stave off creditors. For example, one participant had pawned his mother's jewellery, another had embezzled a legal payment to his sister, another stole from work, while another had used money for a deposit to gamble. In these cases, family members commonly bailed the gambler out, or supported the gambler in their continued deception at work or with family members from whom they have stolen. In these ways, significant others effectively became accessories in criminal activities, bearing an associated emotional burden of anxiety and guilt. Yet, these familial cover-ups were not undertaken with any intent to deceive but rather out of pure love and an associated ill-conceived sense of obligation to protect a family member.

Likewise, partners – and in some cases children – accepted responsibility for control of the gambler's access to the Internet, for example by changing passwords, removing modems and being present when the gambler was online to check what they were doing. Gamblers recounted times, however, where they continued to engage in Internet gambling by working out 'sneaky ways' of getting around blocks or controls on their access that bear parallels with the way young children often resist adult rules and boundaries (Valentine, 1997).

Networks of surveillance were also commonly established in families, with adult parents, and siblings as well as partners working together to keep an eye on the gambler, alert for 'signs' or 'symptoms' such as moodiness, secrecy or unexplained absence, that the gambling may have restarted.

> My partner found out about five years ago . . . and she controlled all my cards. It was a bit demeaning in a way but it had to be done, you know. If I had a tenner to put some petrol in she wanted the receipt and I had a [few] pounds a day for the canteen for some tea and toast, but that's what had to be done [edit later] she's good with computers as well so kept a check on me basically, you know all outgoing phone calls were monitored on the phone bill, even though they'd been free phone numbers to ring off the internet bets. And she knew what she was doing and if I'd been on sites and basically kept a check on me.
>
> (Man, forties, sports betting)

In this way, family members took on responsibility for 'diagnosing' resurfacing problem gambling. Their panoptican-style scrutiny of the gambler reshaped respective roles and responsibilities within the family. In particular, the relational dynamic between partners shifted and entailed corresponding shifts in power relations in which problem gamblers' were often effectively infantalized. This interviewee describes the change in her relationship with her husband:

> I mean it's an awful lot of money, but, you know, we'll settle . . . from a practical point of view, you know, I can kind of cope with that . . . It's the high end of emotional things that you go through, what a change you see in your relationship with your partner from one day to the next, you know, because it really . . . did feel like I was going from being with a partner and [several] children to . . . the whole responsibility and much more debt than I thought we had and having one more child . . . I couldn't understand why anybody would do that. Why anybody from a non-gambler's point of view, it's such a selfish thing to do to lock yourself away for hours . . . and, you know, spend thousands of pounds that you didn't have, which is taking money away from the family. And, you know, it just seemed so selfish and I was really after an answer to why would anyone do that.
>
> (Wife of a gambler)

As this quotation illustrates, this woman redefined her relationship to her husband, and described him as becoming like another child. The point of disclosure for her was the point at which she lost her partner, and gained another 'child'-like responsibility. Here, gamblers' levels of responsibility resemble a child: they operate in relation to other people who have more power, more capacity and more access to resources than they do.

Adult parent–child relationships are essentially about the continued negotiation of a balance between dependence and independence. This usually gradually shifts over time from the parent caring for the child, to the adult child caring for the older parent. Yet, the disclosure of a gambling problem, however, can disrupt this balance of responsibilities such that the adult child 'shrinks' back to a position of vulnerability and dependency in their parents' eyes, becoming in effect, infantalized. While some gamblers' welcomed this escape from responsibility, for others it afforded them the possible to keep gambling and undermined their self-esteem and self-efficacy, reproducing their dependency in other relations too. Noel, who is in his thirties, explains his continued relationship of dependency on his parents:

INTERVIEWER: How do you feel about your parents always having paid off your debts or dealt with whatever problems that have arisen?

NOEL: It's really annoying, 'cos I get weak and I want them to do it, and then it just takes away the problem, but then gives ten times the problems back. And it gives them an unhealthy hold on me. It means that they feel that they then deserve to contact me more, to make decisions for me, to you know, because it's just keeping the adult–child relationship going, you know. Most people when they get older, then they develop a new relationship, but I'm still their 5-year-old kid, and every time they pay off [his gambling debts], it means that I'm still their 5-year-old kid, and that's just keeping it going. You know, so it's not . . . yeah, it might pay off the debt and it might give me an easier life, but emotionally it gives me a hellish one. So I think it's not worth it in the long-run to be honest.

(Man, thirties, sports and online games)

Correspondingly, for the children of Internet gamblers their parent's 'problem' often meant that they effectively 'grew' in other's eyes by taking on new responsibilities, such as keeping a parent's gambling problem a secret from others, monitoring their parent's use of the home computer or recognizing the financial constraints on the family budget and choosing to forgo particular opportunities. In such ways, parent/child roles were effectively reversed with the children demonstrating their maturity and competence by protecting their 'vulnerable' and 'irresponsible' parent from harm.

The familial management of problem gambling required constant attention and development over time as what was seen as the problem by not only the gambler but also their significant others changed over time. In particular, '*problem migration*' commonly occurred. As families gained control of the debt, the gambling was often reframed as neglect and harm of the family. Money spent on gambling was reframed as evidence of the gambler's lack of responsibility, wasted opportunity for other members of the family, and a lack of shared values between the gambler and their significant others. Often, 'the problem' became a problem of time – the time the gambler spent on the Internet, and therefore away from their families (Hughes *et al.*, forthcoming). This time spent away from families was seen as a lack of involvement and integration in family activities, and signified a lack of emotional commitment to children and/or partners. As financial problems migrated to emotional problems new strategies were required for managing 'the problem'.

The notion of identity was crucial in understanding what the gambler needed to do in order to stop problem gambling. Not only did they need to *become* somebody else in their own minds, but they needed to *recover* who they were, their 'spoiled' identity, for their families. In order to recover spoiled identities (such as partner, child or parent) they re-engaged in family practices such as doing more with their children, doing the ironing, being there at mealtimes, engaging more with the wider family. In doing these things, the gambler was simultaneously signifying reintegration in family life and intimate relationships and family activities more generally. Through *being there* they were able to develop a sense of being a good partner/parent/child again, and in this way move beyond a problem-gambler identity. In turn, family members began to shift back certain responsibilities, such as providing cash or a cheque book, and given online access. Additionally, through 'doing it together', a sense of revived togetherness, and improved familial relationship was experienced. This woman describes how she has worked at her relationship with her husband:

> We've made a good attempt to do things together, going out more . . . for example, on Friday night he came home from work, I said 'Right let's take the car out . . . I fancy a fish supper'. We left about seven and got back about half past nine. We'd done nothing special but we did it together, you know, that's what counts . . . sort of really sort of working at things together rather than separate.
>
> (Woman, fifties, poker)

Conclusion: family – intimacy across the life course

In this chapter we have suggested that children's geographers have tended to focus either on individualized experiences (i.e. addressing children's experiences alone) or on the binary relationship between pre-adult children and their parents; and as such geographers have neglected the importance of wider sets of familial relationships (with siblings, grandparents, etc.) and the importance of 'the family' (particularly the parent–child relationship) throughout the life course rather than just in childhood.

Notably, transitions from childhood to adulthood in Western societies have become more extended and more complex in the late twentieth and early twenty-first centuries (Furlong and Cartmel, 1997; Valentine, 2003; Valentine and Skelton, 2007). The expansion of higher/further education and reduction in benefits to which young people are entitled, as well as rising housing costs, mean that many young people live with, or are semi-dependent on, their parents for financial support into their mid twenties and sometimes beyond (Jones, 1995). Moreover, even when adults leave the parental home the family is still the site through which many of our individual biographies and expectations are routed in adulthood. In this chapter, we have used the example of problem Internet gamblers to demonstrate how families – with their traditional ties of love and care – remain a crucial entity, continuing to play a key part in the intimate life of most individuals throughout their adult lives even when they are physically distant from each other. This is most vividly demonstrated by the extent to which online gambling was contained and self-corrected within families, which suggests that the scale of problem Internet gambling may be going unrecognized in the wider public domain.

As such, the evidence of this chapter is that there is a need for geographers to pay more attention to: how intimate relationships ebb and flow over the life course; the extent to which they may be more or less meaningful to different generations during different moments in time; the complex ways that such relationships may span different spaces and scales; and the implications of such relationships for individuals' personal identities through out the life course.

Acknowledgements

We are grateful to the ESRC for funding the research upon which this chapter draws. The argument about the importance of family across the life course was developed in the paper by G. Valentine (2008), 'The ties that bind: towards geographies of intimacy', *Geography Compass*. We are grateful to the publishers for permission to reproduce some edited elements of this paper in the opening section of the chapter.

Note

1 All the names included are pseudonyms; other information which could compromise the anonymity of the informants has been amended or removed to protect the disclosure of their identities. All the quotations used are verbatum. Three ellipsis dots indicates that a minor edit has been made to remove repetitions or verbal stumbles in order to enable the quotation to be more readable. Where a more substantive edit has been made this is marked in the text in square brackets.

References

Beck, U. and Beck-Gernsheim, E. (1995) *Normal Chaos of Love*. Cambridge: Polity Press.

Beck, U. and Beck-Gernsheim, E. (2002) *Individualization*. London: Sage.

Bell, D. (1991) 'Insignificant others: lesbian and gay geographies', *Area*, 23: 323–9.

Brannen, J., Moss, P. and Morley, A. (2004) *Working and Caring over the 20th Century*. Basingstoke: Palgrave Macmillan.

Charles, N. and Kerr, M. (1988) *Women Food and Families*. Manchester: Manchester University Press.

Cole, J. and Durham, D. (eds) (2007) *Generations and Globalisation*. Bloomington, IN: Indiana University Press.

England, K. (ed.) (1996) *Who Will Mind the Baby? Geographies of Child-care and Working Mothers*. London and New York: Routledge.

Finch, J. (1989) *Family Obligations and Social Change*. London: Routledge.

Finch, J. and Mason, J. (1993) *Negotiating Family Responsibilities*. London: Routledge.

Furlong, A. and Cartmel, F. (1997) *Young People and Social Change: Individualization and Risk in Late Modernity*. Buckingham: Open University Press.

Giddens, A. (1991) *Modernity and Self-Identity: Self and Society in the Late Modern Age*. Polity Press: Cambridge.

Giddens, A. (1992) *The Transformation of Intimacy: Sexuality, Love and Eroticism in Modern Societies*. Cambridge: Polity Press.

Gillis, J. R. (1996) *A World of their Own Making: Myth, Ritual and the Quest for Family Values*, Cambridge, MA: Harvard University Press.

Griffiths, M. (2004) 'Betting your life on it', *British Medical Journal*, 329: 1055–6.

Holloway, S. L. (1998) 'Local childcare cultures: moral geographies of mothering and the social organisation of pre-school education', *Gender, Place and Culture*, 5: 29–53

Holloway, S. L. (1999) 'Mother and worker? The negotiation of motherhood and paid employment in two urban neighbourhoods', *Urban Geography*, 20: 438–60

Holloway, S. L. and Valentine, G. (2003) *Cyberkids: Children in the Information Age*. London: RoutledgeFalmer.

Hughes, K., Valentine, G. and Kenten, C. (forthcoming) 'The time of our lives: towards a space-time understanding of internet gambling', *British Journal of Sociology*.

Jamieson, L. (1998) *Intimacy: Personal Relationships in Modern Societies*. Cambridge: Polity Press.

Jamieson, L. and Toynbee, C. (1989) 'Shifting patterns of parental authority, 1900–1980', in Corr, L. and Jamieson, H. (eds) *The Politics of Everyday Life*. London: Macmillan.

Jones, G. (1995) *Leaving Home*. Buckingham: Open University Press.

Krishnan, M. and Orford, J. (2002) 'Gambling and the family: from the stress-coping-support perspective', *International Gambling Studies*, 2: 61–83.

Lesieur, H. (1984) *The Chase: The Career of the Compulsive Gambler*. Cambridge, MA: Schenkman Books.

Lorenz, V. C. and Yaffee, R. A (1988) 'Pathological gambling: psychosomatic, emotional and marital difficulties as reported by the spouse', *Journal of Gambling Behaviour*, 4: 13–26.

McKie, L. Bowlby, S. and Gregory, S. (eds) (1999) *Gender, Power, and the Household*. London: Macmillan.

McKie, L. Bowlby, S. and Gregory, S. (2001) 'Gender, caring and employment in Britain', *Journal of Social Policy*, 30: 233–58

Morgan, D. (1996) *Family Connections: An Introduction to Family Studies*. Cambridge: Polity Press.

Phillipson, C. R. (1998) *Reconstructing Old Age: New Agendas in Theory and Practice*. London: Sage.

Pratt, G. (1999) 'From registered nurse to registered nanny: discursive geographies of Filipina domestic workers in Vancouver, BC', *Economic Geography*, 75: 215–36.

Valentine, G. (1997) '"Oh yes I can." "Oh no you can't.": Children and parents' understandings of kids' competence to negotiate public space safely', *Antipode*, 29(1): 65–90.

Valentine, G. (2003) 'Boundary crossings: transitions from childhood to adulthood', *Children's Geographies*, 1: 37–52.

Valentine, G. (2004) *Public Space and the Culture of Childhood*. Aldershot: Ashgate.

Valentine, G. (2006) 'Globalising intimacy: the role and information and communication technologies in maintaining and creating relationships', *Women's Studies Quarterly*, 34: 365–93.

Valentine, G. (2008) 'The ties that bind: towards geographies of intimacy', *Geography Compass*, 2(6): 2097–110.

Valentine, G. and Skelton, T. (2003) 'Coming out and out-comes: negotiating lesbian and gay identities with/in the family', *Environment and Planning D: Society and Space*, 21: 479–99.

Valentine, G. and Skelton, T. (2007) 'Re-defining norms: D/deaf young people's transitions to independence', *Sociological Review*, 55: 104–23.

Vanderbeck, R. M. (2007) 'Intergenerational geographies: age relations, segregation and re-engagements', *Geography Compass*, 2: 200–21.

Women and Geography Study Group (WGSG) (1984) *Geography and Gender: An Introduction to Feminist Geography*. London: Hutchinson.

Wood, D. and Beck, R. J. (1994) *Home Rules*. Baltimore, MD: Johns Hopkins University Press.

10 Negotiating children's outdoor spatial freedom

Portraits of three Parisian families

Olga den Besten

Introduction

> [O]ne in four eight- to ten-year-olds have never played outside without an adult and one in three parents will not even allow older children, aged eight to fifteen, to play outside the house or garden. [. . .] Despite strong evidence that playing freely strengthens friendships, keeps children healthy and helps them to cope with risky situations . . . opportunities for children to do so have been falling rapidly.
>
> Asthand and Revill, *The Observer* (2008)

A number of news stories such as this one (see also, for example, for the UK: Eason, 2007; Easton 2007; for France: Legrand, 2005; Hofnung, 2009; Blanchard, 2009), as well as academic sources in children's geographies, sociology and psychology (see e.g. Ward, 1978; Valentine and McKendrick, 1997; O'Brien *et al.*, 2000; Prezza *et al.*, 2001) point to the fact that children's unsupervised mobility and play in public outdoor space has dramatically decreased in contemporary Western societies. As it is mostly parents who have the authority to restrict whether and where their children can go out for a walk or play, we can assume that parental control has, simultaneously, increased. Research confirms the predominant role of parents (as opposed to, for example, public provision of play facilities) in determining the degree of children's access to independent outdoor play (see Valentine and McKendrick, 1997).

The thesis about increased parental control, however, contradicts a by now well-known position in social sciences and philosophy, which insists that in contemporary families discussions over children's lives do take place and that children do have a say in them. Authors write about the detraditionalization of family life (Giddens, 1990; Beck and Beck-Gernsheim, 1995; Mac an Ghaill and Haywood, 2007): the changing of family relations towards more democratic, or 'reflexive', where 'men, women and children are . . . much more equal not only before the law, but also in practice' (Giddens, 1991: 135–6). Supporting the idea that relationships within a family are undergoing substantial democratization is the argument that the relationship between children and parents is increasingly characterized by negotiation, which is replacing an authoritative parental style. Negotiation is considered as being 'a contested and conflict driven arena where parents and teenagers adopt different strategies when reconstructing their reflexive relationships' (Williams and Williams, 2005: 315).

This paradox between the positions about increased parental control over children's outdoor mobility and a more relaxed, democratic parent–child relationship has led the author of this chapter to investigate the nature of parental restrictions of their children's spatial freedom. This qualitative investigation is meant to answer the following questions. What possible factors determine the degree of parental control over children's spatial mobility? How do parents ensure their children's safety outside? What types of parental styles, in terms of spatial control, can be identified?

An attempt to explore these questions was made through research in three different families in 2005–2006 in Paris. Such in-depth, family-based research had been planned as a part of a broader study of children's perceptions and representations of their urban areas (see den Besten, 2008; 2010).[1] Parents of the children who participated in the school-based part of the research were contacted by means of a letter from the researcher, which the children would pass to their parents at home. Out of eighty-one families, these three families were, unfortunately, the only ones who expressed their willingness to take part.[2]

Methods used in this family-based research included questionnaires, semi-structured interviews with the children and their parents, the children's subjective maps, photos of outdoor spaces taken by the children and the researcher, and child- and parent-guided walks in the area. Such multi-method approach served the purposes of triangulation: data from different sources – such as, for example, the child's answers along with the researcher's own observations – and of different types, such as visual as well as verbal, were cross-examined. This was done to reinforce the validity of the researcher's interpretation of the participants' perception and behaviour and to get complementary insights and understandings (see Darbyshire *et al.*, 2005).

The research is obviously limited by the fact that only three families were studied and by the above-described reason as to why it is these families who came to take part in the research. Still, the 'portraits' of the three families, constituted as a result of this study, happen to represent a variety of parental attitudes to and children's practices of outdoor mobility. Because of the limitations of the study, however, these 'portraits' should be considered as an initial attempt to explore the issue, rather than an exhaustive typology. I further proceed to present and discuss these 'portraits' one by one.

Portrait 1. 'Mother-hen' *(mère-poule)*: the boundaries of trust

In the first family under analysis, the parent interviewed by the researcher was Caroline, aged 37, who is the mother of two sons: Pierre (14) and

Olivier (10). Together with her sons and her husband, a driver in a delivery service, Caroline lives in a Parisian suburb, just outside the ring road. She comes from a white working-class family with 14 children. According to her, when she got married, her own family first lived in a very small flat subsidized by the state. Then the family applied to the local authority for a more spacious accommodation, which they were lucky enough to get. This is how Caroline described a new flat in an interview:[3]

> When we saw the flat, we were all chuffed . . . It's a big flat, the children could run, move in the flat. Where we were before, they couldn't. We had a fridge in the living room, a table and an armchair – and we couldn't move around. [. . .] The kids had just one room – just one for two boys, and they couldn't play there as they wanted too . . . So when we saw the new flat . . . 117 square meters with a balcony!

The new flat was in a different neighbourhood (*quartier*, in French), so the young family had to move. Although the former neighbourhood can be seen from a window of her current flat on the fourteenth floor, Caroline is nostalgic about the *quartier* where she spent her youth and which she 'would have wanted [her] kids to discover'. After ten years of living in the current *quartier*, her attitude to it is still ambiguous. She says:

> Here it's different, although after some time we've found friends, we go along well . . . one just shouldn't mess with anybody here, criticize anybody . . . Children say hello to me, because they go to school with Olivier, so there is certain respect between parents and children, they say hello when we bump into each other in the street, I think it's great . . . but when there're stories among the big kids, you should never meddle in . . . There are pros and cons . . . When there are stories between families and kids, you'd better keep your nose out, otherwise the family comes to see you, and there are stories, it can come to blows . . . But then, it's good that you can really have fun with children of the neighbourhood. I spoke, laughed, even played a ball with them, and it made them laugh because it's a mom who hits the ball. And me, I adore that.

As the above interview excerpt evokes, Caroline draws a line between two social groups in her *quartier*: those who she calls 'the little kids' (*les petits*) – children, pre-teens and early teens – and 'the big kids' (*les grands*), who, according to Caroline, are further divided into groups of teenagers of 15–16 years old and young adults of 20–23 years old. Between the groupings of 'the big kids' there are often disagreements, which can be followed by fights. Caroline calls such conflicts 'stories' (*histoires*) – in which one 'shouldn't meddle'. However, according to her, 'it stops there', because 'the big kids' still have 'a certain respect': they are 'careful' in the *quartier* because 'they know that there are babies and little children here'.

At this point it should be noted that speaking about her current *quartier*, Caroline makes it synonymous to *cité* or *dalle* (the words that she also uses) – a mostly asphalted courtyard formed by three tall blocks of flats of social housing. This synonymy is not incidental: Caroline's *quartier* is limited to the courtyard, and the courtyard is also the limited territory of her sons' play or hanging out (Plate 10.1). Olivier's photo reveals the separation of the worlds of 'the little kids' and 'the big kids' in his own perception, too. He explained that he took the picture because of the small children's playground: 'It is a small park, little children play there, and I like it'.

Even before our interview with Caroline, these boundaries, imposed by the mother and internalized by the children, already came clear through the research questionnaire filled in by Olivier along with his classmates at school. Olivier is in the last year of primary school, which is situated just across the street from his building. And yet, according to his answers in the questionnaire, he is accompanied by his parents to school every morning and picked up by his mother from school after classes. His answers also indicate that when Olivier is outside, he is always accompanied by his parents. Characteristically, he leaves blank answers to the questions like 'Where do you usually go for a walk?' and 'Where do you like to hang out most?'

Asked about the existence of such boundaries in the interview, Caroline replies not in terms of space, of spatial boundaries, but rather in terms of the children being accompanied as opposed to being on their own. However, her answer is clearly about the *dalle* – the above mentioned courtyard:

Plate 10.1 Olivier's photo of the courtyard with children's playground in the background.

RESEARCHER: Are there any boundaries, beyond which the children are not allowed to go?

CAROLINE: Well, the boundary is that they won't come down to play a ball when I am not with them. Although Pierre is 14 and Olivier is 10. But I don't trust people who can be down there . . . I let them on their own once, and Pierre got slapped across the face by a woman whose old mother was hit by somebody's ball in her leg, and he got slapped [for nothing] . . . And Olivier is too much influenced by others. A fellow would say, 'Come with me . . . let's go . . . to another place', and I don't know where he is.

Yet, as we will see further on, these psychological and spatial boundaries are rather porous, they are largely dependent on the evolution of the mother's sense of trust. As the passage above implies, the degree of the mother's control over her children's outdoor mobility also depends on the perceived personality of one son as opposed to the other. Further into the interview, we learn that Pierre is allowed a greater freedom not (just) because of his age, but also because of his (perceived) personal qualities:

But well, Pierre, *I fully trust him*, because he goes to *collège* [a secondary school], it takes him about 10 minutes to get home; I know that after 10 minutes he's here. He comes straight back home. And if there are friends who ask him to go out, I say yes, because I know he won't follow them. So he can go have a walk with his friends, no problem, *I trust him*. If he doesn't know the person – he won't go see this person. *In fact, he doesn't trust anybody either.* As for Olivier, he'd take the risk, he'd follow everybody. Even when crossing the road, he doesn't look . . . His head is in the clouds, he lets himself be influenced a lot.

(emphasis applied)

'Trust' is a key word in Caroline's story. First, it is trust in her sons' reasonable behaviour vis-à-vis contingencies of the street. This trust can be, according to her, 'deserved' – by the precedents of reasonable behaviour, such as coming home from school on time. Second, it is the degree of trust in her *quartier*, which grew bigger in the course of the years of living there. And finally, it is trust or distrust in certain neighbours, in terms of whether she could entrust minding her sons down in the courtyard to them:

Down there, there's always someone to keep an eye on children. When something goes wrong, I can give a call to the parents, tell them that your son has slipped, your daughter's unwell, she's down here with me, come pick her up . . . But as for me, there are parents who I don't trust. I need to trust the person who'd mind my sons, so that I am sure that she's going to be there to take care of them . . . I have one friend, she minded Olivier a lot. She'd say: 'Caroline, Olivier will go to *Auchan* [a supermarket] with me' or 'He's down here with Jacob and Sophie'. So I know that she'll keep an eye on him. And me, I'd mind her children, if she's not there . . . But there are many parents, who say, 'Yes, we're keeping an eye on your son' and then . . . I am not sure if they even realize that the child is with them. Because they can go away and come back without letting the child know.

As the above excerpt and further interview text show, Caroline's 'childminding exchange' with her neighbours is asymmetrical. She does not trust most of the parents to mind her children, while she is, in her own words, 'attentive to any child, who comes up to me' and is ready to help if needed. A key to the explanation for this particular sensitivity to children and their safety, on the one hand, and distrust in most parents but herself in terms of minding her own children, is found in Caroline's biography. She told me that it is after the loss of her first child – the one who was there before Pierre – that she became extra careful and overprotective: 'Since I lost my little one, I am very much of a "mother-hen" (*mère-poule*). I am very attentive to children, even to children of others . . . So the parents trust me because of that'.

Caroline's story shows how a major biographical event can set priorities in life and lead to the development of a certain parental style. Caroline declares that her utmost priority is children; hence, she has chosen not to be in the paid employment, but to stay at home to take care of them and to protect them from eventual dangers of the street.

Portrait 2. 'Progressively permissive'

Our next parent interviewee, Philippe, aged 40, is the father of two girls: Anne (10 years old) and Lilie (8). He is a company employee, while his wife Michelle has a serious chronic mental health condition so she stays at home. This white family has moved to a Parisian suburb for the sake of having a larger space (at the time, the couple were expecting their first baby). They obtained a bigger flat through a scheme of subsidized rent provided by the company where Philippe works.

The interview with Philippe shows the family's satisfaction with their current living area:

We are very lucky to be by the river, we are privileged to live in such a place. Quiet, green and then, there is a sort of pleasure of life (*douceur de vivre*), which is rarely to be found in *Ile-de-France*, and even more rarely in Paris. To use a literary word, it is bucolic. Tranquil. It seems like we are already in the countryside a little bit.

However, Philippe sounds somewhat ashamed, when he says that there is no real sense of community: '[I]t is a little bit individualistic, everyone lives their own life . . . We have some contact with just 2–3 neighbours . . .'

Yet, according to him and Anne, the girls have quite a few friends of their own – those children who go to the same school and live in the same building. Together with their friends, they usually play in a sort of a passage, or in their own words, a 'corridor' (*couloir*), just outside the back of their four-storied residential building. Sometime they also play on the other side,

Figure 10.1 Anne's drawing of her 'territory' around the building where she lives ('*notre immeuble*') with the emoticon of a heart indicating the preferred places for play.

in front of the building, but, according to their father, 'there are cars there, so, as far as we can, we try to make them play here' (Figure 10.1). The advantage of the girls playing in the passage is also that their parents can see them through the window most of the time, and if they cannot see them, they can always call out for them.

Such spatial parental restrictions are, however, rather flexible in this family. This flexibility is based on certain confidence in mental capability of the children, which, according to Philippe, evolves with their age:

> But well, they have grown up, they are no more like little children, it is a bit less risky now, they know things, so if there is a car coming, they won't cross like this and throw themselves [under it] . . .

Philippe is consciously planning to gradually give more autonomy to the children:

> Go for a walk outside the building? Oh no. Not yet. They are still very little. Since the beginning of the school year, their mother has allowed them to walk to school 4–5 times on their own . . . When I'm here I like using my car. Anyway, they are too little to be completely autonomous. Well, we'll see. We are doing this progressively. This year they already walk to school on their own from time to time, and next year we'll see how it went this year.

As for the girls, an interview with Anne (10) has revealed that they are very well aware of the options available to them, in terms of which spaces and distances they are allowed to go and how this can progress:

RESEARCHER: You wrote here [in the questionnaire] that you either go to school alone, or with your parents, or with your sister. So, how does it happen?

ANNE: Well, if my sister is sick, I go all alone, because my Mum has to take care of my sister. If both my parents are at home, I either go with them both and my sister by car . . . or we all walk . . . or we can walk, just my sister and me, when my Mum lets us go . . . sometimes we ask if we could go on our own, and then we go together, my sister and me.

Anne also expressed a regret of having to miss dance classes sometimes just because the girls cannot go there on their own:

ANNE: The place where we do dance is a little bit far, so we go there with my Dad; but when he's not there, we don't go at all, because my Mum doesn't want to walk there, then come back home, then go again, it would be too many round trips . . .

RESEARCHER: And with your father, do you go by car?

ANNE: Yes, when he's here, but sometimes he's at work.

RESEARCHER: Do you often miss your dance class?

ANNE: Well, for example, we won't go there next Thursday. We'll come home, we'll do our homework. Life will go on, but well . . .

The girl hopes that they'll be able to walk to their dance class on their own in the future, and the interview material gathered in this family shows that this is achievable, step by step.

Portrait 3. 'Letting children enjoy their neighbourhood to the maximum'

Our third parent interviewee, Marie, aged 38, has come to live in Paris very recently. Marie is black and was born in one of the French overseas territories, but lived in Venezuela for most of her life. After a separation from her husband she decided to come to France to give better education to her elder daughter Graziela (12 years old). Graziela does not do very well at school, and Marie believes that in France there exist more options for an alternative to university, specialized professional education – options that, according to Marie, are not widely available in Venezuela. Her motivation to move to a new place is thus very different from the two previous cases: she has moved in search of better opportunities for her children, not better housing. Indeed, the family occupies a small studio flat that they have managed to rent through friends. Worsened housing condition, however, led to a process opposite to the one we have come across in the first family under study: here, constrained by the limited inside space, the children are allowed to explore the outside world. In Marie's words:

> In Venezuela, I had a house, with a garage for three cars, with four rooms and two toilets . . . My kitchen was the size of this studio . . . It's now very hard for the children. This is also why I let them go out. When I feel that . . . there are moments . . . when it gets quite heated up, and they ask me . . . 'Can we go?' I say, 'Yes, come on', so they go for a walk.

Back in Venezuela, Marie worked as a teacher of computer science. In Paris, she lives on a state welfare and is looking for a job. Although the family do not have enough money, Marie tries to use cultural opportunities offered by Paris and in particular, by their local area. The family use the local public library, as especially the younger daughter, Manuela (10), likes to read. Marie has signed up her daughters for sports activities that are free during school holidays and takes her daughters out to a cinema at the time of the day when it is cheap.

The studio flat, which they have managed to find through friends, happens to be situated rather centrally, in what is considered a largely 'bourgeois', relatively well-off area. In the interview, Marie has told the researcher how she came to the conclusion that the *quartier* is suitable for the children's unsupervized outdoor play and walks:

> The neighbourhood reassures me a lot, I used to come down with the girls, stayed there with them, but then I realized that it is very very very quiet. [. . .] And the children go for a walk, they know quite a lot of people, they play together with others . . .

When Graziela and Manuela took me for a walk (they were on their roller-skates), I discovered that their subjective *quartier* – a territory within whose limits they usually stay when outside – is much larger than Pierre's and Olivier's in the first family under study, or indeed the boys' mother's. The girls showed me the spaces they liked or disliked and explained why and how they used them. For example, they didn't appreciate so much the lovely park shown in Plate 10.2, as 'you can't jump or run there . . . because you can make [little] children fall down [unintentionally]'. For such activities as running and especially for learning 'how to do zigzags' on roller-skates, the girls preferred to use another space (Plate 10.3), which is destined, in Manuela's words, 'for the big kids, and for the medium ones as well'.

In our 15-minute walk through various spaces of the *quartier* we reached the street which served as an invisible border, which, according to the girls, they do not cross on their own. A later walk with Marie revealed that she and the girls also often go for a walk together, so she knows the 'routes' her children take and the boundaries, outside which they would not go.

Plate 10.2 A photo of a public space taken by Graziela.

Plate 10.3 A photo of a public space taken by Graziela.

The boundary at which we stopped during our walk, could be negotiated: providing that I was with them, Graziela suggested we should go together to see a landmark situated further out, but that we should first come back and tell their mother about our plans. Thus, letting the mother know is one of the 'safety strategies' used in this family.

Another such strategy is checking on the children at certain time intervals. According to Marie:

> When I feel it's been an hour and I haven't seen them, I come down! I stay there a little bit, and come back home. But normally they come home every time. Get some water to drink, take off their roller skates, put on their sneakers because they want now go running, come back and put on their roller skates again . . . so they come and go, I see them every 40 minutes . . . They come home, I look at them, 'So what have you been doing?' 'We've done this, this and this'. 'Ok, be careful'. And then they get some juice, some water, and some biscuits and off they go again. So it reassures me . . . I see them every time. I asked them to do this, too.

Marie is proud about the fact that her daughters are very well oriented in the area; they go shopping on their own if they need to buy some small everyday things for themselves. According to Marie, her children's street competence, or 'street literacy' (Cahill, 2000), is sometimes better than her own (for example, it was Graziela who first discovered an alternative route to her school and showed it to her mother). Indeed, Marie considers this increasing familiarity of her daughters with their local environment as an important part of their emotional stability and a successful integration in their new country of residence:

RESEARCHER: Do you want to stay in this *quartier*, even if it's expensive [to rent the flat]?

MARIE: Yes, because I think most of all about the children's stability. Because if we move here and there, it'd be hard for them to adapt, to make friends, to have their points of reference. They orientate well, they tell me: 'Well, Mum, we're going to *Monoprix* [a supermarket]', they go on their own . . . to buy something they need . . . Graziela loves her school, she loves her way to school, she even has two options: if the bus is not there, she takes a tube, if the tube is not there, she considers taking a bus . . .

Conclusions

Previous research has demonstrated that the degree of children's independent mobility/play outdoors is influenced by various factors, such as the child's age (see e.g. Matthews, 1992), gender (e.g. McMillan, 2006), ethnicity (e.g. O'Brien, 2000), dis(ability) (Pyer, 2007), as well as environmental factors (for example, whether children live in a big city or a small suburban town, in a block of flats with a coutyard or in a private house – see O'Brien, 2000; Prezza *et al.*, 2001).

The chapter argues that such factors actually exert their influence through a prism of parental perception and evaluation of all of the above, as well as of many other factors, such as the child's personality (especially in comparison with the siblings or peers), the level of security of the neighbourhood, and the prospective or desired education and social status of the child. Examples from the practices of three Parisian families, used in the chapter, show that parental perception and evaluation of these factors is very much conditioned, for instance, by the parents' previous housing and neighbourhood experience (such as in the case of Marie), dramatic biographical events (such as the death of the first child in the case of Caroline), or current personal surcumstances (chronic illness in the case of Michelle).

The chapter thus draws attention to the importance of biographical study for understanding different parents' practices and attitude towards the possibility of outdoor independent mobility for their children. For example, such a study can help unpack the reasons for the so-called 'authoritative', or 'traditional' (Tomanović, 2003), parental style by revealing extreme, sometimes subconscious, parental anxiety behind it. There is also a need to study dynamic processes of negotiation of children's spatial freedom within families. This can lead to a better understanding of the seeming contradiction between the discursive and democratic nature of relationships in a contemporary family, on the one hand, and increased parental control, on the other.

Notes

1 This research was made possible with a generous support through the Scientific Scholarship of the City of Paris and with the guidance of Prof. Florence Weber at the École Normale Supérieure.
2 The author is grateful to the participant families, whose personal details are changed for the publication.
3 The excerpts from the interviews and questionnaires were translated from French to English by the author of the chapter.

References

Asthana, A. and Revill, J. (2008) 'Is it time to let children play outdoors once more?' *The Observer*, 30 March 2008. Available at: http://www.guardian.co.uk/society/2008/mar/30/children.health (accessed 3 March 2009).

Beck, U. and Beck-Gernsheim, E. (1995) *The Normal Chaos of Love*. Cambridge: Polity.

Blanchard, S. (2009) 'A Paris, les enfants ne s'amusent pas avec la neige', *Le Monde*, 7 January 2009. Available at: http://www.lemonde.fr/web/recherche_breve/1,13–0,37–1064988,0.html (accessed 1 October 2009).

Cahill, C. (2000) 'Street literacy: urban teenagers' strategies for negotiating their neighbourhood', *Journal of Youth Studies*, 3(3), 251–77.

den Besten, O. (2008) 'Cars, dogs and mean people: environmental fears and dislikes of children in Paris and Berlin'. In: K. Adelhof, B. Glock, J. Lossau, M. Schulz (eds). *Urban Trends in Berlin and Amsterdam*. Berlin: Humboldt Universität, pp. 116–25. Available at: http://ssrn.com/abstract=1154559 (accessed 12 October 2010).

den Besten, O. (2010) 'Mapping emotions, building belonging: how children with different immigration backgrounds experience and picture their Parisian and Berliner neighbourhoods'. Special issue 'Children and migration: mobilities, homes and belongings', *Childhood*, 17(2), 181–95. Available at: http://ssrn.com/abstract=1355288 (accessed 12 October 2010).

Darbyshire, P., MacDougall, C. and Schiller, W. (2005) 'Multiple methods in qualitative research with children: more insight or just more?' *Qualitative Research*, 5(4), 417–36.

Eason, G. (2007) 'When should children walk alone?' BBC News, 7 June 2007. Available at: http://news.bbc.co.uk/2/hi/uk_news/education/6731743.stm (accessed 7 May 2009).

Easton, M. (2007) 'Analysis: rearing children in captivity.' BBC News, 4 June 2007. Available at: http://news.bbc.co.uk/1/hi/education/6720661.stm (accessed 7 May 2009).

Giddens, A. (1990) *The Consequences of Modernity*. Cambridge: Polity.

Giddens, A. (1991) *Modernity and Self-identity*. Cambridge: Polity.

Hofnung, T. (2009) 'Les bandits du chemin de l'école', *Libération*, 30 August 2009. Available at: http://www.liberation.fr/societe/0101594151-les-bandits-du-chemin-de-l-ecole (accessed 1 October 2009).

Legrand, C. (2005) '*La ville est-elle faite pour les enfants?*' *La Croix*, 17 February 2007. Available at: http://millepattes34.free.fr/spip.php?article171 (accessed 1 October 2009).

Mac an Ghaill, M. and Haywood, C. (2007) *Gender, Culture and Society: Contemporary Feminities and Masculinities*. London: Palgrave Macmillan.

McMillan, T. (2006) 'Johnny walks to school – does Jane? Sex differences in children's active travel to school', *Children, Youth and Environments*, 16(1), 75–89.

Matthews, H. (1992) *Making Sense of Place: Children's Understanding of Large-scale Environments*. Hemel Hempstead: Harvester Wheatsheaf.

O'Brien, M., Jones, D., Sloan, D. and Rustin, M. (2000) 'Children's independent spatial mobility in the urban public realm', *Childhood*, 7(3), 257–77.

Prezza M., Pilloni S., Morabito C., Sersante C., Alparone F.R., Giuliani M.V. The influence of psychosocial and environmental factors on children's independent mobility and relationship to peer frequentation. *Journal of Community and Applied Social Psychology*. 11 (6): 435–50.

Pyer, M. (2007) 'The difference that difference makes: play, space and teenage wheelchair users'. Paper presented to the Royal Geographical Society (with Institute of British Geographers) Annual International Conference, London, 28–31 August 2007.

Tomanović, S. (2003) 'Negotiating children's participation and autonomy within families', *The International Journal of Children's Rights*, 11, 51–71.

Valentine, G. and McKendrick, J. (1997) 'Children's outdoor play: exploring parental concerns about children's safety and the changing nature of childhood', *Geoforum*, 28(2), 219–35.

Ward (1978) *The Child in the City*. London: Architectural Press.

Williams, S. and Williams, L. (2005) 'Space invaders: the negotiation of teenage boundaries through the mobile phone', *The Sociological Review*, 53(2), 314–31.

Theme III

Cities and/or public spaces

11 Children living in the city

Gendered experiences and desires in Spain and Mexico

Mireia Baylina, Anna Ortiz Guitart and Maria Prats Ferret

Introduction

This chapter aims to examine the different experiences of children living in cities and the role public spaces play in their life from a gender perspective. We compare the results of two studies developed in two medium-sized cities in Spain and in Mexico City.

First we briefly analyse the connections between the geography of gender and the geography of childhood from a conceptual and methodological standpoint. After this, we focus on the study cases that are on children's assessments about their everyday lives, their use and appropriation of public spaces and playgrounds and their social, spatial and environmental perceptions of the city. Public spaces are very important in the everyday lives of children, in their processes of socialization, integration and acquisition of autonomy, as well as in their physical and mental well-being (Valentine, 2004; Ortiz, 2007). These processes can vary depending on the age, gender and geographical setting (Coutras, 1996; Karsten, 2003; Spilsbury, 2005). Public spaces are also places were different interests are confronted, for instance, many parents are reluctant to leave children to play outdoors to gain autonomy while children would like this (Karsten, 1998; McNeish, 2005; Nayak, 2003; Valentine, 1997).

Studying public spaces enables us to discover to what extent the needs of children are taken into account in the processes of urban planning and the design of the areas. In this research we are interested in finding out about children's use of public spaces, how and when, and what activities they perform. Finally, we also want to include the opinions, wishes and requests of both the children themselves and their parents with regard to the issue in order to compare them with the vision of the architects, urban planners and politicians involved in creating and maintaining these urban spaces (Baylina *et al.*, 2006).

Gender and children's geographies: some conceptual and methodological connections

Since the 1990s, the debates in the social sciences have been marked by the issues of identity and difference and by the interest in other social groups that had in the past been ignored or not deemed important in social and geographic research. From this perspective, geography and gender studies address the social dimensions that differentiate women and men and how they vary among social classes, ethnic groups, ages, sexual preferences and places (McDowell, 1999; Domosh and Seager, 2001). In parallel, geographical studies have appeared that highlight the spatiality of children's experience (Holloway and Valentine, 2000; Matthews, 2003). Studies on the geographies of childhood start from the idea that children are important for constructing the world in which they live; they take into account how age and gender intersect with other categories of differentiation to reflect specific experiences; and they show how place matters with regard to behaviours and opportunities (Matthews, 1995, 2003).

The consideration of otherness, the importance of place in constructing knowledge and the key role of the spaces of everyday life for learning about and understanding people's experiences are very familiar focuses of interest for feminist geographers. One of the main concerns of feminist geographers is the social construction of space and place and how gender is involved in these constructions. Therefore, they are interested in such issues as women's access, both individually and as a social group, to places and their capacity to act in them.

One of the most important contributions that feminist geography can bring to social studies of childhood is demonstrating that place matters (Holloway and Valentine, 2000). First, place reminds us that conceptions of childhood are specific in space and time. Several studies performed to date demonstrate how childhood is a social invention and that defining it using biological criteria is the foundation upon which several cultures have launched a particular version of what it means 'to be a boy or girl', thus removing a social group (girls) from action or competence (Valentine, 2004). Place is also the social, economic and cultural context where people's everyday practices are inscribed. In this sense, children's relationship with place are articulated structurally (political system), culturally (locally specific values and norms) and individually (personal resources such as education, ambition, etc.), and the intersection between them would give rise to local and regional differences.

Place in its local sense is also understood in connection with the global (Massey, 1994; Paasi, 2002; Aitken, 2004). It is an area that is not linked to any scale, without stable boundaries, a network of past and present social relationships that create a specificity when articulated. Only by giving a global sense to the local can we understand the character of different places today.

The concept of place is also applicable to the spaces of everyday life. By viewing the city from below, one realizes that everyday life can become a demonstration of resistance (Hubbard, 2006). The interest in the everyday as a subject of study has been present in geography and gender studies from the outset and this interest is also present in studies on the geographies of childhood, such as the vulnerability of childhood in public spaces, local cultures of parenthood in relation to the spatial upbringing of children, and the exclusion of children in urban planning processes (Katz, 2004; Valentine, 2004; Thomson and Philo, 2004).

The main methodological connection between geographies of gender and childhood is the use of the qualitative methodology. Qualitative methods allow us to listen and give a voice to groups that have traditionally been ignored in geography. Positionality, reflexivity and intersubjectivity seem to us central to any gender or childhood study and even more when we intersect both issues.

Study areas and methodology

The comparative research presented is based on two studies performed during 2006 and 2007 in two different urban settings. The studies share common goals, contents and methodologies. The comparison is between three areas: the medium-sized cities of Manresa and Sant Feliu de Llobregat in Catalonia (Spain) and Mexico City, one of the biggest cities in the world. The urban setting in Mexico City expresses a different scale and everyday reality from those found in Catalonia. Despite this, we believed that the everyday facts in the life of children inhabiting both urban settings share certain features, such as the centrality of play and the concern and desire to live in a friendlier city.

The results were obtained by qualitative methods, namely by open-ended questionnaires and drawings administered to children. First, we contacted the headmasters and teachers of every selected class group of the schools to explain them our project and ask their consent to perform a few exercises with the students. When we came to schools to do the fieldwork we informed the students about the aims of the research, we asked for their participation to include their point of view and we answered any questions they had. Their attitude was very positive and collaborative, and all of them agreed to participate. In summary, as many authors suggest, we tried to develop empathetic, respectful and non-authoritarian research (Holt, 2004a, 2004b; Matthews and Tucker, 2000; Valentine, 1999).

We selected students in fourth, fifth and sixth grades in primary schools. This age group, which mainly includes children aged ten and eleven, was chosen because they are both users of public spaces and are able to have and express their own desires and needs. Likewise, these are ages in which children may become more autonomous and move more freely around, and make greater use of, the city; although this depends largely on the setting and other variables, as discussed below.

The exercise proposed to students had two parts, in the first part they responded in writing to questions, and in the second they sketched their ideal playground. The questionnaire was previously tested with a small group of children and then it was distributed to the study group and filled out by a total of 265 people (151 boys and 114 girls).

The questions referred to free time, characteristics of play, extracurricular organized activities, autonomy in moving around the city, and finally, their ideal model of city in which to live. The questionnaires omitted the names of the respondents but not their sex, in order to distinguish the results by sex when performing a gender analysis.

Play, autonomy and free time in urban spaces in Spain

Play and free time

The questionnaires filled out by the children at the different schools begin with a very general question, in which they are asked to outline what they do in their free time. The main activity that the children identify with their free time is playing, in the most generic sense of the word. When they mention a particular game, computer games appear at the top of the list. The second activity most often cited, especially among girls, is studying. Other prominent activities include going to the park, reading, watching television and playing football, all of them without major differences between girls' and boys' preferences, except for football, as we shall discuss below.

Considering that playing is the main activity that children do in their free time, we attempted to get more in-depth information by asking specifically how they played. Here football was the most popular activity, with more than twice as many boys citing it as girls. It is interesting to point out, however, that the number of girls and boys playing other types of ball games is more balanced, showing that these games have a greater ability to integrate both sexes. Computer games were also mentioned frequently, especially by boys. Then comes the most popular traditional game: hide-and-seek, which is the only game that was really cited by many girls and some boys. After that, there is a long list of active games, yet each was mentioned by very few children. They include jumping rope, tag, racing, chasing the wall, etc. Even though both boys and girls participate in all these active games, girls cite them more often, perhaps because football occupies such pride of place among boys in terms of their activities and time. This difference is even more pronounced in role playing games or make-believe (dressing up, teachers, adventures, restaurants, homes, parents, witches or veterinarians), which are highly popular among girls and only cited occasionally by boys. There is a similar lack of gender balance with board games, which are clearly much more popular among girls.

The clearest conclusion is that there is still a striking gender gap between the types of games played by boys and girls, a difference that persists despite the schools all being coeducational and despite the efforts by the teaching staff to foster non-sexist education in recent years (Karsten, 2003; Valentine and McKendrick, 1997). All told, girls' playtime activities are more diversified, and they encompass a greater variety of activities, both sedentary and active, both indoor and outdoor, both individual and group. Meanwhile, for boys apparently the popularity of football as the main activity tends to outshine the opportunities for other alternative activities. Likewise, just as in the adult world, girls are more likely to join these games than boys are to join games that are clearly classified as for girls. Here we should look further into the question of to what extent football is key in developing a male identity from childhood on.

The play takes place both inside homes and in outdoor spaces. At home, the favourite place to play is the bedroom, followed by the living room. Open spaces at home like patios, yards, terraces and balconies are also mentioned quite frequently, especially by girls. Outside the home, the most popular space is the park, chosen as the first choice by girls, followed by squares or just outside in general. Other spaces mentioned include school playgrounds or sports fields.

The children's most common playmates are friends, followed by siblings. Playing alone was another popular option, especially among boys, despite it not being a suggested option in the questionnaire. In terms of the rest of the family, we find first parents (mainly fathers), as well as other family members, especially cousins. Worth noting was the fact that the children cite their fathers as playmates more often than their mothers. Even though mothers tend to spend more time with their children, they tend to split this caregiving activity with other household chores and are thus less available for playing.

The extracurricular activities to which we refer include both those done at school itself, organized by the parent–teacher associations, and those that take place in other parts of the city. The availability and location of the activities can be determining factors. Another factor to be taken into account is whether the activities entail a cost for the families, in which case factors like purchasing power and number of children also come into play.

In our study cases, most of the children participate in extracurricular activities. Approximately two-thirds of the children do some type of regular activity, the main ones being sports, once again with football in the lead. Yet a significant number of children also participate in other sports, such as basketball, swimming, gymnastics and skating. Another type of very common activity is the arts, such as music, dance, drawing and theatre. With regard to educational activities, the most common ones are languages, especially English, and computers, while the scant availability of school reinforcement activities is surprising. Along with all these more popular activities, there are many others that very few children take part in, but that prove the wide variety available, such as catechism, groups promoting local culture, typing, scouting, and so on. In terms of gender differences, once again the same general rule detected when referring to play also holds true: football is the male activity par excellence, with only two girls playing it, while dance in its diverse variations is the main female activity, in which no boys take part.

Gaining autonomy in daily life

In terms of children's possible autonomy on their way to and from school, half the children made the trip alone, while the other half went with someone, which indicates that the children are at an age when they are at the threshold between dependency and autonomy from adults. Generally speaking, the girls tend to go alone less often than the boys. The people who most frequently take the children to school by far are their mothers, followed by both parents and siblings. Other figures also mentioned are the fathers alone, grandparents, classmates, neighbours and babysitters. In some cases we have come upon comments on the experience of going to and from school alone, such as the one by two girls aged 11 who had something to say about their feelings of comfort and safety in public spaces. In response to the question 'Do you go to school alone?', they express different feelings: 'No, and if they let me go alone I wouldn't feel safe', and 'Yes and no. I feel fine when I'm walking outside.'

The majority of children answered that they are allowed to go outdoors alone. After that, the most frequent answers were 'sometimes' and 'no', the latter mainly coming from girls. Two girls also specified that they were only allowed to out alone 'during the daytime'.

The places where the children are allowed to go include parks and shopping areas. Other destinations are mentioned less often, such as outdoors in general (to take a walk) and the homes of friends and family members. There were no significant differences by sex in the most common destinations, although girls tended to mention more different places and specified more detail (aunts'/uncles' homes, library, walking the dog, conservatory, etc.). In some cases, outings were mentioned that point to some type of household chore, such as walking the dog or throwing away the rubbish.

Thinking about the city

In response to the question of what they would like their city to be like, the children offered many and varied responses. The children would like a city with more parks, clean and spacious. The reference to parks and green spaces in general was significant in the entire sample polled, which shows their desire to have places that are appropriate for their favourite activity, playing facilities adequate for different ages (some even clarified their responses by specifying 'amusement parks' and 'less infantile parks') as well as their sensitivity to environmental matters. The children also revealed their desire for nature, trees, space, public space, rivers, mountains, forests, peace and quiet, fountains, light and even beaches (Figure 11.1). The environmental factor is closely tied to cleanliness as well. The children were concerned about issues of cleanliness and city maintenance, and they expressed their discomfort with pollution, too many cars and motorcycles, dog excrement, rubbish on the ground and graffiti. They also expressed their stance against too many construction sites, buildings and factories, something that might be associated with environmental pollution (acoustic and visual) and a criticism of current urban growth and the model of city in general. The level of specificity and detail of the responses showed a great deal of logic

Imagina't el millor espai per jugar, com hauria de ser? **Dibuixa'l**

Figure 11.1 The best place to play (girl, 10 years old, Spain).

and common sense, and demonstrated to what extent they experience their places.

Besides these main issues, the children also wish for more sports facilities: football pitches, basketball courts, baseball fields, skating courses, swimming pools, bicycle lanes, ice rinks, volleyball courts and ping-pong tables (Figure 11.2). They also mention other facilities and services, such as larger schools, more shops, more videogame stores, hospitals, more cinemas, more theatres, rubbish lorries, rubbish bins, metro, senior citizens' homes, traffic lights, public toilets, areas for dogs and even zoos.

There are other factors mentioned less frequently, yet also related to

Imagina't el millor espai per jugar, com hauria de ser? **Dibuixa'l**

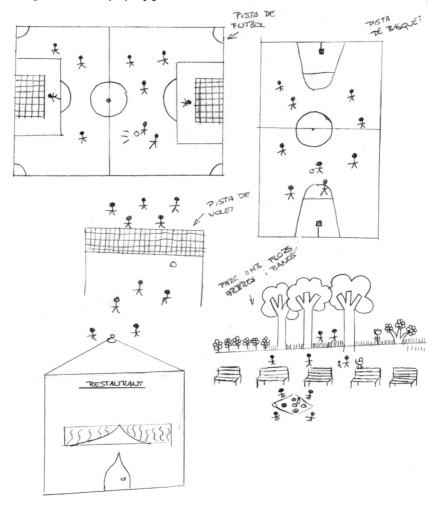

Figure 11.2 The best place to play (boy, 10 years old, Spain).

the aesthetics of the city (pretty, spectacular, modern, reformed, perfect), economic values (more active, more advanced, technological, wealthier) and human values (with good, generous, friendly people; with peace, happiness). It is interesting that in some cases issues of rights were mentioned, such as 'universal right to schooling and having money, a home . . .' or 'a place where children and adults have the same rights' and to fostering the public part of cities (more public spaces, more city swimming pools). Only in two cases of the population studied were aspects related to a lack of safety or crime mentioned ('without thugs', 'with few criminals').

Play, autonomy and free time in Mexico City

Play and free time

In the case of the Mexican children, the activities they prefer to do in their free time vary greatly depending on gender. Thus, while half the boys responded to the question of what they like doing best by saying playing with video games and playing football, the girls tended to answer 'play' more generically, followed by watching television and/or listening to music. No girl mentioned video games, and only one girl claimed to play football and volleyball. Other activities mentioned by boys included reading, talking with friends, drawing, playing with their dog and 'ringing doorbells'. Some girls mentioned dolls, talking and chatting with their friends. Thus, we can see that a good part of boys and girls spend their free time doing sedentary activities like playing with electronic games and watching television, and that the activities that require movement are related to sports (Figure 11.3).

With regard to where they play, two-thirds of the children stated that they usually play at home, either in indoors (bedroom or living room) or outdoors (the patio or yard). On the other hand, more than half said that they also played in open spaces in their block of flats, either in the squares or on the football pitches, as well as on the streets. They mentioned parks to a lesser extent as parks are located somewhat far from their homes, and to reach them the children would have to be accompanied and use public or private transport. As a result, they mainly go to parks at weekends.

Figure 11.3 The best place to play (girl, 9 years old, Mexico).

There were also gender differences with regard to their favourite place to play. The boys mainly responded that their favourite places were nearby open spaces (square and sports fields within their block of flats) or the streets near their homes. They listed two main reasons: there is more space for running and playing, and they run into their friends there ('in the little square with my friends because we can run there and don't get so bored'). The remainder said they felt better at home 'because I feel more relaxed' or 'in the yard of my home because it's large and much safer than the street'. The girls' preferences were divided between the park, because it has more space for playing and because 'I like being outdoors' (as several girls responded), and their house, listing the same reasons as the boys ('because I like being there better' or 'because it's safer, because I might get robbed and I might have a lot of accidents'). Unlike the boys, only two girls said that they preferred the square within their block of flats, and only one said the streets. As we shall see below, the girls do not go out to play alone in these nearby spaces, and when they go to the park it is with family members.

Family members (especially brothers/sisters, but also parents and cousins) are the people with whom the children play the most during their free time, both at home and in the park. Their friends, too, are their playmates, more often for boys than for girls. This difference can be explained by the fact discussed above that boys and girls have different access to the nearby spaces, where the boys meet up with their friends to play football.

After school is out (it runs from 8 a.m. to 2 p.m.), the children go back home accompanied mainly by their mothers and other family members (fathers and grandparents), and they mainly go on foot, but also on public transport and in private vehicles. At home, the children have a snack, do their homework and play. Watching television is one of the specific activities mentioned most often by the children. Only four boys and one girl participate in extracurricular activities (dance and guitar classes and football).

Gaining autonomy in daily life

In response to the question 'Do your parents let you go outdoors alone, and if so where do you go?' we once again find gender differences. The majority of girls responded that they only go out alone when they go shopping at the stores located near their home (especially the newsagents and the bakery) and fewer girls said that they go out alone when they go to their friends' houses to play, or to visit family members. Some only go out if they are accompanied by friends. The remainder, four girls, never go outside alone: 'because my father takes good care of me', 'because they don't like me to go out alone' and 'because they say I'm going to be robbed or run over'. There are also boys who are not allowed to go out alone. The reasons are similar to those cited by the girls: 'because they think I'm going to get robbed' and 'because there are thieves in my block'. These children repeat the same expressions they have heard from their parents about their fears or insecurities about letting their children go out alone in the blocks or neighbourhoods where they lived. The physical and social characteristics of the blocks where some of the interviewees lived – with poorly lit streets, or where drugs were sold and used – as well as the news in the Mexican media helped to forge this sense of insecurity in the city and generate discourses around the lack of safety in public spaces. Just like the girls, the rest of the boys surveyed may go outdoors alone when they need to buy something (they go to the newsagents or to buy sweets), and their parents send them shopping at nearby stores (they go for *tortillas* and bread) which are 'just around the corner' or 'only a few blocks away'. However, the main gender difference observed is the reason for going and the time spent outside the home.

In response to the question 'Do you think that there is enough space for playing in your neighbourhood?', two-thirds of the boys and half the girls have a positive perception of the amount of space available for playing, and they refer to gardens, parks, squares and football pitches. Meanwhile, the remaining children think that there are not enough spaces 'because there are many homes and few places to play', as one boy said, or 'because it's dirty and there are bad people', as another girl stated.

Thinking about the city

Finally, the last question on the questionnaire referred to what they would like their neighbourhood to be like, and what a better place to be would be like for them. For both girls and boys, the main concern was the environment,

Plate 11.1 Playground under the motorway in Mexico City.

and for this reason they would like to live in a place with more green spaces (especially more trees and plants), in a cleaner place ('where there isn't as much rubbish') and without air pollution ('where there were fewer cars') and noise pollution ('less noise from lorries and cars', 'where they don't play music and don't yell because there are people sleeping') (Plate 11.1). After that, they were concerned about the safety of their neighbourhood, and for this reason they would like to live in a place 'without thieves', 'without robbers', 'without criminals', 'without attackers or drug addicts' and 'without corrupt police officers'. Other children would like their neighbourhoods to have more play areas, to be 'lit up at night' and to have 'people who are friendlier and not so rude'.

Creating child-friendly neighbourhood environments

This study has shown the importance of the geographical and cultural setting when analysing the everyday lives of children in urban areas, showing that certain aspects are shared while others are different.

Children are not irresponsible or incompetent, as much of society would like to paint them. In our study, the results show behaviours, wishes and needs that are different for boys and girls. As part of urban planning and the design of playgrounds, these differences are often ignored or translated into certain gender biases. Children are perfectly aware of the everyday problems of urban spaces and they are able to express highly realistic needs and wishes very clearly.

Play is the children's chief free-time activity. In this study, football clearly stands out as the boys' main playtime activity in both geographical settings. Girls' playtime options are much more diversified, especially in Spain. In terms of participation in extracurricular activities, vast differences were noted, as many children living in the Spanish cities signed up for these activities, while they are an exceptional practice in Mexico. This contrast can be explained by the following variables: the range of activities available, the difficulty reconciling work and school times, the different educational expectations and the different socio-economic level of the families. The outdoor public spaces (parks, squares, streets) are key in children's everyday lives in both settings. Not only are they the places where the children play the most, they are also the aspect most often mentioned in children's wishes for their city. Even though they are critical of the existing spaces available, children tend to spend a great deal of time in these areas.

As previously mentioned, children enjoy different levels of autonomy depending on their age, gender and geographical setting. Going outside and to school alone show fewer gender differences in Spain, while in Mexico the girls go out alone less often or they do so in the company of their friends. The perceived lack of safety in Mexico City is a feeling that permeates all layers of society, even in childhood, as expressed in these children's concern for this matter. In different studies, many authors highlight that public spaces are increasingly becoming adult spaces in the sense that children are less and less present (Valentine, 2004; Katz, 2006). As we have seen, especially in the case of Mexico, many parents are too frightened to allow their children to play out unsupervised.

Finally, we highlight that children's wishes for their city were related to environmental matters. In both areas, children expressed the wish for a cleaner city, less polluted, with more places for playing and more green areas. In any event, it was clear that the level and variety of requests for improvements in the city were much greater in Spain than in Mexico, despite that the environmental and urban planning status of the latter is worse. This might be due to the fact that Catalan children are more aware of their right to grow up in cities that are designed with them in mind.

In conclusion, we have shown that children have a great deal to say about the public spaces and playgrounds in their cities and that therefore their opinions should also be taken into account in urban planning and participatory processes on a local scale.

References

Aitken, S. (2004) 'Placing children at the heart of globalization', in D. Janelle, *et al.* (eds) *WorldMinds. Geographical Perspectives on 100 Problems*, Dordrecht: Kluwer: 579–83.

Baylina, M., Ortiz, A. and Prats, M. (2006) 'Children in playgrounds in mediterranean cities', *Children's Geographies*, 4(2): 173–83.

Coutras, J. (1996) *Crise urbaine et espaces sexués*, Paris: Armand Colin.

Domosh, M. and Seager, J. (2001) *Putting Women in Place*, London: Guilford press.

Holloway, S. and Valentine, G. (eds) (2000) *Children's Geographies*, London: Routledge.

Holt, L. (2004a) 'The "Voices" of children: de-centring empowering research relations', *Children's Geographies*, 2(1): 13–27.

Holt, L. (2004b) 'Children with mind-body differences: performing disability in primary school classrooms', *Children's Geographies*, 2(2): 219–36.

Hubbard, P. (2006) *City*, Londres: Routledge.

Karsten, L. (1998) 'Growing up in Amsterdam: differentiation and segregation in children's daily lives', *Urban Studies*, 35(3): 565–81.

Karsten, L. (2003) 'Children's use of public space: the gendered world of the playground', *Childhood*, 10(4): 457–73.

Katz, C. (2004) *Growing Up Global. Economic Restructuring and Children's Everyday Lives*, Minneapolis: University of Minnesota Press.

Katz, C. (2006) 'Los terrors de la hipervigilancia: seguridad y nuevas espacialidades de la niñez', *Documents d'Anàlisi Geogràfica*, 47: 15–29.

Madge, C., Raghuram, P., Skelton, T., Willis, K. and Williams, J. (1997) 'Methods and methodologies in feminist geographies: politics, practice and power', Women and Geography Study Group of the IBG (ed.) *Feminist Geographies. Explorations in Diversity and Difference*, Essex, Longman: 86–111.

Massey, D. (1994) *Space, Place and Gender*, Minneapolis: University of Minnesota Press.

Matthews, H. (1995) 'Living on the edge: children as "outsiders"', *Tijdschrift Voor Economische en Sociale Geografie*, 86(5): 456–66.

166 *M. Baylina* et al.

Matthews, H. (2003) 'Coming of age for children's geographies', *Children's Geographies*, 1(1): 3–5.

Matthews, H. and Tucker, F. (2000) 'Consulting children', *Journal of Geography in Higher Education*, 24(2): 299–310.

McDowell, L. (1999) *Gender, Identity and Place: Understanding Feminist Geographies*, Minneapolis: Minnesota University press.

McNeish, D. (2005) 'Stop, look & listen: how real is our commitment to evidence based policy?', *Children's Geographies*, 3(1): 115–18.

Nayak, A. (2003) '"Through children's eyes": childhood, place and the fear of crime', *Geoforum*, 34: 303–15.

Ortiz, A. (2007) 'Geografías de la infancia: descubriendo 'nuevas formas' de ver y de entender el mundo', *Documents d'Anàlisi Geogràfica*, 49: 197–216.

Paasi, A. (2002) 'Place and region: regional worlds and words', *Progress in Human Geography*, 26(6): 802–11.

Spilsbury, J.C. (2005) 'We don't really get to go out in the front yard. Children's home range and neighborhood violence', *Children's Geographies*, 3(1): 79–99.

Thomson, J.L. & Philo, C. (2004) 'Playful Spaces? A social geography of chidren's play in Livingston, Scotland', *Children's Geographies*, 2(1): 111–30.

Valentine, G. (1997) '"Oh yes I can." "Oh no you can't": children and parents' understanding of kids' competence to negotiate public space safely', *Antipode*, 29(1): 65–89.

Valentine, G. (1999) 'Being seen and heard? The ethical complexities of working with children and young people at home and at school', *Ethics, Place and Environment*, 4(2): 141–55.

Valentine, G. (2004) *Public Space and the Culture of Childhood*, Hants: Ashgate.

Valentine, G. and McKendrick, J. (1997) 'Children's outdoor play: exploring parental concerns about children's safety and the changing nature of childhood', *Geoforum*, 28(2): 219–35.

12 Dredging history

The price of preservation at La Jolla's Children's Pool

David Lulka and Stuart C. Aitken

> If the judgment of a people hardens . . . and history's service to the past life is to undermine a further and higher life; if the historical sense no longer preserves life, but mummifies it, then the tree dies unnaturally, from the top downward, and at last the roots themselves wither.
>
> Nietzsche (1949, 20)

> San Diego City Attorney . . . yesterday said he is seeking state legislation that would allow a colony of harbor seals to stay at Children's Pool permanently. . . . Yesterday's hearing [the last in a series of protracted discussions] was supposed to address San Diego's plans . . . to restore the beach for humans' use.
>
> Lee, *San Diego Union-Tribune* (2008)

Not one to mince words, Nietzsche's comment sets forth a problem that is relevant to a current conflict surrounding a small stretch of beach in La Jolla, California, a conflict wherein advocates for seals are pitted against others who want to see the beach restored for use by children. La Jolla is a community within the city of San Diego, but the controversy over this beach (known as Children's Pool) is now in the hands of state legislators and may, in due course, find its way to a federal court of appeals. The questions this protracted legal battle raises for us relate to the ways public space is constructed, how history is used in that construction, and the implications of that use for the complex relations between children, adults and nature. Nietzsche's challenge to history outlines concerns relevant to children's agency, the historical sense being integral to complex relations within families and within society that frequently bolster or marginalize children's capacities and interests.

After nearly two decades of research emphasizing a sociology of childhood wherein children's agency is paramount (James *et al.*, 1998), new scholarship suggests that more attention should be paid to the complex relations between children, families, public space and nature. For example, Ruddick (2007) notes that a focus on children's agency, although well intended, tends to reproduce myopic, modernist concepts of agency that insinuate autonomy, independence, monadism and self-cohesion. This conception of agency inadvertently supports the marginalization of children, young people and nonhumans who cannot voice an ideal of autonomy and individuation. This is not to suggest that children do not have agency but, rather, that contemporary conceptions (1) marginalize rather than empower some children, and (2) tend to soft-pedal the important dependent relations of all children and all adults. Holt (2006) notes further that this focus on agency underplays the importance of complex relations between young people and the contexts within which they live, including relatively structured institutions and seemingly unstructured nature. The legal battle over the use of Children's Pool brings these dynamics into sharp relief, as the agency of individuals – including children – encounters a series of cultural, governmental, and material forces that work to reshape the landscape.

Though strident in tone, Nietzsche's critique of the role of history in society is worth reconsidering, as it presents a challenge to discourses that purportedly utilize history for the betterment of future generations. Although Nietzsche was referring generally to the role of history as a promoter of ideals, as a force that evaluated the present by means of the past, and which was used by some to portray the present as the logical outcome and culmination of the past, spatial ramifications can clearly be drawn from these same impulses. In particular, Nietzsche's critique has bearing upon the presence of the past in contemporary landscapes that may be used by young people. As material instantiations of the past, we must ask what function do historical places play in the constitution of the present and future? To illustrate these points, this chapter will examine recent events at the Children's Pool in La Jolla. Over the last decade, an increasing number of harbor seals have utilized the Children's Pool for hauling out of the Pacific Ocean and giving birth to pups. The pattern of use by the seals has conflicted with the traditional designation for, and use of the pool by, children, of itself creating a transformation that diverges substantially from the past. Not surprisingly, this has generated disagreement and conflict among the residents of La Jolla and San Diego County. Over a series of council meetings, an interesting rhetoric evolved that pitted children against seals, using issues of rights and agency to substantiate the status of human and nonhuman "stakeholders" in the drama. Amid this discussion was, to paraphrase Nietzsche, an uneasy historical sense about what constitutes the past's proper service to the future. In 2005, San Diego City Council recommended dredging the pool to get rid of the seals and restore the site to its traditional use. Importantly, if enacted, the dredging process is not to be conducted indiscriminately, but is rather intended to bring the landscape into conformance with the original state of the pool in 1941 (Elwany, 2008). Since then, this protracted legal battle has continued, with a change of scale culminating in the placement of the issue before the California State Legislature.

In this chapter, to put these events in perspective and examine the tensions noted above, we first step back and examine the use of historical preservation through Nietzschean eyes to better understand the general dilemma modern society finds itself in. Following upon this theoretical discussion, we look in more detail at recent events at the Children's Pool to assess how they relate to Nietzsche's critique of history and the ways young people and seals are contextualized within the conflict. We then conclude by offering an alternate trajectory for (re)constructing landscapes that prioritizes flexibility.

Dredging up history

The idea of preservation

Historic preservation has become a significant feature of modern society (Tishler, 1979; Carlson, 1980; Lowenthal, 1989; Archer, 1991). In the United States, many sites have been designated in law as points of historical significance. According to the National Register of Historic Places, there are now more than 80,000 sites listed in the registry. According to the National Historic Preservation Act of 1966, sites designated for preservation should be 50 years old or more (Sprinkle, 2007). In part, the 50-year rule was developed so that the passage of time could allow historical perspective to emerge before making any judgment on a particular site and to eliminate the influence of politics that would assuredly accompany sites of contemporary importance. In either case, this perspective certainly differs from Nathaniel Hawthorne's contention that, "All towns should be made capable of purification by fire, or of decay within each half-century" (cited in Lowenthal, 1989, 70). Though less vehement, similar opinions have been expressed throughout modern times, expressing a concern that individuals in contemporary society would be increasingly forced to live amid the rubble and antiquities of the past (Lowenthal, 1989).

Historic designations typically include sites tied to specific cultural events, prominent individuals, or regional idiosyncrasies. Though linked more strongly with the physical environment, the designation of U.S. national parks and similar areas reflects this same tendency. Though numerous in themselves, these formally designated sites do not stand alone. Innumerable places possess significance for local inhabitants, yet have not been legally designated as historical sites. These latter are simply a colloquial part of the texture that defines a region. Consequently, most cities (and many smaller communities) in the United States are pock-marked, to a greater or lesser degree, with historical sites, some of which retain deeply held meaning for the regional citizenry.

The general impetus behind preservationism is to control or contain the transformative power of modern society and its technology. There is a general concern that modern economic and cultural processes will obliterate all remnants of past life, be it human or nonhuman. As Schwarzer (1994, 2) notes:

> The dominant, though contested, philosophy of historic preservation has perpetuated a mythic bifurcation of American society into the

permanent metropolis and the transient frontier. In practice, it has often resulted in the polarization of American cities and towns into zones of static monumentality and unregulated market activity. A reactive strategy, the myth of permanence proposes an alternative idea to the myth of mobility or transience.

For many, effacing the past is ill-advised, not only because modern practices may generate problems of their own, but also because past cultural and material formations have real or potential value in their own right. This perspective aligns in fundamental respects with the general valorization of cultural diversity during the last few decades (Datel, 1985; Hayden, 1988). Thus, Schwarzer (1994, 9) notes that, "From an initial emphasis on patriotism, preservationists have expanded their conception of what it means for a building, district, or site to be of historic importance." Although the temporal aspects of cultural diversity are prioritized in this designation process, the spatial ramifications of preservation cannot be excised from these designations. Historic preservation lends sites a "sense of place" (Ford, 1974), a feeling which is spatial if not quite territorial. In either case, the motives of preservationists are generally well intentioned and particularly difficult to dispute given the increasingly marginal presence of any particular historic era as time proceeds.

Of this process, however, there are many questions to be asked. What types of places are designated as historically significant? What political, economic, and cultural factors influence the process of designation? In what ways is preservation itself realized, and to what extent is it successful? Although important, none of these questions will be addressed in this chapter. Instead, we are concerned here with a more fundamental question, namely, the effect that the imperative of historic preservation has upon the vitality of a place. Let us be clearer, for historic preservation has frequently been used as a means for revitalizing localities, particularly in urban locales that have experienced economic downturns, population losses, and decay of infrastructure (Laurie, 2008; Campbell, 2005; Nelson and Talley, 1991). Commonly, it should be added, these policies of redevelopment have worked, generating tourism, job growth, and new residential patterns. This is "the stuff" of urban geography. We may suggest briefly here, however, that the common mode of development is a superficial form of vitalization, since it is often predicated upon cultural stereotypes and commodifications that are stagnant in their own right. What remains to be seen is whether these historic sites, these repositories of public memory, truly generate, in Jennifer Wolch's (2002) terms, an "anima urbis." By this, she recognizes that a city's sense of place is embodied in its animal as well as its human life forms. Of importance to what we are saying here, she argues that there is a need to consider animals and the urban moral landscape so that competing rubrics of planning practice are assessed with regard to animal as well as human occupants.

The specter of history and public memory is also particularly ominous for children, not because today's children were not part of that history, but because public space has been an adult space. By necessity, therefore, preservation (in formal designations or otherwise) will simply reify the predominance of adult space rather than redistribute it among present-day generations. Thus, it seems, the process of prioritizing the past can devitalize a region. Consequently, the dynamic of preservation needs to be examined in greater detail.

Nietzsche and history

Nietzsche (1996) is well known for developing a genealogical perspective that is ultimately progressive in character. The post-structural take on this perspective has been to accentuate the unbounded character of its ethics, seeing the present and future as an unhinging from the past, particularly with regard to the orthodoxies of religion. There is reason for this assessment. Nietzsche's suspicion of the past also pertained to academic and scientific worldviews. For one, Nietzsche is critical of Hegel's idealism, for he saw in its process of negation the creation of a historical trajectory that was predetermined (and hence lifeless). Similarly, as Grosz (2004) observes, Nietzsche held a certain antipathy toward Darwinism, because he viewed it as prioritizing mere survival at the expense of the present's potential. And, as in Nietzsche's *The Use and Abuse of History*, historians are not exempt from this critique. Yet, as complex as the post-structural utilization of Nietzsche is, it nonetheless misses the central nugget of Nietzsche's objective.

As the aforementioned title of his text indicates, history has a use even though it is more commonly abused. Consequently, the present's relation to the past cannot be partitioned so easily as some might suggest. Indeed, in his valorization of humanity (in comparison to other species), Nietzsche notes that history has played a prominent role in the development of the human. History provides resistance, in a sense, from which individuals gather insight and motivation. Thus, Nietzsche (1949, 8) states:

> [W]e must know the right time to forget as well as the right time to remember, and instinctively see when it is necessary to feel historically and when unhistorically. This is the point that the reader is asked to consider: that the unhistorical and the historical are equally necessary to the health of an individual, a community, and a system of culture.

What, then, is the past good for? "The knowledge of the past is desired only for the service of the future and the present, not to weaken the present or undermine a living future" (Nietzsche, 1949, 22).

Nonetheless, since valorization of the past was the norm of his time, as we might say it is for us today, Nietzsche spent most of his energy articulating the abuses of history. What is positive can quickly turn into a negative force: "Historical study is only fruitful for the future if it follows a powerful life-giving force, for example, a new system of culture – only, therefore, if it is guided and dominated by a higher force, and does not itself guide and dominate" (Nietzsche, 1949, 12). Nietzsche was, in many respects, a man of his time, speaking of health and vigor and foregrounding humanity, a trait typical of emerging modernity; this timeliness also brought him under the umbrella of Darwinian thought. One might say, despite his misgivings about Darwinism, that the evolutionary dynamics of Darwinism lent him the material basis for substantiating his own propulsive vision of humanity.

Although Nietzsche viewed nonhuman animals as eminently unhistorical, there is no reason to conclude that animals play no role in the empowerment of humans. Though his anthropocentric leanings now seem misguided, the intertwining of species cannot be separated from his concern for human empowerment. Thus, when Nietzsche (1949, 69) states, "Excess of history has attacked the plastic power of life that no more understands how to use the past as a means of strength and nourishment," we can take this statement to have quite broad application. The "environmental" aspect is clear in his assertion that, "The unrestrained historical sense, pushed to its logical extreme, uproots the future, because it destroys illusions and robs existing things of the only atmosphere in which they can live" (Nietzsche, 1949, 42). This has bearing upon the conflict surrounding Children's Pool and children's access to nature more generally.

It is here that we want to connect Nietzsche's thought with the historic preservation of landscapes, and urban planning more generally. Wolch, in particular, has tried to rectify this situation by attempting to reintegrate other species into urban settings on their own terms. She has referred to this reconfiguration as a "zoöpolis" guided by a "transspecies urban theory" (Wolch, 1996; Wolch et al., 1995). Her idea is to revitalize urban settings through the inclusion of nonhumans, whereby she refers to an "anima urbis" that is more biologically comprehensive than most urban models (Wolch, 2002, 2007). How historic preservation, which is often utilized to revitalize communities, relates to this enlarged anima urbis is thus an important question to consider, for they may not automatically align. Though Wolch's conception of anima urbis does not explicitly deal with relations between children and nature, we can bring it to bear on that topic. Thus, in the following section, we examine the contentious relationship between the Children's Pool, harbor seals, young people and other residents of La Jolla, seeking to point out the structures and rigidities that prevail and the potentially stultifying effects of historic preservation.

The construction of a children's pool in the context of taming wild places and wild animals

Ellen Browning Scripps first developed the idea of constructing a children's pool in 1921 in response to the dangers posed by local ocean currents (Hollins, 2005). On June 1, 1931, Scripps donated the land to the City of San Diego (2006) for a "pool" that comprised a breakwater that extended out from the coastline and created a protected cove shielded from oncoming waves. Initially, a pool of shallow ocean water extended well into the cove. In the decades that followed, the Children's Pool became a popular site for local residents and a part of the local heritage (Plate 12.1a).

Plate 12.1a Children's Pool Beach around 1980.

Plate 12.1b Children's Pool today, with signage and surveillance cameras.

A modest number of harbor seals also utilized the site during this earlier period. Over time, however, the composition of the pool began to change. The breakwater diminished the strength of the wave action, leading to the deposition of sand within the cove. Gradually, the sand filled in a substantial portion of the cove. While this created a broader beach for humans, it also formed an ideal site for seals to haul out of the water and give birth to their pups. Nonetheless, according to a recent court decision, "There is no evidence of any concern about or discussion of seals in the Children's Pool area until July, 1992" (O'Sullivan v. the City of San Diego, 2005, 6). By 1997, however, the peak number of seals counted at the Children's Pool was 172 animals (Lecky, n.d.). This was not exactly equivalent to Hawthorne's fire of purification, but these changes did alter the local setting and set the stage for cultural change.

In 1994, the city council of San Diego created the Seal Rock Mammal Reserve adjacent to the site for a trial period of five years. In 1997, the beach was closed to human use due to high coliform levels produced by the feces of the seals (Plate 12.1b). Since that time, a debate about the status of the Children's Pool has persisted. If anything, political dynamics in the city council have tended to weigh against the seals in recent years. As noted earlier, in 2005, the city council voted to dredge the interior of the cove. Although the seals still remain at Children's Pool, their position is tenuous at best. The decision to dredge, though still not enacted due to budgetary constraints, hangs over the seals' heads.

That Children's Pool lies within the City of San Diego is not an irrelevant fact, for there is a history of nature-based development in the region. However, unlike the antagonism brought out by the dilemma of the children's pool, most of this nature-based development drew a positive connection between children and animals. The Panama California Exposition of 1915 was perhaps the pivotal event in San Diego during the first half of the twentieth century. The exposition fostered the creation of Balboa Park and brought many exhibits from around the world. Notably, some exhibits included exotic animals, many of which were subsequently abandoned when the exposition ended. In response to this situation, residents of San Diego decided to form a zoological organization with the goal of establishing a noteworthy public zoo. The culmination of activity was the creation of the San Diego Zoo in 1916 in the middle of Balboa Park. Children played a pivotal role in the zoo's early growth. In 1923, John Spreckels donated two elephants to the zoo and presented them to the children of San Diego (Wegeforth, 1953). An early proponent of the zoo stated that:

> Building the Zoo was easy . . . after we found how much the children of San Diego were interested in the new and strange animals we brought from foreign countries. The original idea called for a small group of animals to provide an interesting place to draw people out of doors on holidays, a sort of social health insurance. But so many children began

to flock in that we were impressed with the possibility of a zoological garden on a large scale.

(cited in Wegeforth, 1953, 55–6)

In 1972, the San Diego Zoological Society opened up another institution called the San Diego Wild Animal Park, which exhibited animals in a more naturalistic fashion. Since their opening, these two venues have become world-renowned institutions that cater to families.

In addition, Sea World opened in 1964. Unlike the other institutions, Sea World is owned by a major corporation (the parent company of Anheuser-Busch), which runs several other amusement parks in the United States. According to Susan Davis (1997, 161), "The universal person in Sea World ideology is the child." Within its confines, Sea World presents a domesticated form of wild nature that conforms to cultural norms. As Davis (1997, 162) notes, "the entertainment department thinks of its productions not in terms of what children want to see; rather, it guesses at what parents and grandparents want kids to see and not see." In this sense, Sea World is a conservative social experiment that monitors the images presented to children. It is family entertainment in the guise of nature.

The affinity between children and animals in these venues makes the conflict between children and seals in nearby La Jolla stand out all the more. At least in part, the domestic quality of these animal attractions accounts for this discrepancy, for it does not unsettle social relations. In contrast, the seals at La Jolla are seen by some as divisive entities, for they are perceived to disrupt parent–child relations loaded with histories of their own.

The weight of history

How can we see the role of history in the proceedings over Children's Pool and its impact on contemporary dynamics over child rights and agency? Are current actions and the debate serving to generate an anima urbis or are they mummifying local children (and the general culture of La Jolla) within a historical landscape? This can be expressed in different ways, alternately biographical, legal, and material.

First, though perhaps unintended, there is at times a tendency to depict Ellen Browning Scripps in rigid terms. Some advocates for the removal of the seals refer to the original intent of Ellen Browning Scripps without noting any social developments that have occurred during the intervening years. For example, Revelle (2001), a descendant of Ellen Scripps, wrote a letter to the California Coastal Commission stating her objection to a proposed five-year extension of the seal refuge. In doing so, she based her views on the original intent of her ancestor, stating that:

In 1931, my Great-Aunt Ellen B. Scripps had the breakwater, that forms the Children's Pool, constructed for the purpose of protecting *children*,

> so they could play on the sand and safely paddle, then learn to swim, in the sheltered water. It has been, during all these years, widely used and appreciated by generations of families.

This reification of Scripps' character is facilitated by Scripps' death not long after the official opening of the pool, a situation which did not permit her to further develop or reconsider her notions of the site.

Alternatively, during a city council meeting in 1999, a resident suggested that if Scripps could have seen the future, she would have appreciated the seals. According to the resident, "My great-grandfather was Jacob Chandler Harper, and he guided some of her philanthropic efforts with respect to the community, and I'm sure that if she were alive today – she loved the sea very much – that she would be in favor of the children enjoying the beach and the seals."[1]

These speculations miss the main theoretical point addressed by Nietzsche. Does it matter what Scripps thought then (or now, if she were alive)? Is original intent ever enough to settle an argument? Are we still beholden to a woman who was born in 1836? Is that a sound basis for any contemporary society?

Notwithstanding the uncertainties that surround Ellen Browning Scripps, legal standards generally favor original intent as the default position. This is not specific to La Jolla, but generally applicable to events in the United States. On the national scene, this is reflected in arguments about the original intent of the founding fathers who wrote the US Constitution, the valorization of "strict constitutionalists," and the rejection of "activist" judges in some social circles. The outcome of this perspective is deference to the past, despite the modern nuances and unforeseen contingencies that have developed in the meantime. The tendency is toward caution, if not conservatism.

We may contrast this latter approach with the views of an 8-year-old fourth grade girl from a local school, who stated at a city council meeting that, "Ellen Browning Scripps gave it to the children of La Jolla and I think that they should have the decision. They should have a voice in the decision." Here, we see a utilization of the past, but for the purpose of empowering the present children, not for subjecting them to the past. Nonetheless, despite the name ascribed to the pool, children have had little input into the decision making process. This situation is not unusual, for as Hinchliffe *et al.* (2005, 645) note, "A problem is that the passions and interests that align with urban wilds are often unarticulated, or are articulated by those who have long since been unheeded by political processes. They include not just the very young and the nonhuman, but also the multitude of acts, skills, and attachments that rarely make it into political discussions."

A picture of domesticity

For others, the original intent of the pool and legal mandates are not as important as their personal experience at the site. Most significant in this regard are residents who learned how to swim at the pool when they were children themselves. For example, in 2004, a longtime resident of La Jolla began his statement at a city council meeting by saying:

> I am a father of four. My first two children, age 22 and 19, learned how to swim in the ocean at the Children's Pool. Again, Children's Pool, not seal's pool. Okay. It angers me as a father, that I cannot take my two youngest children, age 7 and 4, down to this place and have them safely, without being harassed by the Save the Seal people, okay or become contaminated and infirmed. Okay, they can't safely swim there where my first two children learned how to swim. This was a marvellous place for families to come down and picnic, to enjoy a safe environment in which they could learn how to swim. This is a tragedy.

What emerges from comments like this is a picture of domesticity. It is a familial space in the traditional sense, where bonds are formed in exclusion to many other worldly concerns. Though contested, these sentiments were not atypical at city council meetings. As above, they draw on a biography for legitimacy, but they draw rather from a much closer source of authenticity – personal experience rather than an historic figure of the past.

Clearly, this father's sentiments cannot be entirely disengaged from the empowerment of his children in the present day. If the San Diego city council acceded to his wishes, his children would possess more capacity to swim in the pool than if the pool were allocated exclusively to the seals. Again, as per Nietzsche, the contention here is not to assert that the past is always debilitating. There is no clean line. A better issue to ponder is the relation between culture, the individual, and empowerment. Specifically, we must ask whether culture is an act of duplication and reproduction or, instead, a mode of being.

At least since the 1980s, identity politics has played a significant role in urban affairs (Mitchell, 2000; Thrift and Whatmore, 2004). One's identity, one's culture, is linked to one's participation in events that reproduce historic practices associated with those identities. Children are frequently enrolled in this process, whether because they are seen as the mechanism for perpetuating the past or due to the "good will" of adults. Despite this good will, these intergenerational dynamics can obviously have a stultifying effect on children. Foucault (1990) famously noted that authoritative powers do not repress identity, but rather produce identity. Certainly, he was correct in noting the power of representation, but his perspective was also too generous to authority figures. He did not adequately acknowledge the non-discursive elements of life that are productive in their own right. The role of affect and immanence, which have become central to non-representational theory, have become core elements of more recent theoretical speculations (Thrift, 2008). Such immanence, which children, adults, and indeed animals embody, is a mode of being that generates culture, not an act of cultural reproduction. Culture is "more-than representational" (Lorimer, 2005), children's behavior being part of this extension. This is the rub for the Children's Pool. We may fairly wonder about the extent to which the father quoted earlier is augmenting the power of his children or, rather, subjecting his own children to his own biography. This is a harsh indictment, and one to be placed in context, but nonetheless one to be taken very seriously, for such stultifying practices creep into life in a multitude of forms.

The same may be said for another citizen, who stated that:

> I love the seals, but I love the children more . . . We seem to have over-blown this thing and feel like that we want people to come from all over the world to see the seals, instead of watching our children play on the beach that was built for them. I think that if you want to see seals, they're available at Sea World. And I know that the price is rather high [at Sea World], but I think the price that we're going to pay to give away the children's beach is even higher.

Not only is some anger about recent changes evident here, but the speaker also reaffirms the position of other cultural forms (i.e. Sea World) that have become a conventional, or naturalized, part of San Diego culture over time.

Nature as a theme park

It is apparent that previous rounds of economic and recreational development play a role in assessing human–nonhuman relationships at Children's Pool. The nature-based entertainment venues have become part of the fabric of family life for those who can afford them, and they are also an aspect of domestic life that is commonly integrated into the temporal dynamics of the family. For some, theme park entertainment tailored for children is seen as an adequate substitute for wildlife, perhaps in part because that wildlife has little connection with a culture that became disconnected from wildlife some time ago. Though not necessarily, this prioritization can constrain children if it helps eliminate other developmental opportunities.

We must add here that history has not only ensnared the nostalgic residents of La Jolla who favor the ouster of seals. In a different fashion, some seal advocates have become locked into their own historical vision. Some claim, for instance, that the seal population pre-existed the human population in La Jolla. This perspective is likely to gain some favor among the public, as it refers to both a pristine nature as well as a marginalized, "indigenous" population. In the urban world, direct observation of habitat loss is not uncommon, and this has led to dismay and self-loathing, resulting in antipathy toward modernism. Furthermore, proponents of the seals argue that the La Jolla seals are the only ones in Southern California, and that the Children's Pool is the only seal rookery between Carpenteria (in Santa Barbara County) and the Mexican border. For such reasons, the San Diego chapter of the Sierra Club, for one, wants to re-designate Children's Pool as the San Diego Coastal and Marine Sanctuary (Hartley, 2007). The "sanctuary" idea, though grounded in nature, is not distinct from aspects of historic preservation movements geared toward the built environment in urban settings.

Memory and nostalgia

The point we want to make is that this debate about seals and children is just as riddled with a sense of loss – of childhood, of nature – that mobilizes a particular form of history that potentially mummifies the vitality of the area. It may be that the proponents of the pool's restoration are mourning the loss of their own childhood more than any tangible activity. Indeed, as one speaker commented,

> As the years have gone by, I've always came back [sic] to my favorite spot to swim and to re-explore the coastline of La Jolla as I did in my youth. Just two summers ago my daughter, now nine years old, learned how to snorkel at this very beach that is now closed to swimmers but is open for seals. Where are our priorities?

Ironically, the vehemence of this speaker's dismay may have been strengthened in part by emergent forms of ecological education that have undercut the superiority of humanity and its privileging in particular places. A city councilwoman with environmental leanings put it this way:

> I agree that it's really sad when there are certain spots that we knew as a child that we can no longer use. I understand that. I remember back in the 50s watching certain spots that I got to use that I don't get to use anymore because of overdevelopment. From areas that used to be places where I could see actual natural habitats, the little places where the lizards ran and the roadrunners, and those are gone due to overdevelopment . . . Apparently, we think it's fine because I don't see the kind of outcry as I see when humans have a certain very tiny spot of beach area that they used to use that maybe they have to share. The type of outrage that I've experienced from that is pretty amazing today.

"Children" are at the forefront of these debates, and yet adults have a different (some might say more comprehensive) knowledge of the stakes involved. Thus, it may be argued that children are mobilized for adultist agendas. Not least amongst these agendas is an elitist predisposition amongst La Jolla residents who want to protect the exclusivity of the beach as part of their community.

Child agency

Child agency is not entirely removed from this debate, however. In the late 1990s, an 8-year-old fourth grade girl from one of the local schools took a poll of her classmates to ascertain their opinion on the issue (Plate 12.2). The results indicated that most of the students wanted the seals to stay, but there is no way of knowing how the polling process or social pressures affected this outcome. In another instance, a group of girls was observed campaigning at the pool in support of the seals. The girls were acting in partnership with a local environmental group (Plate 12.3). Once more it was unclear what social pressures were placed upon them. Although it is unlikely that they were advocating a position they disagreed with, the fate of the seals may not have been one of their top priorities in life.

We are thus presented here with a situation in which two histories, or rather two material concretions, that of the children's aquatic environment and that of the wildlife sanctuary, are dueling for the present. Proponents of each are asserting the priority of their preferred material concretion. Again, Nietzsche is helpful here, for he realized that no historical concretion has ultimate legitimacy, as the search for origins is hopeless. There is only a changing sense of what is natural, commonsensical, and taken-for-granted, that is, the proper state of things. This generates an element of indecisiveness that blends well with the nature of political affairs. As Nietzsche (1949, 22)

Do YOU think the seals should get out of here???

Children's Pool was created for the children of La Jolla shouldn't we have a voice in this decision?

SIGN HERE IF YOU WANT THE SEALS TO BE ALLOWED TO **STAY**

SIGN HERE IF YOU WANT THE SEALS TO BE FORCED TO **LEAVE**

Total:
911
K-6 students
(Torrey Pines,
Bird Rock,
La Jolla)

Total:
131
K-6 students
(Torrey Pines,
Bird Rock,
La Jolla)

Plate 12.2 The result of an 8-year-old child's "advocacy."

Plate 12.3 Young women exercising their civic 'rights' in favor of the seals at Children's Pool.

states, "The consolation is the knowledge that this 'first nature' was once a second, and that every conquering 'second nature' becomes a first." Due to this lack of origins, Nietzsche's conceptualization places alternate depictions of place (of histories) at loggerheads without allowing for an indisputable means of deciding between the parties by dint of their own properties. We must look elsewhere.

Mortar and mortification

Another way of conceiving the impact of history on the life of La Jolla is to look at the structure of Children's Pool itself. As Latour (2005) and others have shown, materialities are forms of agency in their own right that impact patterns of social organization. Kärrholm (2007), in turn, has linked this notion with the concept of territoriality. Such material forces may be particularly important, because they can remain relatively constant over long periods of time, thus withstanding the vagaries of social developments that might signal a desire for change.

According to Hollins (2005), the breakwater of the Children's Pool is 328 feet long. A trench for the foundation of the walkway was cut into a pre-existing rock reef to a depth of 10 feet. Altogether, 1,304.5 feet of holes were drilled into the substrate, and 3,125.5 barrels of concrete were used to construct the breakwater. These statistics hint at the formidable girth of the project. According to Hiram Savage (1931, 9), the architect of the pool, if constructed according to plan, "it would stay until 'Kingdom Come'."

It is easy here to draw some comparisons and contrasts. The weight of the structure can be correlated with the conceptual weight of history, as figured through the eyes of local residents. The rigidity and imperviousness of the breakwater can be contrasted with the crashing of waves and the lolling of tides and currents. From this, we may sense that the hardened structure is grafted onto the ephemeral, or that a second nature is fixed upon a first nature. Such is, in many respects, true. The materiality of the breakwater functions at a different timescale than that of its surroundings, and thus the past extends, and indeed dominates, the present by virtue of the durability of the materials employed to construct the breakwater. The breakwater is not only an object that stretches across space, but also a thought or vision materially extended through time. Stated differently, the original vision of the pool is as long-lived as the coherent materiality of the concrete mixture.

It is against this material historical background, which is part of the past yet nonetheless ever present, that children, seals, and adults must engage and carry out their lives. Typical of organic life, there is an element of animation in each of their modes of being that distinguishes them from their surroundings. For individuals of each group, the material history of the site has presented opportunities and limitations. At this point in time, the seals are the main occupants of the pool. The small beachhead was initially desired as a resting spot for children, but, as it grew in extent due to the effects of the breakwater, seals came to appreciate its qualities. Looked upon generally, seals are quite a stolid group, spending much of their time laying upon the sands, leading, it may appear, a lazy life. A closer look reveals that their days are filled with much more activity. There are minute struggles for space between one another, battles with pestering insects, seemingly indiscriminate urination, and caretaking of pups. Added to this, of course, are the not so infrequent excursions into the water and out of the water. The seal population is a mosaic of sorts, constantly shifting in multiple ways that make it difficult to conceptualize its entirety since it is never completely at rest.

Children (and adults) are largely absent from the sands of the pool at the present. This stands in contrast to historical associations between children and the beach, which enumerate a series of childhood activities that possess a certain vibrancy of their own (Dekker, 2003). That children have been conceived as animals in need of civilization (confer to Myers, 1998) has probably reaffirmed these connections in another way. For such reasons, strong connections have been drawn between children and nature, whereby children seem ideally attuned to, and in place within, nature. This cultural association has undoubtedly had an impact on the strength of opposition to the seals and the desire to return the pool to its original form and function, for the seals are seen as coming between children and nature more generally.

Recent events indicate that the vibrancy of seals and children is imperiled by the historical legacies associated with the site. On the one hand, there is clearly a sense among many that the pool lies within the human domain and is thus subject to human priorities. Materially, this is evidenced by the mortar used to cobble together the large, impervious structure of the breakwater. Mortar is not wholly foreign to the site, for it is made up partially by sand and water in itself. Indeed, it is the initial pliability of mortar, not its firmness, that allows blocks of inexact conformation to congeal together and become one. Yet, mortar ultimately brings a whole new quality to a site by solidifying it, making what was fluid – sand and water – into what is solid. The construction was the means by which a second nature became a new first nature, through human habituation, enculturation, and naturalization over time. There are echoes here of John Locke's theory of labor, in which men come to legitimately possess land by mixing it with their labor. There are also connections with historic dispossession of indigenes, whose own labor (or, rather, way of life) was unrecognized and denied by colonizers who were accustomed to fences and other permanent structures as signs of inhabitation (Cronon, 2003). Through this labor, a legacy is built that extends through time. The political process in San Diego has become steeped in this materiality, as some seek to sift out (quite literally, through dredging) those materials that do not align with certain objectives. In the process of dredging out the sands of the pool, some are hopeful that the seals will also become dispersed like grains of sand, thereby reclaiming the site for a specific suite of children's activities. From this dynamic, a hierarchy emerges that leaves marginal populations, such as the seals of La Jolla, in a tenuous state.

On the other hand, children have also had their use of the pool curtailed in recent years. While many children benefit from observing the seals from the solid structure of the breakwater, they do not interact directly with the sand and waters of the pool. This, of course, is not generally of their own doing, as they are usually under the supervision of an adult. Although adults do restrain children from utilizing the beach because they themselves appreciate the presence of the seals, some most likely restrain their children because they themselves are subject to social pressures. Most of the time, advocates for the seals oversee the pool, making sure that no one harasses the seals by discouraging visitors from venturing onto the sands. Usually, a video camera is in place to videotape anyone that does walk down to the beach. Given the success of this approach, one might say that many adults have become mortified by this surveillance. By mortification, we are not referring to an exaggerated moment of crisis, but rather to a more general form of abstinence that reflects the words traditional meaning. To be mortified not only means to give death to flesh (by abstaining from various corporeal pleasures), it also means to feel shame and embarrassment about oneself. Although it is the parents who are mortified through their greater awareness of social expectations, children are indirectly affected by this denial of interests and redirection of passions.

Neither/nor

Each of these outcomes shows how history, alternately figured, has come to jeopardize, if not actually quell, the actions of contemporary inhabitants. This signals a problematic balance between the past and the present, in which the past comes to weigh excessively on the present to the point of incapacitating individuals. The past is not used as a fulcrum to propel further development, but instead retards action. The simple solution to this problem is to disavow history and let the seals, children, and adults settle this matter among themselves without reference to the past. That would indeed privilege the moment, and, by virtue of that, privilege existence. But such an approach would likely produce problems of its own, whether that is harm inflicted upon children by seals or the dispersal and demise of the seal population, neither of which appears beneficial to contemporary inhabitants. Most observers believe that shared use is not truly an option since the beach inside Children's Pool is quite narrow in width, a physical reality that would probably lead to seal bites, abandoned pups, and other negative consequences.

A reasoned approach would contend that a successful outcome to such dilemmas is the ability to hold onto what once was (whether a safe swimming pool or idyllic environment). Perhaps this speaks to the privileged position of property in Western culture or, similarly, the notion of identity as one's own possession. But looked at from a more heretical viewpoint, success is more adequately defined as the ability to carry on, irrespective of its resemblance to the past. This position is diametrically opposite to the ethos of historic preservation. If Nietzsche's genealogical approach tells us anything, it is that our power comes from an ability to generate new social arrangements. This conclusion is actually reassuring, since in the present context of Children's Pool, we cannot, it seems, preserve both legacies of the past. We are not forced to fail by virtue of a constrained set of options. It is not a matter of either/or.

If we are to change our focus and look forward then, the dictates of success look different. The present becomes not one of choosing between dwindling remnants, but rather becomes a moment of flexibility that opens outward into unknown (though not unbounded) possibilities. This wording is not incidental, for definitions of humanity frequently revolve around heightened conceptions of flexibility, whether in relation to language or tool making (so-called *Homo faber*). These high estimations of humanity place great demands upon adults (and, to a lesser degree, children). What we might offer here as a standard for decision-making, therefore, is a simple demand that we meet our own characterizations of ourselves by being the flexibility we imagine ourselves to be. In the present context, then, success is not based on the ability to secure a space for children or seals (a traditional form of conquest), but rather on the ability to remain fluid and undetermined. By such means, the dynamic of this antagonism can be altered, for we can thus be self-centered in a way that is actually beneficial to others. We can do this by prioritizing our capacities, but in ways that do not portend possession that incapacitates others: namely, muted children and voiceless seals.

Recourse to flexibility outlines a challenge for adults in particular to find another way, but it also sets parameters for determining an advisable path of development in relation to children and nonhumans. To be balanced and not transform a difference in degree into a difference in kind (among generations or among species), we might place similar expectations on children and other species based upon our admittedly inexact estimations of, and experience with, their own flexibility. The deciding factor in any instance, in any place, is not the historical root from which we sprung (from nature or culture), but rather being the threshold of flexibility that the respective parties appear to embody in themselves. Our attitude toward seals and children, in this instance, is not based upon kindness per se, but on a valuation of each party's potential to adapt.

In brief, those who are the most flexible (whether by means of physical strength, intelligence, or capital) will have the greatest burden placed upon them. This criterion carries an uncertain relation to children (and nonhuman animals). Due to a lack of enculturation, children may be more flexible or less flexible depending upon which attributes one is assessing (Low and Hollis, 2003; Mouchiroud and Lubart, 2002; Burnard, 1999; Russ, 1996). More certainly, children are less flexible due to physical limitations. In either case, distinct manifestations of flexibility enable children to become what we, as adults, did not become or have difficulty becoming in retrospect. Similarly, nonhuman animals exhibit their own forms of flexibility. This latter tendency manifests itself in what we know as evolution. In all cases, there are obvious resonances with the notions of affect and immanence noted earlier.

It is not so much that adults, children and animals possess flexibility, but that they are flexibility, something that is not limited by an either/or scenario. Nietzsche intimated as much when he came up with the figure of the "overman," the being which humanity, never fully formed, was to become. We would expect children to benefit from this criterion, for they are generally less flexible than adults in a substantive way, and thus must be accounted for by placing greater demands on adults. That said, we would also expect children to lose out in some circumstances, as when they are reasonably expected to be more flexible than others. This method of adjudication has obvious implications for urban planning and the constitution of public space.

Conclusion

We cannot stress enough that the foregoing thoughts on historic preservation are not a rejection of history or the sites associated with it. This would simply create another set of dilemmas to address. Rather, we see the objective of accentuating flexibility over history as a manner of engaging with the world more thoroughly. In a very real sense, this means engaging with historic sites not because they are historical, but instead because we recognize that they have relevance to contemporary life. In short, though of a distant time, these sites may have a role in substantiating our flexibility and livelihood. At the same time, we are not beholden to the historical nature of these sites, for that would truly prioritize the abstract over the real.

The conflict at Children's Pool is a specific example of problems that may be generated by too much reliance upon historical precedents. Although many historic sites may have a neutral effect on the inhabitants of a region, Children's Pool illustrates in a clear fashion how real lives may be adversely impacted. This result moves the conflict beyond concerns about the mere build-up of rubble and should instigate other modes of evaluation. Although unique in its specifics, we also believe that such impacts are widely migratory, extending, often unseen, into many aspects of contemporary life. Many "communities," loosely defined, are undoubtedly affected by this social impetus to preserve or recreate an area's vitality for future generations. We see the present dilemma as a moment for bringing this aspect to light, and balancing the scales of analysis toward a pragmatism that is inherently flexible. Finding a suitable relationship between the historical and the unhistorical, the human and the nonhuman, the adult and the child is a means of realizing the greater benefits of flexibility.

Note

1 All quotes cited from San Diego City Council meetings were transcribed from official recordings of council meetings that occurred on August 4, 1999, and September 14, 2004.

References

Archer, M.C. (1991) "Where we stand: preservation issues in the 1990s," *Public Historian* 13: 25–40.

Burnard, P. (1999) "Bodily intention in children's improvisation and composition," *Psychology of Music* 27: 159–74.

Campbell, H. (2005) "The Socorro Mission: culture, economic development, and the politics of historic preservation along the Río Grande/Río Bravo," *Latin American Perspectives* 32: 8–27.

Carlson, A.W. (1980) "An analysis of historic preservation in the United States as reflected by the *National Register of Historical Places*," *Journal of American Culture* 3: 245–67.

City of San Diego (2006) "San Diego Municipal Code: Section 63.0102 (b) (10)." Available at: http://docs.sandiego.gov/municode/MuniCodeChapter06/Ch06 Art03Division01.pdf (website uploaded October 24, 2007).

Cronon, W. (2003) *Changes in the Land,* New York: Hill and Wang.

Datel, R.E. (1985) "Preservation and a sense of orientation for American cities," *Geographical Review* 75: 125–41.

Davis, S.G. (1997) *Spectacular Nature: Corporate Culture and the Sea World Experience*, Berkeley: University of California Press.

Dekker, J.J.H. (2003) "Family on the beach: representations of romantic and bourgeois family values by realistic genre painting of nineteenth-century Scheveningen Beach," *Journal of Family History* 28: 277–96.

Elwany, H. (2008) "La Jolla Children's Pool: Sand Excavation and Placement Plan." Unpublished document. La Jolla, CA: Coastal Environments.

Ford, L. (1974) "Historic preservation and the sense of place," *Growth and Change* 33–7.

Foucault, M. (1990) *The History of Sexuality: Volume 1*, New York: Vintage Books.

Grosz, E.A. (2004) *The Nick of Time: Politics, Evolution, and the Untimely*, Durham: Duke University Press.

Hartley, J. (2007) "San Diego Coastal & Marine Sanctuary: an urban wildlife experience," *Hi Sierran* 66 (January/February): 7.

Hayden, D. (1988) "Placemaking, preservation and urban history," *Journal of Architectural Education* 41: 45–51.

Hinchliffe, S.K., Matthew, B., Degan, M. and Whatmore, S. (2005) 'Urban wild things: a cosmopolitical experiment', *Environment and Planning D: Society and Space* 23: 643–58.

Hollins, J. (2005) "'Until kingdom come': the design and construction of La Jolla's Children's Pool," *Journal of San Diego History* 51(2): 123–38.

Holt, L. (2006) "Exploring other childhoods through quantitative secondary analyses of large scale surveys: Opportunities and challenges for children's geographies', *Children's Geographies* 4: 143–55.

James, A., Jenks, C. and Prout, A. (1998) *Theorizing Childhood*, Hoboken, NJ: John Wiley.

Kärrholm, M. (2007) 'The materiality of territorial production: a conceptual discussion of territoriality, materiality, and the everyday life of public space', *Space and Culture* 10: 437–53.

Laurie, J. (2008) "Historic preservation and cluster based economic development," *Economic Development Journal* 7: 38–46.

Latour, B. (2005) *Reassembling the Social*, Oxford: Oxford University Press.

Lecky, J.H. (no date) "Whose beach is it anyway? Managing seals at Children's Pool," La Jolla, CA, Unpublished document, National Marine Fisheries Service. Available at: http://www.mmc.gov/reports/workshop/pdf/lecky.pdf (accessed September 30, 2010).

Lee, M. (2008) "Aguirre wants state measure to help seals", *San Diego Union-Tribune*, October 25 2008, B-1.

Lorimer, H. (2005) "Cultural geography: the busyness of being 'more-than-Representational'," *Progress in Human Geography* 29: 83–94.

Low, J. and Hollis, S. (2003) "The eyes have it: development of children's generative Thinking," *International Journal of Behavioral Development* 27: 97–108.

Lowenthal, D. (1989) "Material preservation and its alternatives," *Perspecta* 25: 67–77.

Mitchell, D. (2000) *Cultural Geography: A Critical Introduction*, Oxford: Blackwell Publishing.

Mouchiroud, C. and Lubart, T. (2002) "Social creativity: a cross-sectional study of 6- to 11-year-old children," *International Journal of Behavioral Development* 26: 60–9.

Myers, G. (1998) *Children and Animals: Social Development and Our Connections to Other Species*, Boulder, CO: Westview Press.

Nelson, A.C. and Talley, J. (1991) "Revitalizing minority commercial areas through commercial historic district designation: a case study of Atlanta, Georgia," *Journal of Urban Affairs* 13: 221–32.

Nietzsche, F. (1949) *The Use and Abuse of History*, New York: Liberal Arts Press.

Nietzsche, F. (1996) *On the Genealogy of Morals*, Oxford: Oxford University Press.

O'Sullivan v. the City of San Diego (2005) *O'Sullivan v. the City of San Diego (Case No. GIC 826918)* (August 25, 2005) Tentative Statement of Decision. Available at: http://www.friendsofthechildrenspool.com/legal_la_jolla_seals/Childrens_082505.pdf (accessed September 30, 2010).

Revelle, E.C. (2001) "Letter to California Coastal Commission," Letter dated March 10, 2001.

Ruddick, S. (2007) "At the horizons of the subject: neoliberalism, neoconservatism and ther rights of the child part one: from 'knowing' fetus to 'confused' child," *Gender, Place and Culture* 14(5): 513–27.

Russ, S.W. (1996) "Development of creative processes in children," *New Directions for Child Development* 72: 31–42.

Savage, H.N. (1931) *Ellen Browning Scripps: Bathing Pool for Children at La Jolla, California*, La Jolla Historical Society Archives.

Schwarzer, M. (1994) "Myths of permanence and transience in the discourse on historic preservation in the United States," *Journal of Architectural Education* 48: 2–11.

Sprinkle, J.H. (2007) "'Of exceptional importance': the origins of the 'fifty-year Rule' in historic preservation," *Public Historian* 29: 81–103.

Thrift, N. (2008) *Non-representational Theory: Space, Politics, Affect*, London: Routledge.

Thrift, N. and Whatmore, S. (2004) Introduction. In: *Cultural Geography: Critical Concepts in the Social Sciences*, N. Thrift and S. Whatmore (eds.), London: Routledge, pp. 1–17.

Tishler, W.H. (1979) "The landscape: an emerging historic preservation resource," *Bulletin for the Association of Preservation Technology* 11: 9–25.

The full reference is:

Wegeforth, H.M. (1953) *It Began With a Roar: The Story of San Diego's World-famed Zoo*. San Diego: Pioneer Printers.

Wolch, J. (1996) "Zoöpolis," *Capitalism, Nature, Socialism* 7: 21–47.

Wolch, J. (2002) "Anima urbis," *Progress in Human Geography* 26: 721–42.

Wolch, J. (2007) "Green Urban Worlds," *Annals of the Association of American Geographers* 97: 373–84.

Wolch, J., West, K. and Gaines, T.E. (1995) "Transspecies urban theory," *Environment and Planning D: Society and Space* 13: 735–60.

13 Filling the family's transport gap in sub-Saharan Africa

Young people and load carrying in Ghana

Gina Porter, Kathrin Blaufuss and Frank Owusu Acheampong

Introduction

This chapter considers the implications of sub-Saharan Africa's transport gap for young people. In urban and rural areas, wherever transport services are deficient, or households lack the economic purchasing power to acquire transport equipment or pay fares, much everyday transport work needed to sustain the family and household is delegated to young people, especially girls. In most regions this involves putting the load in some sort of receptacle – perhaps a plastic container, metal bowl, hessian sack, cardboard box, or a locally woven basket – and then balancing it on the head, which is often protected by a small coil of cloth to make the burden more comfortable. Water and fuel commonly predominate among the loads being carried, even in urban areas, because of the widespread absence of piped water and electricity, but other items such as agricultural produce and groceries are also regularly transported in this way. Loads are carried to sustain the household directly, in terms of providing water, fuel and food, but also to enable participation in the cash economy.

Load carrying as an activity undertaken by children has been largely invisible in studies of African economies, since children's work activity as a whole has been commonly subsumed under women's or family labour, especially in rural contexts. Drawing on some preliminary empirical research in southern Ghana, we examine the scale of load carrying and consider its potential impacts on young people's education, health and well-being, bearing in mind that there may be much more to carrying than mere physical weight: load carrying is embodied and arguably performed and enacted as social position.

Young people, gender and load carrying in the literature

The recognition of African women's load-carrying efforts in the development literature can be traced back to key papers by Doran (1990) and

Bryceson and Howe (1993), which drew on village-level transport surveys and broader research on gendered labour patterns to reveal the predominance of women in rural household transport across many African societies. By contrast, however, there has been remarkably little recognition of children's and young people's contribution to load carrying (Porter *et al.*, 2007; for a rare exception see Malmberg Calvo, 1994).[1] Children and young people's domestic transport work is commonly subsumed under women's work. In part this may be attributable to the fact that African youth has only recently begun to move towards centre-stage as a focus of social research in African societies, despite their long-standing position as major players in the continent's predominantly informal economies (De Boeck and Honwana, 2005: 1). The most detailed information on young people's contribution as load carriers to date probably comes from studies of girl porters in Accra (Agarwal *et al.*, 1994; Grieco *et al.*, 1996).

It is important to reiterate, at this point, the significant gender dimension to load carrying, since this affects patterns of porterage among youth as well as adults. Load carrying, as a low-status activity, seems to be regarded culturally as a 'female' activity in most African societies (Malmberg Calvo, 1994: 9). As a Birom man on the Jos Plateau, Nigeria, observed to one of the authors, as he walked, load-free and without apology, alongside his heavily burdened and heavily pregnant young wife, 'to see a man carrying things on his head in our culture is not allowed'. Young boys are often to be seen carrying water and firewood with their sisters in this as in other regions but, so far as domestic supply of goods like water and fuel wood are concerned, boys older than about 15 years usually only head-load in emergencies (e.g. Doran, 1990: 30; Malmberg Calvo, 1994: 28; Potgieter *et al.*, 2006: 15). When transport technology is introduced, however, boys or men commonly take over transport tasks (Flanary, 2004; Mahapa, 2000). Any work associated with mechanized transport, including driving and working as a minibus call boy or mechanic tends to be viewed as a male preserve (Porter, 2008).

Young people as load carriers in southern Ghana: evidence from traffic and load-weighing surveys

This chapter is based principally on work conducted in Gomoa, one of Ghana's poorest districts. The coastal savanna district is largely dependent on agriculture (maize, cassava, peppers and tomatoes) but suffers from unreliable rainfall, lack of credit for farmers, strong fluctuations in agricultural prices, high input costs and poor roads. Labour shortage is also a problem: many young men have migrated out to the forest zone where they can participate in more lucrative cash crop cultivation. Research focused on four off-road settlements, located between 3 and 8 kms from a paved road. All are primarily Fante villages, though in each there are some stranger farmers from other parts of Ghana. We also worked further north in a fifth (forest zone) village, Aworabo, in Assin district.[2] Assin has a much stronger emphasis on cash crops than Gomoa; cocoa is an important and relatively lucrative local crop. In Aworabo, 25 km from the nearest paved road, there is ample farm land and consequently the Twi-speaking indigenes have been joined by settlers from other areas, including Gomoa.

Our attention to the issue of load carrying among young people first came about as a result of research we conducted on women's access to markets in these five villages in the late 1990s.[3] We undertook a series of traffic surveys, which drew our attention to the remarkably large number of children carrying loads. When we had the opportunity to extend the work with an action research project focused on introducing and monitoring the impact of Intermediate Means of Transport (IMTs) in the villages, in 2000–2003, we incorporated load-weighing in the research design. The action project involved a range of transport equipment (principally locally made push carts and bicycles) and was aimed at assisting women to access local markets.

Loads were weighed in the course of traffic surveys conducted both prior to the introduction of IMTs in 2000, and approximately 20 months after their introduction in June/July 2002.[4] Head loads were counted and weighed, on both a farm day and a market day, along farm and market routes. The weighing (by a team of assistants from two local universities) commenced as dawn broke and continued until 6 p.m. June/July was the most appropriate time of year for this exercise because we wanted to capture conditions in the harvest period, but prior to the September peak when people would be too busy to stop. Weighing points were situated on approach routes to the village, but beyond the principal village water points (because our main focus was on agricultural produce movements).

In the period between the two load-weighing exercises we also charted the impacts of the IMT intervention on the lives of village children. Additionally, we conducted interviews about load carrying with over 30 individual school children (outside school), children who do not attend school, groups of primary and junior secondary school (JSS) children in class, and individual parents and teachers. We tried to keep the interviews with children as informal as possible: they were easily intimidated and in the initial interviews only the bravest in a group would speak. We asked about time spent headloading, the nature of the journeys undertaken, the perceived impact, any income or other benefit, and parental and teacher attitudes to headloading. The interviewing on children's travel (with and without loads) was subsequently extended to include another two junior secondary schools and two senior schools serving the study districts.

In our load-weighing surveys we found that, despite the positioning of the weighing points beyond the water points (which were the focus of many more shorter journeys by children carrying water for domestic supply), the load-carrying journeys of children and young people under the age of 18 were almost as numerous as load-carrying journeys by men over 18 years (though women over the age of 18 years undertook almost half of all load-carrying journeys; see Table 13.2). Thus, women overall undertook 47 per cent of load trips, men 27 per cent, girls under 18 years 12 per cent and boys under 18 years 14 per cent. The adult men we recorded carrying loads were mostly carrying cash crops for onward sale rather than goods for domestic use.

In terms of individual weights carried, girls under 18 years were carrying loads of up to 36 kg[5] and boys in the same age-range up to 39 kg (Table 13.1). During our fieldwork we observed that girls of 15 years and older were regularly carrying 20–30 kg. The commonest head loads carried by young people and adults were cassava, maize, firewood, vegetables and charcoal. The heaviest loads were recorded at Abora, where firewood and wooden pestles are carried regularly to the district headquarters for sale. Young men may help their wives and mothers to carry firewood intended for sale, but will leave the village before dawn in order to avoid observation (since wood carrying is considered inappropriate for men.) Consequently, they were largely unrecorded in the survey: they deliberately left before the recorders arrived at the settlement on the survey days.

The practice of load carrying among young people in the study area: their own and others' perspectives

It is evident from the interviews with young people that they simply expect to headload. Children are widely perceived as a domestic resource by adults

Table 13.1 Maximum loads carried by children according to age

Age	Male (load in kg)	Female (load in kg)
0–6	7	6
7–8	8.5	12
9	10	11
10	10	18
11	15	17.5
12	19	18
13	18	22
14	20	27
15	28	21
16	26.5	36
17	39	34
18	25.5	35

Source: Data from weighing exercise, Gomoa and Assin districts, June–July 2000.

Table 13.2 Number and percentage of head/cycle[1] load trips on specific village routes, June–July 2000

Village name and route F = farm day M = market day	Women		Men		Girls (under 18 years)		Boys (under 18 years)	
	n	%	n	%	n	%	n	%
Gomoa-Abora:								
Apam path F	57	55	22	21	12	11.5	13	12.5
Ankamu road F	27	27	21	21	23	23	28	28
Brofoyedur F	22	37	16	27	11	18	11	18
Apam path M	104	76	11	8	11	8	11	8
Gomoa-Adabra:								
Farm path F	49	55	28	32	10	11	2	2
Akoti junction M	22	59	9	24	4	11	2	5
Gomoa-Lome:								
Well path F	127	44	65	23	41	14	54	19
Nduam road F	95	40	57	24	30	13	54	23
Oguan road F	75	45	51	29	24	14	20	11
Gomoa-Sampa:								
Brofo junction F	46	43	38	35	14	13	10	9
Okye river path F	39	45	40	46	4	4.5	4	4.5
Akropong junction M	110	53	53	25	22	10.5	24	11.5
Brofo junction M	38	70	10	18	4	7	2	4
Assin-Aworabo:								
Japan bridge F	51	39	43	33	18	14	20	15
Farm path F	34	44	29	38	2	3	12	15.5
Odumasi path M	29	41	34	48	7	9	1	1.5
Total	925	47	527	27	237	12	268	14

1 Cycle loads consist solely of three loads in all, all ridden by men in their twenties and thirties. The survey indicates the remarkably low usage of cycles for load carrying in the study area.

and are required to carry a range of loads for their parents and other family members. This applies to both girls and boys (though as noted above, boys will usually not carry loads such as firewood and water intended for domestic use beyond the age of about 15 years.) At Abora, the study village most heavily involved in commercial firewood trade, both boys and girls from the age of about 10 say they regularly carry large loads of firewood to the district headquarters (about 5 kms away) and sell it there before they come to school: a journey of around 10 kms.

I sell [firewood I've collected myself] on the weekend or when I've no money on me. I write some notes that I'm sick [(to explain absence from school]. I started selling when I was 10 years old. [*prompt*] I carry about three-quarters of a woman's load. In Apam I get 3000 or 3500 cedis for

> every head load . . . if I have no firewood to convey [my parents] give me
> theirs to sell – I share the load with my junior brother then.
>
> (Kofi, 14 years, Abora)

Younger children accompany their mothers to the market early in the morning, carrying their own small firewood load to sell – some give the proceeds
to their mothers, others are allowed to spend it themselves: 'if the little ones
get 1000 cedis for selling wood, they may use it to buy things and to hire
bikes – it's all gone before they return home to Abora' (Essi, young mother
c. 20 years, Abora).

Although the data from our traffic surveys suggested that girls carry more
regularly and that their loads are often heavier than those carried by boys
of the same age, children both in class and informal discussions often disagreed (and not always in accordance with their gender) about whether boys
or girls carry the heaviest loads. In Aworabo, where we conducted a class
discussion on travel and headloading with class six primary school pupils, of
the 23 pupils (all aged between 12–15 years), 21 said they regularly carried
goods for their mothers. The two exceptions were both boys. The heaviest
loads they carry are cocoa and, above all, firewood. The boys were happy
to be involved in carrying cocoa, a commercial crop, saying 'we have the
strength', but complained that they disliked carrying firewood (which in
this village is principally for domestic use). This attitude accords with the
common male view regarding carrying products for domestic as opposed
to commercial use. One 15-year-old boy remarked, 'we feel shy to carry the
firewood because the girls will be laughing at us'. In another discussion
group with young in-school and out of school boys (all under the age of 15)
in Lome village we were told,

> here it is not the work of men to carry firewood, but sometimes we can
> carry it from the farm to a certain place for the woman to bring home
> . . . From 13 to 14 years . . . our mothers know that we should not carry
> firewood, so they would not load us any longer, but we can still carry it
> to a certain point [unobserved] for them to bring home.

The common parental attitude to load carrying among children and young
people is that this is a necessary and normal contribution to the household.
The load weight will be increased as the child grows older and stronger. Tiny
children of three or four years, especially girls, will often be given a small
plastic bowl of water to carry. A number of parents suggested (very similar)
guidelines regarding loads they would expect a child to carry at particular
ages, roughly as follows: a child of 4–5 years, whether boy or girl, should be
able to carry half a rubber of maize (4 kg); a child of 8 should be able to
carry a full rubber of maize (8 kg) this being approximately one-quarter of
an adult load; a child of around 10 could carry two rubbers (16 kg) or a full
tray of cassava (perhaps 20 kg), and before the age of 15 years they may be

expected to carry four rubbers (32 kg). One mother suggested that stature could influence load-carrying ability; her ten-year-old daughter could not carry as much as others her age: 'because she is very short I don't want to load her'. None wished to distinguish different load capacities by gender for the younger age groups, though one mother observed that 'girls start [carrying] from 5 years, [the] boy can start if he chooses to do so at the same age, but you can't force him . . . my 6-year-old does not carry at all, because he is stubborn'. By the age of 15 a girl is expected to be able to carry a full adult's load, ranging from around 40 to as high as 70 kg, whereas boys are thought to mature later to a full adult's load. The maximum loads carried by children of different age groups we weighed (Figure 13.1) conform roughly to their observations.[6]

Comments in informal discussion with adults in the villages suggested that often it is foster children who experience the heaviest burden – a load perhaps 'beyond their age' in terms of headloading, as in many other domestic duties (Bledsoe and Brandon, 1992). More research is needed on the specific burdens faced by fostered children.

Educational and health impacts of load carrying on young people

The impacts of load carrying on children and young people's educational attainment may be substantial, especially in areas where the transport gap is significant. Much load carrying is undertaken on the way to and from school, particularly in rural locations. Indeed, in our study area young girls seem to be more commonly observed carrying a bucket of maize or a bag of groceries on their head than a school bag or school books. Corn or other grains for the grinders, for instance, will be taken on the way to school, then picked up afterwards. Thus Felicia, a girl from a satellite village, described how she carries a bucket of rice from home every day 3 km to the grinders in the village, Aworabo, where her school is located.

Such multi-purpose journeys may substantially lengthen both route and journey times to school. School teachers working in the five study villages complained that these domestic transport tasks undertaken before or on the way to school delayed children's arrival and in some cases made them late, a punishable offence. Only in the case of Assin Foso, a local town, did we find an exception to this pattern of load carrying on the journey to and from school. While parents still expect children to carry for them after school, there is apparently less need in this urban context for most (town-based) children to combine the school journey with other tasks to the same degree evident in the villages, because most services lie in relatively close proximity to urban homes.

In our study villages, load carrying, especially on market days may require absence from school for the whole day (as in Kofi's case, above). Particularly around harvest time and on market days, the need to transport large quantities of goods from village to market often led to children being required by their parents or other family members to go to market instead of school:

> [During the cocoa harvest] some from distant villages stay away – you have to give them time to rest – they complain of tiredness. If parents need goods to market at Odumasi, children don't come to school. So there's lower attendance on Wednesdays.
>
> (Male JSS teacher, Aworabo)

In some cases children were carrying goods to market to earn money from other villagers who needed assistance. Where the market is distant from the school attended, or the child's presence is needed to move goods around within the market, or to mind the stall during the day, truancy may be preferable for the child to arriving late at school, given the punishments that are likely to follow.

Regular lateness and truancy will inevitably impact on many village children's performance at school and has been noted as a common cause of withdrawal from school in Ghana, especially among girls (Avotri *et al.*, 1999: 51, 122–3). Additionally, some teachers (perhaps significantly mostly young teachers without children of their own) and many children in our study villages observed that carrying such heavy loads impairs pupils' subsequent work in school, due to tiredness, headaches and associated lack of concentration. One (male) teacher suggested that load carrying affects girls' educational attainment more than boys because they are expected to carry more on the way to school.

The health impacts of load carrying are more controversial: we certainly encountered some mismatch between the discourse of parents and young people where this topic is concerned. The parents we interviewed in our five village study were usually keen to stress the way loads are graduated according to age and the value of children's work in general as a mode of socialization into adult life. Girls, in particular, we were told are trained in load carrying from an early age: there is no issue for the majority (though occasional maltreatment of fostered children was recognized in this respect). The children and young people we spoke to also clearly accept their labour responsibilities in household maintenance, but when we enquired about their experiences of load carrying, they frequently referred to head ache, waist pain, neck pain, and the exhaustion. As noted above, some teachers and children suggest the pain and exhaustion is sufficient in some cases to impact negatively on school performance. In the class discussion with 12- to 15-year-old pupils at Aworabo, all 23 children who regularly carried loads for their mothers said they often suffered neck, waist or head pains from carrying produce. Two of the girls and one boy said they had missed school in the previous few weeks because they were too tired from headloading. However, other questions arise: are there longer-term consequences of carrying heavy loads through childhood which are felt in adulthood or old age? Are there particularly significant impacts on females, if they have carried heavier loads than males in childhood? Are there consequent intergenerational impacts?

A review of transport-related literature provides occasional reference to potential areas for concern, especially regarding girls and women in pregnancy and women in later life. Bryceson and Howe (1993) refer to Kenyan medical sources showing high incidence of backache among Masai women and treatment of 'Kikuyu bursa', osteo-arthritis of the soft tissue of the knee caused by load carrying (citing Curtis, 1986) and women fuelwood carriers in an Ethiopian survey who reported high rates of miscarriage. Doran (1990: 58) suggests that energy-intensive work can be detrimental to foetus formation and breast-milk capacity. Malmberg Calvo (1994) notes that vertebral column deformation may occur, while a pamphlet produced by WaterAid (1996), suggests impact of water loads has especially serious implications for girls, given their immaturity – notably damage to head, neck and spine. It notes that deformity of the spine in extreme cases can lead to problems in pregnancy and child birth. Agarwal *et al.*'s (1994) study of girl porters in Accra referred to earlier does not distinguish among the 'many health problems' (p. 8) but notes that many self-medicate regularly to numb pain and allow continued work. Much of this material is limited in terms of the scale of enquiry and in some cases hypothesizes impact rather than providing firm evidence: this is an area where more detailed research is needed.

Intermediate means of transport (IMT): a potential low cost substitute for headloading?

In our action research study we introduced a set of IMTs which would substitute for headloading at relatively low cost (compared to motorized transport). These were offered to villagers on credit, with women given priority. It is useful to outline some of the findings relating to young people, because of the policy implications regarding IMTs as a possible substitute for headloading.

When the IMTs were introduced in the project, we had not adequately appreciated the importance of child labour in headloading, nor children's potential contribution to the IMT operations. After the IMTs were introduced, many children were found to have used the equipment (notably bicycles and push trucks) for a variety of different purposes, including leisure. This prompted further investigations with teachers, school-going and out-of-school children and their parents. Households who took project IMTs were mostly those with child labour available to operate them. As one old women pointed out, 'If you have children to operate it [push truck] it is easy to collect one, but if there is no child you cannot operate it.' (Lome, January 2002). Whereas young boys undertake headloading as a duty, they were found to treat IMT operation as a game:

'it is very fantastic when you push'; 'we enjoy it very much and push willingly'; 'since the truck is there I find it easier to work on the farm'; 'we were not enjoying the work at the farm, but now because of the truck we want to go there.'

(Group of young boys, Lome, July 2001)

Unfortunately, because we had not anticipated child operation and thus did not provide adequate safety training for children at the outset of the project, some minor accidents occurred. Interestingly, as is the case with technology more generally, the operation of the push trucks was very quickly appropriated by young boys: 'My grandson just takes the truck out and ten boys will be there straight away to go to farm . . . after the farm work is done the boys play on it until it's time to fetch water' (older man, Adabra, July 2002). Girls were reportedly not involved because they are 'not as strong as boys' and because 'girls should be working at the kitchen' (men's group, Lome, July 2002).

We attempted a preliminary assessment of the substitution impact of our project IMTs for headloading, including headloading among young people, 20 months after their introduction. The traffic surveys conducted in June/July 2002 suggested that project IMTs may have reduced maximum load size for young people under 18 years, and this was supported to some extent by qualitative findings which indicated that young people now did less headloading, although the boys were heavily involved in operating the push trucks. At village review workshops, young people's work loads were specifically observed in two of the villages to be lower as a result of IMT adoption. In Adabra, men argued that the children had more time to play now, rather than less, because of the reduction in headloading, while at Abora the children were said to do less work because now they could just go once per day for water, instead of making three or four trips. At Aworabo women observed that whereas boys used to play football after school, they now helped operate the IMTs (which offers another type of play). However, so far as girls are concerned the reduction in headloading may not be entirely beneficial, if they previously earned money as porters, a point made by some JSS schoolgirls at Sampa: 'Previously we helped people to convey maize and we got maize (in payment), but now with the truck people do not call us again'.

Conclusion

In Ghana, children carrying loads are perceived by adults to be performing a natural function of youth. The carrying they are expected to do, in the absence of alternative cheap and reliable transportation, can be interpreted as embodied, performed and 'naturalized' social position. Portering is a very low status occupation. Children and young people tend to occupy the lowest rung in the Ghanaian social hierarchy (Porter and Abane, 2008). Young porters do not merely perform their tasks but, through the bodily positions they take up, are seen to enact their social position as servants to their (adult) masters. Carrying is arguably a daily reaffirmation of mobile servility. The complex intertwining of perceptions about physical capabilities and gender stereotyping supports this interpretation: trucks are too hard for girls to push, yet girls are expected to contribute more than boys when it comes to porterage. Girls, in particular, are trained in the embodied skill of headloading because it is a skill on which they will be expected to draw throughout their lives. The load they carry is increased gradually over time, in this careful body management. They can be construed to be building up body capital (Jackson and Palmer-Jones, 1998): flexibility, muscle tone and strength will all be developed over years of hard work.

However, as we have discussed, long hours spent carrying loads may be extremely damaging in terms of young people's future life chances. Children's time expenditure on headloading in the survey villages appeared to be very substantial, though variable according to gender, age and season, so that we were unable to quantify this. Our evidence for impacts on both education and health is limited by the scale of our enquiry. Carefully disaggregated studies of women's, girls' and boys' load-carrying effort in different cultural and environmental contexts are urgently needed across sub-Saharan Africa, given the potential implications of load carrying for health and educational achievement.[7] Perhaps specific kinds of IMTs such as push trucks and load-carrying cycles could reduce the burden of carrying, but we will not know their potential, including the gendered impacts of uptake, without more detailed research.

Appendix 1

Maximum headloads carried on specific routes in each village by age group

Village name F = farm day M = market day	Women (load in kg)	Men (load in kg)	Girls (under 18), age indicated if under 16 years (load in kg)	Boys (under 18), age indicated if under 16 years (load in kg)
Gomoa-Abora:				
Apam path M	58	21	34	36
Apam path F	61	52	22	31
Ankamu road F	30.5	27	20.5	21.5
Brofoyedur road F	36	23.5	15 (12 years)	21.5
Gomoa-Adabra:				
Farm path F	33	45	9 (14 years)	15
Kumakope M	42	45	22	22
Akoti junction M	40	32	22	20
Gomoa-Lome:				
Well path F	48	43	22 (13 years)	39
Nduam road F	24	38	36	34 (15 years)
Oguan road F	43	45	25	25 (15 years)
Gomoa-Sampa:				
Brofo junction F	32	23.5	24	23.5
Okye river path F	42	31	18 (13 years)	19 (14 years)
Akropong junction F	42.5	46.5	25	19.5
Brofo junction M	44.5	10.5	26	24.5
Assin-Aworabo:				
Japan bridge F	37	26	30	18 (15 years)
Odumasi path M	36	35	12 (14 years)	11

Source: Data from weighing exercise, Gomoa and Assin districts, June–July 2000.

Notes

1 Though there are many broader studies of children's work (e.g. Robson, 1996).
2 We originally intended to confine our study to Gomoa but were requested to include a village in Assin district by the Ministry of Agriculture, which was collaborating in the project.
3 The earlier market access research was conducted by Gina Porter with Frank Owusu Acheampong as research assistant. In the second study Kathrin Blaufuss and Frank Owusu Acheampong were both RAs.
4 We comment here principally on weighing and traffic data for 2000 because this relates to conditions before our project transport equipment was introduced and is thus more representative of load-carrying conditions in the region than post-intervention data.
5 Doran (1990: 11) refers to women's 'normal' loads of 25–35 kg, 'though loads of up to 60 kg have been reported'.
6 In a related study in northern Ghana, Flanary (2004) weighed loads for one day within two compounds during the rains. In the compound where there were many young children, girls aged 8–14 years carried 72 per cent of water, with individual loads of 13–26 kg carried over about 0.5 km.
7 Gina Porter is currently leading a research project on child mobility which includes further work on children and young people as load-carriers (see www.dur.ac.uk/child.mobility/).

References

Agarwal, S., Attah, M., Apt, N., Grieco, M., Kwakye, E.A. and Turner, J. (1994) Bearing the weight: the kayayoo, Ghana's working girl child. Paper presented at the UNICEF conference on the girl child, Delhi, February 1994.

Avotri, R., Owusu-Darko, L., Eghan, H. and Ocansey, S. (1999) *Gender and Primary Schooling in Ghana*. Sussex: Institute of Development Studies.

Bledsoe, C. and Brandon, A. (1992) Child fosterage and child mortality in sub-Saharan Africa: some preliminary questions and answers. In E. van de Walle, G. Pison and M. Sala-Diakanda (eds) *Mortality and Society in sub-Saharan Africa*, pp. 279–302.

Bryceson, D. and Howe, J. (1993) Rural household transport in Africa: reducing the burden on women? *World Development*, 21(11): 1715–28.

Curtis, V. (1986) *Women and the Transport of Water*. London: IT Publications.

De Boek, F. and Honwana, A. (2005) Children and youth in Africa: agency, identity and place. In A. Honwana and F. de Boek (eds) *Makers and Breakers: children and youth in postcolonial Africa*. Oxford: James Currey: pp. 1–18.

Doran, J. (1990) A moving issue for women: is low cost transport an appropriate intervention to alleviate women's burden in sub-Saharan Africa. Norwich: School of Development Studies, University of East Anglia, Gender analysis discussion paper no. 1.

Flanary, R.M. (2004) Gender and embodied mobility: learning in Tarsaw, northern Ghana. PhD thesis, University of Durham.

Grieco, M., Apt, N. and Turner, J. (1996) *At Christmas and on Rainy Days: transport, travel and the female traders of Accra*. Aldershot: Avebury.

Jackson, C. and Palmer-Jones, R. (1998) *Work Intensity, Gender and Well-being*, Geneva: UNRISD Discussion Paper 96, October 1998.

Mahapa, S. (2000) Carting in the Northern Province: structural and geographical change. *Development Southern Africa*, 117(2): 235–48.

Malmberg Calvo, C. (1994) Case studies on the role of women in rural transport: access of women to domestic facilities. Washington DC: World Bank, SSATP Working Paper 11.

Porter, G. (2008) Transport planning in sub-Saharan Africa. Progress report 2: putting gender into mobility and transport planning in Africa. *Progress in Development Studies*, 8(3): 281–9.

Porter, G. and Abane, A. (2008) Increasing children's participation in African transport planning: reflections on methodological issues in a child-centred research project. *Children's Geographies*, 6(2): 151–67.

Porter, G., Blaufuss, K. and Owusu Acheampong, F. (2007) Youth, mobility and rural livelihoods in sub-Saharan Africa: perspectives from Ghana and Nigeria. *Africa Insight*, 37(3): 420–31.

Potgieter, C.-A., Pillay, R. and Rama, S. (2006) *Women, Development and Transport* in rural Eastern Cape, South Africa. Cape Town: HSRC Press.

Robson, E. (1996) Working girls and boys: children's contributions to household survival in West Africa. *Geography*, 81(4): 43–7.

WaterAid (1996) *Children and Transport*. London: WaterAid.

14 Adult anxieties versus young people's resistance

Negotiating access to public space in Singapore

Tracey Skelton and
Nafisah Abdul Hamed

Introduction

In this chapter we explore the ways in which access to Singaporean public space, particularly at night, is controlled and surveilled by adults in ways that seek to constrain young people's movements in and through such spaces. However, we show that control is never absolute but contested in a range of ways (Foucault, 1977). We consider adults' motivations behind their attempted constriction of young people's night wanderings and the ways in which young people engage in processes of negotiation, strategization and the use of tactics (de Certeau, 1984) to establish resistive actions so that they can spend time in their neighbourhood public spaces such as streets, neighbourhood shopping malls and void decks[1] (see Plate 14.1).

The Singaporean state government is dominated by one party, the People's Action Party (PAP), which has controlled the nation-state since its independence from Malaysia in 1965. Singapore has some elements of democracy such as a parliamentary system of government, an elected president, regular, free, well-administered elections and universal suffrage. However, the PAP controls political action and participation, has legislation designed to limit civil and political rights and controls the freedom of the press (Mauzy and Milne, 2002). Nevertheless there is a strong focus on social provision: public housing is available for mortgage at subsidized rates; national education is free and of a high standard in terms of provision, professionalism of teachers and administration by the Ministry of Education; and health care delivered through affordable insurance schemes is widely available and accessible. The government has a strong sense of providing for its citizens but expects responsible, loyal and obedient behaviour from them. Consequently, conformity is a very dominant social and political discourse that filters down through all political and civil institutions – schools and the family included. Hence, in Singapore, teenagers aged 13 to 16 (our focus) are not only trained and monitored by the police and their parents, they also have to follow strict regulations imposed by schools which expect high degrees of

Plate 14.1 Void deck space at night.

conformity and discipline their behaviour within, to and from schools.

In 2006, the government became anxious about teenagers appearing to commit crimes such as snatch thefts, as well as becoming victims of such misdemeanours (Tan, 2006). It instructed the police to implement a controversial measure to keep teens off the streets after 11 p.m. As shops and food outlets in local and central malls and hawker centres are often open until 10 p.m. and public transport runs until 11.30 p.m. or 12.30 a.m., then 11 p.m. is considered 'late enough' for teenagers to be out. The authorities assured the public that this was not a curfew (Channel NewsAsia, 2006a, 2006b), but rather police checks aimed to 'protect potential victims' (Teo, 2006). In a bid to 'partner parents' police send letters to parents of teenagers below the age of 17 caught loitering in public places. This 'non-curfew initiative' shows how the regulation of young teenagers' spatial autonomy not only lies in the hands of parents, but also other authoritative figures, such as the police and the state. It also demonstrates the ways in which the state intervenes in family parenting practices.

In this chapter we critically engage with literature on young people and public space, making an argument for a less-Western approach. We outline adults' anxieties, concerns and tensions about the ways young people use and access public spaces in the night-time.[2] We examine how adults control young teenagers in Singapore and impose regulatory regimes. Finally, we consider the approaches young people take to establish spatialities of freedom from the adult gaze, control and discipline of their night-time mobilities, in turn forming their own resistive identities.

Young people and public space

Where children and young people go, how they get there and what they do when they get there occupies the minds of parents, authorities and academics. There has been a tendency to construct teenagers' behaviour and spatial practices as universal with the Western / Minority World perspectives dominating debates. Several geographers focusing on young people and children have more recently noted that Western ideals of childhood and youth need to be interrogated and critically examined (Holt and Holloway, 2006; Punch, 2002; Robson, 2004; Skelton, 2009). It is imperative to be aware of the danger of subsuming the multiple experiences of a diverse range of young people under a single, dominant meta-narrative. Social and political constructions determine the diverse constraints young people experience in various spaces and places, hence highlighting the need to account for the heterogeneity of experiences in the geographies of young people. Nevertheless, dominant discourses produced in the Minority World have strong reach and influence practices way beyond their geography, consider, for example, the influence of the UN Convention on the Rights of the Child (Skelton, 2007). Singapore, constructing itself as both Western and Asian (Ang and Stratton, 1995), has been particularly susceptible to Western influences, particularly in approaches to public space. However, the authorities have attempted to disguise or adapt Western strategies, hence the introduction of 'police checks' rather than a formalized 'curfew' as utilized in Western countries (Matthews *et al.*, 1999; and see Collins and Kearns, 2001 for a detailed discussion of curfews as legal mechanisms in the USA and New Zealand).

Young people are known the world over to 'hang out' and geographers (and other social scientists) have investigated the ways in which young people establish a presence in public spaces (Chatterton and Hollands, 2002; Pain *et al.*, 2005; Thomas, 2005; Toon, 2000; White, 1993; Young, 2003). There have been studies that specifically focus on the street (Cahill, 2000; Gough and Franch, 2005; Matthews, 2003; Skelton, 2000, 2009; Watt and Stenson, 1998) and shopping malls (Anthony, 1985; Koskela, 2000; Matthews *et al.*, 2000; O'Dougherty, 2006; Vanderbeck and Johnson, 2000). One of the dominant themes that run through these studies on young people and spaces is how they often face adult regulatory regimes. Matthews *et al.* (2000) showed how adults feel that the visible presence of young people in spaces of the mall is inappropriate. Young teenagers are found to challenge the adult hegemony of public spaces (Skelton, 2000; Valentine, 1996). Several studies examine the exclusion of young people in public space and the policing of their movements (Collins and Kearns, 2001; Morrow, 2002; Ruefle and Reynolds, 1995).

Yarwood (2007) argued that attention should be shifted from 'the police' towards 'policing'. This is because an increasing number of agencies, other than the police, are performing policing, such as the state, private, and voluntary actors and seeking to impose regulatory regimes on young people. Sibley (2003), has shown how adults desire more direct control over spaces through the direct exclusion of particular groups such as young people. Children and young people are also often restricted by parental concerns about their safety in public spaces (Valentine, 1997; Valentine and McKendrick, 1997; Pain, 2006). Nevertheless, research on young people and public space is predominantly centred on Western experiences and practices. In this chapter we want to explore particular aspects of adult control over public space (namely adult anxieties) and young Malaysian-, Chinese- and Indian-Singaporean's resistive tactics and strategies within an Asian geography. First, though, we outline the context of the research, geographically and methodologically.

Teenagers in Singapore

Singapore has a total population of 4,839,400 of which 3.64 million are Singaporean citizens and permanent residents (Population Trends, 2008). The ethnic composition of the resident population is 74.7 per cent Chinese, 13.6 per cent Malay and 8.9 per cent Indian. There are 517,000 Singaporean residents aged 10–19 (data specifically for 13- to 16-year-olds are not available) hence they constitute 14.2 per cent of the total population. By ethnicity this age group is 70 per cent Chinese, 18 per cent Malay and 8.5 per cent Indian (the percentage of Malay youth aged 10–19 is slightly higher than the proportion for the overall population). Singaporean authorities are pro-population growth and provide a range of resources to support parents of children (although unmarried parents get minimal support). Education is compulsory for children aged 6–15 (although, children with special needs are exempt) and Singapore spends about 20 per cent of its national budget on education. Parental costs to send children to state schools are very low.

Research was done with both young teenagers and adults in the northern part of Singapore. Participants were recruited through an after-school tuition centre catering for secondary school students. Eighty young people aged 13–16 and 80 parents and other adults completed questionnaires. The northern part of Singapore is an area where Malay Singaporeans constitute a relatively high proportion of the population and so they are slightly over-represented compared with total population statistics (see Tables 14.1 and 14.2). Twelve teenagers and six parents/adults agreed to be interviewed in-depth and all interviewees were given false names. Additionally, discourse analysis of the Singapore media's (print and television) discussions about young teenagers was conducted.

Interviews with parents provided a deeper understanding of why they imposed regulations on their teenagers; interviews with teenagers garnered

Table 14.1 Profile of young teenagers

		Survey sample		Interview sample	
		Number	(%)	Number	(%)
Sex	Male	42	52.5	8	66.7
	Female	38	47.5	4	33.3
	Total	80	100	12	100
Ethnic group	Chinese	26	32.5	3	25
	Malay	47	58.75	8	66.7
	Indian	7	8.75	1	8.3
	Total	80	100	12	100

Table 14.2 Profile of adults and parents

		Survey sample		Interview sample	
		Number	(%)	Number	(%)
Sex	Male	35	43.75	3	50
	Female	45	56.25	3	50
	Total	80	100	6	100
Ethnic group	Chinese	31	38.75	2	33.3
	Malay	44	55	3	50
	Indian	5	6.25	1	16.7
	Total	80	100	6	100

their perceptions and experiences of being regulated and how they negotiated restrictions. These interviews (and to some extent the questionnaires)
revealed interesting contradictions between the opinions of adults and
young people. Hence this chapter contributes to the, as yet limited, debate
within young people's geographies about the roles, rights, responsibilities
and authority of parents and adults in the context of children's lives (but see
Ansell, 2009; Matthews and Limb, 1999; Vanderbeck, 2008).

Adult anxieties

Here we examine the regulatory regimes that are being imposed on
Singaporean teenagers and the motivations behind them. In the Singapore
media, teenagers have rarely been featured in a positive light; the central
focus is on acts of delinquency. Additionally, there are commentaries on

parent–child relationships and the fact that parents have to take responsibility for their child's behaviour. Moral panics about children beyond the control of parents have been used to justify regulations imposed on teenagers. In our study 95 per cent of parents felt that the police checks were necessary and 61 per cent felt that regulations should be placed on young people and provided a range of responses as to why they felt this (Figure 14.1).

While the reasons most often cited for imposing regulations on young teenagers' spaces were notions of safety (69 per cent of adults felt that young people were vulnerable to dangers in public space), we argue that adults simultaneously seek to maintain a spatial hegemony over young people by regulating the spaces they can access. These structural exclusions of young people are increasingly hidden within rhetorical proclamations of serving the best interests of the child. There is a need here to problematize this assumption given the nature of adult–child relations and the uncritical acceptance of the shielding and protective role of adults over children and young people. The notion of protection is very heavily supported in Singaporean discourses about young people, with less emphasis on provision and limited, to no emphasis, on participation.

The 'others' who were seen as a threat to teenagers were in part identified as other teenagers. However, other threatening influences included the media, Western culture, dangerous strangers and a change of housing form (from kampong village-style dwelling to high-rise HDB apartments[3]).

Mdm Hanisah (Malay mother of two teenage daughters) and Mr Tan (Chinese father of a 15-year-old son) illustrate these points (all quotations are written verbatim and reflect Singaporean grammar):

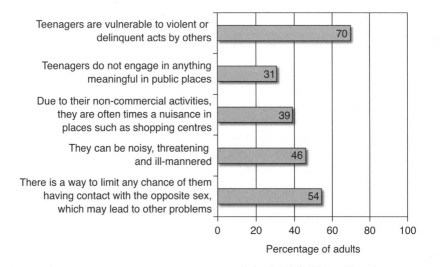

Figure 14.1 Reasons for imposing regulations on young teenagers' spaces.

I am very strict with my two daughters. They have to be back by a certain time and I wouldn't allow them to go out unless there is truly a need to. They're still young girls, you know. They don't understand how dangerous the outside world can be. Just the other day, I saw a sign by the police about an outrage of modesty.[4] Those sickos, they always target young, innocent girls. So, if they need to be back late because of school, I would ask their Dad to pick them up. It's not safe nowadays. We used to stay in kampong houses last time [before], we know everyone in the village. So our parents do not worry about us too much. They knew there'll always be other adults watching over us. Now not anymore.

(Mdm Hanisah)

For this parent, even the close neighbourhood is not seen as safe. Clearly she feels her daughters need protection, escorting and a family curfew to keep them safe.

Mr Tan asserts his adult authority in the home in order to be sure he can protect his son from the dangers of the Internet, but also relates this to minimizing distractions from school work. In Singapore educational success is an extremely powerful discourse and aspiration (hence the plethora of after-school tuition centres). For many young Singaporeans there is intense pressure to succeed academically and parents become very anxious if they have a 'failing child'.

It's difficult for parents nowadays. We're trying our best to protect our children but there's all these violence and inappropriate scenes being shown on TV and the Internet, right in our own home, and that's where they get all the negative influences. I wouldn't allow him (his son) to have a computer in his bedroom. I told him, you're still schooling, and as long as you are, you would have to abide by the rules in this house. He has to learn to listen to the one in charge here.

(Mr Tan)

Adults in the survey had very clear views as to who should determine accessible spaces for teenagers and that taking such responsibilities were seen as aspects of good parenting, but also as a response to their own surveillance by, and expectations of, other adults and the state (Figure 14.2). In some cases it is 'good grand-parenting' that increases the control as parents of parents exert control over how children should be disciplined. In Singapore there are very strong intergenerational family ties and grandparents play important roles in their grandchildren's lives (Vanderbeck, 2007).

Mdm Norin (Malay) stated:

Sometimes, my mother calls me up in the evening and asks if my son's home. There was once he wasn't and she nagged saying how I should not let him out till so late at night and all. It was only about 6 or 7 p.m.

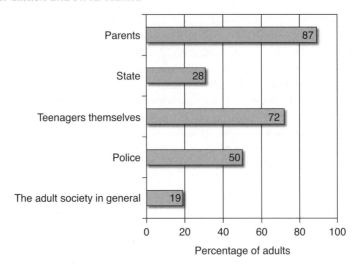

Figure 14.2 Adults' opinions on who should be involved in determining accessible spaces for young teenagers.

actually, but you know, the older generation's more traditional. So to please her, I agreed to make sure my son would come home earlier. I know she's just being concerned about her grandson.

Despite the sense that adults, particularly parents, should determine young teenagers' access to public space, it is worthy of note in Figure 14.2, that 72 per cent of adults felt that teenagers themselves should determine which spaces were appropriate for them. This therefore hints at processes of negotiation and dialogue between parents and teenagers.

There is a range of state imposed age restrictions for public places in Singapore; for places serving alcohol it is 18; for gaming arcades it is 16 and there is no entry for children in school uniform. Bars and clubs are constructed as sites for 'adult' leisure and pleasure; teenagers are unwelcome and seen as out of place. There is a sense of adult territoriality (Sack, 1986):

> I am glad there are age limits to these clubs and discos. Those are spaces where adults enjoy and relax after working hours. There's alcohol, and smoking and basically other 'adults' stuff. That's the last place teenagers should be at.
> (Mrs Chan, Chinese, mother of three children aged 17, 14 and 9)

Parents also construct adult territoriality (which can be highly gender inscribed) in the home-space; 88 per cent felt they should regulate teenagers' spaces and activities within the home:

My kids know what they must do when I'm having a conversation with friends or family members. The girl usually will be at the kitchen with her mum preparing drinks, while my son will be in his room. But, when the guests come, they must come out to the living room to greet them. That's basic courtesy.

(Mr Ahmed, Indian, father of two aged 13 and 15)

Adult and state control of spaces, as we have seen, is not only due to the protection of 'innocent' young people in 'adult' spaces. Such uncritical acceptance of 'protection' by adults conceals larger issues of the social and spatial marginalization of young people through processes of territoriality. It is important to uncover other reasons that motivate adults to exclude young people from various socio-spatial activities and how these help to maintain adult hegemony in and through space. Accepting these naturalized discourses will ultimately lead to the persistence of the marginalization of young people's access to spaces. This is due to unequal power relations between the adult and child that constantly place childhood in opposition to adulthood (which is also reflected in the state and citizen power relations of Singapore). These unequal power relations are materialized in space as adults practice forms of territoriality in order to exclude young teenagers from certain places.

Regulations too act as a manifestation of parents' ability to carry out constructed and idealized notions of 'good parents'. This demonstrates that regulations are not always about the best interests of the child but contribute towards the best interests of adults. Singaporean adult anxieties can therefore be read not only as protective but also as territorial and prescriptive.

Young people's resistance

While adults (parents, teachers, police, the state) attempt to constrain young people's access to public space, teenagers are not passive recipients of such adult hegemony around spatial practices. This section explores some of the resistive practices young Singaporeans use to get to the places they want to go. However, it is very important to note that the majority of young people in this study, 67 per cent, said that they did not try to escape regulations by police and/or parents; 33 per cent stated that they did. However, all participants follow some element of resistance to adult regulatory practices.

Where teenagers go and why

In Singapore hanging out in public spaces is common and expected. It tends to be gendered: boys hang out in basketball courts and gaming arcades; girls tended to identify hanging out in their own or friends' homes (Table 14.3). Ironically, one of the few youth-specific state provisions for young people, the Youth Park, built in 1996 costing about SG$8.8 million (about £4 million), was the least used space and none of the girls in this study ever go there.

Table 14.3 Questionnaire survey results of frequent teenage hangouts

Teenage hangouts	Total Percentage (n = 80)	Breakdown by Gender (%)	
		Boys	Girls
Shopping centres	58/80: 73	30/42: 71	28/38: 74
Own home	47/80: 59	21/42: 50	26/38: 68
Void decks	45/80: 56	28/42: 67	17/38: 45
Friend's house	38/80: 48	17/42: 40	21/38: 55
Public parks/beaches	30/80: 38	15/42: 36	15/38: 39
Fast-food restaurants	29/80: 36	17/42: 40	12/38: 32
Library	24/80: 30	9/42: 21	15/38: 39
Soccer/basketball courts	22/80: 28	20/42: 48	2/38: 5
Cafés/restaurants	20/80: 25	9/42: 21	11/38: 29
Arcades/LAN gaming stations	19/80: 24	17/42: 40	2/38: 5
Pool/billiard outlets/ bowling alleys	19/80: 24	9/42: 21	10/38: 26
Streets	14/80: 18	8/42: 19	6/38: 16
Car parks	7/80: 9	3/42: 7	4/38: 11
Youth Park at Orchard Road	6/80: 8	6/42: 14	0/38: 0

However, what is evident is that the most popular place for both boys and girls were shopping centres. Contrary to practices in Western cities, young people in Singapore are very much tolerated and welcomed in shopping malls; all Singaporeans use these air-conditioned spaces intensively and shopping is described as a national pastime. Gatherings of teenage groups of friends are not seen as problematic. Asked why he liked to hang out in shopping centres Hasyim (Malay, 15) stated:

> It is a meeting port for me and my friends and a hangout place for teenagers. I go there to get to know new friends [*pauses*] . . . more like girls [*laughs*]. You know how girls love shopping right, so guys like me and my members go shopping malls to meet them. That's just us.

The notion of a 'port' symbolizes a sense of fluidity, a coming to a place and a moving through and away from it, but resting awhile. Hasyim is keen to identify the gender distinction between hanging out (boys) versus shopping (girls). He also feels that certain places in the centre give him a sense of lifestyle:

Oh I love hanging out in cafés like Gloria Jeans and Coffee Bean. It's more of a higher standard and there's like class, you know. Makes me feel older with all the working adults around. But the problem is that I'm still a student and I don't have money to go there often.

While such a sense of adulthood is potentially consumable it becomes easier to understand why young people are tolerated so widely in Singaporean malls – they are training grounds for consumption practices. Additionally, coffee shops are particularly important for young Muslim youth, as they are religiously acceptable spaces. Sarah (Malay, 15), identified a Starbucks café in her local mall as her favourite hangout space partly because she felt it gave her 'class' and 'maturity' to be there, but also because as a Muslim it was allowed:

I'm basically allowed to go anywhere as long as I know my limits as a Muslim. My parents always remind me how as a Muslim we must do this, do that . . . remember to pray, don't go out with boys, only eat at halal places, blah blah blah [*laughs*]. Pubs, clubs and such are out of the question. Even when I'm legal [18], I won't be allowed to go those places.

In some cases shopping malls are linked to other spatial practices (football) that are important in young teenagers' 'hanging out time'. Adam (Malay, 16) illustrates this about Adelphi Mall at City Hall:

Everyone knows Adelphi Mall is where skinheads are. We call ourselves the Adelphi Crew, since we're always there. We even have a soccer team named Adelphi FC. That place is like our home ground, home turf.

Young people felt that their immediate neighbourhood spaces were safe – hence their own homes, void decks and friends' houses being the next most popular hangouts after malls. This feeling of safety and familiarity means that they resent being surveilled in their own neighbourhoods:

Well, I understand why there's this police check thingy. But it's just that it can be annoying and irritating sometimes. We're not babies who need to be babysitted you know. We know our limits and how to take care of ourselves. Can't we just hang out around our neighbourhood with our friends? It's definitely safe there as compared to Orchard Road [the busiest, most central shopping street in Singapore].

(Premala, Indian, 15)

Such resentment leads to resistive practices and tactics to attempt a negotiated access to public spaces at night.

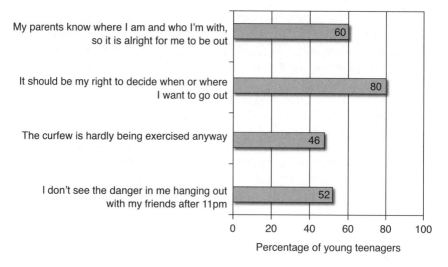

Figure 14.3 Reasons for not following the curfew.

Resistive Strategies, Practices and Negotiations

Teenagers in the study were split over their commitment to compliance to the police checks conducted after 11 p.m.; 56 per cent stated that they follow it, 44 per cent said they didn't. They provided the following reasons for not following the curfew:

Eighty percent of the 44 per cent who said that they did not follow the curfew argued that it was their right to decide when and where they can go. This is an interesting (and we argue encouraging) response in a national state context where there is little public discourse on young people's rights. Andy (Chinese, 16) put his feelings thus:

> I disagree with this act. I feel angry whenever someone does not believe in me. The police checks show that they do not trust young teenagers like us. They have no right to check us. They should be minding their own business. They should be doing their own jobs like catching thieves or something. Not checking young people out as if they are some perverts.

Andy felt criminalized by the checks; he resented the control that they symbolized. He felt that he was 'old enough' to make his own choices and knew his neighbourhood well enough to stay out late into the night.

One-third of teenagers stated that they attempted to escape regulatory practices of the police and parents. They adopt various tactics to appear more 'adult', or try to steer clear of the adult gaze altogether. Such strategies allow them to resist adult regulations and create their own micro-spaces of hanging out (Figure 14.4). In some cases there is direct non-compliance with adult rules of entry.

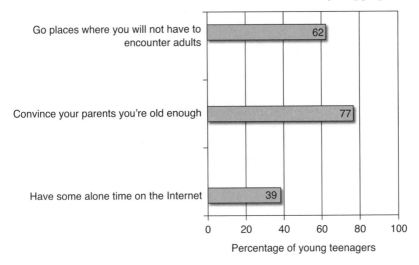

Figure 14.4 How young teenagers try to escape from adult regulations.

> I like playing pool. It's actually for [ages] 16 and above, but my friends and I don't care. We got into a fight once with the owner cause he won't allow us in . . . the next time we just got a friend who's older to bring us in.
>
> (Hasyim, Malay, 15)

Resistance can revolve around a strong sense of being in place (in this case the HDB block void space) and the right to question adult authority:

> We were just chit-chatting and this old lady came to us and started nagging. She said young girls like us shouldn't be seen hanging around in public like that. She started questioning us . . . which school we were from, whether our parents knew where we are . . . we thought she was crazy, it was only around 8 at night! We tried to reason with her, but she was just going on and on. One of my friends got irritated and shouted at her. She threatened to call the police but we were not scared. We were not doing anything wrong. What, just because she's older? Doesn't mean we have to listen to her.
>
> (Amanda, Chinese, 13)

In other contexts young people perform versions of their identity in ways that can dispel adult anxieties and suveillance (in this case in shopping centres). They know that by looking older and behaving in a mature way they are less likely to come under scrutiny.

> They'll follow us around the shop, as though we were going to steal something from them. Like as if we cannot afford it or something. It's

so irritating. That is why I don't like to go shopping malls right after school. They'll know we're still students and wouldn't want to entertain us. I'll change into something nice first.

(Farah, Malay, 15)

Exhibitions of maturity and displays of trustworthiness built around demonstrable practices are important tactics used in negotiations with parents to stretch time and access rules:

I try to gain my parents' trust. At first, I'll just go by their rules. Then, bit by bit, I'll ask for extensions. Like can I come home one hour later today, that kinda thing. I'll keep arguing I'm already 16 and when my brother was this age he was allowed to go out much later than me.

(Daniel, Malay, 16)

I'll make sure I finish all my schoolwork before I go out. If not, my mother will never let me out. Or, I'll just say I have to discuss homework with a friend. She can't say no then.

(Khairul, Malay, 13)

My parents are really religious. So I'll convince them I'm only meeting a group of girls, no boys. They'll feel more secure in letting me out I think.

(Sarah, Malay, 15)

One final strategy is to deliberately choose to spend time in a place that parents and police cannot really object to, void decks (although some neighbours might). Void decks exist at the base of all HDB blocks and are designed to provide community space. They are effectively substitute spaces for the house yards and gardens denied high-rise dwellers.

Void decks are cool cause no one will tell us to leave. Unlike in coffee places and all, once you finish your drink, you'll be sort of, expected to leave. And one drink costs like how much? Umm 5 or 6 dollars. At the void deck we can buy drinks from the provision shop and hang out for as long as we want. So convenient also. So close to home.

(Hakim, Malay, 14)

My home is right beside the void deck. How dangerous can it get? If the police comes, I'll just say I live right next door. I'll ask my friends to convince their parents it's totally alright to come over to my deck. We're just doing homework, chit-chatting and having a good time. If anyone weird comes along, we'll just scream and my parents will be able to hear us [laughs].

(Kimberly, Chinese, 14)

Conclusion

Singaporean young teenagers use particular places for pragmatic and social reasons: They choose places where other people their own age hang out; because they can spend as much time there as they want without being asked to leave; the place affords them some privacy; they feel safe; and they have a sense of belonging with a place because it is somewhere they have always gone. Hence it can be seen that they have quite similar expectations of what they can expect from the spaces they frequent, as do their parents.

In this chapter we have shown that adults tend to attempt to constrain young people's access to public space (particularly in the evenings) based on a premise of safety for the teenagers but that in reality it is often related to hegemonic constructions of public space as adult space. Young people recognize the power inequalities of some of these adultist strategies and develop their own tactics to circumvent the control. However, what is evident within the resistive practices of Singaporean youth, is that a considerable amount of negotiation and performance of trustworthiness is utilized between parents and children to enable young teenagers freedom in their neighbourhoods within certain spatial and temporal boundaries.

Notes

1 Void decks are unique structures and sites of public space. In Singapore more than 80 per cent of the population own apartments in Housing Development Board (HDB) properties. No apartments are on the ground floor, instead there is a shaded, open public space usually cooled by natural breezes – a void deck. Residents in the blocks (and neighbouring blocks) can use the void decks to socialize, sit, exercise and play. Ball games, cycling and skateboarding are usually banned. Good neighbourly behaviour is expected and enforced.

2 Singapore is just slightly over 1 degree north of the equator and night falls quickly and at a similar time throughout the year (around 7.30 p.m.). The temperature is tropical (between 26° and 32°C) and so outdoor movements are not restricted by seasonal changes; only heavy rainstorms temporarily constrain 'going out' practices.

3 *Kampong* is the Malay word for village and was the predominant form of housing in Singapore. There were bungalows with gardens and interconnecting paths. In the 1960s kampongs began to be cleared in order to meet increasing demand for affordable housing and the building of HDB high-rise blocks.

4 Singapore enforces strict laws pertaining to the propriety of behaviour between people and the modesty of individuals. The law 'Outrage of Modesty' is defined as an assault or use of criminal force on any person intended to, or knowing it to be likely to, outrage the modesty of that person. Penalties include imprisonment for up to two years, a fine and/or caning. It includes inappropriate touching, flashing, offensive name-calling, sexual suggestion and so forth.

Bibliography

Ang, I. and Stratton, J. (1995) 'The Singapore way of multiculturalism: Western concepts/Asian cultures', *Sojourn*, 10(1): 65–89.

Ansell, N. (2009) 'Childhood and the politics of scale: descaling children's geographies?' *Progress in Human Geography*, 33(2): 190–209.

Anthony, K. H. (1985) 'The shopping mall: a teenager hangout', *Adolescence*, 20: 307–12.

Cahill, C. (2000) 'Street literacy: urban teenagers' strategies for negotiating their neighbourhood', *Journal of Youth Studies*, 3(3): 251–77.

Channel NewsAsia (2006a), 'New police check not meant to infringe youths' personal freedom: minister', *Mediacorp News Pte Ltd*, 3 March 2006. Available at: http://global.factiva.com.libproxy1.nus.edu.sg/ha/default.aspx (accessed 11 September 2007).

Channel NewsAsia (2006b), 'Police checks on loitering youths after 11 pm not a curfew', *Mediacorp News Pte Ltd*, 22 February 2006. Available at: http://global.factiva.com.libproxy1.nus.edu.sg/ha/default.aspx (accessed 11 September 2007).

Chatterton, P. and Hollands, R. (2002), 'Theorising urban playscapes: producing, regulating and consuming youthful nightlife city spaces', *Urban Studies*, 39(1): 95–116.

Collins, D. C. A. and Kearns, R. A. (2001) 'Under curfew and under siege? Legal geographies of young people', *Geoforum*, 32(3): 389–403.

de Certeau, M. (1984) *The Practice of Everyday Life*, trans. S. F. Rendall, Berkeley, CA: University of California Press.

Foucault, M. (1977) *Discipline and Punish*, Paris: Gallimard.

Gough, K. V. and Franch, M. (2005) 'Spaces of the street: socio-spatial mobility and exclusion of youth in Recife', *Children's Geographies*, 3(2): 149–66.

Holt, L. and Holloway, S. (2006) 'Editorial: theorising other childhoods in a globalised world', *Children's Geographies*, 4(2): 135–42.

Koskela, H. (2000) '"The gaze without eyes": video-surveillance and the changing nature of urban space', *Progress in Human Geography*, 24(2): 243–65.

Matthews, H. (2003) 'The street as a liminal space: the barbed spaces of childhood', in P. Christensen and M. O'Brien (eds) *Children in the City: Home, Neighbourhood and Community*, London: Routledge.

Matthews, H. and Limb, M. (1999) 'Defining an agenda for the geography of children: review and prospect', *Progress in Human Geography*, 23: 61–90.

Matthews, H., Limb, M. and Taylor, M. (1999) 'Reclaiming the street: the discourse of curfew', *Environment and Planning A*, 31: 1713–30.

Matthews, H., Taylor, M., Percy-Smith, B. and Limb, M. (2000) 'The unacceptable Flaneur: the shopping mall as a teenage hangout', *Childhood*, 7(3): 279–94.

Mauzy, D. K. and Milne, R. S. (2002) *Singapore Politics under the People's Action Party*, London: Routledge.

Morrow, V. (2002) 'Children's rights to public space: environment and curfews', in B Franklin (ed.) *The New Handbook of Children's Rights*, London: Routledge.

O'Dougherty, M. (2006) 'Public relations, private security: managing youth and race at the Mall of America', *Environment and Planning D: Society and Space*, 24(1): 131–54.

Pain, R. (2006) 'Paranoid parenting? Rematerializing risk and fear for children', *Social and Cultural Geography*, 7(2): 221–43.

Pain, R., Grundy, S. and Gill, S. (2005) '"So long as I take my mobile . . .": mobile phones, urban life and geographies of children's safety', *International Journal of Urban and Regional Research*, 29(4): 814–30.

Population Trends (2008) *Department of Statistics, Ministry of Trade and Industry*, Republic of Singapore.

Punch, S. (2002) 'Youth transitions and interdependent adult-child relations in rural Bolivia', *Journal of Rural Studies*, 18(2): 123–33.

Robson, E. (2004) 'Hidden child workers: young carers in Zimbabwe', *Antipode*, 36(2): 227–48.

Ruefle, W. and Reynolds, K. M. (1995) 'Curfews and delinquency in major American cities', *Crime and Delinquency*, 41(3): 347–63.

Sack, R. D. (1986) *Human Territoriality: Its Theory and History*, Cambridge: Cambridge University Press.

Sibley, D. (2003) 'Psychogeographies of rural space and practices of exclusion', in P. J. Cloke (ed.) *Country Visions*, Harlow: Prentice Hall / Pearson.

Skelton, T. (2000) '"Nothing to do, nowhere to go?" Teenage girls and "public" space in the Rhondda Valleys, South Wales', in S. Holloway and G. Valentine (eds), *Children's Geographies: Playing, Living, Learning*, London: Routledge.

Skelton, T. (2007) 'Children, young people, UNICEF and participation', *Children's Geographies*, 5(1–2): 165–81.

Skelton, T. (2009) 'Children's geographies/geographies of children: play, work, mobilities and migration', *Geography Compass*, 3(4): 1430–48.

Tan, B. N. S. (2006) 'Police act to keep teens off streets after 11 pm', *Straits Times*, 16 February 2006. Available at: http://global.factiva.com.libproxy1.nus.edu.sg/ha/default.aspx (accessed 28 December 2007).

Teo, X. (2006) 'No curfew, just letters for some: Police will only alert parents of teens who are "exposing themselves to crime risk or bad influence"', *Today*, 23 February. Available at: http://global.factiva.com.libproxy1.nus.edu.sg/ha/default.aspx (accessed 28 December 2007).

Thomas, M. E. (2005) 'Girls, consumption space and the contradictions of hanging out in the city', *Social and Cultural Geography*, 6(4): 587–605.

Toon, I. (2000) '"Finding a place in the street": CCTV surveillance and young people's use of urban public space', in D. Bell and A. Haddour (eds) *City Visions*, New York: Pearson Education.

Valentine, G. (1996) 'Children should be seen and not heard: the production and transgression of adults' public space', *Urban Geography*, 17(2): 205–20.

Valentine, G. (1997) '"Oh yes I can." "Oh no you can't": Children and parents' understandings of kids' competence to negotiate public space safely', *Antipode*, 29(1): 65–89.

Valentine, G. and McKendrick, J. (1997) 'Children's outdoor play: exploring parental concerns about children's safety and the changing nature of childhood', *Geoforum*, 28(2): 219–35.

Vanderbeck, R. (2007) 'Intergenerational geographies: age relations, segregation and re-engagements', *Geography Compass*, 1(2): 200–21.

Vanderbeck, R. (2008) 'Reaching critical mass? Theory, politics, and the culture of debate in children's geographies', *Area*, 40(3): 393–400.

Vanderbeck, R. M. and Johnson, J. H. (2000) '"That's the only place where you can hang out": urban young people and the space of the mall', *Urban Geography*, 21(1): 5–25.

Watt, P. and Stenson, K. (1998) 'The street: "It's a bit dodgy around there": safety, danger, ethnicity and young people's use of public space', in T. Skelton and G. Valentine (eds) *Cool Places: Geographies of Youth Cultures*, London: Routledge.

White, R. (1993) 'Youth and the conflict over urban space', *Children's Environments*, 10(1): 110–23.

Yarwood, R. (2007) 'The geographies of policing', *Progress in Human Geography*, 31(4): 447–65.

Young, L. (2003) 'The "place" of street children in Kampala, Uganda: marginalisation, resistance, and acceptance in the urban environment', *Environment and Planning D: Society and Space*, 21(5): 607–27.

15 Socio-spatial experiences of young people under anti-social behaviour legislation in England and Wales

Rachel Manning, Robert Jago and Julia Fionda

Introduction

Anti-social behaviour (ASB) continues to enjoy considerable prominence in public, political and academic discourse. Moreover, young people remain central to many ASB concerns. Yet while much is written around a wide range of issues relating to ASB and young people, the voices of young people directly affected by ASB legislation are rarely heard. In this chapter we explore the socio-spatial implications of anti-social behaviour legislation in England and Wales. Working from an interdisciplinary perspective we draw on socio-environmental psychology to highlight the socio-spatial impact of ASB legislation, and use this to explore the experiences of young people who have been made subject to Anti-social Behaviour Orders (ASBOs). First we set out the policy context and note key features of the legislation as it is relevant to the socio-spatial regulation of young people. We then briefly highlight a social psychological framework to examine the impact of this legislation on young people's experiences of socio-spatial restriction. We then go on to illustrate this framework through the presentation of themes raised by a series of interviews conducted with young people and their families who have been subject to ASB legislation. Ultimately we argue that, given that the ASBO was designed originally for use against adults, its encouraged use against young people by the government (Labour Party, 1995; Home Office, 1997) has had and will continue to have untold consequences in the future.

ASB and young people

Since its inception following s 1 of the Crime and Disorder Act, 1998, the ASBO, a key tool in the fight against declining cities, has enjoyed a considerable public profile. Despite the fact that the government's aim was to protect the 'old, disabled, vulnerable, poor or [those] from a particular ethnic group' (Michael, 1998) as potential victims of ASB, a brief perusal of reported ASBOs on www.statewatch.org reveals, somewhat ironically, that these groups tend most often to be the recipients of ASBOs. However, the ASBO has become most synonymous with urban youth. This is clearly evident in popular discourse, but also from the fact that self-report surveys conducted by the Home Office in an attempt to count youth crime now also attempt to count and explain causal factors relating to ASB (see *Offending, Crime and Justice Survey*, Roe and Ashe, 2008).

The ASBO is a civil order which requires an application for the order to be made in a magistrates' court by the police or local authority (as extended). Magistrates then have to decide whether, on the balance of probabilities, a person aged ten or over has acted in a way which is deemed to be anti-social. 'Anti-social' is defined in s 1(1)(a) of the Act as being 'a manner that caused or was likely to cause harassment, alarm or distress to one or more persons not of the same household as himself'. Due to the victim-defined nature of ASB, various commentators have pointed out that, 'virtually any activity can be anti-social depending on a range of background factors, such as the context in which is occurs, the location, people's tolerance levels and expectations about the quality of life in the area' (Whitehead *et al.*, 2003: 3–4). When introducing the Crime and Disorder Bill in the House of Lords, Lord Williams, a Labour peer, stated that 'those who suffer anti social behaviour do not need to have it defined; they know what it is and experience it daily.' (Lord Williams HL Deb, 5th ser., vol. 584, 16 December 1997, col. 550). In doing so, he also reminded us that: 'Anti-social behaviour is a menace on our streets; it is a threat to our communities.' (Lord Williams HL Deb, 5th ser., vol. 584, 16 December 1997, col. 513). Thus from its inception, ASB is placed firmly in the realms of 'public space' (Valentine, 1996) and, moreover, threatens that most delicate of public goods: the 'community', which we will return to again below. We are thus alerted to the potential for competing understandings of public space, and the relative privileging of particular claims over appropriate space use (Valentine, 1996).

Whilst the authority of the ASBO lies in the civil law, breach of the order becomes a criminal offence. The ASBO is effectively a civil injunction as it only imposes negative prohibitions but it is criminal in outcome should those prohibitions be breached. This gives the order its hybrid status. This was a deliberate ploy to combine the best features of both the civil and the criminal law. The initial aim was to use the civil law with a lower burden of proof and the avoidance of many of the requirements of Article 6 of the European Convention on Human Rights. This has since been qualified by the House of Lords where they confirmed that although they are civil orders, the criminal standard of proof should apply when making an application for breach of an ASBO. However, in the same ruling, the Lords stated that the assessment of whether an order is necessary to protect people from ASB 'does not involve a standard of proof: it is an exercise of judgement or evaluation', (*R (McCann) v Crown Court at Manchester* [2003] 1 AC 787), which might appear to be a useful way of bypassing any real restriction to making an ASBO.

While Lord Hope of Craighead has confirmed that the prohibitive restrictions in the order are imposed for preventative reasons and not for punishment, (*R (W) v Commissioner of Police of the Metropolis and another* [2005] EWHC 1588 (Admin)), in practice there have been a variety of terms attached to ASBOs. Although the examples range from the fantastic (a 13-year-old was banned from using the word 'grass' for six years) to the tragic (a woman prevented from attempting to kill herself again) there has been particular concern over the use of the ASBO with attached conditions which act as preventative prohibitions. Conditions have included bans on associating with particular people and geographical exclusions (Macdonald and Telford, 2007). An example of where this is truly counterproductive is where an 18-year-old youth was given an ASBO, the condition of which was to prevent him from associating with three or more youths. He then found himself arrested when he entered a local youth club, one of the very devices set up to manage young people's time in a more purposeful way. A further problem with the legal elasticity of definition is also informative here. As Macdonald (2006) points out, 'no distinction is made between anti-social behaviour perpetrated by the defendant and behaviour which is necessarily prior to his anti-social behaviour' (198). This problem is illustrated by the ASBO conditions being used to attempt to ban a pirate DJ from entering buildings more than four storeys tall to prevent him assembling an aerial to enable him to run his pirate radio station. The ban applied to *all* four-storey buildings regardless of the purpose for visiting them. Thus ASBOs can be used to regulate the presence of particular people in particular places – or particular *types* of places – regardless of the behaviours exhibited there.

As noted, it is in relation to young people where this issue of spatial restriction is most evident. It had long been thought that the ASBO would have a disproportionate impact upon young people and their ordinary patterns of behaviour. Burney (2002) commented that 'young people are not primarily perceived as victims; rather youths hanging about have become the universal symbol of disorder and increasingly menace' (469). Back in 1998, Ashworth *et al.* articulated their concern that the 'bus stop kids' who routinely gathered and socialized around the public areas of bus stops, shop entrances and street corners would be targeted and discouraged from such gatherings due to a perception, rather than a real, incidence of ASB. As Padfield (2004) argues, the ASBO is the ultimate in 'Nanny-state' provision – offering unnecessary protection to us all from a series of perceived threats which often do not bear empirical scrutiny.

The perceived threat of young people in public space is further illustrated by the Anti-social Behaviour Act 2003. Here, under Part 4, a new dispersal order was introduced to disperse groups of people of any age whose behaviour in public places is harassing, alarming or distressing. Section 30(6) specifically gives police or community support officers, the power to remove from any public place people under the age of 16 if they are out and not under the control of an adult between the hours of 9 p.m. and 6 a.m., regardless of whether their behaviour is causing concern to members of the public. While we have previously explored this control of young people's use of public space (Fionda *et al.*, 2006), such measures underscore the way in which the mere presence of young people in public space is deemed problematic (Holloway and Valentine, 2000; Millie, 2008; Valentine, 1996) and can thus be legitimately regulated. If the use of public space is seen as a key aspect of human experience, and a marker of citizenship (Painter and Philo, 1995), the use of ASB legislation to regulate the use of public space by young people in particular is additionally problematic. The courts have considered these attempts to restrict young people's movements in this way, (see *R (W) v Commissioner of Police of the Metropolis and another* [2005] EWHC 1588 (Admin)), and Crawford and Lister conducted a case study of three areas and concluded that, 'Dispersal orders . . . convey stark negative messages to young people about their status in society and how they are perceived by adults' (Crawford and Lister, 2007: 69), emphasizing young people as 'the risk' rather than 'at risk' (see also Holloway and Valentine, 2000; Valentine, 1996).

Young people and 'community'

A key part of the enforcement of this agenda against ASB is the role of the 'community' in enforcing the terms of an ASBO. To do this effectively the 'community' needs to know what the terms of an ASBO are. Although there is a presumption in favour of anonymity in criminal proceedings for a child, the use of the ASBO under the civil regime sidesteps that valuable limitation and actively encourages the public to be vigilant and to assist the state in policing a young person's use of public space. Home Office guidance encourages publicity of the ASBO and its terms and defends this on the basis of the need for the public to have confidence in public services and deterring other potential young people considering breaching the conditions of their ASBO. Indeed, ASBOs can only work in the light of what Garland (1996) calls 'responsibilisation' since we rely on the public or the 'community' to police themselves in the light of the 'limits of the sovereign state' to effectively control burgeoning crime and disorder. The 'naming and shaming' of ASBO recipients is supposed to reassure the public that their behaviour is being controlled. However, reliance on public surveillance of their own community may result not in greater community coherence, but rather in the community's greater suspicion of its neighbours and the further isolation of untolerated social groups.

Young people who are already marginalized within the community that they live may thus potentially be pilloried and further isolated. The rhetoric talks of the ASBO being a 'badge of honour' but the reality may be that it is more like a scarlet letter. Braithwaite (1989) has previously argued that the shaming process can do little to encourage integration. The ASBO may therefore reinforce the marginalization that took place before it was made.

Thus Hodgkinson and Tilley (2007) argue that the over use or misuse of the ASBO can have a detrimental effect on the young person as secondary deviance may occur if a person is labelled as deviant because the 'bestowed identity is embraced' (393). Our suggestion here is that socio-spatial restriction is at the core of this bestowed identity.

A socio-spatial perspective on identity

We have seen how policy and rhetoric around ASB can involve concerns around the appropriate use of space, and most notably young people as 'out of place' (Cresswell, 1996) in various public settings. We have previously made the case for the way in which a spatially informed social psychology can contribute to our understanding of some of the processes involved in the experience of ASB legislation (Fionda *et al.*, 2006). In particular, such an approach allows us to focus in particular on the identities and subjective perceptions involved in the contested nature of space in relation to ASB (Aitken, 2001; Millie, 2008).

Drawing on the social identity (SI) perspective (Tajfel, 1978; Turner *et al.*, 1987), we are sensitized to the perceptions and experiences of young people themselves, rather than simply perceptions of or pronouncements about them. Echoing concerns of the 'bias of perspective' inherent in earlier approaches to crowd behaviour (Reicher and Potter, 1985), we can similarly interpret ASB through this intergroup perspective. Moreover, it is young people as a group, or in groups, that are often stereotypically problematic in terms of ASB, drawing on additional assumptions around the effects of the group on individual responsibility and control. Thus, one of the common restrictions attached to ASBOs given to young people is that of association. As we have set out elsewhere (Fionda *et al.*, 2006), recent developments in the SI perspective also point to the way in which the actions of groups, particularly powerful ones, towards other groups can change the ways in which people understand their collective identities and norms of behaviour. It is therefore an empirical question as to how young people who have been affected by ASB legislation perceive it and react to its use. It is for this reason that we conducted empirical research which examines the experience of such young people.

Although a SI perspective sensitizes us to the importance of the collective experience of young people, contemporary social psychology is increasingly concerned with providing an adequate spatial dimension to its theorizing (e.g. Dixon and Durrheim, 2000). The work of Dixon *et al.* (2006) in particular is informed by cultural geography to provide a psychological analysis of place transgression. In examining infractions of the moral order of public space they foreground the notion of ideological dilemmas (Billig *et al.*, 1988) – the idea that ordinary people's reasoning about controversial topics echoes and reworks wider ideological traditions, and that these are often contradictory in nature. For example, Dixon *et al.* (2006) discuss the 'ideological tension between freedom and control' in relation to the production of the public domain. This has particular resonance with our examination of ASB. Thus we might suggest that it is the contested nature of public space itself that is at issue in rhetoric, policy and practice relating to the regulation of ASB.

Given the socio-spatial dimension of both perceptions of ASB, often involving disputation of appropriate use of public space, and sanctions for ASB, involving spatial and social restrictions, the spatial features of the experience of ASB legislation deserves investigation. Moreover, the rhetoric of community and the location of the 'problem' of ASB in public, largely urban, spaces points to the need for further investigation. Indeed, the perception of who belongs where, and what their legitimate actions are there, are fundamental to understanding the impact of the imposition of ASB legislation in relation to young people. We now turn to the perspective of those considered to be 'out of place' themselves.

Socio-environmental experiences of young people

In order to examine the everyday impact of ASB legislation, our data come from a series of interviews conducted with young people in the South of England who had been given ASBOs, and their parents. The majority of the interviews were carried out in the homes of these families; however, three of the interviews were conducted with young people who were in a Young Offenders' Institution (YOI).

Before looking at the accounts obtained, and in order to set up an initial contrast of perspectives, it is instructive to note a local newspaper story that ran prior to our interviews. The story involved three young people involved in our research, and illustrates concerns of young people and their families, together with the practical application of the legislation set out above. The front page of the newspaper carried the headline 'ANIMALS!', followed by photographs of the three young people, all boys aged between 14 and 16 years old, that the headline was referring to. The article described how the young people were banned from the town centre in which they lived and explained the headline as emanating from the local youth court judge. On the following two pages further photographs were provided, which were accompanied by a picture and description of the geographic restrictions given to the three young people as conditions of their ASBOs. The publication of this story and these images thus allowed the rest of the local population (the 'community') to take part in the surveillance that ensured the spatial regulation of these young people. While our concern here is not a detailed analysis of media representations, such examples are nonetheless instructive in examining the regulation of young people and their use of space.

The publicity of ASBO restrictions, for use by 'the community' in informing the authorities of breaches, can have a number of implications from the young person's perspective. The young people's perceptions of their ASBOs varied, but socio-spatial restriction was a theme throughout all of them. One young person, Sam,[1] spoke of how, 'If I go outside now yeah, say you're a nob and that, the police could nick me for it, for breaching my ASBO'. However, as the remainder of the extract below illustrates, Sam's perception of this restriction indicated that he felt his presence in public space *anywhere* would result in arrest:

SAM: Even if it was Greenmouth they'd arrest me.
INTERVIEWER: So even in another city?
SAM: Yeah.
INTERVIEWER: So if you went to London they could still do that?
SAM: Yeah.
INTERVIEWER: You believe that would be a breach of your ASBO?
SAM: Yeah.
INTERVIEWER: Although it is just Nightingale Close?
SAM: I'm not allowed to cause harassment or distress, everywhere.

Other young people we spoke to similarly explained how their ASBO restrictions resulted in an extreme curtailment of their use of public space. The potential threat of arrest is thus universal – even in a city many miles away such as London the restrictions were in place, and any 'nob' could cause Sam to be arrested. This example paints a picture of spatial restriction as a result of ASBO conditions that go considerably beyond the original intention of those restrictions. The scale of restriction reaches beyond the localities specified in ASBO conditions, as perceived by these young people. The conditions do not simply keep them from places where they might be involved in anti-social behaviour, but rather are interpreted as meaning that their mere presence anywhere in public space is problematic and subject to sanction.

Indeed, some of the young people we spoke to, when faced with the complexity and perceived omnipresence of the threat of arrest due to their presence in public space, simply withdrew. The interviewer had been asking Paul about his reaction to being wrongly accused of breaching his ASBO.

INTERVIEWER: Has it changed you?
PAUL: Yeah.
INTERVIEWER: In what way?
PAUL: I don't go out anymore.

Paul went on to explain how he was looking forward to the end of his ASBO so that he could walk down the street. Others spoke of how they would only venture outside in the presence of a parent. Of course, one might suggest that such effects are illustrative of the efficacy of ASBOs, in line with the use of geographical restrictions. While not wanting to devote space to the discussion of such claims here, we will simply question the assumption of the home as a necessarily unproblematic exclusive location for young people, and, moreover, of the legitimacy of excluding the mere presence of young people from public space. For others, ASBO restrictions influenced their identity in public space, and the types of spaces they used: they became invisible, and increasingly used liminal spaces, or attempted to negotiate particular public spaces anonymously or undetected. Such 'coping strategies' speak to the ways in which the imposition of particular identities by others are reacted to and reworked. Their behaviour, coupled with their (hidden) identities, change in line with the prescriptions and proscriptions of powerful others in terms of their use of space.

In this next extract, we can see the broader social effects of the ASBO restrictions given to young people. The impact of the restrictions, as extensive as they might be, are not limited to the young people themselves, but clearly impact on parents and other family members. In spite of the supposed individualized nature of the punishment, ASBO restrictions can be seen to have collective effects.

INTERVIEWER: Normally he would have gone to St Luke's. I can't get my head around the fact that he's got an ASBO and the school that he needs to go to is in that restriction. How does that work out? Did Peter carry on going to school?

SARA: He was half time and all this lot. What they expected me to do, was walk Peter into school, which I had to walk all the way round like I said, come all the way back round [through the woods] and then I had to go from Peter's school, go and get the other kids, which is miles down the road from Peter's school, come back from there, go and get Peter, come back from there, go home and then go all the way back down there again, they expected me to do this every day and it got too much. As I was doing all that everything else was getting on top of me. I got ill, nearly had a brain haemorrhage and after that all this happened. In one year I've gone through hell. I wouldn't wish it on anybody. My dog got run over and everything in one year. Ongoing bad, bad luck.

Sara is the mother of Peter, who is 14. As a result of sanctions toward Peter's behaviour, Sara was evicted from her council house. There are a number of interesting features of Sara's account. First, the interviewer asks about the everyday practicalities of the ASBO restrictions given to Peter – the school that Peter had (sometimes) been attending was located in a restricted area. Clearly, the use of geographical restrictions that make school attendance more difficult for young people who may already be experiencing problems with school attendance must have questionable utility. Sara's account in response to this question highlights the practical implications of this restriction. Moreover, these implications necessarily impact on others. The use of restrictions that proscribe young people from being in particular places alone, or with specified troublesome others, in practice has an impact beyond the individual young person. Sara here talks about the impact on her spatial practices – accompanying her son to school, separately from her other children, and having to take a substantially longer route.

While restrictions on association often meant that the young people could no longer see (or be seen with) friends that they had had for many years, geographical restrictions could also mean that friends or other family members could not be visited. Indeed, such was the impact of the geographical restrictions on the lives of whole families that two of the families we spoke to had 'swapped' houses, in order that they might effect a manageable solution to the newly configured spatial context in which they lived. For another of the young people we spoke to, the impact of geographical restrictions was such that it removed them from the family context completely. Following the death of one parent with whom he had been living, he was unable to live with the surviving parent as their house was in an area that was proscribed by the terms of their ASBO. (At the time of the interview the young person was in custody in a YOI.)

The difficulties in managing the restrictions put on these young people as a result of their ASBOs were thus often constructed in terms of being a deliberate attempt to criminalize the young people – they had a 'target on their head', and were being 'set up to fail' through conditions being set in the knowledge that they would be breached. Injustice permeated the accounts that we obtained. This was highlighted in accounts of breaches of ASBOs. As we have noted above, the conditions were often perceived as unmanageable, and breaches – and therefore arrest or court appearance – an inevitable consequence of being 'targeted' in this way. However, accounts of the behaviours that brought about the geographical breaches were notable in terms of their form, often narratives of active citizenship and contribution to the well-being of others. Young people would talk about their presence in proscribed places as being due to concern over the safety of others, such as girlfriends who felt scared, thus positioning themselves as moral actors in those places in contrast to the transgressive nature of their presence there in the eyes of the law, due to ASBO restrictions.

Similar accounts were also given by mothers. Here we see Sara again describing Peter's recent breach of his ASBO geographical restrictions.

SARA: My little 'un got run over in January and he breached it then 'cos he went over right outside the shop. My son was unconscious on the floor, being hit by a Land Rover and they banned Peter. I've got millions of witnesses to say that because they were all there.

Thus Sara explains Peter's breach in terms of him going to the aid of his younger brother who had been hit by a car, drawing on an audience of 'millions' who could support this version of events. Peter, the young person with an ASBO, who had appeared in the local newspaper under the banner of 'ANIMALS!', is presented as an active citizen in public space, who is punished for this action. The contrast in these accounts of civic engagement with the restrictions to 'ordinary' activities imposed by ASBO restrictions – indeed, the punishment of those who attempted to engage in such activities – is informative in terms of understandings of morality and competing perceptions of appropriate place use, demonstrating the ways in which identities are bound up in space use and spatio-moral orders. This contrast of proscription and active engagement points to the complexity with which these young people and their families engage with public space, and highlights the bluntness of geographical restriction as a punitive instrument.

Conclusion

In order to begin to examine the dynamics involved in the regulation of space use through ASB legislation we have presented a selection of extracts from our interviews that illustrate impact of this legislation on young people's socio-spatial experiences. We are also sensitized to the contested nature of breaches of geographical ASBO restrictions, as young people and their families construct legally proscribed space use as active citizenship. While these extracts could be read simply as 'bad' families attempting to challenge the sanctions imposed upon them and presenting a revised version of events that implicates others, their accounts and concerns were often echoed by various professionals who had contact with the young people and/or their families.

We are not claiming that these stories are representative of all young people who are given ASBOs, or their families. However, they are illustrative of the creative strategies utilized in reaction to the restrictions (Skelton, 2000), in what were often already challenging circumstances, and the contested nature and utilization of public space. Thus while Simon talked of how being given an ASBO made him want to 'get back at them, like the police or whatever', he also explained how 'we should be given more opportunities of doing good stuff and being lively and not just sticking us in here [YOI]. Helping out old people and stuff like that innit'. Such sentiments might sensitize us to the difficulties with the way in which 'the community' are being enlisted in the fight against ASB, and how this is perceived and experienced by young people themselves. Moreover, the experience of these young people and their families as affected by ASBOs was not universally presented as negative – some effects, such as new housing, were referred to as having had a positive effect on the young people and their families as a whole.

The use of this legislation, nonetheless, is instructive in terms of the appropriation of public space (or adult spatial hegemony, Valentine, 1996) and the place of young people in British society. Young people are positioned as 'out of place', and are charged with negotiating considerable spatial restriction – which can result in withdrawal from public space, or can be challenged through the claiming of active citizenship in the face of possible sanction. And it is 'communities' themselves that are charged with managing this sanction. If 'communities' are to be positioned as bringing about the detention of young people who claim to be active, moral citizens in public spaces, then we might question the nature of these 'communities' and the powers with which they are being entrusted.

Ten years after the first ASBO was made it has become clear that the government has preferred to focus its attention on the enforcement of the ASBO and its potentially restrictive prohibitions rather than making any real in-roads in dealing with the underlying reasons that young people engage in ASB in the first place. The focus of enforcement is the community itself and this, according to Garland (1996), is part of the responsibilization strategy which expects the community to round up its young people who are behaving in a way which is inconsistent with its own expectations and restrict their development as a way of controlling their very own enemy within. If the strategy is to eradicate this enemy then on final analysis it appears to be left wanting. If ASB signals that a community is in decline (Hodgkinson and Tilley, 2007) then the way a community deals with its perceived problem will be the measure of that community. The government made no secret of the fact that Wilson and Kelling's 'Broken Windows' theory (1982) informed the ASB policy. In fixing broken windows, the community face a choice between a zero tolerance judgemental approach (Kelling and Coles, 1996) or a more reintegrative and holistic, preventive approach. We argue here that the former is clearly evident in ASB policy and practice. However, judgment comes with significant responsibility and whilst the problem of disorder maybe apparent, the unforeseen consequences of this continued marginalization may be far greater than the problem ever was.

Note

1 Pseudonyms have been used throughout.

References

Aitken, S. (2001) *Geographies of Young People: The Morally Contested Spaces of Identity*, London: Routledge.

Ashworth, A., Gardner, J., Morgan, R., Smith, A. T. H., von Hirsch, A. and Wasik, M. (1998) 'Neighbouring on the oppressive: the Government's anti-social behaviour order proposals', *Criminal Justice*, 16: 7–14.

Billig, M., Condor, S., Edwards, D., Gane, M., Middleton, D. and Radley, A. (1988) *Ideological Dilemmas: A Social Psychology of Everyday Thinking*, London: Sage.

Braithwaite, J. (1989) *Crime, Shame and Reintegration*, Cambridge: Cambridge University Press.

Burney, E. (2002) 'Talking tough, acting coy: what happened to the anti-social behaviour order?', *Howard Journal*, 41: 469–84.

Crawford, A. and Lister, S. (2007) *The Use and Impact of Dispersal Orders: Sticking Plasters and Wake-Up Calls*, Bristol: The Policy Press.

Cresswell, T. (1996) *In Place/Out of Place: Geography, Ideology and Transgression*, Minneapolis: University of Minnesota Press.

Dixon, J., and Durrheim, K. (2000) 'Displacing place-identity: a discursive approach to locating self and other', *British Journal of Social Psychology*, 39: 27–44.

Dixon, J., Levine, M. and McAuley, R. (2006) 'Locating impropriety: street drinking and the ideological dilemma of public space', *Political Psychology*, 27: 187–206.

Fionda, J., Jago, R. and Manning, R. (2006) 'Conflicts over territory: anti-social behaviour legislation and young people', in B. Brooks-Gordon and M. Freeman (eds) *Law and Psychology*, Oxford: Oxford University Press.

Garland, D. (1996) 'The limits of the sovereign state: strategies of crime control in contemporary society', *British Journal of Criminology*, 36: 445–71.

Hodgkinson, S. and Tilley, N. (2007) 'Policing anti-social behaviour: constraints, dilemmas and opportunities', *Howard Journal of Criminal Justice*, 46: 385–400.

Holloway, S. L. and Valentine, G. (eds) (2000) *Children's Geographies: Playing, Living, Learning*, London: Routledge.

Home Office (1997) *Community Safety Order: A Consultation Paper*, London: Home Office.

Kelling, G. and Coles, C. (1996) *Broken Windows, Restoring Order and Reducing Crime in Our Communities*, New York: Free Press.

Labour Party (1995) *A Quiet Life: Tough Action on Criminal Neighbours*, London: Labour Party.

Macdonald, S. (2006) 'A suicidal woman, roaming pigs and a noisy trampolinist: refining the ASBO's definition of "Anti-Social Behaviour"', *Modern Law Review*, 69: 183–213.

Macdonald, S. and Telford, M. (2007) 'The use of ASBOs against young people in England and Wales: lessons from Scotland', *Legal Studies*, 27: 604–29.

Michael, A. (1998) House of Commons, Standing committee B, 28 April 1998, col 37.

Millie, A. (2008) 'Anti-social behaviour, behavioural expectations and an urban aesthetic', *British Journal of Criminology*, 48: 379–94.

Padfield, N. (2004) 'The Anti-Social Behaviour Act 2003: The ultimate nanny-state Act', *Criminal Law Review*, 712–27.

Painter, J. and Philo, C. (1995) 'Spaces of citizenship: an introduction', *Political Geography*, 14: 107–20.

Reicher, S. and Potter, J. (1985) 'Psychological theory as intergroup perspective: a comparative analysis of "scientific" and "lay" accounts of crowd events', *Human Relations*, 38: 167–89.

Roe, S. and Ashe, J. (2008) *Young People and Crime: Findings from the 2006 Offending, Crime and Justice Survey*, London: Home Office.

Skelton, T. (2000) 'Nothing to do, nowhere to go? Teenage girls and "public" space in the Rhondda Valleys, South Wales', in S. Holloway and G. Valentine (eds) *Children's Geographies: Playing, Living, Learning*, London: Routledge.

Tajfel, H. (1978) *Differentiation Between Social Groups: Studies in the Social Psychology of Intergroup Relations*, London: Academic Press.

Turner, J. C., Hogg, M. A., Oakes, P. J., Reicher, S., and Wetherell, M. (1987) *Rediscovering the Social Group: A Self-categorization Theory*, Oxford: Blackwell.

Valentine, G. (1996) 'Angels and devils: the moral landscape of childhood', *Environment and Planning D: Society and Space*, 14: 581–99.

Whitehead, C. M. E., Stockdale, J. E. and Razzu, G. (2003) *The Economic and Social Costs of Anti-social Behaviour*. London: London School of Economics.

Wilson, J. Q. and Kelling, G. (1982) 'Broken windows: the police and neighbourhood safety', *Atlantic Monthly*, 249: 29–38.

Theme IV

Institutional spaces

16 Tears and laughter at a Sure Start Centre

Preschool geographies, policy contexts

John Horton and Peter Kraftl

Preface: tears

A mother and son (aged 3) describe a visit to a Sure Start Children's Centre, March 2009.

> 'We went [to the Sure Start Children's Centre] one time but it frit [i.e. frightened] him half to death . . . He cried his guts out. I've not been since.'

> 'It [the Sure Start Children's Centre] was horrible and *poo*ey!'[1]

Introduction

This chapter focuses upon a particular institutional space purpose-built for children aged 0–4: a new Sure Start Children's Centre in the English Midlands. Specifically, we explore how young children inhabited, and variously cared, worried or even cried, about this venue. In so doing, we make three key, related points. First, we draw attention to the children's geographies which are, of course, at the heart of all institutional and policy contexts constructed for children; we contend that the particularities of these geographies have, ironically, often been effaced in chief discourses about and from such institutions and policies. Second, we foreground the geographies, experiences and viewpoints of children within contemporary UK state provision for 'preschool' children (aged 0–4 years); indeed, we note a more general silence, ranging across diverse contemporary policy and research contexts, regarding the everyday cares, critiques and practices of children in this age range. Third, we emphasize the importance of everyday, bodily, multisensuous and affective registers in understanding the success or otherwise of institutional spaces and policy contexts; that is, we insist that small, quotidian, emotional, perhaps pre-verbal experiences – tears, laughter, even the prefatory '*poo*ey'-ness – should be taken more seriously when attempting to understand or evaluate such spaces and contexts.

The following section provides a brief introduction to the policy context of Sure Start, and the discursive and practical status of young children therein. The main body of the paper draws upon evaluative research conducted with 50 children aged 0–4 years old at a Sure Start Children's Centre in Northamptonshire, UK, during February–May 2009. Following an introduction to our project, we identify four ways in which working closely with these children afforded new understandings of – albeit small, but hitherto unnoticed – ways in which the Centre worked, or not, for its target demographic. In conclusion, we reflect upon some implications of these findings.

Sure Start, and the ambivalent political status of preschool children

Sure Start was launched by the UK government in 1997–99 as a 'landmark' policy intervention to improve children's well-being and 'life chances' in 'deprived' communities (see Glass, 1999). The strategy sought 'to work with parents-to-be, parents and children to promote the physical, intellectual and social development of babies and young children – particularly those who are disadvantaged – . . . and thereby break the cycle of disadvantage' (Sure Start, 2000: 1; also Sure Start, 2002a). In practice, the policy entailed the constitution of locally managed, integrated childcare, education and healthcare programmes for 0- to 4-year-olds, and their parents/carers, in England's most 'deprived' neighbourhoods. Typically, these programmes are physically located within a purpose-built or refurbished institutional space: a 'Sure Start Children's Centre'. As of June 2009, more than 3000 such centres were in operation (Sure Start, 2009).

Ostensibly, discursively, children aged 0–4 are positioned as central to the policy, practice, and success of Sure Start. The founding principles of Sure Start strongly emphasized the importance of working *with* children in the constitution of provision and spaces principally driven by *their* needs (Sure Start, 2004, emphases in original). Each Sure Start Children's Centre would comprise 'joined-up' services, activities and built environments designed *around* children (DfES/DWP, 2006: 23), affording 'personalised' provision 'effectively tailor[ed] . . . to individual children', and more broadly 'plan[ned] . . . to meet the needs of children and families in the local area' (Sure Start, 2003a: 4). To this end, guidance for the establishment and practice of Sure Start Children's Centres highlights the importance of ongoing, careful consultation with children and their parents/carers (Sure Start, 2003b: 2). As such, Sure Start should be understood as a materialization and microcosm of broader contemporary UK policy contexts, wherein the need for state-provided services and institutions 'to be shaped by and responsive to children, young people and families', wherever salient, has become a prominent ideal (DCSF, 2007: 6; also HM Treasury, 2003). In particular, Sure Start is discursively located as key to the realization of a 'culture change' in the care/education of UK preschool children: a policy framework which, ostensibly, 'values and celebrates babies and children', 'recognises their individuality, efforts and achievements', and locates them as 'social beings, . . . competent learners from birth' who 'learn when they are given appropriate responsibility, allowed to make . . . decisions and choices' (Sure Start, 2002b: 4–5).

However, despite the centrality of 0- 4-year-olds within these policy discourses, we suggest that children have, in practice, overwhelmingly been afforded limited agency and responsibility within the spaces of Sure Start Children's Centres. This is perhaps most manifest in the evaluative and consultative processes which are infrastructural in the regulation of Sure Start, and individual Children's Centres. First, the National Evaluation of Sure Start (NESS) is a rolling, UK-wide study, comprising five substantial stands of – largely quantitative – data collection regarding Sure Start's effectiveness (see Belsky *et al.*, 2007). Second, each Sure Start Children's Centre is statutorily required to undertake an annual 'local evaluation', which is typically conducted by centre staff, or commissioned from external consultants/ researchers. As we have outlined elsewhere (see Horton and Kraftl, 2009a, figure 16.1 and table 16.1), these processes comprise limited, circumscribed encounters with the children who are – notionally, rhetorically – central to Sure Start. For on one hand, NESS 'measurement instruments' are solely predicated upon observation, and/or standardized testing/scoring, *of* children, and consultation with parents/carers *about* children. On the other hand, fewer than 5 per cent (14/344) of local evaluative projects in the public domain entailed any direct consultation with children; a greater proportion of projects employed observations *of* children (120/344), or questions *about* children in diverse consultations with their parents/carers. Preschool children thus have an ambivalent status in this policy context: ostensibly prioritized as central and agentic, and yet, in practice, located as *objects of* observation and care, and typically absented from interactive consultative practices.

This limited apprehension of children's own viewpoints is problematic and, in our view, telling. It is problematic because, for example, in our research with parents/carers who opt *not* to use their local Sure Start Children's Centres, children's own attitudes and complaints were explicitly important in around one in five 'non-users" decisions to avoid their local Centre (e.g. the mother quoted in this chapter's preface). That is, children's personal, subjective experiences were actually critical to the 'reach', and therefore sustainability, of particular Children's Centres (and, as such, of Sure Start itself).

Moreover, we suggest that the ambivalent status of children within Sure Start should be understood as telling, and exemplary of a broader problematic: a broad failure, ranging across manifold contemporary policy and research contexts, to attend closely, openly and carefully to preschool children's *own* everyday practices, cares and critiques. This lacuna – also critiqued, within social-scientific contexts, by Løkken (1999, 2000a) and Gallacher (2005, 2006) – may have several, related explanations. First, it might be understood as an intensified form of the well-documented marginalization of children's voices/agency in many contemporary contexts

(Matthews, 2000). Second, similarly, it may represent an intensified form of the deferral of children's agency and decision-making to adult advocates and/or 'experts' (Valentine, 1999). Third, it may reflect a particular methodological heritage, wherein a particular 'toolkit' of observational and quantitative standardized-testing techniques – derived, mainly, from developmentalist psychological, educational and clinical practice – have become normalized and predominant in research encounters with preschool children: hence, for example, the form of the aforementioned NESS Impact Study (see Avis, 2007). Fourth, conversely, it may refract a lack of expertise or confidence amongst qualitative social-scientific researchers when it comes to working with very young children. This may betray anxieties occasioned by the 'otherness' of children (Jones, 2009), or doubts about young children's capacity to contribute meaningfully and rationally to research, especially where it relates to a large and/or politicized topic. Fifth, scholarly accounts of institutional spaces for young children have often taken a particular, notionally 'Foucauldian', line: substantially chronicling the disciplining and control of children, whilst relatively overlooking their own experiences, agency and critiques. Finally, as Løkken (2000b, 2000c) and Gallacher (2005) suggest, circumscribed apprehensions of preschool childhood are, perhaps, effected by an habitual neglect of small-scale, multisensuous, haptic, everyday experiences, and 'playful', vital, 'fun' affective registers, within diverse domains of research, policy and practice (see also Harker, 2005; Horton and Kraftl, 2006).

Evaluating a Sure Start Children's Centre *with* preschool children

In 2008–2009 the authors were part of a team commissioned to conduct the inaugural local evaluation of a recently opened Sure Start Children's Centre in Northamptonshire, UK. Whilst scoping the evaluation with the Centre's management board, it was agreed that it should involve consultation with the young children who visited the Centre,[2] and for whom its spaces, services and activities were principally designed. To this end, a programme of qualitative research was conducted with children aged 0–4 who visited the Centre during January–May 2009: fifty children were consulted, in groups of 2–4, during this period. We developed a reasonably simple 'multisensory evaluation' process to be used in these sessions: this is outlined in Figure 16.1. This method was based on the principle that, although young children may lack verbal capacity or confidence – perhaps especially when confronted with adult strangers posing questions – they are very often virtuosic in using gestural and sensory play to make points, enquiries and critiques (Løkken, 2009). In effect, we sought to afford such play within the Sure Start Children's Centre, and register and 'translate' it into languages and formats 'useable' within the required evaluation criteria and report template. While this kind of process – essentially codifying playful affects and events

All activities conducted by researcher plus a Centre worker, with prior consent of parents/ carers (who can join in, if they wish). The researcher had been introduced to children, and participated in Centre activities, earlier in the day. The following prompts were intended to be adaptable to different children's ages, abilities and levels of engagement.

1) Let's go for a walk
Start sitting on a bench just outside the Centre's door. Explain that we will ask two questions, then walk inside the Centre. Ask:
1) What things can you *see*? Do you like it? What do you (not) like about it?
2) Do you like this place? Why do you say that?
Stand and walk together up path towards the Centre. Just outside the door, pause, kneel and ask:
3) How do you *feel* when you come here? Why do you say that?

2) Show me around
Inside the Centre, each child is given a laminated ☺ and ☹ face. Explain that we want them to use the faces to show us something they really like, and something they don't like, in the Centre. When they show us a ☺ or ☹ face, adults have to play at guessing what they like or dislike. Different children respond to this task differently: some run around flashing cards many times; others spend a long time thinking and then place their faces in just one place.

3) Let's relax
All sit/lie on beanbags arranged on floor. All take part in short breathing/relaxation exercises led by Centre worker. When everyone is relaxed and quiet, ask:
4) What can you *hear*? Do you like it?
5) What can you *smell*? Do you like it?
6) Can you *remember* the first time you came here? What was the best thing? Was there anything you didn't like?

Figure 16.1 Multisensory evaluation project conducted with 0- to 4-year-olds at the Sure Start Children's Centre.

into reportable 'data' – is unquestionably problematic (Kraftl and Horton, 2007), it *did* afford some new realizations which enabled staff to make small adjustments to the Centre's material spaces in direct response to children's hitherto unnoticed issues. In the remainder of this chapter, we highlight four such realizations.

Children's geographies of a Sure Start Children's Centre: four realizations

The following sections present examples of key findings from these research activities. We focus upon four 'realizations', wherein hitherto overlooked issues and concerns were revealed.

Realization 1: the 'Spiderman balls'

'The Spiderman balls are *amazing* . . . but you can get pushed.'

'I always have the other balls – it's not as good as the Spiderman balls.'

'[It's] *very* noisy about here [just next to "ball box"].'

'People *hurt* somebody here [just next to "ball box"].'

'I never get the one [ball] I want – you can sometimes feel left out.'

All of the children indicated that they enjoyed, and cared about the Centre a great deal (see Postscript). Tables 16.1 and 16.2 summarize their responses to the 'show me around' task in which they indicated things they liked/disliked about the Centre. In the remainder of this chapter we will elaborate upon some key points from these tables.

Consider, first, the value attached to toys – and, especially, *particular*, individual toys – by the children consulted. Sure Start Children's Centres typically contain reasonably large, diverse stocks of toys and play equipment. Most days in the life of a centre entail a period when children are allowed to select a toy with which to play. For the children consulted in our research, these trips to the Centre's 'toy shelf' or 'ball box' were a notable, much-anticipated highlight of visits to the Centre. Specific toys – 'the princess' doll, the 'counting blocks' and, most evidently, the 'Spiderman

Table 16.1 What children liked about the Sure Start Children's Centre, Spring 2009

Best thing about the Centre	Frequency* (n = 50)
Playing games	23
Toys	22
'Spiderman balls'	21
'The princess' [doll]	21
Having fun	20
'Counting blocks'	19
Meeting friends	18
'Everything'	18
Spending time with parent/carer	12
Centre staff	9
Painting/drawing activities	6
Music/singing activities	6
Dancing	5
Snacks/drinks	5

Note: * Children were able to list as many positive features as they wanted. Since many children listed more than one thing they liked about the Centre, the frequency column sums up to more than 50.

Table 16.2 What children disliked about the Sure Start Children's Centre, Spring 2009

Worst thing about the Centre	Frequency* (n = 50)
'Nothing'	18
'Rough' play	14
Not able to play with certain toys	12
Approach/entrance to Centre	11
Centre is 'for babies'	10
'Nasty' smells	10
'Nasty' textures/materials	10
Not enough outdoor play	7
Not enough computers	4

Note * Children were able to list as many negative features as they wanted. Since many children listed more than one thing they disliked about the Centre, the frequency column sums up to more than 50.

balls'– were especially valued. These latter toys – four plastic balls of different sizes, bearing images from the recent *Spiderman* movies – belonged in the 'ball box' adjacent to the Centre's 'toy shelf'. As far as adult onlookers – staff, researchers, parents/carers – were concerned, the well-stocked ball box contained plenty of balls to go around on any given day; there was no particular reason to suspect that particular balls were considered especially desirable. However, children made plain that the 'ball box' was the focus for a clear, shared set of preferences: the 'Spiderman balls' were 'amazing'; all 'the other balls' were 'not as good as the Spiderman balls'. In this context, the daily trip to the 'ball box' and adjacent 'toy shelf' had sometimes resulted in 'pushing', 'noise', 'people hurt[ing] somebody'. Indeed, this was a key cause of the 'rough play' described by children in Table 16.2. For some children, the 'ball box' was a site of disappointment, anxiety and exclusion: 'never get[ting] the one I want', 'always hav[ing] the other balls', feeling 'left out'.

Recent work by children's geographers has explored how children's play can often be characterized by politics, normativity and/or exclusions (Harker, 2005) and how, therefore, spaces of/for play are always already social geographies of inclusion/exclusion (Thomson and Philo, 2004; Thomson, 2005; Holt, 2007). Such work should remind us that particular socialities and spatialities exist at the heart of all policy and institutional spaces for children. Certainly, the daily interactions around the 'ball box' can be interpreted thus, in the wake of children's comments. Notably, in this context social geographies and exclusions emerged from, and were attached to, very small spaces, and individual material objects: indeed, as we note in the following section, such geographies even emerged from the microscopic hapticity of specific objects. Notably, too, all of this proceeded largely unseen by the adults who staffed and visited the Centre: although children were closely attended at all times, small disappointments and anxieties around the 'ball box' were largely tacit, and perhaps beyond the ken, away from the concerns, and occasionally beneath the eyeline, of adult onlookers. Certainly, issues relating to the 'Spiderman balls' appeared idiosyncratic and irrational to the Centre's staff, and us as researchers: there appeared no rationale for 'Spiderman balls' being 'better' than the twenty other – equally colourful, similarly sized, similarly branded – balls in the 'ball box'. For the children consulted, however, this preference was simply matter-of-fact: the 'Spiderman balls' were just 'amazing'.

Realization 2: textures

'I hate the handles on some scooters. It is *sticky*.'

'Some [balls] are too *squidgy*.'

'Some toys are *rough*. People rush around and hit because they don't want *those* [toys].'

'The green carpet is horrible – it feels *uggh*.'

'Outside it is too rough . . . The grass is too long and wet. It is too *bumpy* to play on. You can't scoot.'

Consultation with children revealed the importance of very small-scale textures, surfaces and materialities in experiences of the spaces of the Sure Start Children's Centre. Such physicalities can be easily, indeed literally, over-looked by adult onlookers who are somewhat aloof from the Centre's floors and surfaces, and seldom in sustained embodied contact with the surfaces of toys and materials. The children with whom we worked, however, articulated several anxieties and problems relating to the 'feel' of the Centre, from their perspective. They drew attention to the unpleasant 'sticky'-ness, 'squidgy'-ness and 'rough'-ness of particular material things within the Centre. These observations – essentially registering slight, textural degradations of plastics – revealed a level of preferences and anxieties which were largely impercep-tible to adults who staffed and visited the Centre. Thus, textural differences in the condition of scooter handles, balls and action figures constituted a set of preferences, and then divisive practices, relating to each of these objects: as a direct consequence, for example, 'people rush around and hit because they don't want *those* [toys]'. Similarly, children noted a range of issues and aversions in relation to floor-level surfaces: the ways in which certain frictive underfoot textures can make one cringe ('*uggh*'), or certain grass-cutting practices can impede playing or scooting.

These findings recall children's geographers' many explorations of the micro-geographies of particular milieus and neighbourhoods. They remind us, more broadly, of the often-taken-for-granted centrality of tactilities in the sensing and experiencing of spaces (Rodaway, 1994; Paterson, 2007). Crucially, here, these tactilities constituted preferences, anxieties and geographies which made a difference to children's experiences, and un/happiness, within the Centre. Thus, children's comments draw attention to the tangible, but easily overlooked, fabric and micro-materialities which literally constitute institutional and policy 'contexts'. Moreover, they suggest the extent to which particular materialities, and sensuous micro-geographies therein/thereof, can produce contingent experiences, moods and attachments or anxieties. Indeed, we might infer how such contingencies (perhaps children 'rush[ing] around and hit[ting]' because they don't want roughly textured toys) can produce outcomes (upset children who feel disinclined to return there) which ultimately affect the success of this centre and, as such, this policy context as a whole.

Realization 3: 'baby smells'

'Nasty baby smells make it [the Centre] poo-ey and dirty . . . [It is] not fun to be with babies.'

'I don't like playing with the babies. The babies do horrible poo! It makes mess! It's *uggh!*'

'*This* smell [near baby changing facilities] is nasty.'

'It is horrible here – it is poo and the *nasty*.'

Most of the older (i.e. 3- to 4-year-old) children with whom we worked felt that the Centre was 'for babies': that is, not principally for themselves. They articulated a sense that the co-mingling of children of different ages between 0–4 was a problematic feature of the Centre: it was 'boring' and 'not fun to be with babies'. They noted a number of ways in which interacting with 'babies' was 'not fun' relating, for example, to differences in preferences for toys and games, and motor and language skills. This aversion to 'babies' was closely coupled to an aversion to 'baby smells'. Indeed, one in five of the children consulted identified 'nasty smells' as their least favourite thing about the Centre. Their comments revealed a distinct set of spatial, olfactory aversions: a smellscape mainly landmarked by 'poo and the *nasty*'. These terms referred, respectively, to the presence of nappy-changing facilities and dispensers of strong-smelling alcohol-based hand-wash (i.e. 'the nasty') in close proximity to the Centre's communal areas. These smellscapes reportedly varied according to season (smells were stronger in warmer weather), time of day (hand-wash smells became amplified, as a result of cumulative usage, over the course of each day), and the number of 'babies' occupying the Centre during any given session.

Whereas adult users of the Centre took its smells for granted, or had perhaps trained themselves to be tactfully accepting of them, many children were unabashedly upset by the Centre's smellscape. Indeed, a number of children articulated a marked sense of distress, hesitancy and abjection in relation to these smells: they found them '*nasty*', '*horrible*', '*uggh!*' These sensations constituted avoidances and anxieties of particular sites within the Centre: thus, for example, children described how they did not 'enjoy things' within nose-shot of the Centre's toilets, nappy-changing tables, hand-wash dispensers. Thus, the Centre's smells were, to some extent, constitutive of activity patterns within the Centre, and therein (re)productive of older children's antipathy towards 'babies' (and, perhaps, broader constructions of early childhood within the Centre's immediate and societal context). That is, these older children distanced themselves – spatially and imaginarily – from 'baby-ish' individuals, spaces and behaviours through an abjection of smells associated with them (see Sibley, 1995). For some children, too, the Centre's 'poo-ey'-ness and 'baby'-ness were inseparable, and extended to a feeling the Centre itself was – as in this chapter's preface – *itself* entirely 'poo-ey' and 'dirty'. Thus, again, small-scale everyday bodily experiences of the Centre – in this case its smell – contributed somewhat to the broader experiencing and conceiving of the Centre itself.

Realization 4: anxieties

'This door [a locked cupboard] is bad. Something bad could happen. I feel sad.'

'Sometimes I don't like to come [to the Centre] . . . This [a locked cupboard] *scares* me. Sometimes I just want mummy.'

'I don't like the walk [to the Centre]. The [Centre's exterior] walls are horrible with blood [i.e. red graffiti] and big dogs go *woof* and scared me.'

'This [drain cover] is frightening for me and this [doorstep] is horrid because of spiders [i.e. cobwebs].'

Children's responses to our research revealed a wide range of emotive anxieties – some shared, some idiosyncratic – relating to their experience of the Centre. These kinds of responses reveal the extent to which children's experiences of the Centre were profoundly affected by fears or uncertainties in relation to specific, ostensibly banal features of the Centre: thus children described a reportedly ominous cupboard, a reportedly frightening drain cover, a cobweb-covered doorstep, and so forth. These fears may seem trivial or irrational to adult onlookers – or elude their notice altogether – yet they appeared to have deeply affected individual children. Certainly, some children described emotional, bodily and behavioural responses to such anxieties, which thus coloured and haunted their times in the Centre: consider, for instance, the clingy feeling of 'I just want mummy' associated with fears about a locked cupboard in the Centre. In such circumstances, ostensibly small anxieties would almost certainly circumscribe engagement with, and enjoyment of, the Centre for both children and, therefore, their attendant parents/carers.

Children's responses also revealed some ways in which anxieties originating *outside* the Centre could affect their experiences once inside. Thus, for example, overhearing an argument at home, or encountering vandalism or 'big dogs go[ing] *woof*' en route to the Centre could result in individual children 'feel[ing] sad' during their time there. These instances revealed the extent to which local, everyday geographies of familial and community lives (Holloway, 1998a, 1998b) could haunt, and matter in, the particular spaces of the Sure Start Children's Centre (see also Jupp, 2007). That is, contra the idea of a 'Sure Start Centre', the Centre was not a neatly bounded space: rather, it was fundamentally connected to, and always affected by, its community, including its relationships (e.g. familial or neighbourhood disputes), issues (barking dogs and busy traffic outside the Centre) and materialities (graffiti on the Centre's exterior walls). In any of these senses – whether prompted by a mysterious, locked cupboard at the Centre, or an encounter with a fearsome dog on the way – the everyday lives of children and their parents/carers intimately affected the tenor of encounters with and at the Sure Start Centre (see also Horton and Kraftl, 2009b). As we have attempted to suggest in this chapter, the everyday particularities and details of life at the Centre – including its textures, smells, toys, tears and laughter – were quite central to the experiencing, and hence the outcomes, of this particular facet of contemporary policy/institutional provision for young children.

Conclusions

This chapter has re-presented several preschool children's geographies, situated within an institutional/policy context ostensibly 'tailored to' them. As we have noted, our work with these children prompted several small revelations about this Sure Start Children's Centre. Each of these 'realizations' existed somewhat 'under the radar' of adult parents/carers and adult workers at the Centre. While, for children's geographers, their observations are perhaps not surprising, these four realizations do 'flesh out' specific, empirical registers through which such 'under-the-radar' geographies take place.

Our four 'realizations' leave us with a twofold anxiety: (1) how could, or should, such small, quotidian, 'toddler'-scaled geographies be conceived as mattering; (2) indeed, how *were* our four 'realizations' conceived as mattering, in practice, in the political/institutional context in which we worked?

The latter part of this question can be addressed most readily. For we can identify two lines of work via which the empirical details part-presented in this paper were registered and taken forward by the policy/institutional context of Sure Start. On one hand, the Centre's staff have already begun to act, with considerable care, upon these small realizations: more balls have been purchased; the 'ball box' has been 'relocated'; instructions have been issued to mow the grass differently; new air-fresheners have been ordered; cobwebs have been swept from the doorstep; and so forth. Moreover, these practitioners have instigating a process of periodic consultation with young users of the Centre, to address future needs and contingencies as they arise. With this attentiveness to minutiae, the staff thus continue to make small, incremental adjustments to the fabric and practices, and perhaps the 'effectiveness', of this policy-instigated, community-based intervention.

Alternatively, the ultimate political import of the findings presented in this chapter could be – indeed has already been – summarized in the following way: '85, 65, 76, 58, 55, 95'. These six integers, inputted into a password-protected spreadsheet, represented the totality of our research 'findings' when translated into 'performance indicators'. These statutorily required quantitative indicators were reported to the Centre's management Board and governing local authority, and subsequently evaluated against salient national averages for reporting to the national Sure Start Unit. To be sure – for researchers committed to rich, detailed, qualitative modes of enquiry – this translation of preschool children's geographies into performance indicators feels brutal, deeply reductive and problematic. Note, too, that these numbers have considerable weight: that '95' will probably ensure that some of the Centre's funding is guaranteed for another twelve months; had it been an '85' an enquiry would have investigated why the Centre was 'Underperforming'; had it been '60' or below, 'Special Measures' could have been implemented, funding could have been withheld, jobs could have been lost, the Centre's future could have been jeopardized.

In both of these respects, then, the ostensibly banal, 'toddler'-scaled geographies of this particular institutional space can be said to be politically instrumental. To many (adult) onlookers, the small happenings re-presented herein may appear inconsequential, or may pass entirely unnoticed. However, as we have suggested in this chapter, these small geographies – and adults' efforts to register and respond to them – should be understood as potentially deeply politicized, and as having potentially significant ramifications. They are central to the efforts of the Centre staff in constituting spaces and interventions which 'work' – which are appealing, engaging, useful, user-friendly, supportive and potentially transformative – for local parents/carers and their children. As our postscript is supposed to evoke, the results of this labour could, sometimes, be marked, affecting, even joyous. Moreover, these preschool children's geographies are, in some measure, central to the success of Sure Start, locally and macropolitically. For geographies such as those witnessed in this paper must be fundamental to the experiences of children and parents/carers who visit any given Centre; these experiences, once minimally registered and codified as performance indicators, are instrumental in the evaluation, governance and planning of Sure Start Children's Centres, and Sure Start per se. As such, they are arguably key to the socially-historically particular, latterly critiqued, 'post-welfarist' approach taken by the UK government in relation to children and their parents/carers (Bristow, 2005; Clarke, 2006; Mizen, 2006).

We come full circle, therefore, to the ambiguous contemporary political status of preschool children. For the geographies re-presented in this paper were at once largely unseen by adults, yet efficacious within a much broader, and perhaps much more problematic, political milieu. We suggest that this ambiguity is deepened by several, related 'gaps' or non-correspondences which haunt this chapter: between the detail and richness and critical, sometimes-revelatory alterity (Jones, 2009) of children's geographies vis-à-vis the reductive representational economies of evaluative enquiry; between the close attention paid to these geographies by Sure Start Centre staff vis-à-vis the minimal registering of these efforts by national performance indicators; between the everyday happenings and contexts of particular Sure Start Children's Centres vis-à-vis the policy agenda of 'Sure Start'. These differences – and the import habitually attached to the latter over the former, in each case – are deeply ingrained. It is challenging to think otherwise: to respect preschool children as potentially politically agentic; to acknowledge small, easily overstepped, otherworldy details and anxieties as mattering within evaluative practices; to think in terms of the quotidian happening of particular policies or institutional spaces, rather than in terms of *a* Policy or Institution. In this chapter, we have argued that social scientists and policy-makers ought to pay more heed, generally, to the politics of the ostensibly banal, perhaps by attending to the challenges posed by preschool children's geographies in/of policy/institutional contexts. For we should take seriously the politics and importance of small spaces, small happenings and all of the everydayness, smells, textures, tears and laughter therein . . .

Postscript: laughter

A mother and son (aged 4) describe a visit to the Centre, February 2009.

'Once he'd had a look around, he loved it. He was a right friendly chatterbox! I've never seen him smile so much, and *laugh*! He couldn't stop laughing.'

'I like it [the Centre]. There was a bear and it made me *laugh*! And you get to play with other children . . .'

Notes

1 The identities of the Centre and its users are protected throughout this chapter. Ellipses in empirical material are represented by three dots (. . .). Italicized text indicates substantial spoken *emphasis*.

2 In total, the evaluation project entailed four key lines of work: (1) collation of baseline data; (2) a questionnaire survey with 40 parents/carers who used the Centre; (3) interviews with 20 parents/carers who were entitled to use the Centre, but did not; (4) qualitative projects with young children using the Centre. Being statutorily required at the time, the project was commissioned from the Centre's core funding. Summaries of 'policy-relevant' findings/recommendations from the project are available from the authors on request.

References

Avis, M. (2007) 'Introduction to health and child development', in J. Schneider, M. Avis, and P. Leighton (eds) *Supporting Children and Families: Lessons from Sure Start*, London: Kinglsey.

Belsky, J., Barnes, J. and Meluish, E. (2007) *The National Evaluation of Sure Start*, Bristol: The Policy Press.

Bristow, J. (2005) 'A Sure Start for the therapeutic state', *Spiked Online*, 22 September 2005.

Clarke, K. (2006) 'Childhood, parenting and early intervention: a critical examination of the Sure Start national programme', *Critical Social Policy*, 26: 699–721.

DCSF (Department for Children, Schools and Families) (2007) *The Children's Plan: Building Brighter Futures*, London: DCSF.

DfES/DWP (Department for Education and Skills/Department for Work and Pensions) (2006) *Choice for Parents, the Best Start for Children: Making it Happen*, London: DfES.

Gallacher, L. (2005) '"The terrible twos": gaining control in the nursery', *Children's Geographies*, 3: 243–64.

Gallacher, L. (2006) 'Making space for excess in the nursery? Or, superheroes in the doll corner', *Paper Presented at the Annual Conference of the Royal Geographical Society with Institute of British Geographers*, London, September 2006.

Glass, N. (1999) 'Sure Start: the development of an early intervention programme for young children in the United Kingdom', *Children and Society*, 13: 257–64.

Harker, C. (2005) 'Playing and affective time-spaces', *Children's Geographies*, 3: 47–62.

HM Treasury (2003) *Every Child Matters*, London: HM Treasury.

Holloway, S. (1998a) '"She lets me go out once a week": mothers' strategies for obtaining "personal" time and space', *Area*, 30: 321–30.

Holloway, S. (1998b) 'Local childcare cultures: moral geographies of mothering and the social organisation of pre-school education', *Gender, Place and Culture*, 5: 29–53.

Holt, L. (2007) 'Children's socio-spatial (re)production of disability within primary school playgrounds', *Environment and Planning D: Society and Space*, 27: 783–802.

Horton, J. and Kraftl, P. (2006) 'What else? Some more ways of thinking about and doing children's geographies', *Children's Geographies*, 4: 131–43.

Horton, J. and Kraftl, P. (2009a) 'What (else) matters? Policy contexts, emotional geographies', *Environment and Planning A*, 41(12): 2984–3002.

Horton, J. and Kraftl, P. (2009b) 'Small acts, kind words and "not too much fuss": implicit activisms', *Emotion, Space and Society*, 2: 14–23.

Jones, O. (2009) 'Approaching the otherness of childhood: methodological considerations', in L. van Blerk and M. Kesby (eds) *Doing Children's Geographies: Methodological Issues in Research with Young People*, London: Routledge.

Jupp, E. (2007) 'The feeling of participation: everyday spaces and urban change', *Geoforum*, 39: 331–43.

Kraftl, P. and Horton, J. (2007) '"The health event": everyday, affective politics of participation', *Geoforum*, 38: 1012–27.

Løkken, G. (1999) 'Challenges in toddler peer research', *Nordisk Pedagogik*, 3: 145–55.

Løkken, G. (2000a) 'The playful quality of the toddling "style"', *Qualitative Studies in Education*, 13: 531–42.

Løkken, G. (2000b) 'Using Merleau-Pontyan phenomenology to understand the toddler', *Nordisk Pedagogik*, 1: 13–23.

Løkken, G. (2000c) 'Tracing the social "style" of toddler peers', *Scandinavian Journal of Educational Research*, 2: 1–38.

Løkken, G. (2009) 'The construction of "toddler" in early childhood pedagogy', *Contemporary Issues in Early Childhood*, 10: 35–42.

Matthews, H. (2000) *Children and Community Regeneration*, London: Save the Children.

NESS (National Evaluation of Sure Start) (2005) *National Evaluation Report: Early Impacts of Sure Start Local Programmes on Children and Families*, London: DfES Sure Start Unit.

Paterson, M. (2007) *The Senses of Touch: Haptics, Affects and Technologies*. Oxford: Berg.

Rodaway, P. (1994) *Sensuous Geographies: Body, Sense and Place*. London: Routledge.

Sibley, D. (1995) *Geographies of Exclusion: Society and Difference in the West*, London: Routledge.

Sure Start (2000) *What is Sure Start?* London: Sure Start.

Sure Start (2002a) *Birth to Three Matters: An Introduction to the Framework*, London: Sure Start.

Sure Start (2002b) *Sure Start: A Guide for Sixth Wave Programmes*, London: Sure Start.

Sure Start (2003a) *Sure Start Guidance, 2004–06. II – Delivery Guidance*, Annesley: DfES.

Sure Start (2003b) *Sure Start Guidance, 2004–06. I – Strategic Guidance*, Annesley: DfES.

Sure Start (2004) *A Sure Start for Every Child*, London: Sure Start.

Sure Start (2009) *Government Celebrates the Opening of 3000 Sure Start Children's Centres.* Available at: http://www.dcsf.gov.uk/pns/DisplayPN.cgi?pn_id=2009_0091 (accessed 30 September 2010).

Thomson, S. (2005) '"Territorialising" the primary school playground: deconstructing the geography of playtime', *Children's Geographies*, 3: 63–78.

Thomson, S. and Philo, C. (2004) 'Playful spaces? A social geography of play in Livingstone, Scotland' *Children's Geographies*, 3: 111–30.

Valentine, G. (1999) 'Being seen and heard? The ethical complexities of working with children and young people at home and at school', *Ethics, Place and Environment*, 2: 141–55.

17 Social and educational inequalities in English state schools

Exploring the understandings of urban white middle-class children

Sumi Hollingworth, Katya Williams,
Fiona Jamieson and Phoebe Beedell

Introduction

This chapter provides a case study of a very particular sample of children living and going to school in three cities in England, UK. Research in both sociology, children's geographies and education, in urban areas, tends to focus on 'marginalised' or 'disadvantaged' youth and their experiences of growing up in cities. However, our research draws on the accounts of a more privileged section of children in the city: a sample of white middle-class children who are attending, or attended, urban state schools. Specifically, this chapter problematizes the role of increasingly prevalent discourses of individualization in these young people's accounts of the inequalities they come across in their experience of schooling.

Background

Individualization in neo-liberal society

Several commentators have argued that the current neo-liberal age is dominated by a prevailing individualism. It has become popular to proclaim the end of 'old' categories of social class, 'race'/ethnicity and gender, and that these categories no longer govern who we are and what we can be in society (Beck, 1992; Giddens, 1990). Beck (1992) claims that we have moved from 'normal' biographies (life courses that have traditionally been shaped by social structures such as ethnicity and social class) to 'choice' biographies, in which individual futures are personally created, in an endless array of possibilities. Placing a new significance on personal agency, individuals need to become 'entrepreneurs of themselves, shaping their own lives through the choices they make' (Rose, 1999: 230). Arguably, individualization is a particularly potent discourse in relation to the education system, characterized by a notion of meritocracy, where children are told that if they work hard and study hard then they will achieve success.

Inequalities in urban education in England

The individualization thesis might have us assume that people now have 'unfettered opportunities' and are free to be whoever/whatever they want to be in life; however, research shows that the constraints of social class, gender and 'race'/ethnicity are not disappearing. Indeed the effects are just becoming more obscure (see Archer *et al.*, 2010). Opportunities are not entirely equal, even if they are presented as though they are. Much research in the UK has highlighted that there are persistent inequalities apparent in the educational system in terms of attainment, opportunities and outcomes, where certain groups of children achieve less well that others. Those who achieve less well (certain boys, some minority ethnic groups, children receiving free school meals and children from certain geographic areas) are popularly referred to as 'underachieving' and policies typically focus on 'raising' their achievement and aspirations. This approach constructs them (and their families) as 'the problem' (Crozier, 2005), while the educational success of white children from professional backgrounds has often been taken for granted (Lucey and Reay, 2000). Meritocracy is underpinned by the idea that those with the best 'ability' or talent in a particular subject or task will be suitably rewarded. However, sociologists of education argue that 'ability' is a social construct and related to structures of power. Who decides or judges what is considered to be 'ability' constrains some groups in society, while enabling others (see Gillborn and Youdell, 2000). In this vein, sociologists of education, dating back to the 1970s, have argued that European education systems privilege middle-class children in various ways, promoting middle-class understandings of what is knowledge, and penalizing or not valuing (ethnically diverse) working-class knowledges and lifestyles (Bernstein, 1996; Bourdieu and Passeron, 1977; Whitty, 2001). Bourdieu (1997) refers to this advantage as cultural and social capital, where (white) middle-class families' resources, knowledge and contacts have more currency in the system.

It is in urban education settings that such inequalities are particularly apparent. In the UK, historically, children in non-selective state schools in urban areas perform less well in national examinations (GCSEs), fewer than average progress into post-compulsory education after the age of 16 and, accordingly, schools in urban areas feature at the bottom end of government 'Performance Tables'. In the current context of increasing gentrification of urban areas in Britain (Butler, 2003), where the numbers of professional middle-class families living in cities are on the increase, geographers and education researchers such as Butler and Robson (2003), Ball (2003) and Reay (2007) have drawn attention to social and ethnic polarization in urban schooling, where urban state schools (populated by predominantly multi-ethnic, working-class children) are 'demonised' in middle-class imaginaries. Ball (2003) highlights how it is the norm for white urban middle-class parents to avoid the local comprehensive school, and seek out 'better' schools: to 'work the education system' by choosing either private fee-paying schools; or high-status selective schools, where there is a critical mass of children like their own. This is a phenomenon increasingly apparent in other global cities also (see Sofer, 2007).

Urban white middle-class children: the research

The research upon which this chapter draws, however, focused specifically on white urban middle-class families who, acting against this norm, chose to send their children to the local inner-city comprehensive school. We carried out qualitative, semi-structured, in-depth interviews with 124 families in three cities in England. In this chapter we focus on the interviews with the children and young people in those families. We carried out 68 interviews with children across the three cities (20 in our northern city we have called Norton, 20 in our western city we have called Riverton and 28 in London). Their ages ranged from 11 to 22 years old.[1] Consequently, some of the young people we interviewed were no longer in compulsory education so are speaking in retrospect about their experiences several years ago. Nevertheless, there are clear continuities with those contemporary accounts, but also perhaps some subtle difference which we shall discuss.

Despite attending schools in the inner cities that other middle-class families shun because standards of achievement are perceived to be low, this had not appeared to affect these children's achievement levels – or not to any great extent. The vast majority of the children in these families were in the top 'sets' (or 'ability groups') at school and a large number had been selected for the Gifted and Talented programme (an urban scheme for high achieving pupils). All (bar two) achieved the benchmark school leaving grades at age 16 (5 A*–C GCSEs), with most far exceeding this and the majority of those beyond school age were either undertaking A levels (the prerequisite qualifications for university entrance) or were at university (with large numbers attending top-performing universities). This was in sharp contrast to their peers, where in the majority of schools in our sample, fewer than half of pupils achieve the benchmark school leaving grades which are necessary to continue into further academic courses. There is very little evidence here to support the ideal of comprehensive education as a means to level out class and ethnic inequalities in attainment opportunities (Pring and Walford, 1997). In addition, these children were in relatively socially privileged situations – virtually all parents were homeowners, most in gentrified areas; very few were single parents; all parents had professional jobs, many in senior positions in the public sector; and children spoke of regular family holidays overseas. In their narratives, this was often set in contrast to their school peers who were more likely to live in single-parent families, unemployed households and in overcrowded social housing.

This chapter explores how these young people came to understand their privileged location within the school and their neighbourhood. While these children were academically sailing ahead of the majority of their classmates, we ask what kind of discourses did they draw on to explain why some children don't do so well in school (and implied within that, why they do). In this chapter we reveal the pervasiveness of neo-liberal discourses of individualization. While we saw a tolerance and respect of 'others' in social terms coming from some of our interviewees, in educational terms the situation was very different. There was less understanding of how the education system reproduces inequality. Young people's narratives were characterized by a psychologized view of social inequalities framed in terms of personal qualities (Gillies, 2005). Success in education was framed in three main ways: natural ability or intelligence; individual hard work/effort; and parental encouragement and support. All of these explanations, we argue, draw attention away from structural and institutional causes. We discuss each of these in turn before going on to argue that these accounts were often interwoven together and often joined with more social explanations for educational inequality. However, we argue that individualized accounts prevailed, and that this is problematic for equity in urban schools and hence urban children's lives.

Understanding social and educational inequality

Many of the young people were beginning to follow their parents in left-of-centre political views (rejecting the increasing privatization of public services, and condemning the war in Iraq to name a few examples); and several espoused an associated ethical environmentalism (concerned with global issues of climate change, fair trade initiatives, ethical consumption) (see Reay *et al.*, 2008). Many, particularly in London, were committed to anti-racism and felt that attending their school had made them more tolerant, understanding and 'open-minded' (in their words) of 'others' from 'different racial backgrounds' 'different religions' and those from poor or 'disadvantaged' groups, such as refugees.

Many agreed with their parents that supporting the local state comprehensive was a moral imperative – rejecting private, fee-paying schools as elitist, exclusionary and/ or damagingly competitive. A number of the young people recognized the inequalities inherent in the education system caused by the presence of private and selective schools which serve to segregate children from different social backgrounds and upset the social balance in so-called 'comprehensive schools' (Hattersley, 2004; Whitty, 2001). In terms of equality issues within schools, pupils in Norton, our northern city, in particular, spoke of how 'setting' practices and the Gifted and Talented scheme were unfair to those who were placed in the lower groups or not selected to the scheme (Gillborn, 2005; Reay, 2004).

Repertoires of individualism and notions of 'ability'

Despite an awareness of inequalities in the education system, these children at the same time drew on individualizing discourses which located the explanation for these inequities within the individual child. This was often constructed in terms of intelligence or 'ability', and a belief that with enough 'hard work' success can be obtained. We discuss how these discourses sit well within a meritocratic framework, which is used to legitimate inequalities under the guise of equal opportunities.

Following Bourdieu's writings on the reproduction of educational inequality, James argues that, in populist thinking:

> Educational failure is usually experienced as a person's own fault for not working hard enough or not being endowed with the requisite genes (or parents), whilst success is celebrated as the fruit of one's labours and perhaps some innate ability.
>
> (James, 2005: 117)

What James is ultimately describing here is the notion of meritocracy. In Young's (1973 [1958]) book *The Rise of the Meritocracy*, the term was intended to be pejorative, and his book was set in a dystopian future in which one's social place is determined by IQ plus effort. We can see the young middle classes in our study routinely drawing on these very discourses that both Young and James critique: that success in life is rationalized as innate 'ability' (intelligence/merit) plus hard work or effort.

Ability

In this study, several young people drew on the concept of 'ability', which in the educational world has become popularized over the notion of 'intelligence'. The word 'ability' implies more agency than 'intelligence' or 'IQ' which historically have been used in a more scientific manner to denote an actual fixed concept: an innate, biological condition. Indeed, according to the Oxford dictionary, one definition of ability is 'having power to do', which implies a sense of agency, but also raises this notion of power – who has the power to do? However, this is not how 'ability' is typically used and understood. This research and others, has found 'ability' being used by people in a very similar way to intelligence: as something innate. In Gillborn and Youdell's (2000) research with teachers in schools, they found this discourse of innate 'ability' rife. Academic ability was seen as something you either have, or you don't have, and there was little reference by teachers to the socially constructed nature of the term 'ability': that the education system defines what skills and knowledge are valued and that this is based on a given context.

Our research findings supported this perception. Sian, a 13-year-old girl in our northern city, for example, when asked why she thought some people achieved better at school than others, felt that it is because some people aren't as able as others. Sian put success down to innate family intelligence claiming that her and her sister are both very 'clever' so it must be in their 'genes'. Similarly, Jason (13), in Riverton, explained of those in the lower 'sets', that:

> It's not their fault that they aren't achieving, it's like they try their hardest but maybe things don't come to them as easily as people in the higher sets.

In these accounts the individual is accountable for their own success, but actually has very little choice if they are unfortunately born with the wrong 'genes' or with lower 'intelligence' or 'ability'. In our research, parents also used the terms 'intelligence' and 'ability' uncritically, unfalteringly describing their own children as 'intelligent', 'bright' or 'clever' and this was often portrayed as something innate or natural in their children (see also Gillies, 2005; Lucey and Reay, 2002).

This belief in a meritocracy was coupled with a belief in equal opportunities. Sian admitted that while some people aren't as able as others, she thinks 'everybody's got pretty good opportunities.' The implied logic of Sian's statement is that it appears everyone in school is given the same opportunities and resources to succeed, therefore, if they don't, it must be because they are not as 'able'. As Francis (1999: 369) observes, 'liberal equal opportunities discourses [. . .] may mask continuing inequality and difference'. This, others have argued (Lucey and Reay, 2002), feeds into a middle-class discourse of entitlement: where the middle classes feel that because they are naturally bright they are deserving of extra resources and attention, educationally.

Hard work

In addition to innate ability, other young people put academic success down to 'hard work' and application, and failure down to a lack of effort. Martha (16) in Riverton explained how she has been successful because she is a strong-minded person with 'a will and a motivation – self-motivation, which a lot of people don't have at my School', whilst Charlotte (16) and Alexa (15) in London explained that peers haven't done well because 'they couldn't be bothered' or they 'mucked about'. Alexa said: 'if you don't muck about then, yeah, you will get a higher grade. It's as simple as that.' Similarly, Lowry (16) in Riverton asserted: 'I think, most of it – at GCSE level – is whether you decide to do it or not, I think it's yourself.'

Francis' examination of the debate in the UK about boys' underachievement found that young people felt that 'different ways of behaving are caused by "different personalities" rather than gender' (1999: 368). Similarly, in this research we can see approaches to and valuing of school work was attributed to personal qualities. Other people, who don't achieve as well at school are perceived as having the 'wrong' personality – they don't have 'self-motivation' or they can't be 'bothered'. Educational success is thus framed as a choice.

Critics of trends of individualization argue that this mode of thinking transfers responsibility for one's own success, and inevitably 'failure,' to the individual: individuals are constructed as architects of their own failure, as Walkerdine (2003) puts it. There is an internalization of educational (success and) failure into an aspect of the self. So, from a neo-liberal perspective, people who don't do well in education 'appear to be unable – or worse, unwilling – to fit themselves into the meritocratic educational system which produces the achievement vital for [. . .] economic success' (Francis, 2006: 193). Thus, as Rose (1999) argues, unsuccessful people are not seen as victims but as 'failures in self governance, unable or unwilling to appropriately capitalize on their lives' (cited in Gillies, 2005: 837).

So differences in achievement at school are seen to be due to differences in (a) 'natural' intelligence or innate ability, or (b) individual choices – i.e. the choice to behave at school, work hard, try hard and be self-motivated. Lowry in Norton argues that her success was down to a combination of both:

> [B]ecause I worked hard and was quite intelligent and had a good rela-
> tionship with the teachers I made it decent, someone who didn't have
> my personal resources behind them, probably wouldn't get what I got
> out of it.

In Lowry's account, both her intelligence and her ability to apply herself, work hard, and get on with the teachers were seen as 'personal resources', again attributing this to individual merit, as opposed to cultural resources or capital brought to her through familial or some wider middle-class advantage (Bourdieu, 1997). We can see this sense of entitlement in Lowry's talk. Discursive constructions of the deserving self become a resource for the middle classes to consolidate their advantage (Gillies, 2005).

Families that don't care

In this section we show that another way in which some of the children in this research explained inequalities tended to draw on pejorative or deficit understandings of 'other' families. Constructing educational success as a 'choice' has the consequence of pathologizing whole groups of people who are seen as not making the 'right' choices.

Previous research on teachers' discourses about educational achievement, has found that teachers' often invoked students' 'backgrounds' as generally problematic and as causal of academic difficulties (Archer *et al.*, 2010; Comber, 1998). This perspective is also seen in much English education policy where working class and some minority ethnic families are conveyed as the main barrier to achievement, and are seen as hindering their children's aspirations (Colley and Hodkinson, 2001; Gerwirtz, 2001). This deficit model constructs the root of the problem as within these individuals rather than as a function of the system itself (see also Whitty, 2001).

One of the questions we asked all the children was if they thought one's family or schooling has more impact on success in education. The vast majority claimed family was more of an influence. Benjamin (17) in Norton explained:

> It depends a lot on the individual because – I mean with our parents, they're very, interested in us doing well in our GCSEs and A Levels, so they talk about it to me like almost daily, and the idea of the GCSE it's

Table 17.1 White middle-class children's classification of different types of families

Characteristics of families of children who do 'well' at school	*Characteristics of families of children who do not do 'well' at school*
'Parents that care' how their children are doing at school	Families 'not caring' about school
'Valuing education'	'Not valuing' education
'Always supporting'	'Not supporting their child at school enough'
'Academically minded'	'Not so academic'
'Bright'	
'Helping' with school work	Who 'don't give much of a damn'
Parents who 'keep in mind' or 'make sure'	Parents who aren't 'making sure'
Providing an environment where 'homework' is central	Where children 'don't have to do their homework'
In some cases providing outside tuition	Where 'nobody gives a crap'
'Pushing you' to work hard	Not pushing their child
Applying 'pressure'	Parents who 'don't hassle you' to work hard
Families with 'determination'	Families with 'no boundaries' or restraint
	People with 'problems'
	'Bad home lives'
	'Disruptions at home'
With some even explicitly suggesting that these are specific traits of 'middle-class' families	. . . and of 'working-class' families

always there [. . .] but there are some people who, you know, their parents aren't as involved in their education, and maybe they would benefit from more pressure.

As Comber (1998: 9) has pointed out, uneven achievement has all too often been constituted as 'problem of motivation and parental encouragement' (citing Freebody 1992: 74). In her research in schools serving 'disadvantaged communities' in Australia, teacher's set up binaries distinguishing wealthy families from poor families where wealthy families are described as 'successful' and 'intelligent', while 'poor families' are described as 'chaotic', having 'problems' and lacking 'support' for their children (1998: 17). These middle-class young people drew on very similar discourses, setting a clear distinction between 'families who care' (like their own) and 'families who don't care' about their children's education, as the defining factor in educational success (see Table 17.1).

We can see from this table the multiple ways in which parents' behaviour and choices are seen as instrumental to their children's success. Responsibility is projected onto working-class parents for failing to equip their children with the right skills for educational improvement (Gillies, 2005).

The 'kaleidoscope of common sense'

It would be misleading, however, to suggest that these young people's explanations were clear-cut – there was a good degree of ambivalence. As has been evident in some of the young people's narratives addressed so far, ability, effort, parental encouragement were often given as multiple explanations. However, with some of the older interviewees reflecting on their experiences, discourses of individualism were sometimes entangled with other, often more social, interpretations for inequalities. Through the interview process we found these young people struggling to make sense of what are complex issues. Billig (1992) calls this a 'kaleidoscope of common sense': a shifting pattern of resources where premises and inferences regularly swap places, where shifts are fluidly made between arguments from principle and practice (cited in Wetherell and Potter, 1992: 92). And, further, as we shall demonstrate, this reasoning and sense-making comes not without anxiety.

Both Frankie (18) and Katrina (14) claimed that individual ability is important, but also that their family background has a big impact. But Frankie goes on to elaborate from his own experience of attending several urban state schools:

I mean if you go to my school where I am now at sixth form I would say about 70 per cent of the families are middle class and like 80 per cent of the people there have, like, their parents help them with work and teach them and some people have like outside tuition and stuff. And at Eastleigh Common [his previous school] where people don't perform that well, it tends to be like 95 per cent were working-class parents who didn't really care, like most of them when they turned 16 or 18 left and just go and work in like a family business or something like a mechanic or something.

I just think if your family doesn't push you . . . I mean, I know for me, if I think how I would have done if my mum hadn't pushed me, I could have got twenty grand a year that is enough money for me to be happy with and I would have been happy just to leave education and not work hard.

His narrative is an entanglement of all sorts of explanations for social class inequalities: family background, individual effort, while also having some recognition of the extra resources that middle-class families have (such as private tuition at home). There is also some recognition of how social class cultures can play a role in influencing young people's choices and decisions, where for some working-class families leaving school and getting a job is the 'norm'.

However, from both of these boys there is no questioning of the middle-class gold standard of educational achievement and economic prosperity: these values are ingrained. As Gillies (2005) argues, the individualized, agentic self, as theorized by Beck and Giddens, needs access to middle-class economic, cultural and social capital (which is not evenly distributed), however is projected as a standard for all to follow.

A couple of young people did try to refute the notion that academic failure is due to families that don't care. Louise (18) explained, from her experience at school:

[A] lot of these people are single mums. They're looking after multiple kids trying to get money in. They haven't got the time *and it's not that they don't care,* but you know, obviously getting food on the table is more important than getting good grades.

(emphasis added)

Louise makes attempts to grapple with some of the structural contributions to educational failure, such as the pervasive effects of poverty: that some parents, freed up from financial constraints, are able to devote more time and energy to their children's education. Similarly, through her further education course in sociology she learnt how certain minority ethnic families or families with English as an additional language, may be disadvantaged through a lack of knowledge of the system.

Natasha (27) compared her educational success to her friend Evelyn who also went to the same school as her. Natasha went to the University of Liverpool, studied education and now works as a primary school teacher in inner London. Evelyn dropped out of college, did not go to university and is now doing 'bits and bobs' work. Natasha, reflecting on her experience when she was at school, placed the blame of her friend's educational failure with the school, not Evelyn's family:

> I mean, I think Evelyn, who I went to primary school with, who was, erm, [*pause*] working-class background, Afro-Caribbean, very, very bright. She did have other issues in her life but she could have done better and I think the school probably did fail her to be honest because she was brighter than I am, much brighter than I am and she didn't do half as well as I did really [. . .]

Natasha has some sense that the system must have failed Evelyn, but she struggles to pinpoint exactly how. She recognizes that intelligence ('brightness') doesn't necessarily translate into success in education – that there are other forces at work. Though she did not use the term cultural capital, Natasha for example recognized that her own family's 'way of being' immediately set her 'at an advantage'.

However, despite a couple of the older interviewees attempting to grapple with some of the structural causes of inequality, the individualist repertoire has lasting salience. The fact that some people are able to achieve in the system, despite multiple structural disadvantage lead some to reason that ultimately it is down to the individual to do well at school. Frankie (18) in London reasoned:

> I think it has something to do with the way you are. I mean there are some people who are born in families who have, sort of, alcohol and drug problems where nobody gives a crap what you do and [they] go and get ten As at GCSE and go on and do really well.

Similarly, William who we mentioned earlier, who talked about how social class culture constrains and enables higher education participation, came back to this notion that: 'If you follow your life how you want it to be, then where you come from shouldn't present much of a handicap.'

And Louise, despite recognizing the damaging effects of poverty on educational success and recognizing how the system may disadvantage certain working-class or minority ethnic groups, still came back to this idea that the ultimate solution is that it is:

> [D]own to the individual, because the individual student knows that the teachers are there to help, but they have to seek it, they have to be motivated 'cos the teacher can't do anything about it if they're not.

The individualist repertoire appears both 'troublesome' and 'valuable' (Jordan *et al.*, 1994: 8). Frankie, William and Louise are still keen to assert the discourse that if you want it enough, and you work hard enough, you can achieve it.

Middle-class guilt

However, for these white middle-class children their proximity to poverty and inequality induced complex anxieties (Crozier *et al.*, 2008). While the meritocratic fallacy enables a sense of entitlement to resources, the neo-liberal ethic of individualized responsibility also creates feelings of guilt about one's own success. These young people espoused a complex entanglement of guilt, luckiness, shock, embarrassment and superiority about their educational success, relative to their peers. Louise, admitted that she felt guilty because she had many resources at her fingertips. She explained:

> Some of my friends came from such disadvantaged backgrounds – I mean abusive childhoods, and, you know, really not good upbringings and in some ways I did feel guilty sometimes. I live in this big house and I'm doing well at school and I'm going to get good grades and go on to further college.

Similarly, a London father told us how his son really didn't get on well in school because he always felt guilty because he was privileged. Deborah (19) very honestly admitted, with hindsight:

> I think they [her peers] looked up to me to a certain extent and I didn't sort of consciously think it but I subconsciously felt slightly superior to them in that I had everything that they didn't have. You know everything that my mum and dad had given me and I was more intelligent than they were and there was more going for me than there was for them.

Deborah's anxiety about living up to her parents' successes was alleviated by the knowledge that she had a lot of advantage over her friends at school – 'had more going for her'. Louise also struggled with these feelings of superiority, and claimed:

> [A]t the same time I saw that as an opportunity to – not to help them in a charity kind of way – but just to be there for them and support them really, as someone that doesn't have so much maybe stuff on their minds to have to deal with.

These extracts demonstrate the almost impossibility of these young people's situation. It can be seen as a modern version of 'the white man's burden', where the colonialists/the rich are seen to have a moral duty and obligation to help the developing world/the poor 'better' themselves, whether they want the help or not; whilst maintaining an inevitable sense of superiority, because of their position of power. Val Gillies (Gillies, 2005: 838) argues that in neo-liberal policy, with its individualized ethic 'the poor must, for their own sakes, be helped or coerced to become included citizens'.

Conclusion

This chapter has focused on a particular sample of white middle-class children and young people with experiences of urban state schooling in attempt to shed light on how proximity to poverty and disadvantage impacts on their understandings of inequalities. What this analysis shows is the all-pervasiveness of neo-liberal discourses of individualism and meritocracy in today's urban children. Despite coming from liberal, left-leaning families, with a commitment to social justice and tolerance in the city, in the context of education, these young people on the whole were not aware that education institutions reproduce inequality. Instead, the repertoires they were able to draw on placed onus on the individual: the individual's ability, hard work, and the 'right' kind of parents, with the 'right' values. This understanding of educational success unsurprisingly resulted in a sense of entitlement for some of these young people at their own educational success and made invisible the knowledge, resources and capitals available to them. A consequence of this shift of responsibility to the individual is that it absolves the state of any responsibility for the reproduction of disadvantage. Not only are those who 'fail' in this system responsible for this failure, the state's failure to foster equal opportunities and level out inequalities is also internalized, as those who 'achieve' are made responsible for the guilt at their own success.

Acknowledgements

This chapter draws on an ESRC-funded research project entitled 'Identities, Educational Choice and the White Urban Middle-classes' (part of the Identities and Social Action Programme) which was led by Diane Reay, Gill Crozier and David James, with Phoebe Beedell, Sumi Hollingworth, Fiona Jamieson and Katya Williams. The authors would like to thank the whole team for their support and encouragement in writing this chapter.

Note

1   One interviewee was 27 years old, but was included in the sample as she was the only child of mixed ethnic heritage and the researchers were interested in her experiences in comparison to the other white children interviewed.

References

Archer, L., Hollingworth, S. and Mendick, H. (2010). *Urban Youth and Schooling: The Experiences and Identities of Educationally 'At Risk' Young People.* Buckingham: Open University Press.

Ball, S. J. (2003). *Class Strategies and the Education Market: The Middle Classes and Social Advantage.* London: RoutledgeFalmer.

Beck, U (1992) *Risk Society: Towards a New Modernity.* London: Sage.

Bernstein, B. B. (1996). *Pedagogy, Symbolic Control and Identity: Theory, Research, Critique.* London: Taylor and Francis.

Billig, M (1992) *Talking About the Royal Family.* London: Routledge.

Bourdieu, P. (1997). The forms of capital. In A. Halsey, H. Lauder, P. Brown and A. Stuart Wells (eds), *Education: Culture, Economy and Society.* Oxford: Oxford University Press.

Bourdieu, P. and Passeron, J. C. (1977). *Reproduction in Education, Society and Culture.* London: Sage.

Butler, T. (2003). Living in the bubble: gentrification and its 'others' in North London. *Urban Studies,* 40(12), 2469–86.

Butler, T. and Robson, G. (2003). *London Calling: The Middle Classes and the Re-making of Inner London.* Oxford: Berg.

Colley, H. and Hodkinson, P. (2001). Problems with Bridging the Gap: the reversal of structure and agency in addressing social exclusion. *Critical Social Policy,* 21(3), 335–59.

Comber, B. (1998). Problematizing 'background': (Re)constructing categories in education research. *Australian Educational Researcher,* 25(3), 1–21.

Crozier, G. (2005). 'There's a war against our children': black educational underachievement revisited. *British Journal of Sociology of Education,* 26(5), 585–98.

Crozier, G., Reay, D., James, D., Jamieson, F., Beedell, P., Hollingworth, S., *et al.* (2008). White middle-class parents, identities, educational choice and the urban comprehensive school: dilemmas, ambivalence and moral ambiguity. *British Journal of Sociology of Education,* 29(3), 261–72.

Francis, B. (1999). Lads, lasses and (New) Labour: 14–16-year-old students' responses to the laddish behaviour and boys' underachievement debate. *British Journal of Sociology of Education,* 20, 355–71.

Francis, B. (2006). Heroes or zeroes? The discursive positioning of 'underachieving boys' in English neo-liberal education policy. *Journal of Education Policy,* 21(2), 187–200.

Freebody, P. (1992). Social Class and Reading. *Discourse,* 12(2), 68–84.

Gerwirtz, S. (2001). Cloning the Blairs: New Labour's programme for the re-socialization of working-class parents. *Journal of Education Policy,* 16(4), 365–78.

Giddens, A (1990) *The Consequences of Modernity.* Cambridge: Polity.

Gillborn, D. (2005). Evidence to the Education Select Committee: race inequality, 'gifted & talented' students and the increased use of 'setting by ability'.

Gillborn, D. and Youdell, D. (2000). *Rationing Education: Policy, Practice, Reform and Equity.* Buckinghamshire: Open University Press.

Gillies, V. (2005). Raising the meritocracy: parenting and the individualisation of social class. *Sociology,* 39(5), 832–52.

Hattersley, R. (2004). The case against selection. In M. Benn and C. Chitty (eds), *A Tribute to Caroline Benn: Education and Democracy.* London: Continuum.

James, D. (2005). The love puddle: a simple story and some difficult questions. *Educational Action Research,* 13(1), 111–18.

Jordan, B., Redley, M. and James, S. (1994). *Putting the Family First: Identities, Decisions, Citizenship.* London: UCL Press.

Lucey, H. and Reay, D. (2000). Social class and the psyche. *Soundings: A Journal of Politics and Culture,* (15), 139–54.

Lucey, H. and Reay, D. (2002). Carrying the beacon of excellence: social class differentiation and anxiety at a time of transition. *Journal of Education Policy,* 17: 321–36.

Pring, R. and Walford, G. (eds) (1997). *Affirming the Comprehensive Ideal.* London: The Falmer Press.

Reay, D. (2004). Education and cultural capital: the implications of changing trends in education policies. *Cultural Trends,* 13(2), 73–86.

Reay, D. (2007). 'Unruly place': inner-city comprehensives, middle-class imaginaries and working-class children. *Urban Studies,* 44(7), 1191–201.

Reay, D., Crozier, G., James, D., Hollingworth, S., Williams, K., Jamieson, F., *et al.* (2008). Re-invigorating democracy? White middle class identities and comprehensive schooling. *Sociological Review,* 56(2), 238–55.

Rose, N. (1999) *Governing the Soul: The Shaping of the Private Self.* London: Free Associations Books.

Sofer, A. (2007). Global city school systems. In T. Brighouse and L. Fullick (eds), *Education in a Global City: Essays from London.* London: Institute of Education, Bedford Way Papers.

Walkerdine, V. (2003). Reclassifying upward mobility: femininity and the neo-liberal subject. *Gender and Education,* 15(3), 237–48.

Wetherell, M. and Potter, J. (1992). *Mapping the Language of Racism: Discourse and the Legitimation of Exploitation.* Hertfordshire: Harvester Wheatsheaf.

Whitty, G. (2001). Education, social class and social exclusion. *Journal of Education Policy,* 16(4), 287–95.

18 De/re-institutionalizing deafness through the mainstreaming of deaf education in the Republic of Ireland

Elizabeth S. Mathews

Introduction

In the last number of decades, education policy has begun to focus on the inclusion of children with special educational needs in their local public school. This population is predominantly composed of those with physical, sensory, intellectual, emotional and behavioural differences. Their inclusion in mainstream schools is driven by ideals of deinstitutionalization, viewing the amalgamation of children with disabilities with their nondisabled peers as a means of promoting social and educational equality, and is influenced by the civil rights movements from the 1960s and the rise of the social model of disability. However, the process of deinstitutionalization is frequently limited to the spatial realm, moving children from previously segregated environments to so-called integrated environments, providing adaptations to the physical school building with less emphasis on staff training or attitudinal changes (Kitchin and Mulcahy, 1999). Subsequently, mainstreaming continues to be heavily influenced by pathological views of disability driven by the medical model, and its variations, which continues to focus on curing disability and normalizing difference (Holt, 2003).

This is particularly evident in the case of deaf education, where mainstreaming of deaf[1] students frequently relies on the ability of that student to communicate through speech, listening and lip-reading as opposed to the use of sign language in the general classroom (Hyde and Power, 2004). Alternatively, adequate access to the curriculum through the means of sign language, as well as instruction for hearing students and staff in sign language can facilitate mainstreaming of deaf students, a situation which occurs frequently in the US. However, in the Irish context, owing to a lack of provision of sign language interpreters in the mainstream environment the former situation is much more common. Subsequently, the mainstreaming of deaf students instead of addressing the stigmatization of deafness by promoting awareness of sign language and Deaf culture, adds to the pathological view of hearing impairment by placing an emphasis on the need to adapt the deaf child to the hearing classroom, often through medical interventions aimed at ameliorating their impairment. Indeed, it could be claimed that mainstreaming, instead of *de*institutionalizing deaf students, is merely *re*institutionalizing them; rearranging their spatial organization away from the brick-and-mortar institutes of segregated residential school-ing into a spatially dispersed institution of local schools, an institution which although it lacks the spatial delimitations of traditional institutions nonethe-less remains overtly driven by institutional ideologies and a medical model of deafness. This medicalization is supported by interventions taking place in the family home, which in the case of deaf children becomes part of the institutional network negotiating the 'treatment' of deafness. Therefore, as Holt (2003) observes 'the [Special Educational Needs] process can be understood as an institution, which operates within and between schools'.

This chapter will examine this process of de/re-institutionalization in the Republic of Ireland, focusing on the example of deaf education, and consists of two broad sections: the first section traces the development of mainstreaming deaf education and highlights the difficulties when deinstitutionalization is approached as a primarily spatial practice. The second section uses empirical findings to examine how mainstreaming is subsequently a process of *re*institutionalization for deaf children, where normalization and medicalization remain highly influential forces. These empirical findings come from a doctoral research project on mainstreaming of deaf education in the Republic of Ireland. The findings presented here are from semi-structured open-ended interviews conducted with either one (usually mothers) or both hearing parents from 20 families with deaf chil-dren. At the time of the first interviews these children were aged between 18 months and 16 years with an average age of 8 years. While there has been much work recommending the inclusion of children's voices, espe-cially marginalized children, instead of consulting parents or teachers on their behalf (Rose and Shevlin, 2004; Porter and Abane, 2008; Schafer and Yarwood, 2008), the consultation of adults remains a justifiable approach to understanding children's geographies. In the context of this research, since the decisions regarding educational placement are largely made by parents when deaf children are still infants or young children, parents are the best sources of information regarding this early phase of their child's life. Parents were recruited through schools, contacts with the Deaf Community, and a series of five information nights held across the country aimed at promoting the research. Interviews with these parents ranged from half an hour to two hours and were conducted in spoken English, recorded using a dictaphone, with the recordings transcribed and coded for analysis. Three of the families interviewed had migrated to Ireland while the remaining families had at least one parent who was Irish.

As well as the interviews with parents, 24 professionals working with deaf children were also interviewed: seven teachers in self-contained units for deaf children in mainstream schools, five general teachers in mainstream schools, two resource teachers in mainstream schools, two principals in main-stream schools, one special needs assistant, one Irish Sign Language tutor, and six other professionals working in service provision and research in deaf education. The vast majority of these professionals were hearing, with only two identifying as Deaf and another identifying as hard of hearing, although not a member of the Deaf Community. Those identifying as Deaf were interviewed in the Irish Sign Language,[2] with the remaining 22 interviewed in spoken English. In line with emancipatory and participatory research methodologies which honour meaningful involvement of communities affected by research (Oliver, 1992), the Deaf Community were informed of and guided this research project through a series of five information nights held in urban centres across the country. The information nights were followed by informal group discussions, and there was one formal focus group meeting with members of the Deaf Community. Seven young deaf people were also included through paired interviews. Because of the nature of this discussion, however, the bulk of the findings reflected upon in this chapter will consist of the interviews with parents and professionals.

(De)institutionalizing deaf education *or* the problem with mainstreaming

From the 1970s on, there has been an increased move towards integration and more recently inclusion of children with disabilities, so much so that as Holt observes, 'there is a growing international hegemony, which identifies the mainstream school as *the* place to educate (most) disabled children' (2003, original emphasis). Mainstreaming policies are supported by legislation on both national and international levels through legislative acts (Government of Ireland, 2004) and statements such as the Salamanca Statement (UNESCO, 1994). All of these legislative acts promote the mainstream school as the ideal educational environment for children with disabilities,[3] in which they will achieve their 'fullest educational progress and social integration' (UNESCO, 1994) by being included in their local mainstream school and provide parents with the legal entitlement to pursue that education for their child. As a result of these policy measures, there has been a noticeable increase in the numbers of children with disabilities being educated in their local mainstream school and a simultaneous decrease in those attending specialized schools. Regarding deaf education, it is estimated that over 90 per cent of deaf children are currently enrolled in mainstream programmes, although this represents a wide range of placements (Kluwin, 1992), from those in full integration programmes (where they may be the only deaf child in the class) to those enrolled in special classes within mainstream schools (where they may attend classes with mainstream peers for certain subjects as well as being integrated for extracurricular activities). In the Irish context, it is the former which makes up the vast majority of mainstream placements with only a small proportion of deaf children attending one of the eight units for deaf children within mainstream primary schools[4] across the country.

This mainstreaming process has, to an extent, been heralded as the end to the institutionalization of children with disabilities and has been welcomed by many, who viewed institutionalized 'special' education as inhibiting the full participation of people with disabilities in their local communities (Griffin and Shevlin, 2007), ghettoizing disability (Smith, 2005), and failing to prepare children for competing in the workforce (Kitchin and Mulcahy, 1999). However, there has also been notable reluctance from some regarding the mainstreaming project, a reluctance which has been particularly felt in the field of deaf education. Several studies have indicated that mainstreaming deaf education can indeed be problematic. Antia *et al.* (2002) highlight several more-than-spatial barriers which prevent the full inclusion of deaf and hard-of-hearing children in mainstream settings across four categories: teacher issues, student issues, administrative and structural issues, and community issues. Minnet *et al.* (1994) observed that preschool children preferred to have friends of the same hearing status in spite of integration while Stinson *et al.* (1996) and Musselman *et al.* (1996) noted that older deaf students continued to relate better to their deaf peers, a fact which was not affected by increased mainstreaming and interaction with hearing classmates. This can be aggravated by difficulties with acceptance from hearing peers (Antia and Kreimeyer, 1997). Skelton and Valentine (2002) found that while deaf participants reported coping with mainstream primary school, their secondary mainstream experience was fraught with bullying, limited academic opportunities, poor communication, and inappropriate life skills training. In Australia, Hyde and Power (2004) have highlighted that while many deaf students may be competitive academically, their social involvement in mainstream school placements remains problematic. Furthermore, for deaf students who have been mainstreamed, there can be difficulty associating with deaf peers as well as hearing peers during third-level education, with feelings of being stuck between both worlds commonly reported (Kersting, 1997), indicating that the effects of mainstreamed education last into adulthood. Overall, research suggests that the linguistic needs of deaf students mean that for meaningful inclusion within mainstream classrooms to occur, both physical and attitudinal adaptations are necessary, in particular instruction in sign language as well as deaf awareness training to both children and teachers within the school (Gaustad, 1999). Thus, the Salamanca Statement which provides guidelines for the mainstreaming movement acknowledges that the example of deaf children may be one where segregated education is more appropriate and beneficial then integrated education (UNESCO, 1994).

These findings point to the fact that in mainstreaming practice, simple physical integration is not enough, and by focusing on spatial proximity to peers we fail to acknowledge the complexities underlying the (de)institutionalization process, in particular the ideological foundations for both segregation and inclusion as they relate to deaf children. The primary concern underlying these criticisms lies in the fact that this approach to deinstitutionalization through mainstreaming has often focused on the spatial, in spite of policy calls to the contrary (see UNESCO, 1994 I: 6), where in practice mainstreaming in its many forms confuses physical integration with social inclusion (Smith, 2005). As Komesaroff and McLean (2006) highlight 'although initially driven by concerns of social justice, inclusion can be viewed as the relocation of students for compliance with policy' and that it has simply become a case of 'add and stir' in managing difference within the school population. However, although highly spatial, (de)institutionalization is by no means exclusively a spatial process, and to focus on it as such is to deny the highly ideological nature of the process.

The institutions central to our society are not spatially fixed neutral entities, but are highly loaded, contested, multi-spatial cites that are often used as a tool for achieving specific political, social and economic goals (Green *et al.*, 2008). The spatial segregation, confinement, and treatment of classified 'others', including deaf children, over the last two centuries required an ideological basis, to be found in the scientific and medical rationalization of the supposed 'superiority' of certain populations over others and the need for normalizing treatment among those deemed 'inferior' or 'deviant'. This rationalization of 'otherness' manifested itself in evolutionism and eventually eugenics policies in the late nineteenth and early twentieth century. At this point, all individuals become susceptible to systematic categorization against a norm driven by a Western, white, patriarchal, able-bodied, middle-class ideal (Davis, 1997). For the Deaf Community, the construction of deafness as a disability was consolidated during this same period when hearing loss became clinically defined and pathologized, and sign language became problematic (Baynton, 1996; Branson and Miller, 2002). Inspired by evolutionism, colonialism and the xenophobia sparked by increased immigration, deaf education began to focus not on knowledge acquisition, but on spoken language development in an attempt to normalize, assimilate, and thus 'raise' deaf people to an elevated 'hearing' way of being (Baynton, 1996; Branson and Miller, 2002). Normalization through speaking and listening became a driving force in deaf education. Sign language became almost extinct from deaf education and children were punished for its use. Teachers who were themselves deaf were made redundant and replaced with hearing, speaking teachers. Students who could not acquire speech were labelled 'oral failures' and were often segregated and relegated to special classes within institutions for deaf children (see Griffey, 1994, for an account of the oralist system in Ireland). So, the process of institutionalization by the middle of the twentieth century was highly ideological, using spatial processes only as a means to an end, promoting the normalization of deaf bodies through speech and listening skills.

This system continued throughout the twentieth century until the 1970s, which saw a resurgence in the use of sign language giving rise to the bilingual-bicultural movement in deaf education (Lang, 2005). However, technological advances in the 1980s and 1990s, including improvements in digital hearing aids and the arrival of cochlear implantation[5] has once again seen a refocus on spoken language acquisition in the educational context. This has been accelerated by mainstreaming policy where deaf children, surrounded by hearing peers, are embedded within a system which 'it can be contended . . . is institutionally ableist, being underpinned by the assumption of a "normally developing child", and locating any "deviation" from this norm within the individual child, rather than examining socio-spatial processes of disablement in schools' (Holt, 2003). For deaf children, this deviation from the norm focuses on their ability to speak and the mainstream environment is viewed as providing greater opportunities to acquire that speech and simultaneously fewer opportunities for that speech development to be 'hindered' by sign language.[6] Subsequently, mainstreaming as it is currently practised in Ireland remains heavily influenced by the medical model, a fact which Branson and Miller highlight for its failure:

> The failure of mainstreaming for deaf people is seen to stem basically from the fact that they are mainstreamed in terms of a medical model of deafness. Despite the overt opposition to the use of clinically based assessments and, thus, to the use of medical models of 'disability,' even the most radical integrationists continue to define deafness as a pathology, as a lack rather than as a cultural difference based in a linguistic difference. Given the overriding ideals of the mainstreaming movement, the mainstreaming of deaf students is a blatant contradiction.
>
> (2002)

It is for this reason perhaps that there is such reluctance towards mainstreaming from the Deaf Community. As Baynton observed:

> [T]he angriest objection to mainstreaming from deaf people is that in the name of liberating children from their supposed 'isolation' in the deaf community, a true and potentially devastating isolation is risked. In the name of inclusion in 'the' community, deaf children are frequently denied true inclusion in any community. For the sake of an abstraction known as the 'mainstream,' deaf children are denied the solid and tangible fellowship, culture, language, and heritage of the deaf community.
>
> (1996)

Mainstreaming, as opposed to an opportunity for meaningful inclusion with hearing peers, is instead viewed as the final stage of normalization, began in the nineteenth century with medicalization of deaf bodies, continued through the twentieth century with pure oralism, and approaching completion in the twenty-first century through surgical intervention and assimilation with hearing peers. Thus, sentiments against mainstreaming are common from the Deaf Community with Crean (1997) blaming mainstreaming for 'destroying the embryo of the Deaf Community' while Ladd states that 'forceful clumsy attempts to mainstream not only deny the facts about being deaf but destroy much that deaf people and their friends have worked so hard to create, and may in the last resort to be seen as genocidal' (in Branson and Miller, 2002).

Mainstreaming and the medical model

This persistence of the medical model, in spite of calls to the contrary from the Deaf Community (Padden and Humphries, 1988; Bienvenu, 1991; Lane *et al.*, 1996; Lane, 2002; Bahan, 2008) is no doubt contributed to by the fact that 90 per cent of deaf children are born to hearing families for whom their first encounter with deafness is constructed through the clinical gaze of the medical model. In Ireland as elsewhere, since diagnosis occurs through the medical system, the professionals to whom parents turn during this time include audiologists, ear nose and throat specialists, and general practitioners. Immediately after diagnosis, families in Ireland with deaf children also receive a referral to the Visiting Teacher Service, an itinerant service provided by the Department of Education and Science to assist with educational intervention. Subsequently, these professionals play a large part in steering early intervention and educational placement with deaf children laying much of the groundwork for mainstreaming. Both medical and educational professionals often promote interventions which focus on ameliorating hearing loss and encouraging spoken language development indicating that they are embedded within a medical model of deafness. For example, the first service provided to all of the children involved in this research was amplification in the form of hearing aids or cochlear implants. Were this early intervention to focus on the social model of deafness, instruction in Irish Sign Language as well as access to the Deaf Community would be provided.

However, it became clear during the course of this research that it is not uncommon to find that parents are not informed of the benefits of using Irish Sign Language as a communication option with their deaf children. In fact, a negative discourse often surrounds sign language and parents are actively warned against its use. For example, over 25 per cent of the parents interviewed for this study were unaware at the time of the interview that there was an Irish Sign Language home tuition service available through the Department of Education and Science. In contrast, all of these parents were aware of and availing of audiology and speech and language therapy services. Of the 75 per cent of parents who knew about the Irish Sign Language home tuition service, most had found out through their own research, and only one parent had been informed of the service by her Visiting Teacher. Furthermore, several parents reported being discouraged from using the service when they raised the issue with medical or teaching professionals:

MOTHER: They said to me that they were against Chris[7] and Ellen getting sign language because he is still gaining, he is still trying to gain language and it could set him back a lot, that's what the new teacher for the deaf was telling me.

PRINCIPAL INVESTIGATOR (PI): That it would set him back?

MOTHER: Yeah, she said it could. Especially because Chris is relying a lot on lip-reading, that the grammar can just go straight downhill, that they just go from here (*gestures downwards*), she said definitely not at the moment.

(Parent 02)

Sign language, instead of being upheld as a valuable mode of language acquisition for deaf children is instead labelled as a 'crutch', making children 'lazy' in their use of speech and causing deterioration in English grammar. While this early intervention often occurs in the preschool years, it paves the way for mainstreaming which is seen as complimentary to spoken language acquisition since deaf children are surrounded by hearing, *speaking* peers from whom they can learn. Indeed, many parents (in particular those whose children have cochlear implants) spoke of their children being under instruction in mainstream classes, not for educational or social reasons, but specifically to optimize their spoken language development:

So they want Amazu and Adanna to be in the mainstream, especially Adanna . . . because at that age they believe you will pick up more sign language, [and] . . . if they are doing the implant they won't want you to sign.

(Parent 15)

Adanna's resource teacher reflected on her psychological report and its recommendations:

TEACHER: [The psychologist], because the brain shuts down to language acquisition at seven the [psychologist] wants them as much as possible in – in mainstream.

PI: Mmm.

TEACHER: So that was her reason for . . .

PI: Okay it's really for speech development then?

TEACHER: It's for speech development yeah.

(Professional 10, unit resource teacher)

This becomes apparent in the adaptations provided to mainstream schools to 'accommodate' deaf children. The most common adaptation is the use of a soundfield system or radio-aid which amplify sound for the deaf child. This is accompanied by speech and language therapy (which often results in absenteeism from school) to assist deaf children to acquire speech. Children may also be seated optimally for lip-reading and viewing the blackboard. However, techniques common among the Deaf Community such as attention-calling, careful turn-taking to ensure that no one speaks when the deaf student is not watching and that the deaf student is involved in all relevant interactions are not so carefully implemented. My field notes from an observation of Marie in her classroom note:

> The speed of interaction in the classroom is very fast. There are a lot of changes in topics, even within one exercise. A lot of incidental learning is used. For example, they did an exercise on a weather map of Ireland. Eoin [class teacher] asked the students to name some of the counties in Northern Ireland. This was not part of the exercise, but instead an improvised moment of learning for the students. However, Marie was not aware of the change in topic, the microphone from the soundfield system was not used for the answers, and it is unlikely that she picked up the information covered during those brief moments. During these 'incidental learning' moments, the vast majority of the class raised their heads from their books and instigated eye contact with teacher and with each other. There were many hands in the air and several students called out the answer. They seem to know that this learning process is outside of the book. However, Marie remained focused on her book, following the sequence of questions there. When Marie notices the other students answering questions, she puts her hand up too. However, when Eoin calls on her to answer, she does not know what the question is. This suggests, to me, that she does not follow a lot of these 'incidental learning' moments when the topic of discussion has moved away from the sequence of questions in the book.
>
> (Field notes)

While Marie is physically present for the exercise, there is insufficient adaption of the teaching strategies used to fully include her in the lesson. In an environment sensitive to deaf awareness, Marie's attention would be gained before such an exercise. Similarly, in an environment where several deaf students are taught together and a deaf-aware teacher is employed, specific strategies would be used to maintain all students' attention for such interactions, such as knocking on the table so it vibrates, flashing lights, or getting students to tap each other on the shoulder to gain attention.

However, due to the complementary nature of speech acquisition and mainstreaming, segregating, or rather *congregating* deaf children together in specialized classes or units is seen to pose a threat to the development of spoken language. Speaking in relation to units for deaf children, one parent observed:

PARENT: You see that's where I'd be afraid, the sign [language].
PI: Yeah, what would you be afraid of?
PARENT: My main worry there – my main worry would be none of them are speaking properly.

PI: Mmm . . .
PARENT: So how can they learn from each other?

(Parent 04)

As a result, the historical institutionalization of deaf children in residential schools is now viewed as a threat to the normalizing goals of the medical model. For the Deaf community, while the residential schools may symbolize an era of oralism and segregation from their hearing communities, they also represented the opportunity for congregating among their own, fostering the development of sign language and Deaf culture (van Cleve and Crouch, 1989). Institutionalization, perhaps ironically, provided a valued path for resisting hegemonic medical discourses of deafness. Deinstitutionalization, on the other hand, fragments the Deaf community and threatens the very core of Deaf identity by prioritizing speech to the detriment of sign language. Subsequently, mainstreaming practice, while it may aim to deinstitutionalize deaf children is merely *re*institutionalizing them in a new spatial arrangement which does little to challenge the medical view of deafness as a pathological condition and in fact may reinforce the medical model more than institutionalized settings did. This medical model is epitomized by the high status afforded to speech, using it as a measure of success for mainstreamed deaf students. One unit teacher spoke of her group of students, some of whom were mainstreamed and one who wasn't:

> But the fact that the boys [who are mainstreamed] aren't profoundly deaf, it's not as if, you know, they're able to talk, they can hear as well. Cormac is fine, but he obviously has problems with language so he wouldn't be able for mainstream, he'd fall behind.
>
> (Professional 13, unit teacher)

For those who 'fall behind', sign language is often implemented as a last resort and the schools for the deaf may be recommended for second level owing to their inability to cope in the (oral) and mainstream (Powers *et al.*, 1998), reinforcing the image of speech as success and sign language as failure in deaf education. One student, diagnosed with a mild learning disability who was struggling with literacy fell into this category:

> Overall, I don't think he'd do well in a mainstream school. I really don't think he would and I think his education would go down, I think for him, life skills would be more important for him.
>
> (Professional 13, unit teacher)

Thus, the mainstream system resorts to the medical model of blaming the individual impairment when integration with hearing peers is not successful:

Em, his speech was a problem last year, very difficult to understand. Most of the time, unless it was something that was very much in context, I couldn't understand him at all.

> (Professional 15, mainstream classroom teacher)

One noticeable exception to this was in the case of a school with a unit for deaf children, where a bilingual policy had been implemented in the school with all hearing children learning sign language. This was quite a unique situation and when asked about interactions between deaf and hearing students, the teacher blamed limited interaction between deaf and hearing students on the communication skills, not of deaf children, but their hearing peers:

PI: Do they interact a lot with the hearing students, like even at lunchtime or do they tend to stick . . .

TEACHER: They would, now they're inclined, to be honest, to keep to themselves, but my 6th class, my older kids have made a lot of an effort to play with the mainstream children. The mainstream children would know a lot about the deaf children, so it depends as well, some mainstream children would be a lot more communicative and would risk more in trying to communicate with them.

> (Professional 14, unit teacher)

In informal discussion with the deaf children from this school, they confirmed that they preferred to play with other deaf children, but only because they didn't have the patience for their hearing schoolmates' slow signing, but that they appreciated their efforts nonetheless. Structured programmes within this school assisted deaf and hearing children in their interactions and, as was noted from the teacher's comment above, as they spent more meaningful time together, their quantity and quality of interactions improved. This indicates that when mainstreaming is carried out in a manner sensitive to deaf children's linguistic needs and with respect to Deaf Culture, it can indeed show benefits.

Conclusion

In her examination of inclusion and exclusion of children with mind/body differences in primary schools in the UK, Holt (Holt, 2003) argues that 'inclusion, rather than signifying a common meaning between educational practitioners, maybe identified as an ambiguous social-spatial construct, evoking a variety of meanings for individuals in different settings, although some shared group understandings may exist'. For deaf children in the Republic of Ireland, there seems to be a shared group experience whereby mainstreaming is synonymous with spoken language acquisition and interaction with peers based on adapting the deaf child. Owing to the lack of sign language and Deaf awareness training, the deaf student is expected to assimilate, accessing the curriculum with adaptations geared towards the child such as audiological treatment of the built environment and personal amplification assisting the child to hear, and speech and language therapy assisting the child to speak. Adaptations among the classroom, curriculum, school structure, teacher, and hearing pupils, in the Irish context at least, are less common. In such a system, the ability to speak becomes synonymous with success, and failure means reverting to sign language and schools for the deaf. Subsequently, the mainstreaming movement in the Republic of Ireland as it relates to deaf education is merely a continuation and indeed progression of the institutionalization project which sought to 'cure' deaf children so they could integrate with hearing society. It is therefore not sufficiently a process of deinstitutionalization, but rather as Branson and Miller (2002) highlight a 'blatant contradiction' whereby children enter into a process of re-institutionalization, continuing to be pathologized under a medical model. The mainstream environment, far from challenging pathological views of deafness is reinforcing this medical model in that it is seen as a valuable opportunity to foster spoken language acquisition by surrounding deaf children with their hearing peers.

Notes

1 There has been much debate in the last number of years regarding the varying use of the terms deaf (lower case), Deaf (upper case), hearing-impaired, hard of hearing, and so forth (see Skelton and Valentine, 2003 for discussion). Throughout this paper, the term deaf will be used highlighting the fact that the majority of participants in this research had hearing losses over that which would categorize them as hard of hearing, and do not yet identify as culturally Deaf, nor do they use Irish Sign Language as their dominant mode of communication. Where the term Deaf is used, it is used specifically to indicate cultural Deafness, identification with the Deaf Community, and use of sign language.

2 Interviews were conducted without the use of an interpreter; the principal investigator is a competent user of Irish Sign Language. Member checks were conducted to ensure the accuracy of English glosses provided to the sign language interviews.

3 Clauses exist should mainstream placement be detrimental to either the child with disabilities or their peers (see the EPSEN Act, section 1, paragraph 2, for example, Government of Ireland [2004]).

4 This research focuses on primary mainstream education only.

5 A cochlear implant is a surgically implanted device which enables those with sensorineural deafness to access sound. It must be complemented by intensive speech and language therapy or audio-verbal therapy for language acquisition to proceed.

6 There is little to no evidence to support the claim that sign language hinders spoken language development (Powers *et al.*, 1998). Nonetheless, it is a commonly used discourse in the medical and educational fields that sign language will make children 'lazy' in spoken language acquisition, a claim which has seen the deliberate denial of sign language to deaf children.

7 All names of participants have been replaced.

References

Antia, S. D. and Kreimeyer, K. H. (1997) 'The generalisation and maintenance of the peer social behaviours of young children who are deaf or hard of hearing'. *Language, Speech and Hearing Services in Schools*, 28, 59–69.

Antia, S. D., Stinson, M. S. and Gaustad, M. G. (2002) 'Developing membership in the education of deaf and hard-of-hearing students in inclusive settings'. *Journal of Deaf Studies and Deaf Education*, 7, 214–29.

Bahan, B. (2008) 'Upon the formation of a visual variety of the human race'. In H.-D. L. Bauman (ed.), *Open Your Eyes: Deaf Studies Talking*. Minneapolis, MN: University of Minnesota Press.

Baynton, D. C. (1996) *Forbidden Signs: American Culture and the Campaign Against Sign Language*. Chicago: The University of Chicago Press.

Bienvenu, M. (1991) 'Can deaf people survive "deafness"?' In L. Bragg (ed.), *Deaf World*. New York: New York University Press.

Branson, J. and Miller, D. (2002) *Damned for their Difference: The Cultural Construction of Deaf People as Disabled*. Washington, DC: Gallaudet University Press.

Crean, E. J. (1997) *Breaking the Silence: The Education of the Deaf in Ireland 1816–1996*. Dublin: Irish Deaf Society.

Davis, L. J. (1997) 'Constructing normalcy: the bell curve, the novel, and the invention of the disabled body in the nineteenth century'. In L. J. Davis (ed.), *The Disability Studies Reader*, 1st edn. New York: Routledge.

Gaustad, M. G. (1999) 'Including the kids across the hall: collaborative instruction of hearing, deaf, and hard-of-hearing students'. *Journal of Deaf Studies and Deaf Education*, 4, 176–90.

Government of Ireland (2004) *Education for Persons with Special Educational Needs Act 2004*. Republic of Ireland.

Green, A., Preston, J. and Janmaat, J. G. (2008) *Education, Equality and Social Cohesion: A Comparative Analysis*. Hampshire: Palgrave Macmillan.

Griffey, S. N. (1994) *From Silence to Speech: Fifty Years with the Deaf*. Dublin: Dominican Publications.

Griffin, S. and Shevlin, M. (2007) *Responding to Special Educational Needs*. Dublin: Gill and Macmillan Ltd.

Holt, L. (2003) '(Dis)abling children in primary school micro-spaces: geographies of inclusion and exclusion'. *Health and Place*, 9, 119–28.

Hyde, M. and Power, D. (2004) 'Inclusion of deaf students: an examination of definitions of inclusion in relation to findings of a recent Australian study of deaf students in regular classes'. *Deafness and Education International*, 6, 82–99.

Kersting, S. A. (1997) 'Balancing between deaf and hearing worlds: reflections of mainstreamed college students on relationships and social interaction'. *Journal of Deaf Studies and Deaf Education*, 2, 252–63.

Kitchin, R. and Mulcahy, F. (1999) *Disability, Access to Education and Future Opportunities*. Dublin: Combat Poverty Agency.

Kluwin, T. N. (1992) 'What does "local public school" program mean?' In T. N. Kluwin, D. F. Moores and M. G. Gaustad (eds), *Toward Effective Public School Programs for Deaf Students: Context, Process, and Outcomes*. New York: Teachers College Press.

Komesaroff, L. and McLean, M. A. (2006) 'Being there is not enough: inclusion is both deaf and hearing'. *Deafness and Education International*, 8, 88–100.

Lane, H. (2002) 'Do deaf people have a disability?' *Sign Language Studies*, 2, 356–79.

Lane, H., Hoffmeister, R. and Bahan, B. (1996) *A Journey into the Deaf-World*. San Diego, CA: Dawn Sign Press.

Lang, H. G. (2005) 'Perspectives on the history of deaf education'. In M. Marscharck and P. E. Spencer (eds), *Oxford Handbook of Deaf Studies, Language, and Education*. New York: Oxford University Press.

Minnet, A., Clark, K. and Wilson, G. (1994) 'Play behaviour and communication between deaf and hard of hearing children and their hearing peers in an integrated playschool'. *American Annals of the Deaf*, 139, 420–9.

Musselman, C., Mootilal, A. and MacKay, S. (1996) 'The social adjustment of deaf adolescents in segregated, partially integrated, and mainstreamed settings'. *Journal of Deaf Studies and Deaf Education*, 1, 52–63.

Oliver, M. (1992) 'Changing the social relations of research production'. *Disability, Handicap and Society*, 7, 101–14.

Padden, C. and Humphries, T. (1988) *Deaf in America: Voices from a Culture*. Cambridge, MA: Harvard University Press.

Porter, G. and Abane, A. (2008) 'Increasing children's participation in African transport planning: reflections on methodological issues in a child-centred research project'. *Children's Geographies*, 6, 151–67.

Powers, S., Gregory, S. and Thoutenhoofd, E. D. (1998) *The Educational Achievements of Deaf Children*. Nottingham: Department for Education and Skills.

Rose, R. and Shevlin, M. (2004) 'Encouraging voices: listening to young people who have been marginalised'. *Support for Learning*, 19, 155–61.

Schafer, N. and Yarwood, R. (2008) 'Involving young people as researchers: uncovering multiple power relations among youths'. *Children's Geographies*, 6, 121–35.

Skelton, T. and Valentine, G. (2002) 'Towards home and school inclusion for young deaf people: ways forward'. *Youth Policy: The Journal of Critical Analysis*, 76, 15–28.

Smith, P. (2005) 'Off the map: a critical geography of intellectual disabilities'. *Health and Place*, 11, 87–92.

Stinson, M., Whitmire, K. and Kluwin, T. N. (1996) 'Self-perceptions of social relationships in hearing-impaired adolescence'. *Journal of Educational Psychology*, 88, 132–43.

UNESCO (1994) *The Salamanca Statement and Framework for Action on Special Educational Needs*. World Conference on Special Needs Equality and Quality. Salamanca, Spain, 7–10 June 1994.

van Cleve, J. V. and Crouch, B. A. (1989) *A Place of Their Own: Creating the Deaf Community in America*. Washington, DC: Gallaudet University Press.

19 'The teachers seemed a bit obsessive with health and safety'

Fieldwork risk and the social construction of childhood

Victoria Ann Cook

Introduction

This chapter seeks to challenge the theoretical notion of the child as a competent social agent. Drawing on research with three state secondary schools in urban northern England into children's experiences of geography fieldwork, this chapter focuses on the theme of risk which was found to be a central concern for those organizing and authorizing fieldwork. Through this analysis it is demonstrated how the management of fieldwork risk may be understood as contributing to the ongoing social construction of childhood, with students' experiences of risk largely determined by teachers' varying assumptions about competency, maturity and autonomy. The varying levels of personal responsibility invested in the students for the reflexive monitoring of risk demonstrate the conflicting standards by which children were deemed (in)competent to make decisions in the field. Furthermore, it is argued that teachers' heightened sensitivity to risk, fuelled by perceptions of a litigious society, frequently informed decisions where aspects of adult authority were maintained. These findings expose some of the uncertainties and ambiguities surrounding the theoretical notion of children's competent agency.

Ideas regarding the socially constructed nature of childhood and the role of children as competent social agents form what Aitken *et al.* (2006, 1013) refer to as children's geographies' recent 'theoretical scaffold'. The idea that childhood is a social construction was first proposed by Ariès in 1960. As Matthews suggested, 'there is no such thing as the unitary child and there is much to learn about the diverse lives of children and their families' (2003, 4). It follows that Western childhood may be characterized by a particular set of cultural values:

> In the twentieth century [. . .] Western childhood has become a period in the life course characterized by social dependency, asexuality, and the obligation to be happy, with children having the right to protection and training but not to social or personal autonomy.
>
> (James *et al.* 1998, 62)

Discussions of the socially constructed nature of childhood have frequently been accompanied by the ontological repositioning of children as competent agents in their own right (Holloway and Valentine, 2000). For example, Prout and James (1990, 8) argued:

> Children are and must be seen as active in the construction and determination of their own social lives, the lives of those around them and of societies in which they live. Children are not just the passive subjects of social structures and processes.

However, the need for further reflection on these core theoretical assumptions has been recognized (Horton and Kraftl, 2005; Vanderbeck, 2008). As Vanderbeck (2008, 397) noted:

> Although the subfield has repeatedly foregrounded children's competent agency, the theoretical/empirical/political case for maintaining aspects of adult authority is rarely discussed. This is curious because some vision of legitimate age differentiation is almost certainly held by many practitioners, given the dearth of straightforward discussion within the subdiscipline of eliminating age differentiation within law.

This chapter seeks to contribute to such debates through a consideration of children and risk. The ideas of childhood's socially constructed nature and children's competent agency are particularly pertinent to discussions of children and risk. Scott et al. (1998) suggested that risk management may be important to an understanding of the social construction of childhood, since adults' judgements of children's competences, vulnerability and (im)maturity inform decisions concerning children's exposure to risk. As Harden argued, 'the element of choice, responsibility and reflexivity accredited to adults in relation to risk is denied to children' (2000, 47). In addition, the specific risks from which we seek to protect children may also define our understandings of childhood and of children themselves (Jackson and Scott, 1999). For example, children's agency may be curtailed by constraints imposed by parents who are reportedly paranoid about their children's safety outdoors (Furedi, 2001, 2002; Woolley, 2006; Pain, 2006). Such anxieties over risk underlie many of the recent reports documenting the decline in children's independent use of public space (Valentine, 1997a; James et al., 1998; O'Brien et al., 2000; Aitken, 2001; Thomas and Thompson, 2004; Valentine, 2004; Woolley, 2006; Malone, 2007). These anxieties, it is suggested, are fuelled by ideologies of children as innocent, vulnerable and incompetent (Jenks, 1996; Pain, 2006; Wyness, 2006) and the view of childhood as a precious space that must be preserved (Jackson and Scott, 1999). Malone (2007), for example, described how the 'bubble-wrapping' of children in some Australian middle-class families has led to a drastic reduction in children's independent spatial mobility and a resurgence of Victorian notions of the innocence of childhood.

This stands in stark contrast to the literature on risk in the 1970s that emphasized:

> [T]he virtues and dignities associated with a modicum of risk, as a stimulus for creativity in solving problems. Exposure to some risk was considered not a privilege but a civil right and was used as an argument against over-protectiveness. To be denied the opportunity to make choices which carried risk was assumed to be anti-therapeutic in raising children.
>
> (Wolpert, 1980, 393)

An exception is Guldberg (2000) who described a project at a Norwegian school where the playground was designed to encourage children to engage in risk-taking and adults were told not to intervene. She demonstrated how a climate of reduced protection and surveillance enabled the students to develop new knowledge and skills. The literature on risk reveals a wide range of debates regarding the role of risk within society. The following section seeks to contextualize the preceding discussion in relation to this literature and introduce the discussion of fieldwork risk.

Safety and risk

Concern over risk is not limited to children. Risk anxiety has been said to permeate modern Western societies (Giddens, 1991; Beck, 1994). For Beck, risk is a 'systematic way of dealing with hazards and insecurities induced and introduced by modernization itself. Risks, as opposed to older dangers, are consequences which relate to the threatening force of modernization and to its globalization of doubt. They are politically reflexive' (1992, 21). The 'risk society' thesis focuses on two key macro-social processes of late modern societies and their relation to concepts of risk: reflexive modernization and individualization. Both these processes are specifically concerned with agency. Individualization, with its associated emphasis on personal responsibility, refers to the erosion of established norms and values (Lupton, 1999). According to Beck and Beck-Gernsheim (2002), lives are increasingly individualized, with collective identities eschewed as individuals construct their own identities. Individualization entails the reflexive monitoring of risks that individuals are expected to assess and manage (Jackson and Scott, 1999). Reflexivity denotes the response of people to risk in contemporary Western societies, where risk anxieties raise questions about contemporary practices (Lupton, 1999). As the preceding discussion demonstrated, not all individuals may be equally reflexive in their monitoring of risk, with adults assuming greater personal responsibility for children's safety.

One important difference between Beck and Giddens' work concerns the relationship between risk and reflexivity to risk. Beck sees risks as greater in the modern era, hence the heightened degree of risk reflexivity. However, Giddens (1991, 123–4) noted that daily life is not inherently more risky than in prior eras, but people are simply more sensitive to risk and thus the number of risks is thought to have increased:

> The point [. . .] is not that day to day life is inherently more risky than was the case in prior eras. It is rather that, in conditions of modernity, for lay actors as well as for experts in specific fields, thinking in terms of risk and risk assessment is a more or less ever-present exercise, of a partly imponderable character.

Educational professionals have increasingly become involved with thinking about risk and completing risk assessments, which are symptomatic of what Ansell describes as UK society's 'modernizing tendencies' toward risk control (2008, 218). The decline of fieldwork in some schools has been attributed to the bureaucracy associated with risk assessment (Education and Skills Committee, 2005; Cook *et al.*, 2006). The same research also demonstrated that the risk of litigation is perceived to be an important barrier facing those organizing and executing fieldwork. Some have sought to reassure teachers that their perceptions of fieldwork risk are false (see, for example, Education and Skills Committee, 2005). However, it is arguably inappropriate to distinguish between 'real' and 'false' risks since risk is socially constructed as well as being a material reality (Lupton, 1999; Beck, 2000; Ansell, 2008). What it is important to consider, therefore, is the effects of these understandings (Lupton, 1999). This chapter seeks to consider the effects of teachers' understandings of fieldwork risk on the social construction of childhood and students' fieldwork experiences.

Research methodology

This chapter draws on a larger study which explores students' personal, lived experiences of fieldwork. The aim of the research was to embed an in-depth analysis of students' fieldwork experiences within a consideration of the wider structural forces operating at local and national levels. The research methodology, which has been discussed in detail elsewhere (Cook, 2008), used a multi-layered and multi-method approach to explore the perspectives of teachers and students experiencing and making decisions about risk. Although this chapter focuses on the actions of individual teachers, it is acknowledged that their power is constrained by the wider structures of the educational system within which they are embedded. Following a questionnaire survey into the level of geography fieldwork provision in the 28 state secondary schools in the research locality, three schools were approached and agreed to take part in the research. Schools with different catchment area and student characteristics were chosen to enable a range of fieldwork experiences to be researched. Crangley and Rishley Schools (which were mixed) were populated by a White majority and Hepleton School (which was all girls) was populated by an Asian majority.[1] In total, 392 students took part in the research. The students were unevenly distributed between the three schools owing to the schools' varying levels of fieldwork provision. All three schools undertook day-long fieldwork visits. Crangley and Hepleton Schools visited Malham in the Yorkshire Dales, while Rishley School visited the east coast of Yorkshire. The results presented here are drawn from participant observation undertaken during each school's fieldwork visits, written post-fieldwork activities undertaken by the students that included questions exploring their experiences and opinions of the day, and in-depth interviews with members of staff.[2]

Responsibility and behaviour

As Beck argued, 'risk and responsibility are intrinsically connected' (1999, 6). The Head of Geography at Rishley School viewed risk management as the teacher's primary responsibility when undertaking fieldwork:

'What is the teacher's role when undertaking fieldwork?'

'[. . .] obviously there is the safety aspect of anything. That's perhaps the primary, most important one. So it's to ensure that they are done safely. So it's risk assessed.'

The Head of Geography from Crangley School also stressed that it was the teachers' responsibility to reflexively monitor risk in the field, partly by controlling students' behaviour:

I think there is also the role of safety and responsibility, the whole risk assessment issue [. . .] you are responsible for those children as the group leader and therefore kind of professionalism and kind of responsible attitude to how the day should be organized and what the kids should and shouldn't do, what's safe and what isn't.

This emphasis on controlling the students' behaviour appears to position the students as potential risk-makers. It is the anticipation of inappropriate behaviour that poses a potential risk. The advice issued to their students in the field further reinforced the students' positioning as risk-makers (Figure 19.1).

This is consistent with Lupton's observation that social actors positioned as risk-makers require 'observation, regulation and discipline' (1999, 106). Crangley School's approach to risk management was underlain by perceptions of a litigious society:

Fieldwork Advice

Listen carefully to all instructions, AND FOLLOW THEM!

Make sure you put all litter in bins, or take it home with you.

Be polite and courteous at all times.

Follow designated footpaths wherever possible.

Stay with your group at all times.

Take care when walking along the route, especially on the limestone pavement.

Act sensible and responsibly at all times.

Do not damage dry stone walls, use a gate or stile.

Enjoy your fieldwork experience!

Figure 19.1 Crangley School's advice for students undertaking fieldwork. Text (with errors) reproduced exactly from original school document.

> I think that like a lot of schools we've become more risk averse in the way that we allow or disallow fieldtrips. I think the society has changed generally hasn't it and people, parents particularly, are far more likely to resort to legal action or something related if things go wrong. And we have to try and cover the school against this.
>
> (Governor, Crangley School)

The positioning of students at Crangley School as risk-makers, subject to the restrictions imposed by competent, reflexive adults, precluded the students' active involvement in the reflexive monitoring of risk in the field. When asked if there was anything they disliked about the day, three students from Crangley School reported that their teachers' concerns over safety had adversely impacted on their enjoyment of the day:

> Not being able to get right near the edge of the limestone pavement.
>
> (Felix)

> Teachers seemed a bit obsessive with health and safety.
>
> (Freya)

> Teachers pestering don't go there.
>
> (Aadi)

Rules for Working on the Coast.
The coastline is a potentially dangerous environment and for your safety you must follow the following rules.

Do not go down on to the beach without the supervision of a teacher.

Walk carefully when near the cliff edge and do not go too close.

Remember that rocks will be wet and slippery so take care when walking on the beach.

Do not throw stones in the direction of other people.

Do not climb the cliffs.

On certain beaches you will be asked to wear a helmet, please wear it properly and keep the strap done up.

Do not go into the sea as it will be very cold and there may be strong currents.

Please follow the instructions that are given to you by members of staff without question.

Behave sensibly at all times.

When in the minibuses you must remain seated with your seat belt on and you must not do anything that could distract the driver.

Please sign below to say that you have read these rules and agree to abide by them.

Signed_____

Figure 19.2 Behaviour contract at Rishley School. Text (with errors) reproduced exactly from original school document.

In comparison, at Rishley School the onus of responsibility for risk management was placed more directly on the students themselves. At the beginning of the fieldwork the students were asked to read the first page of their workbooks entitled 'Rules for Working on the Coast' (Figure 19.2). This was essentially a behaviour contract to ensure that their time on the coast was as safe as possible. Each student had to sign their copy of the rules to show that they had read them and agreed to abide by them.

This behaviour contract appears to establish the students as actively involved in the prevention of risk, making them personally responsible for the management of their own behaviour. Having invested their students with this personal responsibility, staff gave their students free time away from their teachers in the field. No such free time was given to the students from Crangley and Hepleton Schools. In their post-fieldwork activities the Rishley School students reflected that they particularly enjoyed having this freedom:

I liked the fact that the teachers didn't follow you everywhere.

(Ruby)

The free time was good as we had time to socialise.

(Lola)

I really liked the view of the beaches and the free time was good to look at the views.

(Sebastian)

The Rishley School students were also given the freedom to interview members of the public, in groups away from their teachers, about their opinions on coastal erosion. This was also a very popular activity:

I found it fun to ask the public their views on coastal erosion.

(Cathy)

[I enjoyed the] free time, the coast in general and asking the public.

(Bruce)

The strategy adopted at Rishley School is more reminiscent of a Foucaultian approach to risk, where an understanding of the discourses surrounding risk is particularly important (Lupton, 1999). According to Lupton, such discourses are directed at the regulation of the body, its movement in space and interaction with other bodies. This is clearly evident from the contents of the behaviour contract. In this sense, the 'micro-physics' of power noted by Foucault had gained access 'to individuals themselves, to their bodies, their gestures and all their daily actions' (1980, 151). These discourses of risk contribute to the constitution of selfhood, or subjectivity, and thus are part of the panoply of 'practice' or 'technologies of the self' (Foucault, 1988). Technologies of the self are those technologies that operate as regulatory mechanisms through which we govern our own thoughts and actions (Foucault, 1988). From this perspective, investing the students with personal responsibility for reflexive risk management in the field may be conceptualized as a technology for empowering the students to govern their own behaviour. Investing students with such agency in the field reflects the process of individualization.

Foucault did not engage explicitly with ideas about risk, but his work on governmentality is relevant for those writing about risk. According to this perspective, 'risk may be understood as a governmental strategy of regulatory power by which populations and individuals are monitored and managed through the goals of neo-liberalism. Risk is governed via a heterogeneous network of interactive actors, institutions, knowledges and practices' (Lupton, 1999, 87). As Lupton explained, the approaches of governmentality to regulating populations include less direct approaches that rely on individual voluntary compliance with the aims of the state. James *et al.* (1998, 65) concluded that:

We have moved, then, from a collective to an individual space, with the public and external experience of shame and degradation transformed into the private and inner experience of guilt. Thus modernity's child, at school, on the street and even at home, becomes its own policeman.

Rishley School's approach to behaviour management reflects a wider drive towards the use of similar behaviour contracts in England and Wales today (for example, see Macleod, 2006; Home Office, 2007). The approach of making the students responsible for policing their own behaviour demonstrates the co-dependency of structure and agency explored by Gallagher (2006). Gallagher suggested that 'structures depend on the agency of their subjects' (2006, 172). In other words, for a structure to achieve its aims the agents that comprise that structure must be willing to adhere to its aims. However, as Gallagher noted, agents can also exert their autonomy and challenge, as well as actively reproduce, existing practices. This often creates a paradox within schools that 'are structured to encourage kids to become independent and self-reliant, yet most institutions curb expressions of nonconformity' (Thomas, 2000, 579). In this case, the successful reproduction of the disciplinary structure imposed by Rishley School was dependent upon the compliance of all the students involved.

In comparison, student behaviour was managed very differently at Hepleton School, which had important implications for inclusion. The Head of Geography at Hepleton School recognized that the issue of student behaviour, coupled with perceptions of a litigious society, posed a potentially difficult quandary for teachers wanting to take certain students on fieldwork:

> I just passionately agree that it [fieldwork] should be there in the curriculum. And it should be there for everybody. But that said the government can make as many noises as they like, as they've been doing recently haven't they, there should be more activities for kids, kids should be getting out more. I'm afraid the way kids are, the way parents are, the way the legalities are, I can't see it ever getting back to the level it was maybe ten years ago because people are scared I think about if anything goes wrong. But I'm afraid that if pupils' behaviour deteriorates a lot more, it's very difficult isn't it? Taking really naughty kids out. But I still think it should happen.

At Hepleton School the students were given a piece of work that they had to satisfactorily complete prior to the fieldwork to be able to attend. As the Head of Geography explained, this 'was a tool to encourage and reward effective learning and to send out a message that laziness would not be tolerated'. However, she also admitted that this approach had the positive effect of ensuring that only the more well-behaved students were taken into the field. Using this method, 16 out of the 22 students in the class were allowed to attend. Whilst this method may be viewed as an indirect form of exclusion, or even self-exclusion, of potential risk-makers, it provides further evidence of how the issue of poor student behaviour can undermine fieldwork's potential role in facilitating social inclusion (Cook *et al.*, 2006; Cook, 2007; Power *et al.*, 2008).

Discussion and conclusion: fieldwork risk and the social construction of childhood

This chapter has explored the empirical case for maintaining aspects of adult authority in the field. In doing so it has challenged the notion of the competent child agent. Ambiguous understandings of children's agency were found to operate between the three schools. The varying levels of personal responsibility invested in the students for the reflexive monitoring of fieldwork risk demonstrate the conflicting standards by which children were deemed (in)competent to make decisions in the field. The different strategies adopted by the schools variously positioned the students as active in the prevention of risk or as potential risk-makers. Underlying these different strategies were implicit assumptions about students' competencies and levels of maturity, which influenced the degree of personal autonomy permitted to the students in the field. At Rishley School the students were positioned as competent social agents, actively involved in the reflexive monitoring of risk. In comparison, the students from Hepleton and Crangley Schools were positioned as passive, innocent dependants, subjected to varying degrees of adult authority and control. These findings demonstrate the fluid and contextually bound nature of children's competence noted by Valentine (1997b). Valentine argued that competence is 'not a stable attribute of a particular age but rather is a fluid context-dependent performance that can be staged by adults and children alike' (1997b, 82). It is this fluid and contextually bound nature of children's competence in relation to the management of fieldwork risk that demonstrates childhood's ongoing social construction. Furthermore, it was demonstrated how teachers' heightened sensitivity to risk, fuelled by perceptions of a litigious society, frequently informed decisions where aspects of adult authority were maintained. This highlights the ambiguous positioning of children in relation to discourses of fieldwork risk.

Students have been silenced in debates about fieldwork risk to date. This research has enabled students' voices within adult discourses surrounding fieldwork risk to be heard. Teachers' varying approaches to the management of fieldwork risk were found to shape their students' fieldwork experiences, with the degree of personal autonomy permitted to the students impacting upon their enjoyment of the day. However, such an incoherent approach to fieldwork risk management fails to acknowledge that all interactions with the world involve a modicum of risk. As Green noted, 'we cannot eliminate misfortune, however sophisticated our strategies for managing it become' (1997, 203). Engaging with risk is an important means through which children may learn new skills and knowledge (Guldberg, 2000; Christensen and Mikkelsen, 2007). By failing to recognize the value of fieldwork for enabling all students to experience and learn about risk we are denying children the dignity of risk (Wolpert, 1980).

Notes

1 The names of the schools and the students are all pseudonyms.
2 All spoken responses are presented in italics and written responses are in a normal font.

References

Aitken, S. C. (2001) *Geographies of Young People: The Morally Contested Spaces of Identity*, London: Routledge.

Aitken, S. C., Gagen, E., Kesby, M., Radcliffe, S., Ruddick, S. and Skelton, S. (2006) 'Author meets critics: a review essay (and response)', *Social and Cultural Geography*, 7: 1011–19.

Ansell, N. (2008) 'Third world gap year projects: youth transitions and the mediation of risk', *Environment and Planning D: Society and Space*, 26: 218–40.

Ariès, P. (1960) *L'enfant et la Vie Familiale Sous L'ancien Régime*, trans. R. Baldick (1962) *Centuries of Childhood*, London: Jonathan Cape.

Beck, U. (1992) *Risk Society: Towards New Modernity*, London: Sage.

Beck, U. (1994) 'The reinvention of politics: towards a theory of reflexive modernization', in U. Beck, A. Giddens and S. Lash (eds) *Reflexive Modernization*, Cambridge: Polity Press.

Beck, U. (1999) *World Risk Society*, Cambridge: Polity Press.

Beck, U. (2000) 'Risk society revisited: theory, politics and research programmes', in B. Adam, U. Beck and J. Van Loon (eds) *The Risk Society and Beyond: Critical Issues for Social Theory*, London: Sage.

Beck, U. and Beck-Gernsheim, E. (2002) *Individualization*, London: Sage.

Christensen, P. and Mikkelsen, M. R. (2007) 'Jumping off and being careful: children's strategies of risk management in everyday life', *Sociology of Health and Illness*, 30: 112–30.

Cook, V. A. (2007) 'Inclusive fieldwork in a "risk society"', *Teaching Geography*, 31: 119–21.

Cook, V. A. (2008) 'The field as a "pedagogical resource"? A critical analysis of students' affective engagement with the field environment', *Environmental Education Research*, 14: 507–17.

Cook, V. A., Phillips, D. and Holden, J. (2006) 'Geography fieldwork in a "risk society"', *Area*, 38: 413–20.

Education and Skills Committee (2005) *Education Outside the Classroom: Second Report of Session 2004–2005: Report, together with Formal Minutes, Oral and Written Evidence*, London: Stationery Office.

Foucault, M. (1980) 'Body/Power', in C. Gordon (ed.) *Michael Foucault: Power/Knowledge*, Brighton: Harvester.

Foucault, M. (1988) 'Technologies of the self', in L. Martin, H. Gutman and P. Hutton (eds) *Technologies of the Self: A Seminar with Michel Foucault*, London: Tavistock.

Furedi, F. (2001) *Paranoid Parenting: Abandon your Anxieties and be a Good Parent*, London: Cassell.

Furedi, F. (2002) *Culture of Fear: Risk-taking and the Morality of Low Expectation*, London: Cassell.

Gallagher, M. (2006) 'Spaces of participation and inclusion?', in E. Kay, M. Tidsall, J. M. Davis, M. Hill and A. Prout (eds) *Children, Young People and Social Inclusion: Participation for What?*, Bristol: Policy Press.

Giddens, A. (1991) *Modernity and Self-identity: Self and Society in the Late Modern Age*, Cambridge: Polity Press.

Green, J. (1997) *Risk and Misfortune: The Social Construction of Accidents*, London: UCL Press.

Guldberg, H. (2000) 'Child protection and the precautionary principle', in J. Morris (ed.) *Rethinking Risk and Precautionary Principle*, Oxford: Butterworth Heinemann.

Harden, J. (2000) 'There's no place like home: the public/private distinction in children's theorizing of risk and safety', *Childhood*, 7: 43–59.

Holloway, S. L. and Valentine, G. (2000) 'Children's geographies and the new social studies of childhood', in S. L. Holloway and G. Valentine (eds) *Children's Geographies: Playing, Living, Learning*, London: Routledge.

Home Office (2007) *Guidance on the Use of Acceptable Behaviour Contracts and Agreements*. Available at: http://webarchive.nationalarchives.gov.uk/20100413151441/http://crimereduction.homeoffice.gov.uk/antisocialbehaviour/antisocialbehaviour058a.pdf (accessed 14 October 2010).

Horton, J. and Kraftl, P. (2005) 'For more-than-usefulness: six overlapping points about children's geographies', *Children's Geographies*, 3: 131–43.

Jackson, S. and Scott, S. (1999) 'Risk anxiety and the social construction of childhood', in D. Lupton (ed.) *Risk and Sociocultural Theory: New Directions and Perspectives*, Cambridge: Cambridge University Press.

James, A., Jenks, C. and Prout, A. (1998) *Theorising Childhood*, Cambridge: Polity Press.

Jenks, C. (1996) *Childhood*, London: Routledge.

Lupton, D. (1999) *Risk*, London: Routledge.

Macleod, D. (2006) 'Freshers sign on the dotted line', *The Guardian*, September 11 2006. Available at: http://blogs.guardian.co.uk/mortarboard/2006/09/freshers_sign_on_the_dotted_li.html (accessed 16 April 2008).

Malone, K. (2007) 'The bubble-wrap generation: children growing up in walled gardens', *Environmental Education Research*, 13: 513–27.

Matthews, H. (2003) 'Coming of age for children's geographies: inaugural editorial', *Children's Geographies*, 1: 3–5.

O'Brien, M., Jones, D. and Rustin, M. (2000) 'Children's independent spatial mobility in the urban public realm', *Childhood*, 7: 257–77.

Pain, R. (2006) 'Paranoid parenting? Rematerializing risk and fear for children', *Social and Cultural Geography*, 7: 221–43.

Power, S., Taylor, C., Rees, G. and Jones, K. (2008) *Out-of-School Learning: Variations in Provision and Participation in Secondary Schools*, unpublished report: Field Studies Council.

Prout, A. and James, A. (1990) 'A new paradigm for the sociology of childhood? Provenance, promise and problems', in A. James and A. Prout (eds) *Constructing and Reconstructing Childhood: Contemporary Issues in the Sociological Study of Childhood*, London: Falmer Press.

Scott, S., Jackson, S. and Backett-Milburn, K. (1998) 'Swings and roundabouts: risk anxiety and the everyday worlds of children', *Sociology*, 32: 689–705.

Thomas, G. and Thompson, G. (2004) *A Child's Place: Why Environment Matters to Children*, London: Green Alliance.

Thomas, M. (2000) 'Guest editorial: from crib to campus: kids' sexual/gender identities and institutional spaces', *Environment and Planning A*, 32: 577–80.

Valentine, G. (1997a) '"My son's a bit dizzy." "My wife's a bit soft": gender, children and cultures of parenting', *Gender, Place and Culture*, 4: 37–62.

Valentine, G. (1997b) '"Oh yes I can," "Oh no you can't": children and parents' understandings of kids' competence to negotiate public space safely', *Antipode*, 29(1): 65–89.

Valentine, G. (2004) *Public Space and the Culture of Childhood*, Aldershot: Ashgate.

Vanderbeck, R. (2008) 'Reaching critical mass? Theory, politics, and the culture of debate in children's geographies', *Area*, 40: 393–400.

Wolpert, J. (1980) 'The dignity of risk', *Transactions of the Institute of British Geographers*, New Series, 5: 391–401.

Woolley, H. (2006) 'Freedom of the city: contemporary issues and policy influences on children and young people's use of public open space in England', *Children's Geographies*, 4: 45–59.

Wyness, M. G. (2006) *Childhood and Society: An Introduction to the Sociology of Childhood*, Basingstoke: Palgrave Macmillan.

Index